EDUCATIONAL

LEADERSHIP

AND PLANNING

FOR TECHNOLOGY

FOURTH EDITION

EDUCATIONAL

LEADERSHIP

AND PLANNING

FOR TECHNOLOGY

Anthony G. Picciano

*Hunter College and Graduate Center
City University of New York*

PEARSON

Merrill
Prentice Hall

Upper Saddle River, New Jersey
Columbus, Ohio

Library of Congress Cataloging-in-Publication Data

Picciano, Anthony G.
    Educational leadership and planning for technology / Anthony G. Picciano.—4th ed.
        p. cm.
    Includes bibliographical references and index.
    ISBN 0-13-119471-2
1. Education—Data processing—Planning.   2. Computer managed instruction—Planning.   3. Computer-assisted instruction—Planning.   4. School management and organization—Data processing—Planning.   I. Title.

LB1028.43.P536 2006
370'.285—dc22   2005002963

Vice President and Executive Publisher: Jeffery W. Johnston
Executive Editor: Debra A. Stollenwerk
Associate Editor: Ben M. Stephen
Editorial Assistant: Mary Morrill
Production Editor: Kris Roach/Alexandrina Wolf
Production Coordination: Thistle Hill Publishing Services, LLC
Design Coordinator: Diane C. Lorenzo
Cover Designer: Terry Rohrbach
Cover Image: Corbis
Photo Coordinator: Lori Whitley
Production Manager: Susan Hannahs
Director of Marketing: Ann Castel Davis
Marketing Manager: Darcy Betts Prybella
Marketing Coordinator: Tyra Poole

This book was set in Cheltenham Light by Integra Software Services. It was printed and bound by Courier Stoughton, Inc. The cover was printed by Courier Stoughton, Inc.

Photo Credits: Anne Vega/Merrill, pp. 1, 238; Ann Bancroft/yourexpedition.com, p. 2; Laura Bolesta/Merrill, p. 16; Scott Cunningham/Merrill, p. 42; Kathy Kirtland/Merrill, pp. 63, 199; Anthony Magnacca/Merrill, pp. 64, 84, 112, 218, 280; Valerie Schultz/Merrill, p. 134; David Mager/Pearson Learning Photo Studio, p. 166; Matthew Ward © Dorling Kindersley, p. 200; Patrick White/Merrill, p. 254; NASA/Finley Holiday Films, p. 303.

Pearson Education Ltd.
Pearson Education Singapore Pte. Ltd.
Pearson Education Canada, Ltd.
Pearson Education—Japan

Pearson Education Australia Pty. Limited
Pearson Education North Asia Ltd.
Pearson Educación de Mexico, S.A. de C.V.
Pearson Education Malaysia Pte. Ltd.

10 9 8 7 6 5
ISBN: 0-13-119471-2

TO SISTER ANNE O'DRISCOLL AND SISTER GENEVIEVE LOVE

ABOUT THE AUTHOR

Anthony G. Picciano is the author of six books in the fields of educational leadership, technology, and research methods. *Educational Leadership and Planning for Technology* is the fourth edition of an earlier work, *Computers in the Schools: A Guide to Planning and Administration.* In 2004, Dr. Picciano published the *Educational Research Primer* (Continuum). In 2000, Dr. Picciano published *Distance Learning: Making Connections Across Virtual Space and Time* (Merrill/Prentice Hall), which extensively covers the field of online learning.

Dr. Picciano is a professor in the Education Administration and Supervision Program in the School of Education at Hunter College. He is also a member of the doc-

toral faculty in the Urban Education Ph.D. Program and the program in Interactive Pedagogy and Technology at the City University of New York Graduate Center. His teaching specialties include educational technology, organization theory, policy, and research methods. From 1994 through 2002, he was a faculty fellow at the City University of New York Open Systems Laboratory, a facility dedicated to experimenting with advanced uses of instructional technology and to providing staff development programs for organizations including public schools, colleges, and private businesses. In 1997, he cofounded CUNY Online, the administrative and faculty development facility for providing online courses for students in the colleges in the City University.

Dr. Picciano has served as a consultant for a variety of public and private organizations including the Commission on Higher Education/Middle States Association of Colleges and Universities, the New York City Board of Education, the New York State Department of Education, the U.S. Coast Guard, and Citicorp. He has received numerous grants and awards from the National Science Foundation, the Alfred P. Sloan Foundation, the U.S. Department of Education, and IBM. His articles on educational technology have appeared in journals such as *The Teachers College Record, The Urban Review, Journal of Asynchronous Learning Networks, Journal of Educational Multimedia and Hypermedia, Computers in the Schools, Equity and Choice,* and *EDUCOM Review.* He lives with his wife Elaine in Pocantico Hills, New York.

PREFACE

This book provides educators with both the theoretical and the practical considerations for planning and implementing technology in schools. Basic concepts of technology and planning that use systems theory are presented. Emphasis is placed on the importance of the total application of technology as opposed to any individual component, be it hardware, software, facilities, personnel, or finances. The book forms a foundation from which educators will provide leadership and become agents for realizing the powerful potential of technology in their schools.

The material is designed for practicing administrators and other educators such as teachers, technology coordinators, and media specialists who are involved in initiating and supporting technology in their schools. The text is most appropriate as a text in a preservice or in-service course on planning technology applications designed primarily for school administrators.

ORGANIZATION

This book is divided into three sections: I, Basic Concepts and Foundations; II, Technology in Action; and III, Planning and Implementation. Although each chapter can be read independently, it should be taught in sequence. Several supplemental sections are presented for reference: Appendix A reviews basic technology concepts and terminology; Appendix B lists educational leader competencies; Appendix C, which is found on the Companion Website (www.prenhall.com/picciano), serves as a sample checklist to help educators evaluate instructional software; and the Glossary provides a quick reference for technical terms used in the text.

Section I: Basic Concepts and Foundations

Section I provides the basic concepts and foundation for an overall understanding of the themes and major issues related to planning for technology in schools and school systems. It is directed specifically to those who are or will be leading their schools in planning for technology. This section concludes with a chapter on pedagogical and social issues related to technology that should be considered as part of the planning process. Readers who are not familiar with basic technology—especially computer concepts or terminology—should review Appendix A before proceeding beyond this section.

Section II: Technology in Action

Section II provides five chapters on the nature of technology applications used for both administration and instruction. Although similar in some respects, enough differences exist in the nature, design, and policies associated with administrative and instructional applications that they require separate treatments. Three separate chapters discuss technologies such as multimedia, the Internet, and distance learning.

Section III: Planning and Implementation

Section III presents the primary components of planning for and developing technology applications in schools, and provides practical information on evaluating and implementing these components. Entire chapters are devoted to the five components of every technology application: hardware, software, staff development, facilities, and finances.

End-of-Chapter Elements

Each chapter concludes with key concepts and questions, suggested activities, and/or case studies to stimulate thought and discussion on the material presented. They also relate the material to situations that exist in schools. The case studies, although having some basis in fact, are fictitious and designed to put the reader in the position of leaders having to make decisions about technology and related issues. Reference lists are also provided at the end of each chapter.

Epilogue

The Epilogue reemphasizes the need for administrators to look to the future and to integrate technology into their visions for their schools.

NEW IN THIS EDITION

Since the first edition was published in the early 1990s, technology in schools has evolved from the predominance of stand-alone computers to a blend of computer, media, communications, and other forms of technology. This fourth edition has been updated to reflect the expansion and integration of these technologies. Other changes include:

- All chapters have been updated to reflect current thinking and advances in technology as applied to education.
- New material has been added on data-driven decision making, distance learning, digital video, and wireless local area networks.
- Four new end-of-chapter case studies have been developed. All other case studies have been updated.
- Text-specific website information found at www.prenhall.com/picciano has been meaningfully integrated into this edition via margin notes, making its connection to chapter content more explicit and cohesive. Website modules include: Suggested Activities, Weblinks, PowerPoints, Instructional Software Evaluation Factors, and Summary.

■ DEFINITION OF TERMS

Technology is a general term applied to various administrative and instructional applications involving calculators, overhead projectors, telephones, television, and so forth. In this book, technology refers to computer as well as other technologies such as data communications, video, and multimedia.

School districts sometimes are referred to as small, medium, or large, depending on their enrollment:

Small: fewer than 600 students
Medium: at least 600 but fewer than 25,000 students
Large: more than 25,000 students

School districts in the United States generally are governed by independently elected or appointed boards of education with the power to raise taxes and issue bonds. Some districts, particularly those in urban areas, are governed by other governmental entities such as a municipality, from which they receive an operating budget. Unless otherwise noted, references to school districts include all school districts. In some cases, the term *municipally governed* is used to refer specifically to those school districts described earlier.

■ ACKNOWLEDGMENTS

I gratefully acknowledge the guidance and assistance provided by the staff at Merrill/Prentice Hall, especially Debbie Stollenwerk, Ben Stephen, Mary Morrill, and Kris Roach. I'd also like to thank Angela Williams Urquhart and the staff at Thistle Hill Publishing Services for editorial and project management assistance.

I am most grateful to a distinguished group of reviewers who took the time to read the previous edition and who made many fine suggestions for this fourth edition: John T. Thompson, Buffalo State University; Joyce P. Logan, University of Kentucky; Karen Lieuallen, Marian College; and John K. Rugutt, Illinois State University.

In addition, I have benefited significantly from my professional associations with a number of colleagues, specifically: the faculty in the Department of Curriculum and Teaching at Hunter College, particularly Janet Patti, Marcia Knoll, and Janell Drone; the faculty in the Ph.D. Program in Urban Education at the CUNY Graduate Center; colleagues at the Alfred P. Sloan Consortium for Asynchronous Learning Networks; and all of the school administrators who provided source material and who are truly leading their schools in creative uses of technology.

Especially important to my efforts were the students in the Administration and Supervision Program at Hunter College. They are an industrious group of future leaders who will make many fine contributions to their schools for years to come.

Lastly, my gratitude to Michael and Dawn Marie, who have helped me to be a better person, and Elaine, who always supports me in everything I do.

Anthony G. Picciano

BRIEF CONTENTS

CONTENTS

xvi Contents

Note: Every effort has been made to provide accurate and current Internet information in this book. However, the Internet and information posted on it are constantly changing, so it is inevitable that some of the Internet addresses listed in this textbook will change.

EDUCATOR LEARNING CENTER: AN INVALUABLE ONLINE RESOURCE

Merrill Education and the Association for Supervision and Curriculum Development (ASCD) invite you to take advantage of a new online resource, one that provides access to the top research and proven strategies associated with ASCD and Merrill—the Educator Learning Center. At **www.educatorlearningcenter.com**, you will find resources that will enhance your students' understanding of course topics and of current educational issues, in addition to being invaluable for further research.

How the Educator Learning Center Will Help Your Students Become Better Teachers

With the combined resources of Merrill Education and ASCD, you and your students will find a wealth of tools and materials to better prepare them for the classroom.

Research

- More than 600 articles from the ASCD journal *Educational Leadership* discuss everyday issues faced by practicing teachers.
- A direct link on the site to Research Navigator™ gives students access to many of the leading education journals, as well as extensive content detailing the research process.
- Excerpts from Merrill Education texts give your students insights on important topics of instructional methods, diverse populations, assessment, classroom management, technology, and refining classroom practice.

Classroom Practice

- Hundreds of lesson plans and teaching strategies are categorized by content area and age range.
- Case studies and classroom video footage provide virtual field experience for student reflection.
- Computer simulations and other electronic tools keep your students abreast of today's classrooms and current technologies.

Look into the Value of Educator Learning Center Yourself

A four-month subscription to Educator Learning Center is $25 but is **FREE** when packaged with any Merrill Education text. In order for your students to have access to this site, you must use this special value-pack ISBN number **WHEN** placing your textbook order with the bookstore: 0-13-226344-0. Your students will then receive a copy of the text packaged with a free ASCD pincode. To preview the value of this website to you and your students, please go to **www.educatorlearningcenter.com** and click on "Demo."

Section I

BASIC CONCEPTS AND FOUNDATIONS

1. Introduction to Technology and Planning

2. Basic Concepts of Planning

3. Technology, Learning, and Equity Issues

Chapter 1

Introduction to Technology and Planning

On February 11, 2001, Ann Bancroft and Liv Arnesen became the first women to cross Antarctica on foot. It took 94 days of walking, skiing, and ski-sailing to complete the 1,700-mile trip in temperatures as low as −35 °F. While the expedition itself will go down in history as a great feat of woman against nature, there are other elements of the Ann and Liv story that are of particular interest to educators.

Ann is from Minnesota and was a former physical education and special education teacher; Liv, a Norwegian, was a former literature and physical education teacher. A significant aspect of their efforts was to share their journey with others—especially schoolchildren. As part of the meticulous planning, they developed curriculum materials that could be shared with children throughout the world. In addition to all of the basic survival equipment (fuel, food, tents, clothes, skiing equipment, stoves) needed to exist on the frozen continent for 3 months, Ann and Liv also carried a good deal of computer and communications equipment that would be used not only to keep contact with their base camp but also to tell their story to children in classrooms. They chose not simply to log their day-to-day activities in a journal but to share them through audio and video files that could be downloaded to Web sites anywhere in the world where children had access to the Internet. When asked why they devoted so much energy and effort to sharing their experience with the world's children, Ann and Liv responded: "to inspire and to touch kids' lives."

Anyone who has had the privilege of being a teacher knows that at one level, teaching is about information, child development, social maturation, and so forth, but at its highest level, to teach is to inspire. The best teachers understand that their most important goal is to be an inspiration to children to learn, to dream, and to try to accomplish. Ann and Liv accomplished their goal well. More than 3 million students in 116 countries learned, followed, and participated (virtually) in their journey.

The story of Ann and Liv is provocative spiritually but also serves as an apt introduction to the main topic of this book: technology in schools. Once on Antarctica, they relied solely on their human strength and endurance to complete their journey—however, to touch children's lives, they were totally dependent upon technology including an Apple laptop computer, a satellite phone, and digital cameras. They used the Internet extensively for communicating with schools literally around the world. Most of their equipment with the exception of their energy packs could be purchased at a local computer store. The Internet of Ann and Liv is the same Internet that most children use to send e-mail, to look up information, and to do schoolwork. The Internet—which has reshaped much of humankind's social, professional, and educational activities—can connect people even in the most isolated places.

Liv, while resting one night in her tent on the ice of Antarctica, reflected:

> It was funny to think that the rest of the world was so accessible to us through this modern technology, and yet, if Ann and I were to be injured in this area, no plane could land here to save us. The terrain was too rough. We were completely connected and completely isolated at the same time. (Arnesen & Bancroft, 2003, p. 8)

Liv's observation is an important one because increasingly it is the nature of digital communications technology to bring people together even when they are miles apart. An important aspect of this book is to present the benefits of technology to connect teaching and learning, to connect students to knowledge, and to connect educators to the powerful potential of modern digital communications, computers, and media equipment for the betterment of schools and schooling.

Ann and Liv's accomplishment was the culmination of years of planning. The key to success was the fact that they had a vision of something they wanted to do and were able to lead and persuade others to help them accomplish it. Thousands of educators in schools around the country are in positions similar to that of Ann and Liv. They are in positions to lead others in developing and implementing projects and programs that will surely touch children's lives. They need vision and resources—but, most importantly, they need the will to share and accomplish their goals with others.

PURPOSE

Explaining the purpose of this book requires a discussion of the purposes of schools and schooling. Educational technology, to be successful, must be integrated into the main functions of schools. Technology for technology's sake is an expensive and generally futile endeavor. However, when integrated into an educator's vision of what children and young adults need to learn about the world and themselves, then technology can be an effective tool in achieving that vision.

Views differ among educators and communities regarding the purposes of schools and schooling. For some, education should focus on the intellectual and emotional needs of children. For others, the focus may be a society's social and economic needs. Fundamental to most of these views is a sense that children, as a result of education, will come away with a desire to learn more about themselves, others, and the world about them. Drawing from experiential theories, a basic assumption is that children are born with a natural curiosity about the world, and the main function of schooling should be to stimulate that curiosity. Once the desire to learn has been instilled, children will learn a great deal on their own. Schooling succeeds when children begin to learn through experiences, and by learning are motivated to experience more, so that a cycle of lifelong learning and experiencing evolves. Seymour Sarason (1995) describes this concept most succinctly:

> If when a child is motivated to learn more about self and the world, then I would say that schooling has achieved its overarching purpose. . . . The student knows that the more you know the more you need to know. . . . To want to continue to explore, to find answers to personally meaningful questions, issues, and possibilities is the most important purpose of schooling. (p. 135)

The role of technology in achieving this purpose can be made evident by briefly describing its relationship to education. For most of the 20th century, technology in education centered on print media. Paper, pens, books, and chalk were critical for communicating ideas, accessing information, and learning about the world. In the 21st century, electronic media have begun to replace print media. Word processing, e-mail, fax-modems, video, CD-ROMs, DVDs, multimedia, and the Internet have become the common tools for communicating ideas and accessing information. The morning newspaper is now read to provide additional insight into what was already seen and heard on the nightly news broadcast. The linearity of the sentence, paragraph, and page is used in conjunction with hypertext branching and searching. The one-dimensionality of the lecture achieves depth and perspective as it is integrated into multiple-interactive dialogues and small-group discussions on local and international data communications networks. Technology is becoming the tool of choice for communicating in, accessing, and learning about our world. It should be integrated with any educational vision or plan that attempts to help individuals, including children, understand this world.

The purpose of this book is to provide educators with both the theoretical framework and the practical considerations for planning and implementing technology, particularly computer applications, in schools. Basic concepts of technology and planning that use systems theory are presented. The book emphasizes the importance of the total application of technology in the educational enterprise more so than any individual component, be it hardware, software, facilities, or staff. This book is meant to form the foundation from which educators will look ahead and become the agents for realizing the powerful potential of technology in their schools.

THE POTENTIAL IN PRIMARY AND SECONDARY SCHOOLS

"For many firms using computers . . . is an absolute necessity." So said James O'Brien (1989, p. 33) about the use of computers in business organizations. His readers would have accepted this statement with little reservation. In the latter part of the 20th century, computer technology became an integral part of most business operations, as fundamental as accounting, finance, marketing, and management. Architects, engineers, bankers, and salespersons routinely used computers for various aspects of their jobs.

The same was true for many organizations in the public sector. High-technology agencies such as the Department of Defense, NASA, and the Federal Aviation Administration have become totally dependent on computers for all aspects of their operations. Weapons systems, the space shuttle missions, and air traffic are controlled almost exclusively by computer technology. Most other public agencies, such as the Internal Revenue Service and the Social Security Administration, also rely on sophisticated information retrieval systems to conduct their operations. Take a walk through a hospital, a library, or a college, and you will likely see technology routinely used to monitor a patient's heartbeat, to borrow a book, or to conduct research.

Those who have studied and observed the use of computers in primary and secondary education see a substantially different picture. Educators are surely interested in the potential of the technology but also express reservations in its implementation. In *Oversold and Underused* (2001), Larry Cuban, a professor at Stanford University and a respected voice in American education, argues that when teachers are not given a say in how the technology might reshape schools, computers function basically as high-speed typewriters and classrooms continue to run much as they did a generation ago. In his studies of early childhood, high school, and university classrooms in Silicon Valley, Cuban found that students and teachers use the new technologies far less in the classroom than they do at home, and that teachers who use computers for instruction do so infrequently and unimaginatively. Cuban further points out that historical and organizational economic contexts influence how teachers use technical innovations. Computers can be useful when teachers sufficiently understand the technology themselves, believe it will enhance learning, and have the power to shape their own curricula.

In June 1997, the journal *Technological Horizons in Education* celebrated its 25th anniversary with a special edition that looked back at educational technology milestones over the preceding 25 years. Articles by major contributors to the field of educational technology celebrated achievements and lamented obstacles. All agreed that technology in education had grown since the 1970s from an object of study to an indispensable tool. However, they also agreed that the potential had yet to be realized and that education was not as far along as other endeavors in its use of technology. For example:

Andrew Molnar, Director for Applications of Advanced Technologies, National Science Foundation
"The world of education has changed from an orderly world of disciplines . . . to an infosphere in which communication technologies are increasingly important. While education is changing, it is not changing fast enough." (Molnar, 1997, p. 68)

Seymour Papert, Developer of Logo and Professor, The Media Laboratory, Massachusetts Institute of Technology
"But with this greater complexity of activities comes greater problems of access to knowledge: the problems and difficulties that come up are increasingly beyond what a teacher can be expected to handle." (Papert, 1997, p. 80)

Alfred Bork, Professor Emeritus, Information and Computer Science, University of California, Irvine
"Replacing our current educational systems with ones that depend on technology is not a simple and inexpensive process." (Bork, 1997, p. 76)

Although schools have started to use technology, these quotes reflect the fact that educators are still cautious and concerned about the impact. We can make airline reservations, buy lottery tickets, withdraw money, or tally a cart of groceries electronically at the push of a button or the wave of a wand. Yet, the vast majority of primary and secondary schools rely on intensive manual efforts to conduct one of our most important "businesses"—that is, the education of children. Why this has occurred is an important starting point for the study of planning and administering technology in primary and secondary schools.

THE BEGINNING YEARS

Primary and secondary schools were effectively excluded in the early years of the computer revolution (1960s and 1970s) for a variety of reasons. Much of the earliest software provided for computers was designed for data processing applications rather than for educational purposes. The exceptions were several scientific software languages and packages that were useful in organized research activities and major military-industrial and space exploration projects. International Business Machines (IBM), which dominated the entire computer industry and provided much of the leadership, developed products for organizations that were already part of an office machine customer base, such as users of typewriters and punch card equipment. Although extremely active in higher-education markets (to familiarize future business leaders and engineers with its products), IBM was not as active in marketing to primary and secondary schools. In a 1988 article in *Think*, an IBM publication, Jim Dezell, the general manager of IBM's Educational Systems, was quoted as saying, "We were way behind, way behind. . . . As recently as three years ago, the only IBM software in education . . . the company was offering was Writing to Read. . . . We had no installed base or customer references" (Grimm, 1988, p. 5).

Schools have a long tradition of being people-oriented rather than machine-oriented. In addition to teaching, schools provide nourishment, health, recreation, and other social services to their students. A fundamental concept of teacher education is to nurture children and to take care of the "whole" child. As a result, in their earliest courses teachers are trained to be child-oriented. Many of them considered most of the earlier computer technology as an impersonal approach to teaching, particularly in the primary grades, and did not embrace it. Furthermore, teachers who received their training prior to 1990 likely did not receive formal training in computer technology in their undergraduate programs. As a result, this technology did not become a routine part of their repertoire of teaching tools.

When major advances in computer technology were being made in the 1960s and 1970s, schools were also going through significant changes. No other organizations in this country were affected as much by the major social issues of the times as were the primary and secondary schools. Racial integration, bilingual education, and the rights of persons with disabling conditions have affected all aspects of society. However, it was the schools that were called on to spearhead changes in the way the United States would resolve these issues. While private businesses and many governmental agencies were gradually changing, major and sudden changes were occurring in the nation's schools. These changes rightfully dominated much of the planning that school administrators and education policy makers did and became the major priorities for improving the schools and their instructional programs.

Although some larger school districts could afford it, most of the 15,000-plus school districts in the nation did not have adequate financial resources to invest in the new computer technology. Businesses were willing to invest resources in designing and developing computer applications, but schools used their available resources for other priorities. Smaller school districts could afford neither the hardware nor expensive support staff that the large mainframe computer systems of the 1960s and early 1970s required. Some districts made pioneering attempts to use time-sharing systems provided by universities, state and local agencies, and educational consortia, but these efforts did not affect the vast majority of teachers and students in the schools. As late as 1980, after reviewing the results of several national surveys, H. J. Becker (1991, 1994) estimated that no more than 50,000 microcomputers or computer terminals were available in the nation's primary and secondary schools. With more than 40 million students and a student-to-computer ratio of 800:1, this technology was surely not a part of their educational experiences.

Without hardware, software, or training and with other more important and pressing priorities, primary and secondary schools did not enter the technology revolution that occurred in the 1960s and 1970s. However, the situation changed in the late 1970s and early 1980s with the introduction of microcomputers. Major new computer manufacturers such as Apple, Commodore, Tandy, and Atari were genuinely interested in marketing their products to schools. They were also interested in the children's market in general and provided hardware and software that could be used in the home for playing electronic games. Teachers and school administrators began to observe that more and more children were becoming computer literate at home. Parents were also becoming more familiar with computer technology as their workplaces began to require them to use it. New software companies such as Sunburst, Broderbund, Tom Snyder Productions, and Scholastic appeared almost overnight with educational software that was more appealing and pedagogically more interesting than any developed in the previous 20 years. As a result, schools finally began to make meaningful investments in computer technology in the 1980s. With the advent of the Internet in the 1990s, schools accelerated their involvement with and investment in technology (as did all segments of society) as they attempted to connect to the communications and data resources of the information superhighway.

Although unquestionably behind other American enterprises, schools are beginning to make significant strides. The time has come for administrators and teachers to take control and harness the power of the technology at their disposal.

This task involves engaging in thoughtful evaluation, discarding or improving what does not work, accepting and building on what does, and carefully planning for new applications.

■ STEADY PROGRESS IN ADMINISTRATIVE SYSTEMS

Technology applications in education can be divided into two major categories: administrative and instructional. Administrative applications support the administrative functions of a district or school. Examples include database management and transaction-processing systems such as student demographics, grading, budgeting, payroll, personnel, scheduling, and inventory control, all of which are designed for and used primarily by administrative staff. Instructional applications support teaching and learning activities that are designed for and used mainly by teachers, school library media specialists, and students. The background, implementation, and planning for these two major categories of applications are different and need to be distinguished.

Administrative systems have progressed more steadily than instructional applications because they are very similar to the data processing applications in private industry and public agencies. Customer and product database management systems in private businesses resemble student and course systems in schools; personnel, payroll, and financial database systems designed for public agencies are identical to those used in schools. As a result, schools were able to draw on the expertise and software products developed for general data processing applications for their own administrative operations. Computer manufacturers, software developers, and data processing service bureaus could market many of the same products to schools, private industry, and government agencies. Many of the larger school districts were able to afford and use the benefits of these data processing applications. For example, school districts governed by local municipalities generally were required to follow the same administrative procedures established for all the other agencies under the municipality's jurisdiction. This was especially true for financial applications such as budgeting, payroll, and purchasing. As municipalities began to computerize these applications, so did the school districts.

In the late 1960s and 1970s, state education departments became much more active in data collection and evaluation activities, partly because of the reporting requirements of the federal government regarding entitlement programs, and partly because of a desire and need to better understand what the schools were doing. Schools were increasingly required to provide data on student demographics, performance, and expenditures. To streamline these data collection activities, some states (e.g., Florida, Minnesota, Texas) established statewide computer networks to assist the school districts. Administrators soon were able to use these networks not only to fulfill the reporting requirements but also to meet their own informational and other administrative needs.

By the 1970s and 1980s, as microcomputers became available, many school districts were converting existing applications or developing new ones to meet their administrative needs. Even districts with very little access to computing before this period were able to draw on the experiences of other districts and utilize established software products.

INSTRUCTIONAL SYSTEMS SHOW PROMISE

The quotes earlier in this chapter that refer to the potential of computer technology reflect the thinking of educators regarding the instructional rather than the administrative uses of computers in the schools. Practically all schools have begun to invest in technology, but many are struggling with it for various reasons in terms of a teaching philosophy, the benefits, and problems in implementation.

Most of the early research and development that went into software development was directed to improving data processing applications that were prevalent in businesses and many public agencies. Such research concentrated on data and information flow and was primarily concerned with improving speed and other transaction-processing features. Although critical to high-volume, service-oriented organizations such as banks, insurance companies, stock brokerage houses, and many governmental agencies, these features were of minimal value to teaching and learning. Several of the early attempts at developing packages for schools consisted of copies and conversions of software developed primarily for businesses and other organizations. For example, the Bank Street College of Education, which enjoyed an excellent reputation for having developed a variety of very interesting educational software packages, started by converting standard word processing (Bank Street Writer) and database management (Bank Street Filer) software for use in primary and secondary schools.

Many of the earliest instructional software applications developed in primary and secondary schools in the 1960s and 1970s were of the drill-and-practice variety and concentrated on providing repetitive exercises for learning basic skills. Although drill and practice is widely used by teachers using flash cards and other manual techniques, when delivered electronically on computers it became the topic of much debate (Gagné, 1977; Trumbull, 1986; Yates, 1983). Although drill and practice has proponents, many teachers were not receptive to the early software developed in the 1960s and 1970s. Some, in fact, were turned off to computing technology in general and viewed it as an impersonal, "Big Brother is watching" approach. Even if schools wanted to use software before 1980, they still had to overcome financial and other technical hurdles. To deliver computing power to the classroom using a large mainframe or even a minicomputer system required a significant organizational commitment. Hardware costs alone made it prohibitive for many school districts. Other problems (e.g., establishing data communications networks to allow student access, attracting and training highly paid technicians, building environmentally controlled facilities) made it impossible for all but some of the larger districts.

In the early 1980s, with the proliferation of microcomputers, some of these problems were overcome. Hardware costs decreased dramatically. Software began to be designed for children. Although intended more for entertainment than education, video games were effective in breaking down the first barriers that prevented children from using computer technology. In addition, video games such as Pac-Man and Space Invaders relied heavily on motion and graphics that significantly added to their appeal to children. As a result, a good deal of software research and development in the 1980s was devoted to improving graphics, not just for children but for adult and business applications also. Thousands of titles of software packages now exist that were designed for children and are very appropriate for use in primary and secondary schools. According to data collected in a national survey by Quality Education Data (1996), 98% of all public schools had acquired some form of computer technology by 1990. By 1999, the vast majority of all classrooms were connected to the Internet and schools had an average of one instructional computer for every 5.7 students (Fatemi, 1999).

THE NEED FOR PLANNING

One of the major issues impeding the establishment of successful technology programs in schools is the lack of careful planning. Although some schools and districts have shown progress, others appear to be struggling. For instance, the November 2003 issue of *Education Week* included an article titled "Budget Crises May Undercut Laptop Efforts" (Trotter, 2003). It described a number of school districts throughout the country that were having second thoughts about participating in "laptop for every student" initiatives. School districts in Maine, Michigan, Washington, and South Carolina had decided not to participate in state-sponsored programs or to withdraw from programs they had already started. The fundamental problem presented was that educational policy makers had invested significant resources on initial funding for the laptop program without considering future costs. It has been well documented that for many technology programs, ongoing costs for staff support, training, repairs, and upgrades frequently equal if not exceed the start-up costs.

At a meeting held in June 2000, in Atlanta, the CEO Forum on Education, a group of business and education leaders, observed in its 3rd Annual Report that new computer hardware flooding into schools "may go to waste" unless educators take time to develop clear plans for how the technology will be put to work for students (Weiner, 2000). In one national survey conducted by *Education Week*, only 20% of teachers indicated that they were well prepared to integrate technology into their lessons (Jerald & Orlofsky, 1999, p. 61). Cheryl Lemke, president and CEO of the Metiri Group, a learning technology consulting firm based in Los Angeles, California, observed a "disconnect" between why policy makers invest money in technology in public schools and what they expect from it once it is there (Trotter, 1998, p. 6).

Problems of hardware cost and software development and acquisition are being resolved, but other problems such as curricular integration and staff development remain. Careful planning at both the district and school building levels would more clearly define these problems and provide alternatives for their resolution. Planning for technology requires concentrating on a total application. By choosing an application and asking what is needed to make it successful, educators will naturally have to consider questions regarding obvious components such as hardware and software as well as other less obvious components such as staff development, curricular integration, facilities, and ongoing maintenance. To emphasize further the importance of planning, the U.S. federal government now requires school districts to have approved technology plans to participate in the Universal Service Fund program, commonly known as the E-Rate program. Most states have also established a similar requirement in order to apply for technology grant programs funded by the No Child Left Behind Act of 2002.

Another important aspect of planning is evaluation and feedback. Although schools have implemented computer applications, few have evaluated them in terms of achieving intended goals or objectives. Evaluation in education is not easy, given the variability of human conditions and skills. However, because they are dealing with new approaches, administrators need to assess what works or does not work in their schools. What is successful in one school or district may not be successful in another. Why this happens is the essence of evaluation, a process that identifies strengths and weaknesses in all the various components of an application within a specific operating environment. For example, excellent hardware with poor software will likely not result in a successful application, nor will excellent hardware and software assure success without staff who know how to use them properly. All components depend on each other, and a weakness in one affects all the others. By the same token, a particular strength in one component may disguise or make up for weaknesses in another component. For instance, some of the early successes of computer applications in the schools involved teachers and administrators who were most interested in and enthused about using technology. Their basic interests and enthusiasm were strengths that made for apparent successful applications even in cases in which software was mediocre or facilities were inadequate. However, as administrators attempted to replicate these applications with less interested or less knowledgeable staff in other settings, the weaknesses frequently became more apparent and the applications failed.

Planning for technology also requires involvement of the people who will ultimately use a computer application, be they administrators, teachers, or clerical staff. For the many reasons already discussed, educators have been cautious and in some cases even antagonistic regarding computer technology. Top-down implementation of computer applications without consultation and involvement will likely increase resistance among staff and may possibly doom entire undertakings. Involvement is critical—particularly in identifying training and curricular needs and other less obvious components of a computer application, to say nothing of securing the commitment of those who will ultimately influence its success or failure. In private industry, public agencies, and other segments of society that have been using computer technology for many years, the concept of planning has become widely accepted. For many organizations, planning resulted from trial and error, like some schools are experiencing today. For others, planning resulted from a gradual change in thinking that evolved as their organizations became more dependent on computer technology. At the same time, systems analysts, software engineers, and information specialists became managers who were increasingly involved in the overall operations. Their prior training in systematic problem solving and analysis allowed them to adapt their analytical skills to broader organizational issues that required planning and evaluation methods and tools.

Conversely, in school systems, with the exception of some larger school districts, systems analysts and designers generally are not present in the administrative hierarchy. As a result, school administrators and teachers must assume the responsibility for planning for technology.

THE SYSTEMS APPROACH

In presenting any topic, a basic framework for study needs to be established. Systems theory is most appropriate for the major topics of this book: technology in primary and secondary schools and the need for planning for successful implementation of technology applications. The basic systems concepts of "input, process, and output" and their interrelationship are generally accepted as fundamental to all aspects of computer technology. For example, the basic configuration of a computer hardware system consists of one input device, a central processor, and one output device. All other hardware configurations are variations of this, whether with multiple input, processor, or output devices or with multiple hardware systems and subsystems working together.

The systems approach is also appropriate for studying schools and school processes, including planning. Many social scientists and sociologists would describe and analyze schools as social systems. Basic concepts of input, process, and output are regularly applied to communities, students, teaching, curriculum, and outcomes in describing school systems. Using systems theory for presenting the technical aspects of computing technology and the planning aspects of school administration makes for a consistent, integrated approach for presenting the material in this book. It would be difficult and perhaps impossible to identify another framework that would work as well.

ORGANIZATION

This book is organized into three major sections. Section I provides the basic concepts and foundation material for an overall understanding of the themes and major issues related to planning for technology in schools and school systems. The foundation of sound planning is conceived as the total application of the technology. Important policy issues in planning for technology are also presented.

Section II presents major applications of technology as used in schools today. A variety of administrative and instructional applications are examined in terms of planning implications.

Section III develops the implementation of each of the five major components of successful computer applications: hardware, software, staff, facilities, and finances. The objective is to relate each of these components to an overall application.

The book concludes with appendices and a glossary of technical terms. Appendix A is designed to provide a review of basic computer concepts. Appendix B identifies the competencies required for educational administrators to be leaders in planning, developing, and implementing technology in their schools and districts. Appendix C, which is located on the Companion Website, serves as a checklist to help educators evaluate instructional software. The Glossary is a quick reference for providing definitions of technical terms.

SUMMARY

This book offers a foundation that educators can use to become the agents for realizing the potential of technology in their schools. The current state of the uses of computer technology for administrative and instructional applications has been briefly described in this chapter. Administrative applications have progressed steadily, but opinions vary as to the benefits of computer technology in regard to instructional applications. Administrators need to plan and carefully evaluate the implementation of computer technology in their schools. The chapter also establishes systems theory as an appropriate framework for examining technology and planning its implementation.

KEY CONCEPTS AND QUESTIONS

1. Schools have not evolved as other organizations have in the use of computer technology. Why?

2. Administrative computer applications are different in design and purpose from instructional or academic applications. Are there counterparts to administrative applications in organizations other than schools? How are they similar or dissimilar? Are there counterparts to instructional applications in noneducational organizations? How are they similar or dissimilar?

3. Administrative applications have progressed more steadily than instructional applications. Why? Is this changing? Will it change in the future? Explain.

4. Planning for computer technology should center on the application rather than on only hardware, software, or other individual components. How and where in a district or school should this planning occur? Who should be the major participants in planning for technology? Explain.

5. Systems theory is appropriate to computer applications in schools. What is the systems approach? Does it apply only to technology such as computer systems? Identify nontechnical environments in which the systems approach is an appropriate framework for describing and analyzing processes.

SUGGESTED ACTIVITIES

To complete the Suggested Activities online, go to the Companion Website at **www.prenhall.com/picciano,** then to this chapter's *Suggested Activities module.*

REFERENCES

Arnesan, L., & Bancroft, A. (2003). *No horizon is so far.* Cambridge, MA: Da Capo Press.

Becker, H. J. (1991). How computers are used in United States schools: Basic data from the 1989 I.E.A. Computers in Education survey. *Journal of Educational Computing Research, 7*(4), 385–406.

Becker, H. J. (1994). *Analysis and trends of school use of new information technologies.* Irvine: Department of Education, University of California.

Bork, A. (1997). The future of computers and learning. *Technological Horizons in Education Journal, 24*(11), 69–77.

Cuban, L. (2001). *Oversold and underused.* Cambridge, MA: Harvard University Press.

Fatemi, E. (1999). Building the digital curriculum. *Education Week, 19*(4), 5–8.

Gagné, R. M. (1977). *The conditions of learning.* New York: Holt, Rinehart & Winston.

Grimm, E. (1988). Coming on fast in the classroom. *Think: The IBM Magazine, 54*(6), 5–8.

Jerald, C. D., & Orlofsky, G. F. (1999). Raising the bar on school technology. *Education Week, 19*(4), 58–69.

Molnar, A. R. (1997). Computers in education: A brief history. *Technological Horizons in Education Journal, 24*(11), 63–68.

O'Brien, J. A. (1989). *Computer concepts and applications with an introduction to software and BASIC.* Homewood, IL: Irwin.

Papert, S. (1997). Educational computing: How are we doing? *Technological Horizons in Education Journal, 24*(11), 78–80.

Quality Education Data. (1996). *Education market guide and mailing list catalog 1996–97.* Denver: Quality Education Data.

Sarason, S. (1995). *Parental involvement and the political principle: Why the existing governance structure of schools should be abolished.* San Francisco: Jossey-Bass.

Trotter, A. (1998). A question of effectiveness. *Education Week, 18*(5), 6–9.

Trotter, A. (2003, November 5). Budget crises may undercut laptop efforts [Electronic version]. *Education Week, 23*(10), 1, 21.

Trumbull, D. J. (1986). Games children play: A cautionary tale. *Educational Leadership, 43*(6), 18–21.

Weiner, R. S. (2000, June 28). More planning needed for school technology. *New York Times,* p. B10.

Yates, D. S. (1983). In defense of CAI: Is drill and practice a dirty word? *Curriculum Review, 22*(5), 55–57.

Chapter 2

Basic Concepts of Planning

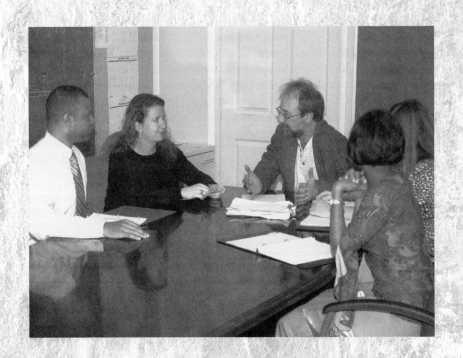

One of the most fully treated topics in educational administration is planning. Numerous books, articles, and guides have been written on how to plan and whom to involve in educational planning. Journals devoted entirely to issues of planning are available to enable administrators to keep up-to-date with the most current thinking. Consultants abound at conferences where sessions are routinely dedicated to planning, its theories, and practices. On the other hand, skepticism exists regarding the value of planning in education, particularly during periods of fiscal constraint and "tight budgets" (Engvall, 1995). The major purpose of this chapter is not to review this extensive literature but to provide a framework for educational planning as related to technology.

First, a generally accepted definition of planning is elusive. In one extensive review of the literature, Adams (1987) provided at least seven different definitions, all of which he considered incomplete. An obvious reason for his conclusion is that planning means different things to different people and is done for different purposes. However, common elements of a definition involve individuals thinking about and developing strategies to prepare their organizations for the future.

Second, planning goes on in all organizations, including schools and school systems, and takes on different characteristics. Planning can be structured, formal, top-down, and nonparticipatory in some cases, versus unstructured, informal, bottom-up, and highly participatory in others. It can involve complex social and administrative phenomena such as economics, personalities, and individual needs.

Third, schools are social systems that in the course of their activities, including planning, consider the social needs of students, teachers, administrators, and communities within the context of the school and the larger social environment.

These assumptions form the basis for constructing a framework to define and describe planning in educational organizations. They may be considered oversimplifications of a very complex topic; however, because this book is written for all who are involved in school administration and technology, these assumptions recognize and respect a variety of existing situations. The implementation of this framework is left to the judgment of superintendents, principals, assistant principals, and other administrators, most of whom know best what will work in their schools. Educational leaders must be aware of the differences that exist within a community and among individual constituents if planning is to be successful in their schools (Engvall, 1995).

SCHOOLS AS SOCIAL SYSTEMS

Various theories and models have been developed to describe and explain the way schools operate in our society. Most of them stem from general organization theory and development. The writings of organizational theorists such as Chester Barnard (1964), Herbert Simon (1945, 1957, 1960), Talcott Parsons (1951, 1958), and Amitai Etzioni (1961) are cited in basic administration courses and form the foundation of much of our knowledge in this area.

The more recent literature in educational administration deals with topics such as organizational culture, strategic planning, environmental scanning, transformational leadership, school-based management, and shared decision making. The common thread throughout this material is the assumption that schools operate, as do most organizations, as part of their larger societies. Teachers, students, and administrators interact with each other in a place called school and also interact individually and collectively with their communities and larger societies.

Figure 2.1 is a simplified version of a social process model developed by Getzels and Guba (1957) that is applicable to any social system and easily adaptable to a school. In this model, a school functions as a subsystem (institution) that interacts with the larger environmental social system. The needs of individuals as well as the expectations (roles) of the school (institution) operating within and responding to the values of the culture of the larger environment (community) are the essential elements. Processes such as teaching, administering, and planning that operate within the schools are social processes involving people and social interactions. This concept provides an important fundamental assumption for understanding educational planning processes.

Using this model, administrators would plan and make decisions based on the human needs of people both inside and outside the school—including students, teachers, parents, and taxpayers. The model also supports the practice of allowing others to participate in administrative processes. Several school systems

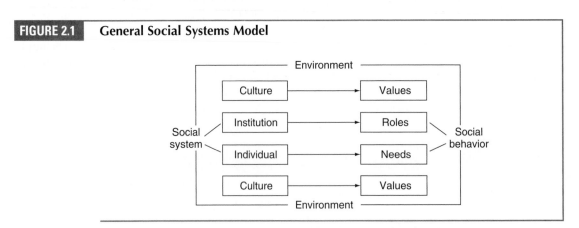

FIGURE 2.1   **General Social Systems Model**

Source: Adapted from the social process model cited by Getzels and Guba (1957).

(e.g., Chicago, Denver, New York, and Miami) have implemented school-based management and shared decision making in their schools; their policies are based on this concept.

As with most theories or models, this one is not perfect. One common criticism is that a social system model is not the most efficient approach for administering complex organizations. Involving many people in administrative processes is time-consuming and leads to more decisions based on consensus and sharing of resources rather than on optimization of resources. Furthermore, people do not always operate in a purely rational manner. They may be focused too much on individual needs and issues and not necessarily on the needs of the school or society as a whole. Indeed, we would be naive to expect a social system model to provide a perfect explanation of how such a complex organization operates. The best way to use this or any other model is to assume that it provides direction focused on a "big picture," that it will not fit perfectly, and that conceptually it exists on a continuum.

EVALUATING THE BOTTOM LINE: THE SOCIAL PROCESS AND RATIONAL MODELS

Figure 2.2 represents a continuum with the social process model on the right and its opposite, the purely economic (or rational) model, on the left. The economic/rational model posits that schools operate similarly to private businesses, with an emphasis on bottom-line profits. In practice, it is a problem to administer schools and other nonprofit social agencies strictly according to this model. Unlike businesses, in which one can compare earnings and costs with a common evaluation measure (the dollar), a school's "earnings" are very difficult to define. "Earnings" in education are imperfect. Evaluation measures such as student academic achievement (as a function of student potential), social development, and other student outcomes do not compare or measure well with their costs. Universally accepted measures for student achievement do not exist. Standardized tests have been the subject of intense

FIGURE 2.2 **Continuum of Economic/Rational and Social Process Models of Organizational Behavior**

Source: Adapted from Luthans (1981).

debate regarding their validity, reliability, cultural bias, and poor administration, and leading education researchers have expressed concerns about their misuse (Vladero, 2000, p. 6). Other techniques for measuring student achievement—such as portfolios and outcomes-based education—are also difficult to compare to costs.

Human talents and abilities are very diverse. One child may be a poor reader with a talent for mathematics. Another child may perform poorly in mathematics but be a gifted writer. Experienced administrators and teachers would probably agree that the most desirable outcome would be for these children to achieve their potential in all subjects while recognizing that they will probably achieve much more in their strengths than their weaknesses. However, attempting to measure these outcomes becomes an almost impossible task given existing achievement measures and assessment techniques.

The wide disparity in school district spending even within the same states and counties, municipalities, communities, and boards of education clearly shows that school districts have very different ideas regarding appropriate costs for their children's education. This further complicates the problem of establishing evaluation measures and attempting to understand and administer school programs according to the economic/rational model.

Instead, what schools do is attempt to serve their children as best they can by offering variety in their curricula and by hiring trained teachers who understand children's diverse needs and talents and can interact with them appropriately. In managing and coordinating schools, administrators interact with teachers and other staff as well as with parents, school board members, state education departments, colleges, and local businesses to try and understand the environment in which these children will eventually use their talents and abilities. However, administrators and teachers will admit that their understanding of this environment is imperfect. Social interaction helps improve our understanding of educational goals and outcomes and the problems in achieving them, but it does not perfect this understanding.

These concepts stem from the foundations of organizational theory. An individual commonly associated with them and whose work is highly recommended for further reference is Herbert Simon (1945, 1957, 1960, 1979, 1982). Simon was awarded the Nobel Prize for Economics in 1978 for his research on decision making in organizations. His theory on the limits of rationality—later renamed "bounded rationality"—posits as its main principle that organizations operate along a continuum of rational and social behaviors mainly because the knowledge necessary to function strictly according to a rational model is beyond what is available to administrators and managers. Although first developed in the 1940s, this theory has withstood the test of time and is widely recognized as a fundamental assumption in understanding organizational processes such as decision making and planning (Carlson & Awkerman, 1991; Luthans, 1981; Peters & Waterman, 1982; Tyson, 2002). Simon (1991) has devoted a good deal of effort during the past 30 years to examining the role that computer technology can play in expanding the knowledge necessary for administrators to be more effective planners and decision makers.

■ COMMON ELEMENTS OF EDUCATIONAL PLANNING

In a review of planning processes, Sheathelm (1991) identified four major elements of successful planning as the four Cs:

- ■ Comprehensiveness
- ■ Collaboration
- ■ Commitment
- ■ Continuity

They are very much worth exploring for developing a framework in planning for technology.

Comprehensiveness

Planning needs to be comprehensive. A total view of a school and what it is supposed to accomplish for students and the community is an essential element. An important distinction here is the difference between having a total view and necessarily having solutions for everything. Part of planning is examining and understanding both the school and the environment as much as possible with the caveat that they cannot be understood entirely. Likewise, providing solutions for problems that are not fully understood is an imperfect if not impossible way of operating. Administrators need to be aware of the needs of individuals (i.e., students, teachers, other administrators, board members) that may be specific and at times very unique. These needs can frequently be converted into goals and objectives on which a plan is formulated. On the other hand, teachers and staff frequently need to have a better understanding of the total enterprise, including objectives and resource availability. The essence of a comprehensive plan links individual needs and objectives into overall institutional goals.

Collaboration

Planning needs to be collaborative. Although administrators generally have a good deal of expertise in education, they need to rely on others to help improve their understanding. Specialists such as science teachers or speech therapists know their subjects better than administrators. Business managers, librarians, counselors, school nurses, and other staff have specific expertise that frequently is more complete and more current than that of a general administrator such as a principal or superintendent. This vast pool of knowledge, expertise, and experience should become a vital part of any planning process.

In addition to the exchange of knowledge, collaboration also allows for greater appreciation of several perspectives of a goal, objective, or need. As Deborah Meier— a nationally recognized school reformer and founder of Central Park East elementary and secondary schools—states, educators need to develop "the capacity to see the world as others might" (1995, p. 40).

Commitment

Through collaboration, securing the commitment of those who are vital in carrying out a plan becomes easier. Commitment is critical because the best plan will not be realized if the people who are expected to implement it are not committed to the task. Commitment comes from being involved with formulating overall goals and objectives and with developing specific courses of action. Collaboration also allows others to understand a plan, a goal, or a course of action and the purposes behind it. Greater understanding generally fosters higher levels of commitment.

The commitment of administrative leaders such as principals and superintendents to planning is also critical. Commitment from teachers, staff, or parents will only come if there is a sense on their part that the administrative leadership is committed to a plan. Administrators must exercise their leadership skills in securing commitment by offering themselves as examples in sharing knowledge, formulating goals, developing objectives, and implementing courses of action.

Continuity

Every planning process is continuous and never-ending. Societies, schools, and people are constantly changing, and plans must change with them. An organization is like a living organism that continually responds and adjusts to environmental stimuli. As the values of a society change, so must the way schools prepare students to live and function in that society. As new tools and technologies are developed, so should our methods of training students to use these tools and technologies.

Planning usually involves developing a written plan as a result of a series of meetings and committee work. However, planning does not begin with these activities and end with the production of the written plan. On the contrary, the written plan is a guideline for everyday activities. Administrators, teachers, and staff follow this guideline and accumulate information on how well the objectives of the plan are being implemented. This new information (including adjustments to the plan) then becomes input for further planning activity.

▊ PLANNING FOR TECHNOLOGY

An overall model for planning for technology in a school district is shown in Figure 2.3, which is derived from the social process model. This model attempts to show planning for technology as proceeding from values defined by the environment toward goals and objectives formulated primarily at the school district level. To achieve these goals and objectives, computer applications are identified as the main courses of action that in turn require hardware and software, staff needs, facilities, and finances to be implemented or provided for at the school building level. Once

FIGURE 2.3   **Model for Planning for Technology**

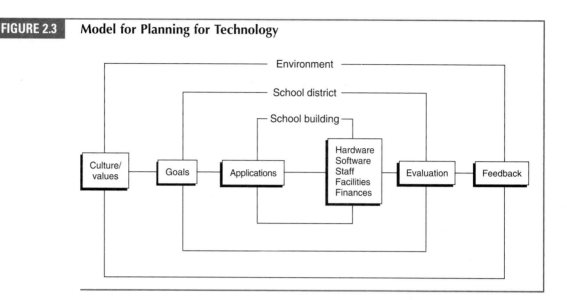

implemented, they are subsequently evaluated, and feedback is provided to the planning process for establishing new goals, objectives, and applications and for revising existing ones. Information flows both ways in this process, from left to right as well as from right to left.

The model requires a good deal of information gathering and idea sharing, which may be done formally through committees as well as informally through ad hoc discussions, observations, visits, and reading the literature. This model fits well and should be integrated with other planning activities in the school district.

An important feature of this model is that it incorporates external *environmental scanning*, which simply means engaging in activities to provide information on the community, state, and society for planning purposes. In addition to understanding societal and community values, environmental scanning is critical for comprehending changes in technology. The fundamental nature of technology includes change and, in the field of electronics and computers, rapid change. For many people involved with technology, this is frustrating but also invigorating. Developing an understanding of trends in hardware and software is important and enables planners to avoid technology that will quickly become obsolete. Successful environmental scanning involves establishing and developing contacts with experts in the community, local colleges, and private businesses. District-wide committees for planning for technology are becoming common and can be used effectively as the bridges between school districts and the communities they serve.

A basic assumption of this model is that an administrator, most likely at the district level, provides the necessary leadership in converting environmental values and conditions into district-wide goals and objectives. Committees may be necessary for specific areas such as administrative applications or instructional applications, which allow for participation on the part of administrative staff and teachers. Identifying courses of action and technology applications, in particular, should also allow for input from sources at the building level. In a study of the progress of a technology committee headed by a principal at an elementary school in Boise, Idaho, Keeler (1996) concluded that cooperation and collaboration were enhanced and the principal was viewed more as "a leader and model of lifelong learning than as a manager of a school" (p. 342). A computer teacher or library media specialist can also function as a coordinator who leads a building-level committee for identifying applications that coincide with district-wide goals and objectives. In large high schools with several thousand students, several such committees might exist representing different subject areas or grade levels.

By allowing teachers, parents, and others in a school to participate, those responsible for planning become more knowledgeable about the alternative courses of action and applications that a district might support. It is thus important to include at various levels the input of a school district's business officer or manager who can provide information on available financial resources. Naturally, planning is easier if the available financial resources can support all the various proposals that are being considered. However, if these resources are not available, then administrators will need to draw on their leadership abilities in bringing committees to agreement on which proposals to include and which to exclude. If true participation has been effected, then priorities should become more evident to all participants.

A plan covers a period of time, frequently from 3 to 7 years, which can allow for more inclusion than exclusion. Administrators should attempt to be equitable and to distribute resources among competing participants. If resources are severely limited, then a major goal of the planning participants should be securing more funds rather than developing applications. In this case, the participation of community representatives may help identify and develop financial support from various sources, including governmental (federal, state, local) and private agencies.

A pivotal step in a planning process using the technology planning model depicted in Figure 2.3 is the development of a written plan. The purpose here is to provide understanding of the plan to all participants. Just as information flow is critical in the formative stages of planning, a written summary of what has been discussed or agreed on is essential for implementing the plan. Participants and others such as board members, administrators, and teachers need to understand what the goals are and what their responsibilities are in achieving them. School districts, in fact, can be creative in presenting and communicating their goals and objectives. Such creativity is desirable and not only helps participants and constituents understand the plan but also builds interest in it. Written summaries also form the basis for the next cycle of planning activities. Figure 2.4 and Figure 2.5 are excerpts from state and school district educational technology plans.

Evaluation and feedback are critical for continuing planning activities from year to year or from planning cycle to planning cycle. Planning participants need information on how well computer applications are achieving objectives. This can only be provided if mechanisms are established for evaluating applications and generating feedback to the planning participants.

FIGURE 2.4	**Excerpt of a State's Educational Technology Planning Guidelines**

Educational Technology Planning Guidelines

"Washington State's education system must prepare students for their futures, not this generation's past. Reflection on the driver for educational restructuring nationally brings a recognition of tension between an education system designed for the industrial age and the reality of an information age.

Technology has changed the very fabric of today's society. It has been a driver of change in such areas as global communications, economics, the arts, politics, and environmental issues. Education must analyze the changing fiber of today's society and weave the reality of the information age into the education system.

Technology is key to learners' achievement of world class standards. First and foremost is the critical need for students to be able to access information, manipulate data, synthesize concepts, and creatively express ideas to others using video, text, and audio media. Technology can virtually bring the world to the child, providing a depth and richness of instructional approaches to reach children of all learning modalities. The child becomes a "knowledge architect" using the rich resources at his/her fingertips through technology to bring personal meaning and expression to knowledge.

Secondly, technology is an administrative tool which can bring efficiency to the management and assessment realms of education. This is especially important as teachers begin to use performance-based assessment to continuously improve the students' learning. The power of the technology allows easy tracking of student work enabling teachers to develop and maintain individual learning profiles for all learners.

Our changing society and workplace demand citizens who can take responsibility for their own learning and well being. Educational reforms which can develop these citizens are dependent on the adequate and appropriate infusion of technology to support the new education system."

Washington State educators have identified seven roles learners will play as they use technology in order to achieve the essential academic learning requirements:

1. The student as information navigator
2. The student as critical thinker and analyzer using technology
3. The student as creator of knowledge using technology, media, and telecommunications
4. The student as effective communicator through a variety of appropriate technologies/media
5. The student as a discriminating selector of appropriate technology for specific purposes
6. The student as technician
7. The student as a responsible citizen, worker, learner, community member, and family member in a technological age

Source: From the Quincy (Washington) Public Schools Technology Plan. Retrieved December 26, 2004, from the Quincy School District Web site (http://www.qsd.wednet.edu/qsdtechplan.htm).

| FIGURE 2.5 | **Excerpt of a School District's Educational Technology Plan** |

Educational Technology Goals

The Groton Public Schools Educational Technology Curriculum is based upon the belief that the ability to utilize technology is an essential life skill. Technology empowers students to be more actively engaged in their learning.

Technology shall be fully integrated across all content areas as a tool which supports all curricula. In order to utilize this tool, students are entitled to a comprehensive and integrated technology curriculum.

The Educational Technology Curriculum is organized into four competency areas each containing six content strands.

1. *Literacy*
Students will be able to identify, define, and explain terms and equipment associated with educational technology in the content strands of networking, video production, electronic communication, publishing and presentation, hardware, and the Internet.

2. *Application*
Students will demonstrate knowledge and skills in the use of technology in the content strands of networking, video production, electronic communication, publishing and presentation, hardware, and the Internet.

3. *Presentation*
Students will use multiple technology resources to access, interpret, analyze, synthesize, apply, and communicate information in the content strands of networking, video production, electronic communication, publishing and presentation, hardware, and the Internet.

4. *Ethics*
Students will understand important issues of a technology-based society and will exhibit ethical behavior in the use of technology in the content strands of networking, video production, electronic communication, publishing and presentation, hardware, and the Internet.

Source: From the Groton (Connecticut) Public Schools Mission Statement. Retrieved December 22, 2003, from GPS Online (http://www.groton.k12.ct.us/itsgpt2.htm).

TAKING A POSITIVE ATTITUDE TO EVALUATION

Undertaking evaluation with a positive attitude is desirable for all involved in the planning process. Unfortunately, educators approach evaluation with caution or reluctance, especially when it is conducted or administered by others or "outsiders." For decades, school and governmental officials have used formal measures such as SAT scores, state competency testing, and other standardized instruments to evaluate school performance. The 21st century ushered in another era of school standards in which testing is used to monitor student achievement and progress. And once again, many view testing as unjustified pressure brought on teachers and children to perform. On the other hand, testing is viewed as the mechanism needed to hold schools accountable for the enormous investment that has been made in public education in this country. The entire issue of standardized testing has and will continue to be hotly debated for years to come among educators, politicians, and government officials.

Educators must not abandon evaluation in their planning but instead should attempt to develop evaluation criteria on which participants (administrators, teachers, parents) can agree. This is especially true for technology planning because resources will be scrutinized even in the most financially able school districts. Large expenditures for equipment, staffing, and facilities are common when implementing technology and justifiably should be evaluated carefully.

In developing evaluation criteria for technology planning, the measures should be appropriate to the goals. Goals for administrative applications frequently require summative evaluation criteria and the establishment of timetables and milestones for accomplishing certain events. Goals for instructional applications may or may not require standardized measures. However, if an instructional goal is directed to student achievement, then testing or other performance measures are appropriate evaluation criteria and should be considered.

For instructional applications involving student achievement, multiple evaluation criteria are highly recommended. As an example, Rock and Cummings (1994) described a project designed to evaluate the implementation of interactive video technology in 15 schools in California, Illinois, Missouri, New York, Pennsylvania, Oregon, Texas, and West Virginia. The program was funded by Optical Data Corporation, a leading provider of multimedia software, but school administrators and teachers were free to design their own evaluation criteria. In every school, a standardized test—such as the Iowa Test of Basic Skills, the Missouri Master Achievement Test, or the New York State Regents Examination—was used in conjunction with some other measure, such as a student attitude questionnaire, portfolio assessment, or classroom observation. Of the 15 schools, 7 used two evaluation criteria, 2 used three criteria, and 6 used four or more criteria. Teachers and administrators reported that the use of videotape to observe and record student involvement and interactivity with lessons was particularly helpful because significant differences were consistently observed between classes using the interactive video technology and those not using it.

Educators and policy makers must also prepare for the reality that not every plan and implementation will be successful. However, good technology planning will minimize risks by establishing basic evaluation criteria early in the process. This is especially important for major technology initiatives involving an entire district. Dick and Carey (1985), Thigarajan, Semmel, and Semmel (1974), and Willis (1993) propose an instructional development research model (see Figure 2.6) that is appropriate for this type of evaluation. This model essentially recommends defining, designing, developing, and disseminating technology in small incremental stages until satisfied that the technology is meeting expected goals on a limited basis before implementing it on a larger scale. Such an approach reduces the risk of making a large investment in technology that may not be beneficial.

FIGURE 2.6   **Four-D Model for Instructional Development**

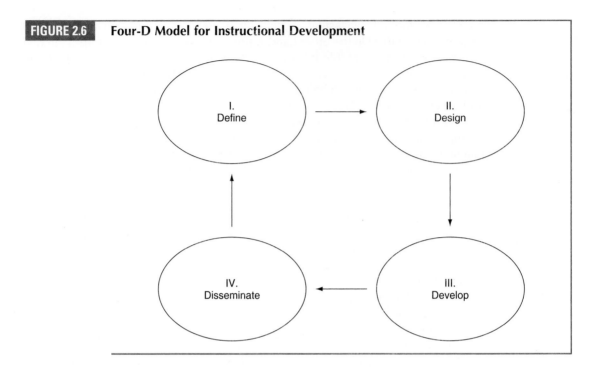

ADMINISTRATIVE AND INSTRUCTIONAL APPLICATIONS

The most important characteristic of this framework for planning is the concentration on technology applications as the fundamental courses of action. Applications simply refer to applying technology to the goals and objectives of the plan. Most important for our understanding is that the identification of these applications precedes the acquisition of their components such as hardware, software, staff development, and facilities. Applications may use existing hardware and software components, but they should not be determined simply because of these preexisting components. Otherwise, planning becomes the classic case of the tail wagging the dog.

In many cases, different types of applications require different components. Administrative applications are different from instructional applications. Within instruction, writing applications are different from science applications, which are different from those for social studies, music, art, and so forth. As an example, when computer technology consisted of large mainframe computers, many users depended on and shared common hardware and software because the costs would otherwise be prohibitive. However, it did not work well then, and it does not work well now. Even with modern, general purpose microcomputers, certain desktop publishing programs requiring high-resolution graphics might work better with Apple Macintosh equipment than with Windows-based machines; standard, commercial database software packages might work more efficiently with Windows-based computers; some science simulation software packages might require custom probe or other specific hardware devices and interfaces.

Planning for Administrative Applications

Planning for administrative applications is different in several ways from planning for instructional applications. The goals, nature of the applications, participants, and evaluation are different. Environmental scanning is helpful in formulating goals, especially for identifying appropriate technology. State education departments, local governmental agencies, accreditation associations, and professional organizations are valuable resources for helping school districts determine the types of administrative applications that are being used in other school districts. Local businesses such as banks or insurance companies, which frequently use current information technology such as database management systems (DBMS), can be helpful in identifying appropriate software for establishing and maintaining computer-based information systems. School districts that are part of larger local or state governmental jurisdictions also need to make sure that they understand the information or administrative system requirements of these governing entities. For example, urban school districts frequently have certain administrative systems such as budgeting, payroll, and purchasing provided to them by municipal agencies. Any planning involving these systems should provide for participation by the municipal agents familiar with the future development of these systems.

In planning administrative applications, the goals of a district can be stated in many different ways, and planners are encouraged to be creative to generate interest in a plan. However, administrative applications frequently relate to common themes such as the following:

- To develop/improve information resources
- To provide/improve new administrative services
- To improve/increase administrative productivity and efficiency

These themes can be stated in many different ways as goals, objectives, and applications in actual planning documents.

Information resources are all aspects of the data collection, storage, and retrieval processes and procedures needed by school administrators to monitor, report, and understand what is going on in their schools. The major data collection and record-keeping applications in most schools pertain to students, curriculum, finances, personnel, and facilities. They typically use database management software systems that are maintained centrally at the district level and that can be distributed to the individual schools.

Providing new administrative services is a broad goal with an emphasis on doing or improving that which is not being done or not being done well. Examples include expanding student grade reports to provide prescriptive information, automating substitute teacher lists, improving general communications to parents and residents, or establishing an online student guidance system. These services may use database, office automation, e-mail, Internet, electronic spreadsheet, or desktop publishing software, and they can be developed centrally at the district level or locally at the building level.

Increasing productivity and efficiency in administrative operations is frequently associated with computer technology and refers to improving information and communication flow. For example, database management systems have been particularly effective in improving reporting and reducing redundant data-gathering activities (e.g., having two or more offices collecting the same information). Providing administrative staff with office automation software such as word processing, e-mail, and electronic spreadsheet programs has also been widely accepted because it helps them become much more efficient in presenting, communicating, and assembling all types of text- and number-based materials.

The major leadership in planning for administrative applications exists centrally at the district level, because applications involving information flow and data management typically are directed and controlled centrally. Building-level administrators and staff should understand and accept the need for central administrative information systems. However, in planning administrative systems, staff at the building level should be involved. They are important resource people who begin the information cycle by collecting source data on students, families, personnel, payrolls, and so on. They will do a better job of data collection if they understand the purposes of their efforts. They will do a spectacular job if they personally can realize some benefits such as less paperwork or less need to do repetitive periodic reports. They can also help planners determine staff development and training needs that are as important for secretaries and administrative assistants as they are for teachers and instructional staff.

Developing evaluation criteria as part of the planning process is usually very straightforward for administrative applications. Initially, it involves determining whether certain milestones in developing an application are being met, culminating with the application becoming operational. For example, the evaluation criteria for the development of a new computer-based financial information system might be to establish dates by which certain modules or subsystems are to be operational. When the system is established, additional evaluation criteria might involve comparing the timeliness and accuracy of critical reports before and after the system became operational.

Figure 2.7 provides a partial example of a school district's plan for implementing a new integrated financial management system. The plan is organized with goals relating well to objectives and the application, and it also shows how planning goals respond to needs emanating from both outside and inside the district. Objectives are clearly stated, and appropriate time frames are established for design, implementation, and evaluation. Focusing on the financial management application, the plan also provides for various components such as hardware, software, and staff development.

Chapter 4 is dedicated exclusively to an examination of the major administrative applications that can exist in a school. There you will find additional information related to planning for these applications.

FIGURE 2.7	**Samples of Planning Goals and Objectives for an Administrative Technology Application**

Background

The following is excerpted from a planning document for implementing an integrated financial management system in a school district. The need for this system occurred because of changes in the way funds were provided by external agencies (i.e., state aid), which increasingly were being allocated later in the school year, requiring the school district to make allocations and adjustments to allocations even later. In addition, demands for fiscal data and accountability had increased significantly from both external funding agencies and internal departments. This application was designed to replace several nonintegrated computer applications that were implemented in the district office in the 1980s.

North Central School District No. 1
Six-Year Technology Plan (1998–2004)

Goals (from district's long-range plan)
Improve financial reporting capabilities to external funding agencies.
Improve financial record keeping within the district.
Improve fiscal accountability within each of the schools in the district.

- •
- •
- •

Objectives (1998–1999)
Design the requirements of a new, integrated financial management system (FMS).

- •
- •
- •

Objectives (1999–2000)
Evaluate computer software products that can meet the design requirements of FMS.
Procure a computer software product that meets the design requirements of FMS.
Evaluate hardware requirements of the central office and schools for implementing FMS.
Evaluate the data communications facilities required to implement FMS in the schools.

- •
- •
- •

Objectives (2000–2001)
Acquire the necessary computer hardware in the central office to implement FMS.
Implement the financial accounting and budget modules of FMS in the central office.
Train all central office staff in the use of FMS.
Acquire the necessary data communications facilities to implement FMS in all the schools.

- •
- •
- •

(continued)

FIGURE 2.7	*continued*

Objectives (2001–2002)
Acquire the necessary computer hardware to implement FMS in the schools.
Implement the financial accounting and budget modules of FMS in the schools.
Train all school staff in the use of FMS.
Implement the purchasing and accounts payable modules of FMS in the central office.
Continue training staff in the central office in the use of FMS.

  •
  •

Objectives (2002–2003)
Implement the purchasing and accounts payable modules of FMS in the schools.
Implement the payroll and personnel modules of FMS in the central office.
Continue training staff in the central office and in the schools in the use of FMS.

  •
  •

Objectives (2003–2004)
Implement the payroll and personnel modules of FMS in the schools.
Continue training staff in the central office and in the schools in the use of FMS.
Conduct an in-depth evaluation of the benefits of FMS to the school district.

  •
  •
  •

Planning for Instructional Applications

Planning instructional applications is similar to planning administrative applications, but several differences do exist. Environmental scanning is just as important, and many of the same agencies—such as state education departments, accreditation associations, and professional organizations—can be excellent resources for information and ideas. In addition, professional organizations such as the National Education Association and the Association for Supervision and Curriculum Development are active in presenting issues on the instructional uses of technology. Local colleges, especially those with teacher education programs, may also possess valuable expertise in developing planning goals and applications.

A school district's goals and objectives regarding instructional applications can be very diverse. Several national studies (Becker, 1994; Sheingold & Hadley, 1990; U.S. Congress, 1995) indicate that instructional uses of computers frequently relate to one or more of the following themes:

■ Preparing students to participate in a technically oriented society

■ Enhancing/improving learning by using technological tools

■ Enhancing/improving teaching by using technological tools

■ Providing technology-based curricula for students with special aptitudes or interests in technology

As with administrative applications, these instructional application themes may be stated in many different ways in actual planning documents.

The first theme—preparing students to participate in a technically oriented society—recognizes that all types of jobs, professions, and everyday routines increasingly use technology. Students should develop basic competency or literacy in using technology during their primary and secondary school programs. Accomplishing this may involve taking specific, dedicated courses in computer software applications or integrating technology with other courses (such as using databases to conduct research in social studies), or a combination of both. In recent years, Internet-related activities such as the use of e-mail and searching for information on the World Wide Web have become important objectives of this theme.

The second theme—enhancing learning by employing technology—refers to students' use of technology in general curricular areas. Examples include using word processing software to teach writing, electronic spreadsheet programs to teach accounting or business subjects, the Internet to learn about other cultures, and electronic encyclopedias to do research. The list of possibilities is almost endless. Increasingly, integrating technology into the curriculum has became a major goal for many school districts in planning instructional applications.

Enhancing teaching by making use of technology refers to teachers incorporating technology in classroom presentations and other teaching activities. Specific examples are the use of large-screen monitors and other multimedia (computers and video) in the classroom. The emphasis here is on the use of technology by teachers for teaching, more so than by students for learning. A popular element of this theme is staff development and the training of teachers to use technology in the classroom.

Providing technology-based curricula for students with special talents or interests in technology is a rapidly expanding theme for many school districts. This includes special vocational programs such as computer operations, computer maintenance, and data communications. These programs can be designed to prepare students seeking employment immediately upon graduation from high school as well as to prepare them for 2-year community college programs. High school programs that offer electives in computer programming for students who are considering a computer science or engineering career can also be included.

The leadership for planning instructional applications should be shared at the district level and at the building level with the teaching staff who possess expertise in the various subject areas. Diverse subject areas and grade levels require different computer hardware and software or specialized staff training. Tens of thousands of instructional software packages are available, which make it increasingly more difficult for central office staff to keep current and maintain a level of expertise. As a result, planning for these applications more frequently allows individual teachers, academic departments, and grade-level coordinators to make specific proposals that might fit an overall planning goal. This process may also involve establishing an ongoing budget and approval mechanism for evaluating, funding, and acquiring instructional software at the building level. In addition to drawing on the expertise of many of the professional staff members, this approach also allows teachers to use technology best suited to their own teaching styles and philosophies. It should also encourage a greater commitment to its successful utilization.

Evaluating the implementation of instructional applications should include a formal assessment. In addition to establishing milestones for implementing instructional applications, a district that uses standardized tests can incorporate these into the overall evaluation criteria. A good student record-keeping system in a district should easily provide these and other student achievement data such as grades and graduation rates for evaluating an application's instructional effectiveness. Other evaluation techniques that should be considered include portfolios, student and teacher attitude surveys, and classroom observations.

Figure 2.8 is a partial example of a school district's plan for implementing multimedia technology; it illustrates several characteristics of a good instructional technology plan. Teachers are actively involved (e.g., Multimedia Coordinating Committee) in planning and implementation. Staff development is continuous and ongoing. Stages of the plan relate to grade levels. It also requires extensive evaluation and review before progressing to each successive stage of the plan.

Chapter 5 is dedicated exclusively to a review of instructional applications, and also presents additional information related to planning for these applications.

FIGURE 2.8   **Samples of Planning Goals and Objectives for an Instructional Technology Application**

Background

The following is excerpted from a planning document for implementing multimedia technology in all the schools in a school district. While several isolated uses of multimedia technology had been implemented at the high school and middle school level, this plan represented the first district-wide concerted effort. The need for this technology evolved from the recommendations of several teachers who had been using videodisc technology and CD-ROM since the early 1990s. As defined by the Technology Planning Committee, a multimedia workstation consists of a high-end microcomputer with a projector, speakers, DVD drive, and high-speed Internet connection.

South Central School District No. 1
Five-Year Technology Plan (1999–2004)

Goals (from district's long-range plan)
To improve teaching by making greater use of multimedia technology.
To enhance learning by making greater use of multimedia technology.

-
-

(continued)

FIGURE 2.8   *continued*

Objectives (1999–2000)

To establish an ad hoc Multimedia Coordinating Committee within the school district.

To conduct exploratory presentations on the use of multimedia in instruction.

To acquire six multimedia workstations and associated software for high schools.

To pilot six multimedia programs in the high schools.

To evaluate the six pilot multimedia programs in the high schools from the teachers' perspective (as a teaching tool).

- •
- •

Objectives (2000–2001)

To continue to acquire multimedia equipment and software for the high schools.

To conduct staff development programs in multimedia for high school teachers.

To acquire six multimedia workstations and associated software for the middle schools.

To pilot six multimedia programs in the middle schools.

To evaluate the six multimedia programs in the middle schools from the teachers' perspective (as a teaching tool).

- •
- •

Objectives (2001–2002)

To continue to acquire multimedia equipment and software for the middle schools.

To continue to provide staff development programs in multimedia for high school teachers.

To conduct staff development programs in multimedia for middle school teachers.

To evaluate multimedia programs in the high schools and middle schools from the students' perspective (as learning tools).

- •
- •

Objectives (2002–2003)

To acquire 12 multimedia workstations and associated software for the primary schools.

To continue to acquire multimedia equipment for the high schools and middle schools.

To continue to provide staff development programs in multimedia for high school and middle school teachers.

To pilot 12 multimedia programs in the primary schools.

To evaluate the 12 pilot multimedia programs in the primary schools from the teachers' perspective (as a teaching tool).

- •
- •

Objectives (2003–2004)

To continue to acquire multimedia equipment and software for all schools.

To provide staff development programs in multimedia for primary school teachers.

To continue to provide staff development programs in multimedia for high school and middle school teachers.

To evaluate multimedia programs in all schools from the students' perspective (as learning tools).

- •
- •

CASE STUDY

PLACE: LOTUSVILLE   YEAR: 2002

Lotusville is a suburban school district in the Southwest with an enrollment of 5,500 students distributed among one high school, three middle schools, and six primary schools. The population has been increasing by approximately 2% per year. The district's tax base has also been rising because of recent commercial development. A formal planning process was implemented in 1985 by the board of education. A district-wide Planning Committee was established and has continued to be active in establishing goals and objectives. The membership of the Planning Committee is as follows:

- Three parents, one of whom is the president of the PTA
- Two school board members
- The manager of the local bank, who is a former school board member
- A teacher who represents the teachers' union and who teaches high school mathematics
- The district superintendent
- The director of pupil personnel services for the district

The district superintendent also acts as a resource person for the Planning Committee and has established formal processes for gathering information for the committee's planning activities.

In 1990, at the suggestion of two of the parents, the Planning Committee established an Advisory Committee for Instructional Technology. Although the Planning Committee had always been supportive of technology in the instructional programs, the resources devoted to it were increasing significantly. The perception was that a need existed to review more carefully the district's future resource allocation. The Advisory Committee has the following membership:

- Two parents
- The manager of a local computer hardware distributing company
- One school board member
- A teacher who represents the teachers' union and who teaches science in the high school and was a former part-time computer coordinator

- The assistant superintendent for instruction
- The principal of one of the middle schools

The Advisory Committee has worked well with the Planning Committee and has been effective in expanding instructional computing in the district.

In the entire district in 1987, there were 40 microcomputers in two computer laboratories in the high school. These were supervised by one science teacher who was released from half of his teaching responsibilities. Pascal, BASIC, word processing, and electronic spreadsheets were taught in elective courses within the high school mathematics program. An instructional technology plan was developed in 1991 that called for a significant increase in the number of micro-computers being used for instructional purposes at all grade levels and the hiring of at least one computer teacher for each school by 1992. By 1995, the district had installed 550 microcomputers, primarily in central laboratories and open access areas in school libraries. Increasingly more units were being distributed to individual classrooms, primarily in the high school.

Currently [2002] each school has at least one full-time technology teacher who supervises the laboratories and teaches technology courses. A full-time com-puter technician has also been hired who maintains the equipment for the entire district. A wide variety of computer software packages is available for all grade levels, including simulation programs, desktop publishing, word processing, spreadsheet, database, Visual BASIC, and MS-Powerpoint. All the schools are con-nected to the Internet including the computer laboratories, libraries, and certain classrooms. All classrooms were wired by 1998. The Advisory Committee has established a technology replacement policy that maintains the number of computers at approximately 550–600 units throughout the district.

A major issue facing the district's Planning Committee is whether the expan-sion in instructional computing has been worth the investment in equipment and personnel. Annual standardized test scores indicate that academic achievement increased slightly from 1995 to 2000 but decreased slightly in the past 2 years. The teachers' representative on the Planning Committee has stated that many of the primary school teachers would like to see more microcomputers placed in the regular classrooms. The district superintendent has been advised by the assistant superintendent for instruction that locating equipment in the regular classrooms would require a major increase in the number of microcomputers and an extensive new staff development program because many teachers, especially in the primary schools, needed more training to use the technology effectively.

Continued on next page

DISCUSSION QUESTIONS

1. Analyze the preceding case study. What observations can you make regarding the effectiveness of the planning process in the Lotusville school district? Do you have any suggestions for improving it? Consider especially the structure, membership of the committees, evaluation, and feedback.

SUMMARY

This chapter describes several basic assumptions and concepts regarding educational planning for technology. A great deal of literature exists on educational planning, much of which has its roots in organization theory and development. One of the more important concepts is the idea that schools operate as social systems and are part of larger social systems. Individuals (teachers, students), organizations (schools), and larger environments (communities, towns, cities) interact with one another through social processes. One way of describing and understanding organizations is to understand that social processes provide the foundation for how they operate.

In applying the social process model, four common elements are identified as important to effective educational planning. Planning needs to be comprehensive, collaborative, and continuous. In addition, it needs to have the commitment of all involved: administrators, teachers, parents, and other community representatives.

Planning for technology can be incorporated into other educational planning activities and processes, following a social process model that involves individuals, the school, the community, and the larger environment. It should allow for participation of administrators, teachers, and staff at the district, school building, and departmental levels. Because of the dynamic and changing nature of technology, planning should extensively use environmental scanning and data gathering on technological trends and developments. Evaluation is critical to meeting objectives, and educators should adopt a positive attitude to using it in planning processes.

In the development of objectives and courses of action, applications become the fundamental building blocks on which hardware, software, staff development, facilities, and financial components depend. Administrative applications are different from instructional applications, and writing applications are different from science applications, which are different from music applications,

2. Compared with your own environment, does Lotusville appear to be more or less effective in the way it plans for technology?

3. Finally, if you were the district superintendent, what courses of action might you consider or recommend to the Planning Committee to help resolve some of the recent issues identified regarding instructional computing?

and so on. Microcomputer technology has matured to the point where specific solutions identified as applications can be provided to meet specific goals and objectives.

KEY CONCEPTS AND QUESTIONS

1. Planning is a frequently used term among individuals, schools, organizations, and government agencies. How do you define planning? What are its common elements?

2. Much has been written and said regarding what is needed for successful planning to take place in complex organizations such as schools. What are the essential elements of an organizational planning process? Are these elements evident in your organizational environment? Explain.

3. Private businesses and governmental agencies use planning processes. Are processes developed for these organizations appropriate for schools? Why or why not?

4. Schools can be described and analyzed as social systems. How do you define a social system? Who are the major participants in this system? What are their roles, if any, in planning?

5. Planning involves the establishment of goals and objectives. In planning for technology, meeting these goals and objectives should center on technology applications rather than on individual application components. What do you consider the essential components of technology applications? Are some components more important than others? Explain.

6. Planning for administrative applications and planning for instructional applications have similarities and differences. Compare the two in relation to objectives, participants, and evaluation.

7. Environmental scanning has become a frequently used term in planning processes. Why is it particularly important when planning for technology?

SUGGESTED ACTIVITIES

To complete the Suggested Activities online, go to the Companion Website at
www.prenhall.com/picciano, then to this chapter's *Suggested Activities module.*

REFERENCES

Adams, D. (1987). Paradigmatic contexts of models of educational planning and
    decision making. *Educational Planning, 6*(1), 36–47.

Barnard, C. I. (1964). *The functions of the executive.* Cambridge, MA: Harvard
    University Press.

Becker, H. J. (1994). *Analysis and trends of school use of new information
    technologies.* Irvine: Department of Education, University of California.

Carlson, R. V., & Awkerman, G. (Eds.). (1991). *Educational planning: Concepts,
    strategies, and practices.* New York: Longman.

Dick, W., & Carey, L. (1985). *The systematic design of instruction* (2nd ed.). Glenview,
    IL: Scott, Foresman.

Engvall, R. P. (1995). The limited value of planning in education: Getting back to
    basics isn't all about curriculum. *Urban Review, 27*(3), 251–262.

Etzioni, A. (1961). *A comparative analysis of complex organizations.* New York: Free
    Press.

Getzels, J. W., & Guba, E. G. (1957). Social behavior and the administrative process.
    School Review, 65, 423–441.

Keeler, C. M. (1996). Networked instructional computers in the elementary classroom
    and their effect on the learning environment: A qualitative evaluation. *Journal
    of Research on Computing in Education, 28*(3), 329–345.

Luthans, F. (1981). *Organizational behavior.* New York: McGraw-Hill.

Meier, D. (1995). *The power of their ideas: Lessons for America from a small school
    in Harlem.* Boston: Beacon.

Parsons, T. (1951). *The social system.* New York: Free Press.

Parsons, T. (1958). Some ingredients of a general theory of formal organization. In
    A. W. Halpin (Ed.), *Administrative theory in education* (pp. 40–72). Chicago:
    University of Chicago Press.

Peters, T. J., & Waterman, R. (1982). *In search of excellence.* New York: Harper & Row.

Rock, H. M., & Cummings, A. (1994). Can videodiscs improve student outcomes?
    Educational Leadership, 51(7), 46–50.

Sheathelm, H. H. (1991). Common elements in the planning process. In R. V. Carlson
    & G. Awkerman (Eds.), *Educational planning: Concepts, strategies, and practices*
    (pp. 267–278). New York: Longman.

Sheingold, K., & Hadley, M. (1990). *Accomplished teachers: Integrating computers into
    classroom practice.* New York: Bank Street College of Education, Center for Tech-
    nology in Education.

Simon, H. A. (1945). *Administrative behavior.* New York: Macmillan.

Simon, H. A. (1957). *Administrative behavior* (2nd ed.). New York: Macmillan.

Simon, H. A. (1960). *The new science of management decision.* New York: Harper & Row.

Simon, H. A. (1979). Rational decision making in business organizations. *American Economic Review, 69*, 493–513.

Simon, H. A. (1982). *Models of bounded rationality.* Cambridge, MA: MIT Press.

Simon, H. A. (1991). *Models of my life.* New York: Basic Books.

Thigarajan, S., Semmel, D., & Semmel, M. (1974). *Instructional development for training teachers of exceptional children: A sourcebook.* Reston, VA: Council for Exceptional Children.

Tyson, C. (2002). *The foundations of imperfect decision making.* Stanford, CA: Stanford Graduate School of Business Research Paper Series. Retrieved January 20, 2004, from the Stanford Graduate School of Business Web site (http://www-gsb.stanford.edu/facseminars/events/economics/pdfs/101002.pdf).

U.S. Congress, Office of Technology Assessment. (1995). *Teachers and technology: Making the connection* (Report No. OTA-EHR-616). Washington, DC: U.S. Government Printing Office.

Vladero, D. (2000). High-stakes tests lead debate at researchers' conference. *Education Week, 19*(34), 6.

Willis, J. (1993). Technology in teacher education: A research and development agenda. In H. C. Waxman & G. W. Bright (Eds.), *Approaches to research on teacher education and technology* (pp. 35–50). Charlottesville, VA: Association for the Advancement of Computing in Education.

Chapter 3

Technology, Learning, and Equity Issues

A s technology continues to expand in the nation's schools, a variety of associated issues are developing with which administrators should be familiar. Some of these derive from the larger issue of the effectiveness of technology in instruction and learning. Others are equity issues, perhaps involving gender or race, that derive from larger societal or educational policy issues. Administrators in all environments should be sensitive to these issues as they plan for and implement technology in their schools.

   This chapter reviews some of the critical issues emerging as technology expands in the schools. Knowledge and understanding of these issues are particularly important during planning activities.

TECHNOCENTRIC EDUCATION

In *Mindstorms: Children, Computers, and Powerful Ideas,* Seymour Papert (1980) revealed his philosophy regarding the beneficial effects of computer technology on learning. This was one of the first major works to weave an educational philosophy into the development of a computer programming language (Logo). In what is perhaps one of the more controversial passages, Papert says, "I am optimistic—some might say utopian—about the effect of computers on society" (p. 26). He then described the benefits of the Logo programming language on children's learning and cognitive development. For many educators, Papert's theories generated unbridled enthusiasm for the use of computing technology in the classroom. Throughout the 1980s and 1990s, Papert's work and philosophy were the subject of great debate and discussion (Becker, 1987; Davy, 1984; Maddux, 1989; Maddux & Johnson, 1997; Papert, 1987; Pea, 1983, 1987; Walker, 1987). The debate revolved around a technocentric approach to teaching and learning in which computers would become the vehicles for solving many of the problems in education. Although several educators, including Papert, have since called for a more cautious and deliberate approach in the use of computers in education, the issue remains open.

   Lewis Perelman (1992), the author of a very successful book titled *School's Out: Hyperlearning, the New Technology, and the End of Education,* called for policy makers to seize an opportunity that was presenting itself in American education. He described classroom teachers as approaching "rapid obsolescence" and stated that their jobs could be done better by technology. He called for a major overhaul of the nation's schools that would transform teaching and learning from the traditional, human interactive activity into a machine-intensive activity. He claimed that teachers could be replaced by computers and that the only reason this had not yet occurred was because the academic establishment and "educrats" were not allowing it to happen. Frank Levy, Rose Professor of Urban Economics at Massachusetts Institute of Technology, and Richard J. Murname, Thompson Professor of Education at Harvard University, disagree with Perelman and posit that teaching and learning involve complex communication processes and expert thinking that computers are not yet able to duplicate. For example, a student can download a lesson on calculus from a Web site—but while the student has access to the information, there is no guarantee that he or she will learn it. To the contrary, the student needs the help of a teacher to translate the information about calculus into usable knowledge (Levy & Murname, 2004). Although many educators consider Perelman's viewpoint extreme, it nonetheless continues to exist and should not be ignored. The use of technology is expanding, and as schools advance, questions are emerging as to how much technology should be employed in the schools. Is more technology better? Can technology replace teachers? Is it more cost-effective?

To provide further insight into this issue, an examination of integrated learning systems (ILSs) would be helpful. These systems represent the most intensive uses of technology in teaching and learning available. They integrate hardware, software, and curriculum and also usually provide sophisticated computer-managed instructional techniques that are able to customize or individualize material for each student using the system. They were designed not to be an adjunct to teaching but actually to perform the teaching function. In schools with ILSs, teachers' roles have been transformed to a certain degree from those of instructors to managers of instruction. However, in the vast majority of these schools, instruction is provided on the ILS for a limited period each week.

In 1990, the Educational Products Information Exchange (EPIE) Institute of Brookvale, New York, conducted a national study of 24 schools with these systems. Field visits were made to each site, and eight different ILSs were evaluated. In general, administrators, teachers, and students supported the use of these systems (Sherry, 1990). For example, 96% of the teachers and administrators interviewed in these schools recommended that other schools install similar systems, and 99% of the students interviewed indicated that they too would recommend these systems for other schools. Longitudinal student performance data based on grades or standardized tests were not collected. The researchers contemplated collecting the data, but they concluded that the outcomes of ILS use were "too difficult or impossible to measure" at the time. The overwhelming support for the ILSs in these schools indicated their general acceptance. The major benefits of ILSs most often cited by teachers and administrators in this study were the individualization of instruction, the extensive reporting capabilities, and the completeness of content.

Should all schools acquire such systems, and should schools with these systems expand their use? Because technology is good, is more technology better? The answer to both these questions is probably no. In addition to careful planning, EPIE recommended caution in investing in ILSs. Administrators, teachers, and students all support and endorsed their use, but their enthusiasm for such systems would not likely endure if ILSs were the primary (or only) teaching delivery system employed in their schools. Although ILSs can be important tools when integrated properly with a district's curriculum, they should not replace that curriculum entirely. Furthermore, teachers must be well trained to use these systems and to integrate them with other teaching activities.

One rationale for employing instructional technology in a school is its cost benefits. While there is a basis for this rationale in certain applications, an administrator needs to approach cautiously if committing to an unbridled infusion of technology. Trotter (2003), for example, reported that several school districts in Michigan and Maine opted not to participate in initiatives that would have provided a laptop computer for every middle school teacher and student. He observed that if given a choice between funding more technology or reducing class size, many policy makers would choose the latter. He concluded that district officials' negative reaction to the laptop initiatives reflected a more mature understanding of the costs of technology than in years past. The issue here was not simply the use and benefits of the technology, but whether the costs would be worth the educational benefits and whether other options such as the reduction of class size would be more worthwhile.

Papert's observation from *Mindstorms*, cited earlier, gave the impression that technology is a utopia for learning and education. However, later in this same passage, he referred to the computer as "a useful educational tool" (1980, p. 27). Like all tools, the value of computers and other forms of technology can vary depending on who uses them and how they are used. Administrators should adopt this "tool" mentality as opposed to a "technocentric" mentality when implementing technology. Though continuing to improve and advance, technology has not yet reached the point of replacing teachers. Administrators should be developing teachers to capture and harness the power of technology so as to integrate it with other teaching and learning activities.

WHEN SHOULD COMPUTER EDUCATION BEGIN?

Upper-grade and high school students have more access to technology than early childhood and elementary school children. Studies (Becker, 1994; Picciano, 1991; Quality Education Data, 1995; U.S. Department of Education, 2000) indicate that junior high and high schools typically have 33% more computer equipment per student than elementary schools. One major reason is that high schools and upper grades adopted computer science and computer literacy courses before the elementary schools did. Also, as students progress in their educations there is a need to start developing career skills. Another important reason entails the debate within the elementary schools as to the appropriate age at which to introduce students to technology. Whereas some schools have adopted an "earlier the better" approach, others indicate that there is no need to rush and children can learn computer skills later on in their education.

One side of this issue is based on the concept that technology is good—therefore, the more (and earlier) students can learn it, the better off they will be. The other side of this issue concerns the readiness of children to use technology. Readiness in this regard can relate to a host of subissues including cognitive development, finger dexterity, eye-hand coordination in using keyboards, comprehension of computer instructions, and integration into content areas.

Papert (1980), who lived and studied with Jean Piaget, believes that children are able to benefit from computer technology at a very early age. The fundamental Logo concept of manipulating a friendly-turtle icon was directed specifically at the young learner and is derived directly from Piaget's theories on cognitive development. Though children develop cognitively at different rates, Piaget (1952) proposed that logical thinking, at least as applied to physical reality, begins at approximately 7 to 11 years of age. The fact that, by the late 1990s, 95% of all elementary schools had acquired microcomputer equipment and were connected to the Internet for instructional purposes suggests that educators believe children are ready to begin using computer equipment at an early age (U.S. Department of Education, 2000).

Logo and its derivatives, such as Microworlds, continue to be popular instructional software packages, and have been used successfully in many elementary school programs. Offered as a content area in which children learn about computer technology, Logo is also commonly integrated with other curriculum activities such as mathematics and problem solving. The success of Logo and other software packages designed for young children also suggests that many children of elementary school age are indeed cognitively ready to use and benefit from computer experiences.

Young children's finger dexterity is not the critical issue it once was because of recent hardware developments and advancements. Although the keyboard remains the major input device for most computer hardware systems, other devices now available—such as the mouse, joystick, and trackball—are easier for children to use and manipulate. Home video games such as Nintendo continue to grow in popularity and expose children to these and other types of input devices. Special instructional input devices—such as the Muppet keyboard, which has oversized letters and keys—have also been designed for use in early childhood education and can be found in prekindergarten classes.

Computer instruction or message comprehension can be a problem in the early years if appropriate software has not been selected. Such errors in selection can result in young children staring at a video screen unable to respond to a command or becoming frustrated because they chose a logic path or continuous loop in a program from which they were unable to escape. Although these frustrating situations can and do continue to occur, even among older children and adults, careful software evaluation combined with proper supervision by teachers can minimize them.

In evaluating software for use by young children, planners should remember that children's reading comprehension level becomes most critical in determining whether they can follow the software's instructions. Educational software packages routinely include as part of the documentation the necessary reading levels required to use the programs effectively. Teachers evaluating software should match these suggested reading levels against those of their children.

In addition, teachers should not leave young children alone for extended periods of time when using technology. Young children need and appreciate regular assurance that they are doing what is expected of them.

Perhaps the most crucial decision regarding when to introduce technology into an elementary school program is its placement within the curriculum. When educational software was less abundant, the availability of software almost dictated the content areas in which computing would be used. In most cases, the targeted areas were basic skills, especially reading and mathematics. However, this has changed dramatically, with elementary schools using computers in a variety of content areas including art, social studies, and science. The abundance of quality software across content areas provides many options, and all of them should be explored. As a guiding principle, the computer should be viewed as a tool that can be integrated into various content areas of the elementary school curriculum, more so than as a subject of instruction in and of itself.

SPECIAL EDUCATION

In the past three decades, American schools have been trying to improve the education of children with special needs. Several pieces of legislation—including Section 504 of the Rehabilitation Act of 1973, the Education for All Handicapped Children Act of 1975 (Public Law 94–142), and the Individuals with Disabilities Act of 1997—prodded education policy makers to reexamine special education in the schools. An outcome of this legislation has been a movement toward inclusion of special education children into general education classrooms. This movement has presented opportunities for educators in preparing these children to participate more fully in American society. It has also presented challenges for educators to provide for the many special needs of these children.

The most fundamental tools used in education are books. Students use them in the classroom and at home to read and write. In addition to the spoken word, they are the primary means of communicating and conveying ideas. Yet, for many special education students, reading a book or writing—even simply turning a page—may be as formidable an obstacle as ascending a flight of stairs is to a person in a wheelchair. Technology is now being used by children who have difficulty learning through conventional means. Regardless of the challenge—whether hearing, vision, mobility, or learning disability—assistive technology is being used to help provide the links to learning that otherwise might not have been available to these children in years past.

For example, technology provides a variety of voice input and output devices that allow visually impaired students to hear and respond to text that is stored on a computer disk or a CD-ROM rather than printed on the pages of a book. In addition, video and text enlargers are available for students with limited vision, as are braille printers that produce embossed paper output. For students with severe motor control impairments who are unable to use their arms or hands, a number of innovative input devices have been developed that allow students to control or respond to a computer using other parts of the body. An electronic switch mechanism can be activated by wrinkling an eyebrow, moving one's jaw, puffing on a tube, or making contact with a metal plate. These switches enable students with disabilities to turn to the next page in an electronic book, respond to yes/no questions, and communicate using Morse code, which is instantly converted and displayed on a computer screen.

For a variety of other challenges including hearing, speech, and multiple disabilities, technology is also being used to provide the primary means of communication.

Special education students are able to have computers in their homes, on their wheel-chairs, and in minivans, in addition to the classroom. For many of them, especially those with severe physical disabilities but unimpaired brain functionality, the computer can become the primary means for communicating with the world around them.

The purpose here is not to review completely the various ways technology is being used in special education, but to emphasize the concept that technology can be used to provide tools that alleviate the hindrances that many special education children experience in their learning. When integrated with other support services and used by well-trained teachers, technology can be as beneficial to the special education child as to the general education child. Depending on the need or challenge, it may even be more beneficial because the special education child may have far fewer options for communicating and functioning in the general classroom environment.

Selecting appropriate technological aids for special education children can be complex. Given the limited market, these devices are also more expensive than other forms of educational technology. However, reimbursement for such technology may be available from governmental as well as private insurance agencies. Administrators and teachers involved with planning for technology should make sure that they have access to individuals and sources who can provide the appropriate expertise. Vocational rehabilitation agencies and national and local support groups can provide invaluable advice and assistance. A growing number of organizations (see Figure 3.1) that specialize in assisting and providing technology to persons with disabilities are available. Highly recommended is the National Center to Improve Practice in Special Education Through Technology, Media, and Materials. The major computer manufacturers such as Apple, Dell, and IBM also maintain services to guide school districts to information sources.

For more information about organizations that provide specialized technologies, go to the *Web Links module* for this chapter on the Companion Website at **www.prenhall. com/picciano.**

FIGURE 3.1   Sources of Information for Technology and Special Education

ACTT (Activating Children Through Technology)
WIU, 27 Horrabin Hall
Macomb, IL 61455

ADDS (Assistive Device Database System)
650 University Ave.
Sacramento, CA 95825

AFTA (American Foundation for Technology Assistance)
Rt. 14, Box 230
Morganton, NC 28655

Alliance for Technology Access
1307 Soans Ave.
Albany, CA 94706

American Foundation for the Blind
15 W. 16th St.
New York, NY 10011

American Printing House for the Blind
1839 Frankfort Ave.
P.O. Box 6085
Louisville, KY 40206

Assistive Devices Information Network
University Hospital, Developmental Disabilities
Iowa City, IA 55242

Braille Institute
741 N. Vermont Ave.
Los Angeles, CA 90029-3594

(continued)

| FIGURE 3.1 | *continued* |

Center for Special Education Technology
Council for Exceptional Children
1920 Association Dr.
Reston, VA 22091

Closing the Gap
P.O. Box 68
Henderson, MN 56044

Communication Assistance Resource Service
3201 Marshall Rd.
Dayton, OH 45429

Don Johnston, Inc.
1000 N. Rand Rd., Bldg. 115
P.O. Box 639
Wauconda, IL 60084-0639

Helen Keller National Center
for Deaf & Blind
111 Middle Neck Rd.
Sands Point, NY 11050-1299

Innotek
2100 Ridge Ave.
Evanston, IL 60204

National Association of the Deaf
814 Thayer Ave.
Silver Spring, MD 20910

National Info Center for Children
with Handicaps
P.O. Box 1492
Washington, DC 20013

On-line Microcomputer Guide and Directory
11 Tannery Lane
Weston, CT 06883

Pass Word
11400 Bacon Rd.
Plainwell, MI 49080

REACH (Rehab/Educ/Advocacy—Citizens
with Handicaps)
617 7th Ave.
Fort Worth, TX 76104

Research Grant Guides
P.O. Box 4970
Margate, FL 33063

RESNA
1101 Connecticut Ave. NW, Suite 700
Washington, DC 20036

SCAN (Shared Communication and
Assistance Network)
8605 Cameron St., Suite 406
Silver Spring, MD 20910

SpecialNet
2021 K St., Suite 315
Washington, DC 20006

TADD Center (Technological Aids
& Assistance for Disabled)
1950 W. Roosevelt Rd.
Chicago, IL 60608

TechLine
Center for Special Education Technology
1920 Association Dr.
Reston, VA 22091

Trace Research Center
University of Wisconsin
Waisman Center
1500 Highland Ave.
Madison, WI 53705-2280

U.S. Society for Augmentative and
Alternative Communication
c/o Barkley Memorial Center
University of Nebraska
Lincoln, NE 68588

United Cerebral Palsy
1522 K. St. NW, Suite 1112
Washington, DC 20005

Washington Library for Blind
and Physically Handicapped
821 Lenora St.
Seattle, WA 98129

EQUITY ISSUES

Since the expansion of technology in the nation's schools in the 1980s, a number of equity issues have emerged that continue to be critical considerations for educational planners. The term *equity,* which refers to qualitative properties (e.g., content or nature of the technology curriculum), is often used interchangeably with *equality,* which refers to quantitative properties (e.g., student access as measured by student/microcomputer ratios). These and other equity issues will be examined in the sections that follow.

Gender Issues

The issue of gender as it relates to the use of computers in education can be complicated, and to a degree it involves larger societal issues and sex stereotyping. Women demonstrate their technical abilities in using technology every day. However, much of the research and literature indicate that differences prevail in the way females and males approach the use of technology during their formative years. Much of this literature comprises two categories—one dealing with the performance of females and males in technology-infused courses, and the other dealing with the attitudes of females and males to technology. Very likely, a relationship exists between the two.

In the past, studies have shown differences in the outcomes of males over females in terms of performance and mastery of computer skills (Fetler, 1985; Hawkins, 1987; Martinez & Mead, 1988). Others show no differences (Linn, 1985a; Robyler, Castine, & King, 1988; Webb, 1985). The subject needs continued research and examination.

A possible explanation of the performance differences that showed boys performing at higher levels than girls is the assumption that technology is a skill that improves with use. If boys tended to use technology more than girls, then over time they would perform at higher levels or show greater competency, particularly in the upper grades (Sacks, Bellisimo, & Mergendoller, 1994). However, even in studies involving very young children who are first introduced to computer activities, the results are inconclusive. Using preschool samples, Schaefer and Sprigle (1988) found no gender differences in mastering Logo skills. On the other hand, Block, Simpson, and Reid (1987) reported gender differences favoring boys in learning Logo in a sample of kindergarten, 1st grade, and 2nd grade students. Campbell, Fein, Scholnick, Schwartz, and Frank (1986) found gender differences in programming style but not in programming mastery in a sample of kindergarten children learning Logo.

Whereas technology performance research comparing gender differences has been inconsistent, research comparing gender attitudes is more consistent. Many studies involving the optional uses of computers indicate that males tend to favor computer activities more so than females. These uses of computing included taking elective courses, joining computer clubs, going to summer computer camps, and majoring in computer science in college (Dambrot, Watkins-Malek,

Silling, Marshall, & Garver, 1986; Gibson & Nocente, 1999; Hess & Muira, 1985; Linn, 1985b; Sanders & Stone, 1986). For example, Gehring (2001) reported that according to the College Board only 15% of those taking the Advanced Placement exam for computer science were girls. The various reasons for attitudinal differences may relate to larger societal factors including parental influence, subject stereotyping, peer influence, and access to computers (including video games) in the home. Shashaani (1994), in a study involving 1,730 high school students in Pittsburgh, concluded that significant gender differences in computer interest, computer confidence, and gender-stereotyped views exist. Furthermore, she stated that parental attitudes and influences are directly associated with student attitudes about computing.

In more recent years, particularly with the proliferation of Internet tools, some of the attitudinal issues may be changing. For instance, although females were slow to be active users of the Internet (fewer than 9% in the early 1990s), they now represent more than half of all Internet users in the United States (Weise, 2000). However, how females use the Internet may be different. Weise (2000) reported that women in general tended to use the Internet more as a productivity tool, whereas men tended to use it "to play around." In a study of 280 high school students enrolled in a computer-enriched science course, Fishman (1999) found that while both female and male students used e-mail at about the same rate for course work, male students made greater use of group e-mail and discussion lists than did female students. Fishman attributed this to males preferring and being more comfortable in participating in the public group e-mail forums than did females. However, Christie (1997) cautioned against reaching firm conclusions on gender studies regarding the use of technology, particularly for communication. In a study of female and male users of e-mail in an elementary school, Christie attempted to study the gender-stereotypical uses of the technology. She concluded that when using computers for communication, such as with e-mail, gender stereotypes cannot be understood as something apart from the social systems of particular classes (Christie, p. 170). The technology is so woven into the social fabric of the class that to try to isolate it as a topic of study is difficult if not impossible.

In developing curricula, planners should keep in mind that these gender-based attitudes toward technology exist and that they most likely were established and reinforced outside the school. If technology is to be an important part of their curricula, schools should attempt to overcome these attitudinal problems. In an extensive treatment of this subject, Sanders (1986a, 1986b) and Sanders and Stone (1986) suggested a variety of strategies for educational policy makers, including the following:

- Require students to take certain technology courses, because girls tend to enroll in much smaller numbers than boys if courses are optional.
- Expand technology curricula beyond mathematics and science courses.
- Integrate technology into the regular academic program.
- Educate parents at parent-teacher meetings to ensure that the home environment does not contribute to stereotyping.

For more
information on
sex equity and
computing, go
to the *Web
Links module* for
this chapter on
the Companion
Website at
**www.prenhall.
com/picciano.**

- Educate the staff so that teachers are aware of the issue.
- Establish positive role models in the schools.
- Review and eliminate software and technology literature that might contain stereotypical characterizations or depictions.

For further information on sex equity and computing, readers may wish to contact the Gender, Diversities, & Technology Institute, the Computer Equity Training Project of the U.S. Department of Education (555 New Jersey Ave. NW, Washington, DC 20208–5646), and GenTech.

Minority Issues

Minority access and utilization is probably the most complex of all issues concerning the use of technology in education. The reasons relate to larger socioeconomic issues, school financing policies, and urban school environments. Much of the published material on these issues tends to focus on three factors: (1) access (e.g., the amount of equipment in the schools or in the home), (2) student performance, and (3) the level of software utilized (e.g., drill and practice versus higher order thinking skills).

In years past, there was definitely a large gap in terms of access to technology among majority and minority schools. Quality Education Data (1991), after conducting three national surveys between 1988 and 1991, concluded that although all school districts had accelerated their acquisition of computers and other technologies, the typical leaders tended to be affluent suburban districts more so than inner-city and rural districts. The U.S. Department of Education (2000) reported that schools with a high percentage (in excess of 70%) of poor students have student-per-computer ratios of 16:1, whereas schools with a lower percentage (less than 11%) of poor students have ratios of 7:1. This point has been a critical part of the problem when discussing minority access to computers. Urban schools, schools in poor rural districts, and larger schools have less computer hardware per student than other schools; they also enroll much higher percentages of African American and Latino children.

More recent research indicates that the access to technology issue may be abating. In a national survey, Park and Staresina (2004) report that the average student-per-microcomputer ratio is 4:1. In high-poverty and high-minority schools, the ratios are 4.2:1 and 4.3:1, respectively. However, it should be noted that within some states and communities, access to technology continues to differ among affluent, largely White suburban communities and minority inner-city schools. Many educational equity issues in technology relate to larger issues of school policy and finance where low socioeconomic schools with high minority enrollment have less access to educational opportunities than do middle and high socioeconomic, nonminority schools. For example, in a 129-page study of California schools conducted by the UCLA School of Education, Oakes (2003) concluded that problems of supply and adequacy of textbooks, curriculum materials, and instructional technology are most severe in schools that have a high enrollment of "the State's most vulnerable students" including low-income, minority, and English language learners. In New York State, Park and Staresina (2004) report that while the total state school population has a favorable student-per-microcomputer ratio of 4.3:1, in high-minority schools and high-poverty schools this ratio increases to 6.2:1 and 5.2:1, respectively.

Access to hardware is not the only issue. The overall educational environment and context in which technology is used is just as, if not more, important. Research on minority student performance vis-à-vis technology is relatively sparse. In an extensive review of the research on equity issues in the use of computers in the schools, Sutton (1991) concluded that the data on "minorities and people of color" were generally lacking and little is known. One of the most extensive studies was conducted by the Educational Testing Service in the 1980s. It involved an evaluation of IBM's Writing to Read program and included 10,000 kindergarten and 1st grade children in 28 different schools (Murphy & Appel, 1984). The overall performance for all students was positive, but the authors also report that the program worked better with White children than it did with minority children and children from low socioeconomic backgrounds.

Robyler and colleagues (1988), based on their own meta-analysis of more than 80 studies conducted since 1980, concluded that computer technology might not be as effective as other nontechnical strategies in teaching Spanish-speaking children. However, other research (Gonzalez-Edfelt, 1990) reported that computing is effective in teaching Spanish-speaking children. The inconsistency reported for Spanish-speaking students may relate more to the limited availability of software appropriate for bilingual students in the 1980s.

Emihovich and Miller (1988) compared African American and White 1st grade children who were assigned either to a Logo class, a computer-assisted instruction (CAI) class, or a control group class. White students outperformed the African American children in the CAI and control groups, whereas the African American children outperformed the White children in the Logo group. Because of the small sample size ($N = 36$), the researchers recommend further study on larger samples. In addition to the differences in the outcomes between African American and White students, this study is most interesting because of the comparison of different types of educational software.

Simmons (1987) suggested that in schools where computers are being used in instruction, the indication is that minority children make greater use of drill-and-practice software to emphasize basic skills, whereas White students use computer programming software to develop higher order thinking skills. Zehr (2001) likewise reported that ESL students use technology in schools in "less meaningful ways" due to a lack of high-quality software or Web sites geared for English-language learners. Judge, Puckett, and Cabuk (2004) also found differences in the way young children were using computers in high-poverty versus low-poverty schools. The quantitative research on software tracking is negligible and is supported more by observations and anecdotes than systematic survey or study. In one survey of 136 schools in the New York City area (Picciano, 1991), such a pattern of inner-city, mostly minority schools using drill-and-practice software and suburban, mostly White schools using higher level programming software was not found. This problem has begun to correct itself as more technology users both in and outside the schools increasingly use tool software such as word processing, spreadsheets, graphics programs, Internet browsers, and databases—none of which require any programming knowledge. By the early 1990s, the educational software industry had begun to develop and market a much broader and creative list of products designed especially for the increasing bilingual, and especially the Spanish-speaking, populations (Smith, 1995). When developing an instructional plan for technology, educators should be cognizant of any bias that might be built into the curriculum favoring particular levels of software for a particular racial or ethnic group.

Minority issues go beyond technology education questions, and educational planners cannot be expected to resolve them simply by virtue of their curriculum and technology access. Nonetheless, educators must be sensitive to these issues as they relate to their schools. They should consider strategies that do not isolate one group from another but instead bring them together. Educators should be seeking to provide opportunities that allow children of all colors and ethnic backgrounds to experiment with technology and experience learning together.

Socioeconomic Issues

National surveys of computer use in the United States indicate that the percentage of households owning a computer is doubling every 5 years. However, this ownership is not even across all family characteristics. Family socioeconomic situations have always had an effect on education and also relate to the issue of ownership and access to technology in the home. For example, in a national study the Kaiser Family Foundation (2004) reports that parents' education, occupation, race, and income all influence ownership.

Kominski (1990) reported that a family is twice as likely to have a computer in the home when children are present, which indicates that parents are increasingly buying computers for their children. Novak and Hoffman (1998) also reported that where a primary, secondary, or postsecondary student was present, home access to the Internet increased significantly.

Race and family income especially relate to technology access in the home. Many agencies, services, and companies have been conducting Internet access surveys and generally they indicate that White and Asian American households have higher percentages of Internet access than do Black or Latino households. For example, Novak and Hoffman (1998) reported that 44.2% of the White households in the United States have access to the Internet, as compared to 29.4% for African Americans. The Business Women's Network (2001) projects that in 2005, 84% of Asian American, 76% of White, 68% of Latino, and 64% of Black households will have access to the Internet. These surveys also indicated that the gap or "digital divide" between the two races was narrowing and that a more significant factor in Internet access was family income. Although all households in the lower income brackets were less likely to have Internet access, Black families in the higher brackets had comparable access to White households. Melinda Bier and colleagues (1997) found that low-income families who were most disadvantaged in terms of computer and modem access were the most enthusiastic users of online services when provided with the necessary equipment in their homes. Critical to this discussion is the fact that much of the data referred to above relates to national trends and samples; greater or lesser differences can exist within school districts and communities. Educational leaders in planning technology programs should consider collecting data on their own students regarding access to technology in the home.

If you assume that technology is good and can be beneficial in education, then students who have greater access may have an advantage over those who do not. This may be dismissed as just another aspect of the effects of socioeconomics on education, in that families with more resources can purchase calculators, typewriters, encyclopedias, or private tutors. However, administrators as part of their planning should consider that the more they implement technology-based education in their schools, the more they should also consider providing access to equipment beyond normally scheduled class periods. Access to hardware also offers access to educational tools and information resources such as the World Wide Web that can significantly facilitate doing homework and research assignments.

As an example, word processing software can provide advantages to students doing compositions or essays. Not only does the final paper look neater and cleaner than handwritten or typewritten work, but modern word processing software packages provide spell-checking, thesaurus, and grammar-checking features. In addition, students using word processors can correct and redo their work many times without the drudgery of rewriting or retyping it. But they should be advised on the judicious use of automated features to make sure that they understand their mistakes and are not simply letting the computer correct their work for them.

Administrators and teachers need to be aware of how many students in their schools have access to technology in their homes and consider doing something for those students who do not. Open access after school to equipment in laboratories, media centers, and libraries is becoming more and more common. However, these facilities are not as beneficial as having a computer in the home. Lending or purchasing equipment for students will likely increase in the future, as smaller portable and notebook computers become less expensive. States such as Maine, Michigan, and New Mexico have piloted programs to provide a laptop computer for every student. Some school districts have initiated similar programs specifically for homebound and other needy students. This equipment is used interactively to provide access to the Internet, e-mail, discussion groups, and other educational software.

For more information on access to technology, go to the *Web Links module* for this chapter on the Companion Website at **www.prenhall. com/picciano.**

With all the concerns that exist in education, access to technology in the home may not be a major consideration. However, with the growing acquisition of personal computer equipment combined with access to the Internet and national networks, opportunities exist for educators to use and provide experiences for their students that in the past simply were not possible. By the same token, educators increasingly will have to consider how they supply these experiences to those children who do not have access to such opportunities in their homes.

For additional information on access to technology, socioeconomics, and "digital divide" issues, the EDC Center for Media and Community maintains a resources Web site that addresses these issues.

CASE STUDY

PLACE: SOJOURNER TRUTH HIGH SCHOOL
YEAR: 2005

Sojourner Truth High School is the pride of Hewlitt County, a suburban community in the South. The community has grown in the past 10 years because the general metropolitan region around it has increased in population and has attracted businesses relocating from the Northeast and Midwest. The Hewlitt County School District is generally regarded as one of the best managed in the state.

Sojourner Truth High School has an excellent reputation. The principal, Mr. Wells, has spent his entire career in Hewlitt County, where he was first hired as a science teacher in 1976. The entire academic program is highly regarded; in fact, the science and technology programs are considered among the best in the state. Students from Sojourner Truth win both national and state awards each year in a variety of competitions, especially in science. In the past 10 years, several students have won the prestigious national awards. In terms of computer education, the student-to-microcomputer ratio is 4:1. In addition to several central laboratories and open access areas, microcomputers with high-speed Internet connections are also located in each classroom.

It is Friday, June 7, and Dr. Lewis, the district superintendent, is finalizing the agenda for the monthly school board meeting that will take place Monday night. At the June meeting, Dr. Lewis usually has Mr. Wells give his annual high school

SUMMARY

This chapter presents several issues regarding the use of technology in education. Although not as obvious as some of the basic hardware, software, and staff development issues, they are nonetheless important. Minimally, educators should be aware of them—but, more important, they should be sensitive to them early in the planning stages when considering the implementation or expansion of technology.

The primary learning issue to be considered is the extent to which technology is desirable in the school. Although enthusiasm about technology is desirable and even beneficial, too much enthusiasm can be disruptive and do more harm than good.

report, during which he always introduces one or two students who have achieved some outstanding distinction. This was an especially good year in that four students (James H., Jason K., Roger S., and Miguel P.) won a national science award for developing a computer simulation program to predict drought conditions in the Southwest.

The telephone rings and it is Mrs. Elena Bodine, who wants to discuss a concern she has about her daughter, Caroline, a junior at Sojourner Truth. She says that her daughter would like to join the school's computer club but is reluctant to do so because she would be the only girl. Mrs. Bodine has had at least three conversations with Mr. Wells about this since last January. He promised to look into the matter but, according to Mrs. Bodine, "he has not done a thing about it." Although Dr. Lewis promises that he will address her concerns, she informs him that if she does not hear from him with an appropriate solution to her daughter's problem by Monday, she will attend the meeting and bring the issue up before the school board.

DISCUSSION QUESTIONS

1. Assuming that you are Dr. Lewis, what actions do you take? Do you think it might be appropriate to change the agenda so as not to embarrass anybody? What additional information do you need?

2. What are some actions or policies that could be adopted to encourage more girls to join the computer club?

Technology in and of itself is limited. But as a tool and when placed in skillful hands, it can open new possibilities and enrich learning regardless of grade levels. Elementary, middle school, and high school students are able to derive benefits from technologically based teaching techniques. Special education children, who because of various impairments are unable to use traditional educational tools, are using computer aids to provide the necessary links to learning.

In addition to educational issues, a number of equity issues are emerging. Administrators and teachers should be cognizant of gender, minority, and socioeconomic factors in their school districts that may affect the success of their academic computer programs. Some of these issues must ultimately be resolved in the larger society; however, educators should try not to add to the inequity that might already exist and instead employ technology to lessen it.

KEY CONCEPTS AND QUESTIONS

1. Technology is being used in all aspects of our society. Use is growing in business, government, and homes. Many components of our society could not function without computer facilities and information systems. Has American education reached the point where teaching should depend more extensively on technology, which, in turn, may form the impetus for school improvement? Or is technology a simple tool that will have little impact on education? Explain.

2. Technology is generally available in high schools and upper grade levels, but major questions persist as to when it should be introduced in the elementary school. What are some of these questions? How would you respond to them if you were involved in planning or implementing technology in an elementary school?

3. Technology is proving to be especially effective for several special education populations. Do you agree with this statement? If so, provide examples. If not, which alternatives are more appropriate?

4. Equity issues and the use of technology relate to much larger societal issues involving gender, minority, and other socioeconomic factors that may be beyond the scope of most administrators' duties. What are some of these issues as they relate to technology in the schools? What strategies would you consider to lessen any inequities that might exist?

5. Computer equipment is increasingly being acquired by Americans for use in their homes. Does this pose any special consideration for educators? Is this a problem or an opportunity? Explain.

SUGGESTED ACTIVITIES

To complete the Suggested Activities online, go to the Companion Website at **www.prenhall.com/picciano,** then to this chapter's *Suggested Activities module.*

REFERENCES

Becker, H. J. (1987). The importance of a methodology that maximizes falsifiability: Its applicability to research about Logo. *Educational Researcher, 16*(5), 11–17.

Becker, H. J. (1994). *Analysis and trends of school use of new information technologies.* Irvine: Department of Education, University of California.

Bier, M., Gallo, M., Nucklos, E., Sherblom, S., & Pennick, M. (1997). Personal empowerment in the study of home Internet use by low-income families. *Journal of Research on Computing in Education, 30*(2), 107–121.

Block, E. B., Simpson, D. L., & Reid, D. K. (1987). Teaching young children programming and word processing: The effects of three preparatory conditions. *Journal of Educational Computing Research, 3,* 435–442.

Business Women's Network. (2001). *Wow facts: Technology Chapter 47.* Retrieved February 10, 2004, at the Web site of Wow! Facts (http://www.ewowfacts.com/chap.html).

Campbell, P. F., Fein, G. G., Scholnick, E. K., Schwartz, S. S., & Frank, R. E. (1986). Initial mastery of the syntax and semantics of Logo positioning commands. *Journal of Educational Computing Research, 2,* 357–378.

Christie, A. A. (1997). Using e-mail within a classroom based on feminist pedagogy. *Journal of Research on Computing in Education, 30*(2), 146–176.

Dambrot, F. H., Watkins-Malek, S., Silling, M., Marshall, R., & Garver, J. (1986). Correlates of sex differences in attitudes toward and involvement with computers. *Journal of Vocational Behavior, 27,* 71–86.

Davy, J. (1984). Mindstorms in the lamplight. *Teachers College Record, 85*(4), 549–558.

Emihovich, C., & Miller, G. E. (1988). Effects of Logo and CAI on Black first graders' achievement, reflectivity, and self-esteem. *Elementary School Journal, 88*(5), 473–487.

Fetler, M. (1985). Sex differences on the California statewide assessment of computer literacy. *Sex Roles: A Journal of Research, 13*(3/4), 181–191.

Fishman, B. J. (1999). Characteristics of students related to computer-mediated communications activity. *Journal of Research on Computing in Education, 32*(1), 73–97.

Gehring, J. (2001, May 10). Not enough girls. *Education Week, 20*(35), 18–19.

Gibson, S., & Nocente, N. (1999). Microcomputers in social studies education. A report of teachers' perspectives and students' attitudes. *Computers in the Schools, 15*(2), 73–81.

Gonzalez-Edfelt, N. (1990). Oral interaction and collaboration at the computer: Learning English as a second language with the help of your peers. In C. J. Faltis & R. A. De Villar (Eds.), *Language, minority students, and computers* (pp. 53–89). Binghamton, NY: Haworth.

Hawkins, J. (1987). Computers and girls: Rethinking the issues. In R. D. Pea & K. Sheingold (Eds.), *Mirrors of minds: Patterns of experience in educational computing* (pp. 242–257). Norwood, NJ: Ablex.

Hess, R. D., & Muira, I. T. (1985). Gender differences in enrollment in computer camps and classes. *Sex Roles: A Journal of Research, 13,* 193–203.

Judge, K., Puckett, K., & Cabuk, B. (2004). Digital equity: New findings from the early childhood longitudinal study. *Journal of Research in Technology in Education, 36*(4), 383–411.

Kaiser Family Foundation. (2004). *Children, the digital divide, and federal policy.* Issue brief of the Henry J. Kaiser Family Foundation, Menlo Park, CA. Retrieved February 15, 2004, from the Kaiser Family Foundation Web site (http://www.kff.org/entmedia/7090.cfm).

Kominski, R. (1990). *Computer use in the United States: 1989* (Current Population Reports Special Studies Series P-23, No. 171). Washington, DC: U.S. Department of Commerce, Bureau of the Census.

Levy, F., & Murname, R. J. (2004). Education and the changing job market. *Educational Leadership, 62*(2), 80–83.

Linn, M. (1985a). Fostering equitable consequences from computer learning environments. *Sex Roles: A Journal of Research, 13*(3/4), 229–240.

Linn, M. (1985b). Gender equity in computer learning environments. *Computers and the Social Sciences, 1,* 19–27.

Maddux, C. (1989). Logo: Scientific dedication or religious fanaticism in the 1990s. *Educational Technology, 29*(2), 18–23.

Maddux, C. D., & Johnson, D. L. (1997). Logo: A retrospective. *Computers in the Schools, 14*(1/2), 1–7.

Martinez, M. E., & Mead, N. A. (1988). *Computer competence: The first national assessment* (Technical Report No. 17-CC-01). Princeton, NJ: Educational Testing Service.

Murphy, R. T., & Appel, L. R. (1984, November). *Evaluation of the Writing to Read Instructional System, 1982–1984: A presentation from the second year report.* Princeton, NJ: Educational Testing Service.

Novak, T. P., & Hoffman, D. L. (1998). *Bridging the digital divide: The impact of race on computer access and Internet Use.* Project 2000, Vanderbilt University. [This paper is a longer version of the article "Bridging the Racial Divide on the Internet," published in *Science,* April 17, 1998.] Retrieved February 26, 2004, from the Web site of Vanderbilt University (http://www2000.ogsm.vanderbilt.edu/papers/race/science.html).

Oakes, J. (2003). *Access to textbooks, instructional materials, equipment, and technology: Inadequacy and inequity in California public schools.* Los Angeles: Graduate School of Education and Information Studies. Retrieved February 28, 2004, online (http://www.mofo.com/decentschools/expert_reports/oakes_report_2.pdf).

Papert, S. (1980). *Mindstorms: Children, computers, and powerful ideas.* New York: Basic Books.

Papert, S. (1987). Computer criticism vs. technocentric thinking. *Educational Researcher, 16*(1), 22–30.

Park, J., & Staresina, L. (2004, May 6). Tracking U.S. trends. *Education Week, 23*(35), 64–67.

Pea, R. D. (1983). *Logo programming and problem-solving* (Technical Report No. 12). New York: Bank Street College of Education, Center for Children and Technology.

Pea, R. D. (1987). The aims of software criticism: Reply to Professor Papert. *Educational Researcher, 16*(5), 4–8.

Perelman, L. (1992). *School's out: Hyperlearning, the new technology, and the end of education.* New York: Morrow.

Piaget, J. (1952). *The origins of intelligence in children.* New York: Norton.

Picciano, A. G. (1991). Computers, city, and suburb: A study of New York City and Westchester County public schools. *Urban Review, 23*(3), 93–109.

Quality Education Data. (1991). *Microcomputer uses in schools: A 1990–91 Q.E.D. update.* Denver: Quality Education Data.

Quality Education Data. (1995). *Education market guide and mailing list catalog, 1995–1996.* Denver: Quality Education Data.

Robyler, M. D., Castine, W. H., & King, F. J. (1988). Assessing the impact of computer-based instruction. *Computers in the Schools, 5*(1), 1–149.

Sacks, C. H., Bellisimo, Y., & Mergendoller, J. (1994). Attitudes toward computers and computer use: The issue of gender. *Journal of Research on Computing in Education, 26*(2), 256–269.

Sanders, J. S. (1986a). Closing the computer gender gap. *Education Digest, 10,* 34–39.

Sanders, J. S. (1986b). Here's how you can help girls take greater advantage of school computers. In J. C. Arch (Ed.), *Technology in the schools: Equity and funding* (pp. 40–43). Washington, DC: National Education Association.

Sanders, J. S., & Stone, A. (1986). *The neuter computer.* New York: Schuman.

Schaefer, L., & Sprigle, J. E. (1988). Gender differences in the use of the Logo programming language. *Journal of Educational Computing Research, 4,* 49–55.

Shashaani, L. (1994). Socioeconomic status, parents' sex-role stereotypes, and the gender gap in computing. *Journal of Research on Computing in Education, 26*(4), 433–451.

Sherry, M. (1990). An EPIE Institute report: Integrated instructional systems. *Technological Horizons in Education, 18*(2), 86–89.

Simmons, W. (1987). Beyond basic skills: Literacy and technology for minority students. In R. D. Pea & K. Sheingold (Eds.), *Mirrors of minds: Patterns of experience in educational computing* (pp. 86–100). Norwood, NJ: Ablex.

Smith, M. M. (1995). The battle over bilingual education. *Electronic Learning, 15*(1), 30–38.

Sutton, R. E. (1991). Equity and computers in the schools: A decade of research. *Review of Educational Research, 61*(4), 475–503.

Trotter, A. (2003, November 5). Budget crises may undercut laptop efforts [Electronic version]. *Education Week, 23*(10), 1, 21.

U.S. Department of Education, National Center for Education Statistics. (2000). *Internet access in U.S. public schools and classrooms: 1994–99,* NCES 2000–086. Washington, DC: U.S. Department of Education, National Center for Education Statistics.

Walker, D. F. (1987). Logo needs research: A response to Papert's paper. *Educational Researcher, 16*(1), 9–11.

Webb, N. M. (1985). The role of gender in computer programming learning processes. *Journal of Educational Computing Research, 1,* 441–458.

Weise, E. (2000, August 9). In a Web first, women are in the majority. *USA Today,* p. 1.

Zehr, M. A. (2001, May 10). Language barriers. *Education Week, 20*(35), 28–29.

Section II

TECHNOLOGY IN ACTION

Chapter 4

Technology in Educational Administration

ince the introduction of microcomputer technology in the late 1970s, much of the literature on the uses of technology in schools has concentrated on instructional applications in the classroom. Thousands of books, professional journals, magazines, and newspaper articles have been written providing insights into the uses of technology for learning and teaching. However, for superintendents and principals, among the most successful technology applications have been those that support their administrative operations. The effectiveness of technology in instruction continues to be debated, but the effectiveness of technology to provide information, manage budgets, analyze test scores, and improve office operations is a foregone conclusion. This chapter reviews major applications of technology in educational administration and provides an integrated framework for planning and implementing them.

KNOWLEDGE IS POWER

History abounds with examples of the concept that knowledge is power: the control of trade routes, the conquest of disease, and the development of the atomic weapons, to name a few. In organization theory, also, the power of knowledge has been well recognized. French and Raven (1959), in a series of studies on administrative management, were among the first theorists to identify "expert power" as a requisite to successful leadership among managers. They defined expert power simply as having access to critical information about one's organization and environment.

This concept that knowledge is power should not be viewed negatively. Because of public control and the number of constituents, schools generally require their administrative leaders to have expert or information power. Parents, teachers, staff, school board members, and the media seek out and rely on administrators to help them understand issues and events in their schools. An important characteristic of the experienced and accomplished administrator is to share freely her or his knowledge with others. Administrators who invest in and develop their information resources are better able to lead and manage their schools in all activities, be they program evaluations, budget presentations, or curricular improvements. Making good judgments in these areas requires accurate information about what is going on both inside and outside the schools.

Given the extensive reporting requirements of various governmental agencies, school administrators need to be able to demonstrate that they have access to and can provide critical data about their schools. Failure to do so can jeopardize budget requests, grant applications, and overall credibility with governmental officials.

Ready access to accurate information is indispensable to the functions of school administrators. Therefore, planning administrative systems for a school district requires the integration of information needs with available computer technology.

THE AGE OF KNOWLEDGE

In the 20th century, we witnessed major breakthroughs in humankind's activities and endeavors. Some of these have come to be characterized as periods of time, such as the age of the airplane, the atomic age, and the space age. The latter half of the 20th century, known as the information age, resulted from advances in the use of computer technology for collecting, sorting, manipulating, and reporting information. However, the information age is evolving into the age of knowledge. Educated people and their ideas, facilitated and augmented by information technology, have become key to our social well-being and a driving force for great change in all social institutions (Duderstadt, 1997). Success and progress will depend upon the ability of institutional leaders to harness and convert information resources into knowledge about what is happening within an organization while monitoring the forces that influence it from the outside. Corporations, government agencies, and schools have made significant investments over the past five decades to take part in the information-knowledge age by developing, expanding, and improving their computer-based information systems.

These systems consist of three broad categories of administrative applications: (1) databases to manage data and information, (2) electronic spreadsheets to manage and manipulate numerical data, and (3) office automation to manage text and communications. Together, these three types of applications form the basis of any plan to develop and improve information systems in organizations.

Databases

Database applications are by far the most important of the three categories mentioned. They involve the management of information about the various activities of a school in the form of data elements, records, and files. Unlike spreadsheets and office automation applications that became popular relatively recently with the introduction of microcomputers, database management systems began evolving on large mainframe computers in the 1950s. IBM became a corporate giant in part because it was the first of the major manufacturers to realize the potential of the computer for managing data files rather than for manipulating and crunching numbers in scientific research and engineering applications.

In the past 40 years, database management systems have grown in complexity and sophistication, particularly for large organizations. The more data needed to be collected, verified, updated, and reported, the more complex and expensive the task of establishing and maintaining an accurate database becomes. However, the alternatives are unthinkable. Not having access to the data eventually becomes a very serious problem and one that leaves an administration vulnerable. Collecting data manually can also be very expensive and prone to problems of inaccuracy and inconsistency. All school districts, regardless of their level of operation, should have as a priority in their plans the development, improvement, or upgrading of their database management systems.

The terminology used for describing databases has been inconsistent over the years, and certain terms mean different things to different people. Identifying and defining some of these terms here may be helpful. The general definition of a database is a collection of files in which data can be created, updated, and accessed. However, a more modern definition requires that data files be interrelated or integrated so that data can be accessed easily across all files and redundancy of the same data be kept to a minimum. The basic concept of databases involves the management of data in an increasingly more complex hierarchy. The members of this hierarchy, from least to most complex, are the *character*, the *data element*, the *data record*, the *data file*, and the *database*. These terms are defined as follows:

A **character** consists of a single letter of the alphabet (A through Z), a single digit (0 through 9), or a single special character ($, %, +).

A **data element**, also referred to as a *data field*, groups these characters to represent characteristics of a person, place, or thing. Examples of data elements include birth date, gender, father's name, family income, grade, course number, or room number.

A **data record** consists of a collection of related data elements for a single entity (person, place, or thing). Examples of data records include the personal record of an individual employee, the inventory record of a single piece of scientific equipment, or the transcript record of an individual student.

A **data file** is a collection of related data records. For example, the records of all employees would comprise a personnel file, or the records of all students would comprise a student file.

A **database** is a collection of data files and records. The database for a school district would encompass student, personnel, course (or curriculum), financial, and facilities files.

A **database management system** is a package of computer programs that allow the user to create, maintain, and access the data on a database. Examples of database management systems include Oracle for large computer systems and Microsoft's ACCESS for microcomputer systems.

Within a database management system, the data should be organized and documented in a **data element dictionary,** which is a table used to identify the content and coding schemes of the database. Table 4.1 is an example of part of a data element dictionary table that would be used to identify the content of a simple personnel record. This table would be stored in a computer file to be used by the database management system software and be included in a documentation manual for reference by the staff and teachers who need to maintain or access this file. Figure 4.1 is a page from a data element dictionary manual that describes the characteristics of one of

TABLE 4.1	Sample Data Element Dictionary Table for a Personnel Record

Field number	Field name	Type	Width	Decimal	Comments
1	NAME	CHARACTER	25		Last, First, Initial
2	SOC-SEC-NO	CHARACTER	9		Social Security Number
3	SCHOOL-CODE	NUMERIC	2		School Assignment
4	DEPT-CODE	NUMERIC	2		Department Assignment
5	STARTDATE	NUMERIC	6		First Date of Employment
6	TENUREDATE	NUMERIC	6		Date Tenure Awarded
7	BIRTHDATE	NUMERIC	6		Date of Birth
8	GENDER	CHARACTER	1		Female/Male
9	STREET	CHARACTER	15		Street Address
10	CITY	CHARACTER	15		City Address
11	STATE	CHARACTER	2		State Abbreviation
12	ZIP	NUMERIC	5		ZIP Code
13	SALARY	NUMERIC	8	2	Current Salary
14	MARITAL-STAT	CHARACTER	1		Marital Status Code

FIGURE 4.1	Sample Page of a Data Element Dictionary Manual

DATA ELEMENT DICTIONARY
NORTH CENTRAL SCHOOL DISTRICT NO. 1
PERSONNEL MASTER RECORD (PMR)

FIELD NUMBER: 14

FIELD NAME: MARITAL-STAT

DEFINITION: The legal status of the employed with
                                                 respect to wedlock.

CODING SCHEME/COMMENTS: S = Single
                                                 M = Married
                                                 D = Divorced
                                                 W = Widowed
                                                 L = Legally separated

the individual data elements in the personnel record represented in Table 4.1. Each data element should have a page in a paper or online manual similar to this.

As databases grow and become more complex, the task of documenting and maintaining a data element dictionary also becomes more complicated. School systems that operate a dedicated information service, data processing, or computer center frequently have full-time staff functioning as database administrators who have these responsibilities. All school districts, regardless of their size, should have someone performing these tasks. Failure to do so may render a database useless after awhile because the staff will forget how to update or access the files.

One of the most important features of database software is the ability to generate reports. A query language is provided that enables users to access data in many different ways. These languages are very powerful for creating customized reports and temporary data files. Designed for nontechnical staff, they give users excellent access to data without having to wait for computer or data processing personnel to perform the task for them.

The number of software developers providing database management systems has grown over the past 15 years. For microcomputer systems, Microsoft ACCESS, Paradox (Borland), APPROACH (Lotus), FOCUS (Information Builders), and FileMaker Pro (FileMaker, Inc.) have proven to be very popular and are reasonably priced. For large computer systems, the selection of a database management system is a serious decision that should be made carefully, with the advice of experienced and trained technical staff. These systems are expensive to acquire and more expensive to implement considering the planning, design, and computer programming required. Some of the major database management systems for large computers are Oracle, Sybase, Informix, IBM DB2, and MS SqlServer.

In reviewing and evaluating information about database management software, administrators will see references to the "data structure" or data organization used. Data structure is the method by which one data element relates to other data elements. Many books and articles explore and compare the benefits of the different data structures and approaches taken by software developers. Among the more popular structures is the relational database. Although a simple structure, a relational database views all data as being stored as tables or matrices, with each data element having access to the other data elements. Figure 4.2 is an illustration of how a student file and a course file might relate to one another in such a structure. In this illustration, the course codes serve to "relate" or link student records to course records.

Figure 4.3 illustrates some of the major administrative database applications. Each application area has a unique role in contributing to the overall data management resources of a school. The student applications tend to be the most complex because of the amount of data that needs to be collected. In addition, student data are volatile and subject to frequent change. Applications such as attendance reporting and scheduling require extensive data collection efforts and careful coordination. Student applications are important because certain areas such as achievement and performance come under a good deal of scrutiny, especially from outside the school. Administrators need to have good access to data such as retention, attrition, graduation rates, and test scores. Student enrollment data are also usually critical for various state and local funding formulae, and accurate data on students in attendance become a necessity for various reporting purposes.

FIGURE 4.2   **Sample Relational Database Structure for Student and Course Files**

Student records

NAME	ID	YEAR	COURSE CODES
SMITH JAN	31122	10	A1,E1,S2,F2
FOX ANN	21667	11	E1,S2,L3,M2
FELD LOIS	11233	9	E1,F1,L1,M1

Course records

COURSE CODES	SUBJECT	CREDITS	ROOM
A1	ART 1	1.0	H100
E1	ENG 1	1.0	H101
E2	ENG 2	1.0	H110
E3	ENG 3	1.0	H102
F1	FRE 1	1.0	L100
F2	FRE 2	1.0	L110
L1	LAT 1	1.0	L103
M1	MATH 1	1.0	L101
S2	HIS 2	1.0	H120

Course codes are used to "relate" student records to course records.

Curriculum and course applications are vital for a school's internal academic operations. Curriculum meetings and discussions are, in many schools, the centerpieces of academic planning. Administrators and teachers collect extensive amounts of data to develop new courses and modify existing ones. Data on student performance tied to curriculum and course enrollment become critical for such planning. A good curriculum and course database is also necessary for developing a student scheduling application, one of the most time-consuming activities when done manually.

Personnel and financial applications are frequently the first database systems to be implemented. In public schools, they may tie into other local governmental agencies for applications such as payroll, accounting, and purchasing controlled at the municipal or county levels. For any administrator, the management of a budget is a critical responsibility. Access to up-to-date and accurate information on budgets and finances is a necessity and affects all of a school's operations. Personnel files are important complements to the financial data files for purposes of managing a budget, because the major costs in school operations are for personnel items such as salaries and fringe benefits.

Facilities are generally the last of the database applications to be implemented. Facilities data are not as critical or volatile and do not need to be as tightly integrated. However, applications such as space utilization, equipment inventory, and supplies inventory should not be ignored because they contribute to overall effectiveness and efficiency.

The database management system software in Figure 4.3 is common to all of the applications and serves as an integration mechanism. By developing such a system, schools greatly enhance administrative cohesiveness because offices become more

FIGURE 4.3 **Common Database Applications**

dependent on one another by virtue of sharing common data files. A single system also significantly improves the consistency of information and eliminates issues involving the accuracy of one office's data versus another's.

In developing an overall plan for database management systems, administrators should assess their ability to collect and maintain data in the five major application areas identified in Figure 4.3. More resources may have to be provided for those areas where data collection has been poor or nonexistent. In addition, all database applications, even the most established, need regular modifications and upgrades. In many cases, the ongoing costs for modifying and upgrading an existing database system, particularly when staff time is considered, may be as much as the original implementation. Administrators believe that the ability to bring order and easy access to their information resources is well worth the price.

Electronic Spreadsheets

Electronic spreadsheets have significantly grown in popularity for applications that require frequent analysis and manipulation of numbers (e.g., budget, accounting, enrollment projections, test scores). Electronic spreadsheets have become indispensable tools for planning and modeling.

Electronic spreadsheet software is an electronic grid or matrix of rows and columns. It replaces the accounting tablet as a tool for organizing numbers into appropriate boxes or cells, and it automatically performs all of the arithmetic operations that were formerly performed manually or with calculators on each individual cell. VisiCalc was the first popular spreadsheet package developed for use on microcomputers in the late 1970s. Presently, Lotus 1-2-3, Microsoft Excel, and Quattro Pro are among the most popular. Packages such as Microsoft Office integrate spreadsheet software with database and office automation software. These packages also provide excellent graphics capabilities that enable users to present their worksheets in colorful and interesting ways.

Figure 4.4 is an example of an electronic spreadsheet for a school district's yearly budget summary and proposal. This figure shows a grid of numbered rows and lettered columns. Entries are made onto the spreadsheet by pointing or moving a cursor to the appropriate cell as identified by grid coordinates (A1, A2, B4, C6, etc.). Each cell can also have a *formula*, or arithmetic operation that uses data existing in any of the other cells. The major benefit of spreadsheet software is that these arithmetic operations can be performed automatically, so that a change in any one cell will almost instantaneously change all other cells that may be affected. This provides for a very rapid "what if?" facility, as popularized by media advertisements. For example, in doing a school's budget projections, if you wanted to know the effect of some percentage reduction on all the various cost centers or departments, this computation could be done almost instantaneously by just changing the entry in one cell. The calculation could also be performed over and over again with different percentages. Financial

FIGURE 4.4   **Sample Spreadsheet (School District Budget)**

	A	B	C	D	E	F	G
1							
2			North Central School District No .1				
3			Proposed Budget 2005/2006				
4							
5			2004-05	2004-05	2005-06	Approved vs.	
6			Estimated	Approved	Proposed	Proposed Budget	
7	Category		Expend. ($)	Budget ($)	Budget ($)	Change ($)	
8							
9	General support		3,888,500	4,222,500	4,100,000	-122,500	
10	Instruction		38,250,500	39,000,000	42,000,000	3,000,000	
11	Transportation		3,555,000	3,550,000	3,600,000	50,000	
12	Plant Operations		5,150,500	5,200,000	5,300,000	100,000	
13	Employee benefits		7,250,000	7,200,000	7,500,000	300,000	
14	Community service		3,050,000	3,150,000	3,100,000	-50,000	
15	Interfund transfer		800,000	800,000	800,000	0	
16	Debt Service		7,200,000	7,200,000	7,000,000	-200,000	
17							
18		Totals	69,144,500	70,322,500	73,400,000	3,077,500	

staff who regularly perform spreadsheet-type applications manually can learn to use an electronic spreadsheet in a matter of hours and become proficient after doing only a few applications. When proficiency has been achieved, electronic spreadsheets typically will replace all similar applications that had been performed manually.

Figure 4.5 provides a chart of some of the major administrative applications appropriate for electronic spreadsheet software. It is by no means a complete list of such applications (which easily number in the hundreds). They are grouped according to the major database file applications that are illustrated in Figure 4.3.

Because optimum management of information resources requires that all data files and applications be integrated where appropriate, the source data for electronic spreadsheet applications should come from the district's database files whenever possible and not gathered anew from other sources. This is generally referred to as downloading data from the database for use by other computer applications. It can be done electronically by creating aggregate data files that can be accessed by the electronic spreadsheet software. Of course, if a database does not exist or if the particular data needed are not available, then they must be gathered from other sources. This is necessary when attempting to do analyses involving phenomena that occur outside the

FIGURE 4.5   **Common Electronic Spreadsheet Applications**

Student
- Enrollment projections
  - District
  - School
  - Class
- Grade analysis
- Test score analysis

Curriculum/course
- Course projections
- Course grade analysis
- Scheduling analysis
- Course requirements analysis

Electronic spreadsheet software

Personnel
- Salary projections
- Staffing projections
- Affirmative action reporting
- Retirement projections
- Sick leave analysis

Financial
- Budget projections
  - District
  - School
- Department budget reporting
- Cash flow analysis
- Revenue projections

Facilities
- Space summary reports
- Equipment cost analysis
- Supplies cost analysis
- Construction
  - Project timetables
  - Cash flow management

schools. For example, an enrollment projection might require data on birthrates or the number of children under age 4 in a district.

Electronic spreadsheet software is effective in manipulating any aggregate data that are typically presented in tabular form. The number of reports using student data in this fashion is endless. Enrollment projections at various levels, test score analyses, and grade evaluations are common applications. For academic planning and scheduling, electronic spreadsheets can be very effective in doing course enrollment projections.

Personnel files are also important sources of data for spreadsheet applications. Staffing projections related to enrollment and course offerings can be routinely done. Personnel costs account for the major portion of the budget, and data such as salary projections are invaluable during budget planning and collective bargaining negotiations.

Designed initially for financial applications, spreadsheets have become commonplace in most accounting and budgeting offices. Entire budget-planning processes are conducted with school board members, superintendents, and others using the printed output from spreadsheets as the basis for discussion. These documents can easily be changed and recalculated many times over the course of the budget negotiation cycle. The graphics capabilities of spreadsheet programs can produce pie charts and bar graphs on budget information (see Figure 4.6 and Figure 4.7). Increasingly, these graphics are being used during public presentations of a budget and in mailings to residents on budget proposals.

Facilities applications such as space utilization reports and projections, as well as equipment and supplies inventory analyses, are also commonly done on spreadsheets. Project management timetables, cost projections, and cash flow analyses for capital construction can also be done effectively.

Spreadsheets are important tools in the presentation and manipulation of data and are most effective when integrated with database management systems. When planning these applications, keep in mind that the benefits of spreadsheet programs will best be realized if they have good data sources from which to draw aggregate data.

FIGURE 4.6   **Sample Pie Chart Using Data from Figure 4.4**

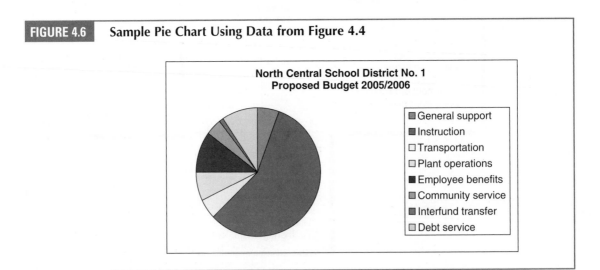

| FIGURE 4.7 | Sample Bar Chart Using Data from Figure 4.4 |

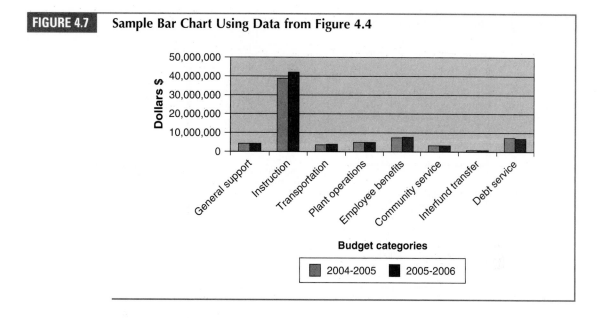

Office Automation

Until the early 1990s, the concept of office automation essentially referred to word processing. It was a major step forward when secretaries and other administrators made the change from typewriters to microcomputers. Word processing continues to be by far one of the most frequently used microcomputer applications worldwide. Developing word processing software has become an industry in itself, with such fine products as Microsoft Word and Corel WordPerfect. Most administrators and teachers have learned the basic features of word processing packages. Although one product might be a little easier to use and another might have a better spelling checker, they all do the job very well and certainly much better than typewriters can.

With the advent of the Internet, office automation applications have moved beyond word processing. Administrators should be thinking about how to use word processing with overall communications tools and integrating it into a "suite" of administrative software packages. In office automation, word processing is increasingly being used in conjunction with other software such as desktop publishing, electronic mail, voice mail, and databases. Word processing creates and edits text while these other software tools print, report, and communicate the text to others. Unlike word processing, which essentially developed as a stand-alone application replacing the typewriter, these other office automation tools require either local or wide area computer networks to be effective. Lotus Notes and Microsoft Exchange are examples of software that links and integrates several office automation packages.

The first use of word processing with other software came with the need to merge data from database management systems with text. The best example is the merging of addresses from a database file with the text of a letter (i.e., mail merge). This not only saved the time that would have been needed to key the addresses but

FIGURE 4.8   **Commonly Merged Text and Data Applications**

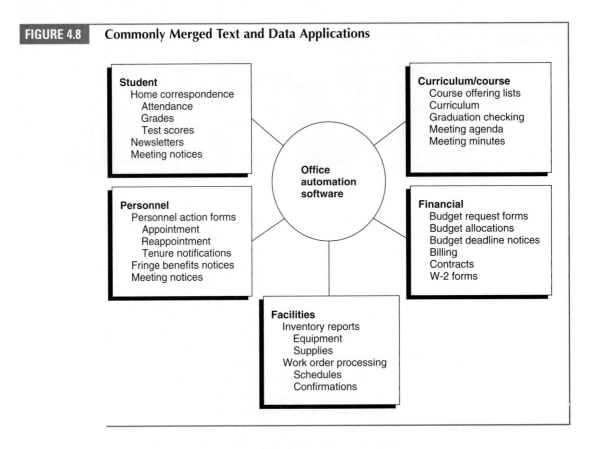

also made good use of the information resources available from the database management system. Today, there is much more merging of text with all sorts of data—attendance records, grades, test scores, and schedules—that are downloaded from databases. In most cases, this is an attempt to personalize the form letter and to relate the contents specifically to the recipients. Figure 4.8 provides a chart of some of the common uses of text with database information that are typically performed in school systems.

Electronic mail (e-mail) systems to distribute messages have grown in popularity. These systems concentrate on the distribution of communications throughout and beyond an organization by means of electronic mailboxes, which are data files containing text data such as messages. These systems also provide software for controlling who can send and who can receive messages and for alerting users when messages are in their electronic mailboxes.

To use these systems, a school district must develop a good data communications network that is used regularly by administrators and staff. Most school districts have begun to establish such systems. Variations of the electronic mail software include electronic bulletin boards and voice mail, which uses digitized voice messages rather than computer text files. The U.S. Department of Education reported that by 1999, 95% of all schools had acquired the necessary communications equipment to connect to the

Internet (U.S. Department of Education, 2000). A good case study of the large deployment of a system-wide communications system for electronic mail is in the Jefferson County Public Schools, the largest school system in Kentucky. Jefferson County built a communications infrastructure that offers e-mail access to every 4th through 12th grade student, teacher, and staff member in the district. As the largest school system in Kentucky and the 26th largest U.S. district, this was no small task. Jefferson County has more than 92,000 students enrolled in its 88 elementary, 23 middle, and 20 high schools.

Desktop publishing software is also growing in popularity and is used increasingly by schools to produce their own printed materials such as newsletters, manuals, and other documents. In addition to providing word processing capabilities, desktop publishing also provides easy-to-use graphics capabilities so that previously simple typewritten notices can include illustrations and become more colorful and interesting to the eye. Some of these publishing packages, such as Adobe Pagemaker, Corel Ventura, Microsoft Publisher, and QuarkXPress, are highly rated and effective in supporting public relations activities. They can also save money by doing printed work in-house rather than sending it to a professional printer. These packages also provide World Wide Web interfaces so that material can be displayed on Web pages as well as printed pages.

The development of document storage and retrieval software that integrates computer and microform technologies is also advancing rapidly. Schools and many other people-oriented organizations are tremendous producers of paper documents that need to be stored and maintained for many years, in some cases "forever." Computer indexing systems help and in some cases replace the extensive paper file systems that are so common in a school's administrative offices. These moderately priced systems provide rapid search capabilities for looking up key identifiers to microform (film or fiche) documents. They assume the existence of a microform system, which would be more efficient if a quick indexing or look-up capability was provided. They should also use existing databases for downloading index keys and other pertinent information.

With the development of optical disc technology, more and more documents that were being converted to microform are now being converted to digital form. These systems are being used mostly in larger school systems that maintain hundreds of thousands of past and current records. However, as this technology becomes less expensive and more readily available on microcomputer systems, with extensive read and write disc storage capacities, most school districts, regardless of size, will start to implement them and eliminate the need to keep paper documents. Using relatively inexpensive optical scanners, almost any paper document can immediately be converted into digital form and stored on an optical or magnetic disk file.

Office support systems that help organize work activities are another type of office automation software. Such systems provide facilities for planning work activities and include electronic calendars, appointment books, address books, notepads, phone lists, and alarm clocks. Several computer manufacturers now include these as part of the standard software package provided on all their microcomputers. Most handheld microcomputers or personal digital assistants provided by manufacturers such as Palm, Casio, Blackberry, and Hewlett-Packard feature these applications and are able to integrate them with the Internet and other large proprietary networks.

The various programming packages that come under the rubric of office automation are diverse and extensive. Many of these packages perform tasks electronically that in the past were routinely done manually. They generally can be time savers and improve communications in a school district. In planning for such systems, administrators are encouraged to integrate them with other administrative systems, especially database management.

SPECIALIZED ADMINISTRATIVE APPLICATIONS

There are several additional specialized computer applications worth mentioning. First, technology is increasingly being used as an external communications tool. With the emergence of the Internet as the major technological communications tool, all organizations including schools are becoming a part of the global digital community. School technology leaders have begun to expand home pages and to develop "portals" or main points of entry to the Internet that provide a full range of Internet services to faculty, staff, and students. Typically a "portal site" has a catalog of Web sites, a search engine, e-mail, access to databases, and other Internet-based services. Most of the administrative applications mentioned earlier in this chapter can be integrated with Internet and World Wide Web software to communicate information and data beyond the school building (school to school, school to school district, school district to government agency, government agency to government agency, school to families, etc.). Using the Internet and other specialized networks, administrators can access a host of databases maintained by federal and state governments as well as other public or private agencies and corporations. Examples include the Educational Resources Information Center (ERIC), which contains the world's largest collection of articles and studies in the field of education; Educational Testing Service Test Collection, which has thousands of descriptions of standardized tests and measures; and LEXIS/NEXIS, which provides access to the full text of articles appearing in all the major newspapers and general-interest magazines. Access to these databases provides administrators with an important research tool allowing them to keep up-to-date on many aspects of the field of education.

Second, statistical software packages such as the Statistical Package for the Social Sciences (SPSS) and the Statistical Analysis System (SAS) can be valuable additions for institutional planning, evaluation, or research offices. They provide inexpensive, easy-to-use programs for doing all types of statistical analyses involving treatments such as *t* tests, analysis of variance (ANOVA), correlation, and regression. They are not meant to replace electronic spreadsheet software for doing simple tables and summary totals, but rather perform the advanced statistical analysis necessary in research and data-driven decision making.

Third, test-scoring equipment and software are common in many schools and provide quick marking of objective tests. Many of these systems are on the market and use some type of optical scanner to read the tests and provide the data to a microcomputer, which in turn provides the test results in the form of a printed report. The better packages also provide summary statistics such as group results, means, standard deviations, and item analysis. Teachers make good use of these systems in grading and analyzing student academic performance. Much of this specialized equipment is also being upgraded and provided by World Wide Web software packages.

Fourth, automatic telephone calling systems that combine telephones, computer equipment, and stored voice message equipment are used in some districts. Originally designed for use in telephone sales or telemarketing operations, these systems have found success in school districts for monitoring student attendance. Such systems generally require that a disk file of telephone numbers of the children absent from school be provided each day. These are automatically dialed, and a recorded message is played informing the parent that her or his child was not in school that day. These systems can also be used to notify parents of special meetings, school closings, and other news.

Fifth, energy management is an important means of generating substantial savings through the use of computer technology. Computer applications support energy management in two different ways. One is simply to use a database management system to keep detailed records on energy consumption by heating zones and time of day. Analyzing these data regularly allows facilities personnel to track down and eliminate wasteful uses of energy. A more sophisticated approach requires a computer system that is directly connected to all the physical plant's control mechanisms for electricity, heating, and cooling. These systems can be programmed to control (reduce, increase, shut down) the amount of energy that is being used in all the various zones. Such systems are expensive to acquire and install but should be considered, especially when doing capital improvements.

INTEGRATING IT ALL TOGETHER: DATA-DRIVEN DECISION MAKING

While all of the major administrative applications mentioned above are critical for the effective operation of a school or school district, they are incredibly powerful when integrated and used to inform decision making. In recent years, the term *data-driven decision making* has become popular in education. The simplest definition of data-driven decision making is the use of data analysis to inform when determining courses of action involving policy and procedures. It is important to note that data analysis is used *to inform* and does not replace the experience, expertise, intuition, judgment, and acumen of competent educators. Inherent in this definition is the development of reliable and timely information resources to collect, sort, and analyze the data used in the decision-making process.

Decision making may be singly defined as choosing between or among two or more alternatives. In a modern school organization, however, decision making is an integral component of complex management processes such as academic planning, policy making, and budgeting. These processes evolve over time, require participation by multiple stakeholders (administrators, teachers, parents), and most importantly seek to provide information that will help all those involved in the decision process. Figure 4.9 illustrates the basic data-driven decision making process. It assumes that

C A S E   S T U D Y

PLACE: LINCOLN MIDDLE SCHOOL, ROCKWELL CITY   YEAR: 2005

Lincoln Middle School is a 6th to 8th grade middle school located in Rockwell City. It has an enrollment of 600 students and its principal, Jan Marson, is generally recognized as one of the more effective school leaders in Rockwell City. Almost 90% of the students regularly pass the state-mandated competency tests. Ms. Marson credits the success of Lincoln mostly to a dedicated teacher corps and an involved community, especially the parents. About 4 years ago she and one of her assistant principals took a workshop—"Using Data to Guide Instruction"—offered by a local college. Both she and her assistant were impressed with the concepts and decided to try implementing some of them at Lincoln. The biggest obstacle was the absence of a user-friendly database system in their school and district. They were required to maintain basic student information on an old database system at the district office, but accessing the data was slow and very cumbersome. Nevertheless, working with data provided by the state education department and with several reports generated by the district, Ms. Marson and her assistant were able to establish a small but

| FIGURE 4.9 | Data-Driven Decision Making Process |

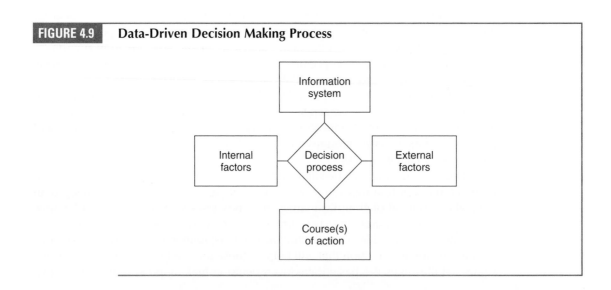

effective database that contained some basic student demographic information as well as performance data on mandated tests. Her assistant, Len Vasquez, was especially attentive in keeping the data accurate.

The following year, Ms. Marson and Mr. Vasquez introduced the concepts of data-driven decision making to the teaching staff. Teachers were generally willing to try it, and in 2003 a data-driven decision making process was implemented with grade 6 teachers. The process is inclusive, with teachers meeting and discussing student performances class by class. Performance goals and strategies for each class are subsequently established for the following year with particular attention paid to individual students who did not pass the state competency tests. Teachers were responsive to the approach and the process was extended to the other grades in 2004.

Mr. Vasquez performs all of the responsibilities of a data analyst and coordinator for Lincoln, and he has had to invest many hours in order to collect and provide the data on a timely basis. He is having some difficulty meeting his other responsibilities and has expressed this to Ms. Marson. Ms. Marson recognizes that he is spending much more time on this than she originally anticipated and she is concerned.

In May, Ms. Marson received a telephone call from the district superintendent, Dr. Elizabeth Cope, asking her to serve on a district-wide committee to guide the development of a new student information system. Dr. Cope indicated that she

Continued on next page

information systems are available to support the decision process, that internal and external factors not available through the information system are considered, and that a course of action is determined.

Operations related to data-driven decision making include data warehousing, data mining, and data disaggregation. *Data warehousing* is another term for a database information system that is capable of storing and maintaining data longitudinally (over a period of time). *Data mining* is a frequently used term in research and statistics, and refers to searching or "digging into" a data file for information to better understand a particular phenomenon. *Data disaggregation* refers to the use of software tools to break down data files into various characteristics. An example might be using a software program such as a database query language to select student performance data on a standardized test by gender, by class, by ethnicity, or by other definable characteristics. The ways data can be used in decision making are endless and can be effective for budgeting, academic planning, curriculum, student performance, or any of the other decisions that educators are called upon to make every day.

chose Ms. Marson for this assignment because Lincoln Middle School is one of the few schools in the district that has managed to collect student information capable of supporting a data-driven decision making process for instruction. In preparation for the first meeting of the committee, Dr. Cope has asked Ms. Marson to write a position paper on her experiences with data-driven decision making at Lincoln and more importantly to provide her views and recommendations on how the district should proceed.

SUMMARY

This chapter reviews the major administrative uses of computer systems. A framework is developed for planning that requires these systems to be integrated with one another as much as possible. Database management systems and the information they provide are critical for this integration; they are the resources on which all the other applications depend.

Database management systems, electronic spreadsheets, and office automation are the major software packages used to perform administrative applications. Extremely sophisticated but easy to use, they are evolving into indispensable administrative software tools. Various examples of the uses of these software packages in educational administration are also presented. In addition, several special-purpose applications of computer technology are described, including access to national information networks, statistical software, test scoring, automatic calling, and energy management systems. The chapter concludes with a discussion of data-driven decision making.

KEY CONCEPTS AND QUESTIONS

1. Developing the information resources of a school district is a critical goal of administrative computer systems. Why is this goal so important to school administrators? Who are some of the regular recipients of information from a school district? Is developing information resources a common goal in all organizations? Explain.

2. Database management systems, electronic spreadsheets, and office automation are the three major categories of administrative software applications. How do you define and compare them? Are they dependent on one another, or do they function independently? Explain. If starting administrative applications from the beginning, what would be your first priority? Why?

3. Database management systems are very complex applications. Identify some of the common database applications that exist in a school district. How do they relate to one another? What staff would be involved in designing a new database management system for student records? Personnel records?

DISCUSSION QUESTIONS

1. Assume you are Ms. Marson. What are your recommendations for the district? Critical to your recommendations are whether or not what has been accomplished in one middle school can easily be adapted to the entire district.

2. Are the issues here simply technological, or are there important personnel considerations as well?

4. Spreadsheet applications are used extensively in number manipulation exercises. Identify some common uses of spreadsheet applications in a school. How are the data generated for these applications? Who might be the major developers of spreadsheet applications in a school?

5. Office automation at one time essentially referred to word processing. How is it changing? What other applications does it include? Who are the major beneficiaries of office automation applications?

6. In addition to database, spreadsheet, and office automation applications, various other special-purpose applications can exist in a school district. Identify several special-purpose applications. For each one, consider (a) whether special hardware or software is required, (b) which individuals in a school would be involved with developing the application, and (c) how important you consider the application to the overall administrative operations.

SUGGESTED ACTIVITIES

To complete the Suggested Activities online, go to the Companion Website at **www.prenhall.com/picciano,** then to this chapter's *Suggested Activities module.*

REFERENCES

Duderstadt, J. J. (1997). The future of the university in an age of knowledge. *Journal of Asynchronous Learning Networks, 1*(1), 78–88. Retrieved March 15, 2004, from the JALN Web site (http://www.aln.org/publications/jaln/v1n2/v1n2_duderstadt.asp).

French, R. P., & Raven, B. (1959). The bases of social power. In D. Cartwright (Ed.), *Studies in social power* (pp. 150–167). Ann Arbor, MI: Institute for Social Research.

U.S. Department of Education, National Center for Education Statistics. (2000). Internet access in U.S. public schools and classrooms: 1994–99, NCES2000-086. Washington, DC: U.S. Department of Education, National Center for Education Statistics.

Chapter 5

Technology in Instruction

D uring the 1980s and 1990s the 15,000-plus school districts in the United States began making a substantial investment in computer technology to support instructional applications. In 1983, the student-per-microcomputer ratio in all public schools was approximately 125:1; by 2004, it was 4:1. However, while the investment in hardware continues, the yield in terms of academic benefits is unclear. In some schools, technology applications have been heralded and showcased as models for delivering instruction. In others, these applications have not lived up to their promises. School administrators can sometimes find themselves caught in the middle, because some members of the school community request more resources for expanding instructional technology whereas others question its value. This chapter provides school administrators with a balanced assessment of instructional technology applications.

INSTRUCTIONAL COMPUTING: A NEW BEGINNING

In 1988, the U.S. Congress's Office of Technology Assessment (OTA) conducted a national study on the uses of computer technology for instruction in primary and secondary schools. Extensively researched and documented, the study provided one of the first glimpses of the investment that schools in all parts of the country were making in instructional technology. Millions of microcomputers costing billions of dollars had been purchased in the 1980s, and almost every school in the country had acquired some form of computer technology. This study was frequently cited in professional journals as evidence of the revolution under way in the schools. The study showed that a major new thrust in instructional computing was indeed occurring.

Based on data provided by Quality Educational Data (QED), the National Center for Education Statistics (NCES), and *Education Week*, Figure 5.1 provides the actual national student-per-microcomputer ratios in the public schools for 1983 to 2004. The 4:1 ratio in 2004 represents a national average. Among the 50 states and the District of Columbia, the student-per-microcomputer ratios ranged from a low of 1.4:1 (South Dakota) to a high of 5.5:1 (California).

The public schools spent approximately $2 billion per year on computer technology in the 1980s. In the year 2004, schools were spending closer to $9 billion per year on technology. These figures are indeed significant considering that in 1975, computers for instructional purposes were nonexistent in many primary and secondary schools, and the expenditures for technology in general were negligible.

| FIGURE 5.1 | **U.S. Public Schools Student-per-Microcomputer Ratios** |

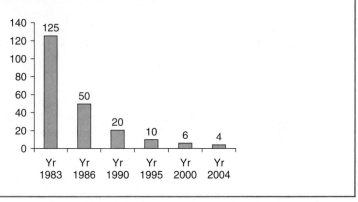

Source: Based on data provided by Quality Education Data (1996), the National Center for Education Statistics (U.S. Department of Education, 2000), and *Education Week* (Park & Staresina, 2004).

Based on the number of machines purchased and the dollars invested, you would assume that computer technology has become an integral part of instruction in our nation's schools. This is debatable. Larry Cuban (2000, 2001), professor of education at Stanford University, observes that many teachers at all levels remain occasional users or nonusers and those who are regular users seldom integrate the machines with core curricular or instructional tasks. In a national survey conducted for *Education Week* in 2004, many teachers considered themselves beginners in the use of technology in their classes. Furthermore, in a survey of 4th grade students, only 63% reported using a computer at least once a week in school (Park & Staresina, 2004).

The question is: Why then do the schools continue to make such a considerable investment in technology? The answer is not simple. If you see instructional technology as a mature activity with many well-known and well-understood applications, making this investment without substantial results becomes questionable. However, if you consider instructional technology as relatively new and, in many cases, experimental, then this expenditure can be supported as a research or development activity, at least for awhile. The presumption is made here that many schools find themselves in the latter situation, still in the developmental stages.

Much of the hardware and software used in the 1970s and early 1980s has little application today. It is true that some of the early pioneers of instructional computing—such as Patrick Suppes, John Kemeny, Donald Bitzer, and Seymour Papert—have seen applications that they designed and experimented with in the 1960s evolve to take a major place in present-day instructional technology. But by and large, they are the exceptions. Computer hardware has changed radically, spurring new approaches to instructional software, most of which has been developed by companies founded after 1990. The advent of the Internet and World Wide Web in the mid-1990s spawned another new wave of instructional technology applications. Schools and most other organizations had to rethink how the resources of the new global network would be used. Schools are in a new beginning vis-à-vis instructional technology. They are still experimenting with and evaluating different applications, and slowly some of these applications are being accepted and added to the schools' instructional repertoire. Given demands for more technology by parents, the business community, and some teachers, administrators will continue to find themselves in positions of nurturing and helping computer applications to mature.

INSTRUCTIONAL COMPUTING: SOME HISTORY

Patrick Suppes is the individual most associated with computer-assisted instruction, or CAI. Starting in 1959 at Stanford University, he conducted various experiments with CAI and eventually developed software especially designed for teaching basic skills such as reading, writing, and arithmetic. He is still actively involved in computer-based education, particularly with integrated learning systems provided by the Computer Curriculum Corporation in California.

In the late 1950s and 1960s, John Kemeny and Thomas Kurtz were among the first to envision personal computers. The product of their vision was Beginner's All-Purpose Symbolic Instruction Code (BASIC), a programming language that was really a variation of the FORTRAN programming language. The importance of BASIC is that it was the first language designed to be used by anybody. Originally required of all freshmen entering Dartmouth College, with which Kemeny and Kurtz were affiliated, BASIC quickly gained wide acceptance throughout the country. When microcomputers were introduced in the late 1970s, most of the manufacturers decided to provide BASIC as part of their operating systems. As a result, it became the most popular programming language ever developed. Microsoft's Visual BASIC, which is used extensively for programming multimedia applications and taught in many advanced high school computer science courses, evolved from the original BASIC language developed by Kemeny and Kurtz.

Donald Bitzer developed Programmed Logic for Automatic Teaching Operations (PLATO) at the University of Illinois in the 1960s. PLATO was the first popular authoring system for developing instructional applications. Designed to run on a large computer network, it sought to bring quality and innovative instructional material to students over wide geographic areas. One of PLATO's unique features was the use of a plasma display tube for producing exceptionally interesting graphics. Bitzer is generally credited with foreseeing the importance of graphics and sound in developing instructional computer applications.

Probably the best known developer of instructional computing software for primary and secondary schools is Seymour Papert of the Massachusetts Institute of Technology (MIT). Logo, which many consider the first language developed for children, embodies his philosophy of experiential and discovery learning. The name derives from the Greek *logos*, meaning "word, thought, or discourse." Although developed and well received in the late 1960s, like BASIC, Logo really became popular when it was made available on microcomputers in the late 1970s and 1980s. Logo Computer Systems, Inc., a company that Papert founded in 1981, has continually improved it—and versions that incorporate multimedia (Microworlds), word processing (LogoWriter), and mechanical interfaces (Micorworld Robotics, Lego-Logo) are commonly used in schools today. Papert's (1980) major book, *Mindstorms: Children, Computers, and Powerful Ideas,* is recommended reading for administrators and teachers interested in instructional computing. It is one of the first books to relate the development of an instructional software package to a particular educational philosophy: namely, experiential or discovery learning.

These software developments are well respected among technology educators, but their impact on academic achievement remains questionable. Although hundreds of studies have been conducted, the acceptance of instructional technology as having a definitely positive effect on academic achievement is not universal.

A BRIEF REVIEW OF THE RESEARCH

Some of the most extensive reviews of the research on computer education were conducted by James Kulik and his associates at the University of Michigan. In the 1970s and 1980s, they conducted a series of meta-analyses of hundreds of studies dealing with the effects of computer education at different grade levels (elementary, secondary, college, and adult). Their general conclusion was that computer-based education had a beneficial effect on academic achievement, although it was not uniformly true at all grade levels (Kulik, 1984; Kulik, Bangert, & Williams, 1983; Kulik, Kulik, & Bangert-Downs, 1984; Kulik, Kulik, & Cohen, 1980; Kulik, Kulik, & Schwab, 1986). However, Richard Clark (1983, 1985) refuted the findings by questioning the research controls of most of the studies that were included in the Kulik meta-analyses. Clark further concluded that the computer was basically a vehicle carrying an instructional substance and that real improvement in achievement only comes with improving the substance, not the vehicle. Clark's position has been challenged over the years by a number of researchers including Kozma (1991, 1994a, 1994b) and Koumi (1994) who see the medium as integral to the delivery of instruction. However, the two differing opinions on this issue remain and the "great debate" continues to this day.

In the late 1980s and early 1990s, educators saw value in providing instructional computer experiences for reasons other than improving student performance. Benefits such as ensuring computer literacy, providing variety in instructional delivery, or releasing teacher time from record-keeping tasks were considered important enough to continue investing in technology. However, even with objectives that might not directly affect academic performance, schools are having problems implementing effective instructional applications.

Sheingold, Kane, and Endreweit (1983) from the Bank Street College of Education identified six issues critical to planning and implementing instructional computer applications:

1. Access to hardware
2. New roles for teachers and administrators

3. Integration of technology into the curriculum, especially at the elementary school level

4. Quantity and quality of software

5. Teacher preparation and training

6. Effects and outcomes of the instructional use of technology (p. 426)

These six issues are still appropriate in helping us briefly assess the conditions that exist when planning and implementing instructional applications in schools today.

Access to hardware, as documented by the QED, NCES, and *Education Week* data cited at the beginning of this chapter, has improved dramatically. Despite progress, however, improving student access to hardware continues to be a priority in schools. Even in school districts with very favorable student-per-microcomputer ratios, the priority among computer coordinators continues to be the acquisition of more hardware—either to upgrade existing equipment or make more machines available to students. Also, the popularity of the Internet and the World Wide Web has forced all technology planners to reexamine their digital communications equipment and infrastructure.

New roles for teachers and administrators have become evident as more and more school districts employ full-time technology coordinators. In districts with many schools geographically dispersed, it is common to have building-level coordinators in addition to district-level coordinators. Graduate schools at many universities across the country have also developed new specialized programs that provide concentrations in technology-related teacher education.

Integration of technology into the curriculum, especially at the elementary school level, is improving but still requires a good deal of attention on the part of administrators. Studies (Becker, 1994; Fatemi, 1999; Park & Staresina, 2004; Picciano, 1991; Sheingold & Hadley, 1990; U.S. Congress, 1995) have continually indicated that this is a most serious issue. Resources, especially for release time, are needed for teachers and curriculum coordinators to do the detailed curriculum design work necessary for successful integration. This issue also relates directly to the need for more teacher training.

Both the quantity and quality of software has improved. Thousands of instructional software products are on the market, with the number of packages increasing every year. The instructional software industry, which only started in the late 1970s, has grown considerably, and the increased competition has forced improvement in quality. Instructional software is also becoming more specialized as small companies attempt to attract a limited market by meeting the needs of particular applications and subject areas rather than trying to develop general-purpose packages. This specialization also yields a better product. Although the quantity and quality of software have improved, as have other aspects of technology, the need for more and better software continues.

Some teacher education colleges have begun to make technology a basic requirement; others have not. In a 1998 survey of 416 colleges of education, the International Society for Technology in Education concluded that teacher preparation programs were not giving future teachers the kinds of experiences they needed to use technology in the classroom (Trotter, 1999, p. 42). Park & Staresina (2004) report that only 15 states require technology course work as part of their colleges' teacher education programs. Regardless, new teachers now entering the education field are more technology-literate than their predecessors. However, the existing teacher corps—particularly those who have had very little, if any, formal technology training—needs ongoing and systematic training and development in the use of technology. Even teachers who take the initiative in learning to use technology still require a good deal of ongoing training to master technology-based practices and to maintain their skills.

In terms of the effects and outcomes of instructional computing, recent studies and reviews of the literature (Archer, 1998; Becker, 1994; Christensen & Knezek, 2001; Robyler, Castine, & King, 1988; Thompson, Simonson, & Hargrave, 1992; U.S. Congress, 1995) continue the debate. One of these, a meta-analysis by Robyler and colleagues (1988), concentrated on more than 80 studies conducted since 1980. Their conclusion: "Computer applications have an undeniable value and an important instructional role to play in classrooms of the future. Defining that role is the task [for the future]" (p. 131). Trotter (1998) defined this role as being beyond student achievement; teaching high-tech skills, providing access to information, making learning more fun, promoting problem-solving skills, and providing individual student attention are among the roles that technology is expected to play in the classroom. Today's administrators are in the pivotal positions in their schools to define further and to expand technology's role.

DEFINING TECHNOLOGY'S ROLE: A TOUCH OF PHILOSOPHY

In defining technology's role in instruction, discussing and identifying an overall philosophy of learning is appropriate. As any undergraduate in an education foundations course will attest, the literature on learning theory is immense. It is not the intent here to cover this extensive literature. School district administrators, school building administrators within school districts, and teachers within schools pride themselves on their own philosophical approaches to teaching and learning that frequently have been developed from their studies and experiences. However, attention should be given to a philosophical framework that has become particularly popular when using instructional technology.

Piaget, Bloom, Gagné, and Vygotsky are well-recognized theorists in the area of learning theory. Piaget (1952), in addition to his contributions in the area of cognitive development in children, makes an important case for experiential learning. *Experiential learning* is defined here simply as learning by doing. Bloom (1956) and later Gagné (1977) established taxonomies of learning that related to the development of intellectual skills and stressed the importance of problem solving as a higher order skill critical to the learning process. Vygotsky (1978) also posited that problem solving and the construction of knowledge were the essence of the learning process. Vygotsky described the learning process as the establishment of a "zone of proximal development" in which exists the teacher, the learner, and a problem to be solved. The teacher provides an environment in which the learner can assemble or construct the knowledge necessary to solve the problem.

Evolving from Piaget, Bloom, Gagné, and Vygotsky is a constructivist theory of learning that stresses the importance of experiences, experimentation, problem solving, and the construction of knowledge. Constructivism draws on the vast experiences of the learner. Applying this to instructional technology translates into presenting problems and learning situations to which the learner can relate as well as providing the materials, media, and informational resources needed to solve the problems. Seymour Papert (1980), in describing the popular Logo programming language, talks about creating a highly interactive, technology-based microworld in which children solve problems by drawing on the resources of a computer. The learner, with guidance from a teacher, can actively access databases, test mathematical equations, or manipulate a geometric figure by using a computer. This concept can be broadened and applied to the design of any instructional technology application. The designer considers the technology-supported learning environment as a microworld in which problems (mathematical, scientific, social issues, case studies, etc.) are presented. A teacher or tutor who acts as a guide is available to the learner, as well as numerous informational tools and resources (World Wide Web, databases, media, analytical tools, written materials) that enable learners to engage in and solve the problems. The learner learns by interacting with the available resources (teacher, tutor, information, media, etc.) and drawing on his or her own experiences to construct the knowledge to solve the problem. In this scenario, the ability to interact with teachers or tutors as well as to access other materials becomes most important—and designers must ensure that the ability to do both is available in the environment. The technology tools become integrated with, and facilitate, the problem-solving activity. Given the vast information and other resources that technology can provide, how this is done is left to the creativity of administrators, teachers, and instructional designers.

CLASSIFICATION SYSTEMS AND DEFINITIONS OF TERMS

Widely accepted classification systems are elusive in education. This is also true in instructional technology. Although various attempts have been made to establish classification systems for instructional software, very little agreement exists. The Educational Software Preview Guide identifies 19 different software classifications or modes as part of its reviews. One of the simpler and better known classification systems, and the one referenced in many standard technology education textbooks over the years (e.g., Bullough & Beatty, 1991; Lockard, 1992; Merrill et al., 1992; Simonson & Thompson, 1997), is Robert Taylor's (1980) trichotomy of "tutor, tool, tutee." In tutor mode, the technology or computer possesses the information and controls the learning environment. In tool mode, the technology is used to assist or act as a tool in the learning activity. In tutee mode, the student possesses the information and controls the learning environment. This trichotomy is a flexible system. It lends itself to overlap in which particular software packages might be categorized in more than one of the classifications. Before examining this in more detail, it is important to establish some basic definitions of instructional technology terms.

Figure 5.2 summarizes most of the commonly used terms and definitions associated with instructional computing applications. Many of these terms—particularly when used by their acronyms such as CAI, CMI, or CBE—have been a source of confusion among educators. In some cases, they are used interchangeably—for example, computer-based education (CBE), computer-based instruction (CBI), and computer-assisted instruction (CAI) are all frequently used to refer to any type of learning environment in which a computer is used. Sometimes, the definition of a term has changed over time—such as that of computer-assisted instruction, which originally was a generic term applied to all instructional uses of computers but now is used more frequently to refer only to tutor-type software. Readers should familiarize themselves with

---

FIGURE 5.2   **Instructional Computing Terminology**

Computer-assisted instruction (CAI). The use of the computer to assist in the instructional process. One of the earliest used terms to refer generically to computer applications in education, it is used now to refer to tutor-type applications such as drill and practice and tutorials.

Computer-assisted learning. *See* Computer-assisted instruction.

Computer-augmented learning. *See* Computer-assisted instruction.

Computer-based education (CBE). A generic term used to refer to the broad array of instructional computer applications.

Computer-based teaching (CBT). The use of a computer by teachers as part of an instructional presentation such as an interactive video.

Computer-managed instruction (CMI). The use of the computer in an instructional process in which student progress is monitored and recorded for subsequent instructions and review. Most CMI applications are also able to adjust material to each individual student's level of understanding.

Computer-mediated communications (CMC). The use of computer systems that incorporate communications software such as e-mail and electronic discussion boards to enhance distance learning and computer-managed instruction applications.

Integrated instructional system (IIS). *See* Integrated learning system.

Integrated learning system (ILS). A single computer package for delivering instruction that combines hardware, software, curriculum, and management components. It is usually supplied by a single vendor.

Intelligent computer-assisted instruction (ICAI). Similar to CAI but also uses a substantial database of information for presenting material and selecting instructional paths.

these terms and establish a basic vocabulary in their own environments for use in discussions and printed materials.

■ TUTOR APPLICATIONS

A very common tool used today, tutor applications trace their beginning to the 1960s. In tutor applications, the computer has been preprogrammed by educators and technicians. Generally, the computer presents some information or subject matter, the student responds, the computer evaluates the response and presents additional or new information, and the cycle repeats itself. There are four subcategories of tutor applications: (1) drill and practice, (2) tutorials, (3) simulations, and (4) instructional games and problem solving. Figure 5.3 provides examples of some of the popular tutor software programs.

Drill and Practice

Drill-and-practice applications are usually used to reinforce a lesson or material that has already been presented to the student. They have been much maligned as too boring and mechanistic. This view is not entirely unjustified in that many of the drill-and-practice applications developed in the 1960s and 1970s could have been more interestingly designed. However, technological limitations existed in the early years of computing that made some pedagogically important features such as graphics and sound difficult to program. Many of these applications have since been improved by making greater use of graphics, motion, color, and sound to keep students interested in the activity.

Teachers regularly use drill and practice manually (i.e., flash cards, work sheets) as part of their normal instructional repertoire. The benefits of a computer drill-and-practice program can include immediate feedback, automatic adjustment of the level of difficulty depending on student responses, and record keeping on student performance that can be reviewed as needed by teachers. In reviewing and planning instructional applications, administrators should assume that some drill and practice is common in most schools' software libraries; however, it should not dominate the collection.

Drill-and-practice computer applications are used in many learning situations at different grade levels. Much of the earliest drill-and-practice software packages concentrated on basic skills and have continued to evolve as the technology has improved. They are most commonly used in mathematics, basic language skills, grammar, and spelling. They are also popular in special education classrooms where they have been combined with specialized speech and visual equipment.

Tutorials

Tutorial applications are similar to drill-and-practice applications in design and appearance. An important distinction between the two is that tutorial programs

FIGURE 5.3	Popular Tutor Software

DRILL AND PRACTICE

Program	Developer	Subject
Cornerstone Reading Comprehension	The Learning Company	Reading
Math Blaster Series	Knowledge Adventure	Mathematics
M_SS_NG LINKS	Sunburst	Language arts
Reader Rabbit Series	The Learning Company	Language arts

TUTORIALS

Program	Developer	Subject
A.D.A.M. Essentials High School Suite	adam.com Software	Biology/health
Rosetta Stone Series	Fairfield Language	Foreign languages
School House Rock Series	Creative Wonders	Science, mathematics
Writing Trek	Sunburst	Writing

SIMULATIONS

Program	Developer	Subject
Amazon Trail	The Learning Company	Social studies
Decisions, Decisions Series	Tom Snyder Productions	Social studies
Math at Work Series	CCI Publishing	Mathematics
Operation Frog	Scholastic Software	Biology
Oregon Trail	The Learning Company	Social studies
Science Court Series	Tom Snyder Productions	Science
Science Explorer Series	Riverdeep Interactive	Science
Virtual Lab Series	Edmark Corporation	Science

INSTRUCTIONAL GAMES AND PROBLEM SOLVING

Program	Developer	Subject
A to Zap	Sunburst	Language arts
Fizz and Martina Series	Tom Snyder Productions	Mathematics
Inspirer Series	Tom Snyder Productions	Social studies
Jump Start Series	Knowledge Adventure	Reading/mathematics
Magic School Bus Series	Scholastic Software	Science
Mighty Math Series	Edmark Corporation	Mathematics
Where in the _____ Is Carmen Sandiego Series	Broderbund	Critical thinking

attempt to teach something new and are not used specifically to reinforce material already presented—although they can do that, too. Tutorial programs have been criticized for the same reasons as have drill-and-practice programs, but they too have improved in recent years. They are used regularly in advanced technologies such as interactive video and integrated learning systems.

In many schools, the emphasis on using computers has been to try to integrate them into a regular curriculum. When used for stand-alone instruction, tutorial programs tend to keep the computer as something separate; they have not been as popular as other software programs for this reason. Tutorial programs can, however, be very effective in certain situations, such as for students who have missed a good deal of class time because of illness, who are homebound, or who live in rural areas where teachers may not be available to teach certain specialized subjects.

Simulations

Simulations attempt to represent on a computer certain real-life situations that would be impossible to duplicate in most classrooms. For instance, scientific experiments, ecological systems, and historical or current events can be duplicated by using computer models to represent the real-life situations. Students interact with the simulation and influence decisions and outcomes. Simulation software keeps growing in popularity, and many educators consider it a more effective use of computers than drill-and-practice programs or tutorial software.

Simulation software is also considered to be appropriate for beginning the teaching of higher order thinking skills. It can easily be used to supplement a lesson to allow students to apply what they have learned to different situations. Increasingly, simulations are combined with instructional games and problem-solving applications.

The Learning Company has been successful in developing a wide variety of stimulating and pedagogically appropriate simulations in social studies (Oregon Trail), ecology (Amazon Trail), science (Discovery Lab), and other subject areas. Tom Snyder Productions has also developed a series of excellent simulations—called Decisions, Decisions—that cover subjects like colonization, immigration, city management, and teenage drug use. Simulation software is also beginning to be used in developing interactive video programs where the use of motion and sound will add significantly to the pseudoreality of the computer models.

Instructional Games and Problem Solving

Instructional games software attempts to make learning fun by combining learning, entertainment, and gamesmanship. Although some instructional games continue to be poorly designed, many are well done and have instructional value. Of the various types of instructional software packages, games are frequently successful in using current technology, especially graphics and sound, to heighten student motivation and interest. Instructional games should be used to supplement other lessons; they are excellent when used to add some variety to a student's day. This is more important in elementary school programs and especially with younger children.

Problem-solving software is frequently subcategorized with instructional games, although it can also be considered a separate category. Problem-solving software is significantly gaining in popularity because of its primary focus on thinking skills. Students typically are presented with situations in which they use and develop cognitive, analytical, and other thinking process skills. In many cases, the material is presented in game format in which students compete with one another or with the computer. The literature on teaching and learning thinking skills is very extensive and open to much debate. For further reading on problem-solving software and higher order thinking skills, readers are encouraged to review Vockell and van Deusen (1989) for an excellent treatment of the subject.

■ TOOL APPLICATIONS

Tool applications, comprising the most frequent uses of computers in classrooms, include (1) word processing, (2) spreadsheet, and (3) database software. Although originally designed for purposes other than teaching and learning, tool software packages are being used effectively in enhancing the instructional process. Common examples include the use of word processing software to assist in teaching writing, the use of electronic spreadsheet programs to assist in teaching scientific formulas, and the use of the World Wide Web to search for information.

The popularity of tool software is primarily due to the fact that it is the easiest of all the various instructional software types to integrate into a curriculum. Teachers can use tool software without making major changes to the established course work. Furthermore, as teachers increasingly use tool software packages for their own professional and personal purposes, they are able to draw on their technical knowledge to use these packages effectively in the classroom. Students likewise increasingly see their parents and older siblings using tool software such as word processing, spreadsheets, and especially the World Wide Web in their homes and may have already begun to use these same programs themselves.

Figure 5.4 provides a partial list of popular tool software packages used for instruction. The nature of database, spreadsheet, word processing, and desktop publishing is also presented extensively in Chapter 4.

Word Processing and Desktop Publishing

Word processing is frequently used to assist in teaching writing. Word processing software makes revisions very easy and avoids the drudgery of handwriting or retyping extensive amounts of text. Students at various grade levels commonly use commercial word processing packages to do writing assignments. In addition, some word processing packages have been developed specifically for use by young children in classrooms.

When word processing is implemented as part of a writing program, questions frequently arise regarding the use of spell checking and grammar checking features. In most cases, these features are optional and can be deleted if a decision is made that these aids are not appropriate for teaching writing. Students exposed to word processing early in school generally continue to use it and become more proficient as they grow older.

A variation of word processing software that has grown significantly in popularity is desktop publishing software, which combines standard word processing features

FIGURE 5.4	Popular Tool Software

TOOL SOFTWARE

Program	Developer	Subject
The Amazing Writing Machine	Broderbund	Word processing
Bank Street Writer	Scholastic	Word processing
Big: Calc	Don Johnston, Inc.	Special education
Co: Writer	Don Johnston, Inc.	Special education
Community Construction Kit	Tom Snyder Productions	Architecture
Easy Book Series	Sunburst	Science reporting
FreeHand	Macromedia	Drawing tools
Graph Action Plus	Tom Snyder Productions	Graphs
HIP Series	Center for Image Processing	Biology images
Imagination Express Series	Edmark Corporation	Book and movie production
In My Own Voice	Sunburst	Poetry/multicultural
Kid Pix	Broderbund	Drawing tools
Map Maker's Toolkit	Tom Snyder Productions	Map making
Math Keys Series	The Learning Company	Mathematics tools
Movie Works	Interactive Solutions	Movie editing
PageMaker	Adobe	Desktop publishing
Performer	Mark of the Unicorn	Music editing
Physics Explorer Series	Riverdeep Interactive	Science laboratory tools
Print Shop	Broderbund	Desktop publishing
Smart Music Studio	Coda Music Technology	Music editing
Statistics Workshop	Sunburst	Graphs and statistics
Student Writing Center	The Learning Company	Desktop publishing
TimeLiner	Tom Snyder Productions	Timelines

ELECTRONIC REFERENCE WORKS

Program	Developer	Subject
A.D.A.M. The Inside Story	adam.com Software	Biology/health reference
American Sign Language Dictionary	Multimedia 2000	Special education
Children's World Atlas	Rand McNally	Atlas
Encarta	Microsoft	Encyclopedia
Eyewitness Series	DK Interactive Learning	Encyclopedia
Grolier Encyclopedia	Grolier	Encyclopedia
Math Resources	Math Resources, Inc.	Mathematics encyclopedia
National Geographic CD-ROM	National Geographic	Geography/wildlife
Romeo & Juliet Center Stage	Sunburst	Drama/literature
Who Built America?	Grolier	American history

with graphics capabilities to produce visually stimulating print material. Desktop publishing can be used to create professional-quality newsletters, school newspapers, and flyers. It can also be easily integrated into course work and extracurricular activities. Typical applications might be clubs doing flyers on recent activities, social studies classes preparing a newspaper article on some important historical period such as the French Revolution or the first landing of men on the moon, or students designing banners for sports and dances. Students usually collaborate on desktop publishing projects, which frequently translates into motivation for completing the final products. In recent years, desktop publishing software programs have advanced to the point where in addition to printed material, they are also able to generate World Wide Web pages. Yancey (2004) reports that desktop publishing programs may be fundamentally changing the way students approach writing. Because of the ease with which photographs and other images can be integrated into writing activities, students are able to express themselves in ways that were not easily possible before the development of word processing/desktop publishing technology. Using both text and visual material makes it easier for many students "to focus on, analyze, and improve their writing" (Yancey, 2004, p. 39).

Spreadsheets

Standard electronic spreadsheet programs are being used for a variety of subjects. Mathematics, the sciences, and business education make extensive use of spreadsheet software for all sorts of instructional applications involving the manipulation of numbers. Almost any subject in which mathematical formulas or statistical analyses are used can integrate spreadsheets into the curriculum. Just as word processing takes the drudgery out of typing text, spreadsheets take the drudgery out of doing hand calculations. They should not be used in courses where it is desirable or necessary for students to do hand calculations as practice in refining their mathematics skills. However, there are many instructional situations where the nature or understanding of a formula is more important than the mathematical practice of adding, subtracting, multiplying, or dividing numbers. In these situations, spreadsheets can be most effective.

Commercial spreadsheet packages also provide easy-to-use graphing features that allow students not only to do a mathematical formula but also to visualize it. Lotus 1-2-3 and MS Excel are some of the commercial packages commonly used in many schools. Integrated packages such as Microsoft Office also provide excellent spreadsheet programs along with word processing and database software. These integrated packages can be particularly effective in instructional applications where data collection using a database is combined with data analysis using a spreadsheet. Examples include research activities on voting behavior, economic forecasting, and local census data.

Databases

Database software is also finding its way into a variety of instructional applications. Data-collecting and data-searching skills are being taught by having students use the

World Wide Web to access databases maintained by government agencies, universities, and research institutions. During research projects students build their own databases with information that they have collected on animals, weather, states, famous people, minerals, places, and so forth. A popular long-term assignment is to have all the students in a class contribute to building a database over the course of a semester or year, and then to do some type of statistical analysis as a culminating experience.

Standard database packages such as Filemaker Pro and dBase can be readily learned by older students. For younger children, it may be more desirable to acquire database software packages such as Friendly Filer, which have been designed specifically for instructional applications. Some of these packages provide databases on a variety of subjects in addition to the software for collecting and manipulating data.

In planning the instructional applications of databases, educators interested in building employment skills should recognize the increasing importance of reference and researching skills, as many professions rely more on the ability to access information from a variety of sources. Online databases are not simply the domain of research organizations and graduate schools but are used routinely in all types of everyday businesses. Students should be prepared to use them along with other standard tool software programs as part of their basic education.

Electronic Encyclopedias and Reference Works

A type of database software becoming standard in most school libraries is the electronic encyclopedia, which is gradually replacing or being used in addition to standard multivolume printed encyclopedias. Examples include Microsoft's Encarta, Compton's Electronic Encyclopedia, and Grolier's Multimedia Encyclopedia. The popularity of electronic encyclopedias stems from the ease of searching for the required material electronically rather than manually. In addition, they provide excellent graphics, sound, and video clips. Other reference works available on CD-ROM or DVD include atlases, dictionaries, literary works, classical music, and works of art.

Specialized Tool Software

Tool software packages are also being developed for special-purpose instructional applications. For teaching music, several products such as Performer and The Music Studio are on the market for composing and listening to music using synthesizers. Broderbund's Science Toolkit uses a variety of temperature, light, and other sensory probes and instruments to collect data for real-life experiments. In special education, as mentioned in Chapter 3, there are a number of technology tools available to assist instruction. As the technology improves, especially in the use of sound and voice, the development and use of specialized tool applications will expand.

■ TUTEE APPLICATIONS

To develop tutee applications, both teacher and student learn to direct or control a computer to perform some task. Usually this involves learning to program a computer. In years past, learning computer programming was also the best way to develop an understanding of how a computer works. It was deemed a worthwhile instructional activity and in many situations, the computer itself became a focus of learning. However this notion has begun to change.

Developing computer programming skills provided several worthwhile instructional experiences. Programming languages such as BASIC and Pascal required students to learn rules, syntax, and logic constructs. The nature of computer programming was also one of problem solving and developing plans (programs) for solutions. It is a higher order thinking exercise formalized via programming instructions that can be visualized to a certain degree on a computer.

Debate persisted, however, regarding the value of a computer programming exercise in actually teaching thinking skills. Some educators, such as Papert (1980) and Luehrmann (1980), supported the use of computers for this purpose. Others, such as Linn (1985) and Pea (1987), accepted programming as a thinking exercise but cautioned that there is no proof that it actually improves the teaching of thinking. Perhaps Vockell and van Deusen (1989) summarized the issue best by making the "chicken and egg" comparison: Do clear and logical thinkers become successful computer programmers, or do people become clear and logical thinkers by writing computer programs? These theorists concluded that computer programming undoubtedly requires and exercises higher order thinking skills, but it is illogical, though tempting, to assume that teaching programming will also *teach* higher order thinking skills. In developing a tutee application, administrators and teachers should feel confident that they are providing a higher order thinking and problem-solving experience for their students. They are also offering one of the better experiences for learning about computers.

In recent years, however, educators have questioned whether programming languages should be taught in primary and secondary schools. One practical reason is that to teach programming well requires a significant amount of class time as well as significant investment in teacher training and development. Furthermore, the technology industry is prone to rapid changes, so that computer programming languages such as BASIC and Pascal that once were very popular are now being used less and less. Increasingly, presentation software and Internet and Web-based software tools are replacing the traditional computer programming activities. A discussion of several popular tutee technology applications follows.

Logo

The most popular programming language taught in primary schools is Logo and its derivatives, which were designed and developed by Seymour Papert of MIT specifically for young children. Logo can be used to experiment and explore or to develop very sophisticated computer programming procedures. Logo was designed so that a "friendly turtle" in the center of the screen became the vehicle whereby children learned to master and control the computer by drawing different shapes, developing geometric patterns, or designing a computer game. However, Logo was sophisticated enough that it could also be used at many grade levels.

For educators wishing to provide programming experiences in the early grades, Logo and its derivatives (LogoWriter, MicroWorlds, Lego-Logo) are among the best software packages available. MicroWorlds, available from Logo Computer Systems, Inc., is a powerful Logo-based multimedia authoring tool that allows students in grades 2 and up to create impressive projects incorporating movies, photos, sound, graphics, text, and animation. In planning to implement Logo into a curriculum, a good deal of computer access on a regular basis is a necessity—as it is with all tutee applications.

High-Level Programming Languages

High-level programming languages such as Beginner's All-Purpose Symbolic Instruction Code (BASIC) or Pascal were once very popular in advanced high school classes. A BASIC programming experience combined with a general understanding of computer hardware served to define computer literacy in the schools throughout the 1980s. Microsoft's Visual BASIC is a derivation of the original BASIC and is still one of the more popular programming languages for doing multimedia programs. However, in response to the way technology has changed in general, schools have replaced BASIC and other programming experience with authoring tool software packages, especially those designed to develop World Wide Web materials.

Authoring Languages

Computer programming over the past four decades has gradually become easier. The computer software industry has been moving in the direction of providing simpler tools and techniques to communicate with a computer. High-level languages such as BASIC and Pascal were easier to use than their predecessor languages, but they could not in any way be considered simple languages to learn. They have their own special syntax, verbs, constructs, and rules for developing logical plans for directing a computer to perform a task. In recent years, simpler software development tools have evolved that are generically referred to as *authoring languages.*

Authoring languages are much easier to use than other programming languages and were originally designed to be used for specific applications by people without special computer training. For instruction, several authoring languages are available to aid teachers in developing lessons, in doing multimedia presentations, and in creating pages for the World Wide Web. They are designed specifically to make it easier to present material, ask questions, and interpret student responses. They can also be used to control other equipment such as CD-ROMs and DVDs to provide a multimedia presentation.

The first authoring languages—such as TUTOR, MicroTUTOR, COURSEWRITER, and PILOT—were designed strictly for instruction, and although some teachers were willing to make the effort to use these languages, the time needed to learn to use them proved burdensome. Authoring languages developed in the 1980s and early 1990s—such as Apple's HyperCard, IBM's Linkway, and Asymetrix's Toolbook—were appropriate for lesson development as well as other applications such as building databases, maintaining inventories, or keeping a telephone directory. Though relatively easy to use, these newer authoring languages were not adopted by very many teachers because they too required a good deal of time and effort to master.

Newer authoring languages—such as HyperStudio and Microsoft's PowerPoint—are designed for doing multimedia presentations. They are more widely used by teachers, especially those who have had some technical training. Using a series of programming objects such as buttons, fields, and graphics, these languages can provide a very stimulating learning environment. They are especially effective in combining graphics and some animation with instructional text and other written material. These languages are fast becoming the basic tools for developing multimedia materials using video and audio. They are also easy enough to use so that technology instructors are teaching students how to "author" or use an authoring language. Authoring languages will continue to evolve and will play a larger role in the future in computer education curricula.

During the late 1990s there was an evolution of authoring software packages for the development of hypertext markup language (HTML) documents for distribution as World Wide Web pages. Dozens of Web authoring programs have been developed that make creating and editing Web pages no more difficult than using a word processing program. In fact, the newest version of Microsoft Word has a built-in Web authoring facility. These authoring packages are becoming very popular in schools where teachers and students are using them for a host of Web-related activities.

INTEGRATED LEARNING SYSTEMS

Integrated learning systems (ILSs) are integrated systems of hardware, software, curriculum, and management components that are generally marketed by a single supplier. Also referred to as integrated instructional systems (IISs), they are probably the most sophisticated examples of computer-managed instructional products on the market. The hardware usually consists of a microcomputer that can function as a file server in a local area network (LAN). The software is generally tutorial and drill and practice. The curriculum provided can range from kindergarten through 12th grade subjects, although many of the most popular ILSs are used for basic skills instruction in language arts and mathematics. In recent years, a number of ILS vendors have converted their materials to be accessed by the World Wide Web. Especially popular are a number of adult education software products designed to improve job and career skills.

Critical to all ILSs is a student management system (computer-managed instruction) that tests students, keeps records on their performance, and adjusts lesson material depending on their progress. The management system usually produces automated individual student and group progress reports that can be used by teachers and administrators for instructional planning.

Many educators consider an ILS as the total solution for implementing instructional computing in their schools. All the major components provided are already integrated. The problems of integrating computer technology into the curriculum are solved because the computer provides the curriculum as well as a major portion of the instruction. Some of the vendors—such as Computer Curriculum Corporation, Jostens Learning Corporation, and Wicat Systems, Inc.—have a great deal of technical and pedagogical expertise and have been developing and refining their systems for many years.

Why, then, have most school districts not acquired these systems? The major reason is their cost. Depending on the number of computer workstations, such systems can easily cost hundreds of thousands and, in some cases, millions of dollars. After the initial investment, there are yearly costs for maintenance and upgrades, which can range from 7% to 12% of the original purchase price. Many school districts simply cannot afford an ILS. To be used effectively, these systems require extensive training of the teaching staff and may require teachers to become managers of instruction rather than simply instructors. On the other hand, an ILS with extensive reporting capabilities can be a powerful tool for monitoring student progress and customizing lessons to individual needs.

In planning to acquire an ILS, administrators need to do a very careful analysis to ensure that the benefits of such a system will be realized in their districts. Because of the costs, administrators cannot afford to experiment; they must be sure that the curriculum provided is appropriate and consistent with their own curriculum goals and objectives. Most importantly, teachers need to be well trained to take full advantage of the many technological and pedagogical tools that an ILS provides.

MULTIMEDIA: A BRIEF WORD

Most of the instructional software packages mentioned above have been available for several years. In some cases, they are in their seventh or eighth versions. Perhaps the most significant changes or improvements from version to version have been the addition of multimedia (sound, pictures, video) to the basic software program.

The power of images and sounds expands every year. Television, videocassette recorders (VCRs), videodiscs, CD-ROMs, and digital versatile discs (DVDs) are common in homes and in schools. Children, especially teenagers, frequently are more knowledgeable about these media than adults. School administrators and teachers need to understand and, where appropriate, tap into the power of multimedia if they have not already done so. In acquiring instructional software, multimedia features are important complements—especially when the program has a good pedagogical foundation to begin with. This will be discussed further in Chapter 6, which is devoted entirely to the topic of multimedia.

DATA COMMUNICATIONS

Data communications provide facilities for a wide range of instructional applications. Local area networks (LANs) are used to support central computer laboratories, integrated learning systems, and other instructional applications. Using a file server, the LAN can provide software programs to all the users on the network, which thereby precludes the need to purchase multiple copies of the same software packages for use on stand-alone machines.

Wide area networks (WANs), in addition to offering all of the services of a LAN, allow access to a variety of instructional applications. The Internet, as will be discussed in greater detail in Chapter 7, emerged in the 1990s as the epitome of the wide area network, providing access to a wealth of resources throughout the world. The Internet has had such an impact on technology that software vendors are preparing to offer World Wide Web versions of many of their products and services. Even before the advent of the Internet, several networks were established to supply specific services directed to teaching and learning that involve the sharing of information not ordinarily available at the local school. Either by way of the Internet or as separate entities, many of these networks are still providing specialized instructional resources and applications that are important to educators.

Probably the most common service provided by national networks is access to databases. Students and teachers can access encyclopedias, research databases, information exchanges, and technical documentation. The most important benefit of databases via national online services is that they provide the most current and up-to-date information. Educational networks such as GTE Education Services provide several services: ED-LINE for general education news; SpecialNet for databases and information exchanges directed to the special education profession; Youth News Service Newsline for news and journalism activities appropriate for primary and secondary school children; and CNN Newsroom for curriculum and other instructional materials based on daily news reports.

Some of these services combine information access with e-mail and bulletin boards so that students can exchange information with other students across the country and across the globe. National Geographic's Kids Network, for instance, provides services for students to share information about the environment, weather, geography, current events, and so forth. National Geographic even provides curriculum material so that teachers can develop research projects and share reports with other schools doing similar projects.

Possibly the greatest potential for WAN services involves integrating them with television and distance learning technologies. Learning Link and IntroLink, for instance, are designed to be used in conjunction with Public Broadcasting Service (PBS) television. Curriculum information and classroom activities based on current PBS offerings can expand the uses of educational television for instruction. Distance learning, which has been emerging as an important educational technology for several years, is greatly enhanced when a two-way communication link is established that allows for interactivity between students and teachers. State education departments in states like Minnesota, Wisconsin, Alaska, Kentucky, and Iowa have taken the lead in developing distance learning facilities for a number of school districts. Most state education departments, if they have not already done so, are planning to provide distance learning facilities for use by local school districts in the near future. This topic will be discussed in greater detail in Chapter 8.

CURRICULUM INTEGRATION AND PLANNING

Curriculum integration is a simple concept but is proving difficult to realize with instructional technology applications. Integrating computer tools into the classroom is conceptually similar to integrating other tools such as chalkboards, overhead projectors, or paints and crayons. Teachers and students have few problems, however, using these other, more familiar, tools in teaching and learning. Furthermore, these tools have limited application, so mastering them is an easy task.

Modern technology—especially the computer—on the other hand, provides more sophisticated, expensive tools, and mastering them is a more complex and ongoing undertaking. Integrating computers into the curriculum starts with making sure that teachers and students have developed a basic understanding and knowledge of computer use. Once this basic understanding has been achieved, mastery involves developing a knowledge base of the many different ways computers can be used. Teachers need to feel comfortable using technology and developing a repertoire of instructional applications. Integrating technology into the curriculum is therefore closely tied to staff development—which is therefore one of the critical components of any technology-based plan, along with hardware, software, facilities, and finances.

Integrating instructional applications is not something that can be accomplished overnight. Quick fixes in implementing technology usually have very little lasting impact and frequently only delay serious planning activities. Administrators should not be thinking about quick fixes but instead should be evaluating whatever instructional technology is already occurring in their schools and building on that which works.

Planning requires the involvement of those who possess expertise and who ultimately may be responsible for implementing new applications. The fulcrum for curriculum integration and planning instructional applications is the teaching staff. The teachers are critical for identifying applications and evaluating software, hardware, and staff development needs. Administrators must work with teachers to provide leadership in these activities, ensuring that resources are available for training, facilities, and staffing, as well as for hardware and software.

Finally, because of the many applications and alternatives available, teachers and administrators need to develop a process in which priorities can be established and plans developed for the long term. No school district in the country—even with the best tax base, the most competent teachers, and most enlightened administrators—can afford to do everything it might wish to do; however, every school district can and does do something well. This should be kept in mind when planning for instructional technology.

CASE STUDY

PLACE: SILICON CITY   YEAR: 2005

Silicon City, an urban school district on the West Coast, has an enrollment of 28,000 students in 41 schools. The population has been increasing significantly during the past 10 years, particularly with students needing bilingual education. The voters approved a bond issue in 1999 to build a new high school. As part of the bond issue, $4 million was budgeted for purchasing new instructional equipment, of which $1.5 million will be used district-wide for educational technology.

A district-wide planning committee was established in 1991 with a standing technology subcommittee. This subcommittee has been very effective in securing funds and helping the district implement technology in the schools. Each school has one or more centralized computer laboratories and a building coordinator. A major goal of the district has been to integrate technology into the regular classrooms rather than providing it only in centralized computer laboratories. The district has a student-per-microcomputer ratio of 5:1.

In addition to acquiring basic computer hardware and software for the new high school comparable to what exists in the other high schools in the district, the technology subcommittee would like to use a portion of the instructional equipment budget to make a major thrust into newer technologies that might benefit the entire district. As part of the planning process last year, the technology subcommittee asked a group of administrators, teachers, and building computer coordinators to develop proposals to help in this regard.

The subcommittee was provided with three proposals, each of which would cost approximately $1 million to implement initially. They were as follows:

Proposal 1: Upgrade data communications in the classrooms. This proposal would allow each school to be wired for higher speed data communications access in each classroom. Presently, some schools have high-speed (T1) access and some have modest (ISDN) speed. In some schools, high-speed access is available in the central computer laboratories but not in individual classrooms. Each microcomputer in each classroom would be wired for higher speeds and equipped with the necessary software for tying into the Internet and other national networks. A variety of instructional applications were identified as benefiting from this upgrade, including accessing databases, monitoring seismographic data, using CNN curriculum materials for teaching current events, and establishing electronic pen pals in Latin America.

Proposal 2: Acquire/upgrade video equipment. This proposal would provide funds so that each classroom would be equipped with a large monitor, videotape, and/or DVD players. Each school would also be provided with funds to expand and update its video library appropriate for the curriculum. It would build on the video equipment and materials that some of the schools have already purchased. This proposal has been very much supported by the science and social studies departments, which use this equipment extensively to demonstrate experiments and to show multimedia programs of cultural productions, current events, and geographic tours of countries.

Proposal 3: Develop an integrated learning system to teach basic skills. This proposal would use the funds to establish a district-wide ILS. Each school could tie into the system via the computer laboratories at all of the schools. Although the ILS could be used for several instructional applications, it would be used initially for basic skills and bilingual education. One ILS vendor based on the West Coast indicated great interest in working with the school district to establish a model for using its products and offered very attractive pricing.

The subcommittee, before it proceeds with making a recommendation to the planning committee, has asked the assistant superintendent for curriculum for her recommendation. It is unlikely that the district could afford to fund more than one of these proposals over the next 3 years.

DISCUSSION QUESTIONS

1. Assuming that you are the assistant superintendent, analyze the three proposals. What observations can you make regarding the appropriateness of the three proposals from technological, pedagogical, and programmatic perspectives?

2. Although you have been provided with only a summary of each proposal, what additional information on each proposal would you consider critical to making a recommendation?

3. Finally, given the information provided and assuming you felt compelled to support one proposal, which would you recommend? Why?

SUMMARY

This chapter reviews the development and issues surrounding instructional technology. All school districts have made some investment in instructional technology, with varying degrees of success. While some question the benefits of this investment, every indication is that this investment will only increase in the future.

This chapter also attempts to provide administrators with a balanced picture of instructional applications: their problems, benefits, and potential. It is evident that with the proliferation of the microcomputer in the 1980s followed by the emergence of the Internet in the 1990s in all aspects of businesses, the professions, and everyday living, schools throughout the country are attempting to ensure that their students are prepared to use this technology.

The research on instructional technology is conflicting. Some researchers conclude that it is beneficial and improves academic achievement, whereas others dispute these claims. Much of the recent literature also identifies implementation problems such as the lack of trained staff, difficulty in integrating technology into the curriculum, and limited resources as the root of many problems. Some of these issues are gradually being resolved.

Looking at the evolution of instructional computing applications, much of the work done in earlier years is not relevant because of the radical changes that have occurred in the technology. Several exceptions, though—including the pioneering efforts of Suppes, Kemeny, and Papert—have continued to evolve, and the fruits of their labor can be seen in many schools today.

Instructional computer applications have grown, with tens of thousands of software and media products on the market. Classifying and developing a framework for understanding the various applications is prone to a good deal of overlap. Robert Taylor's "tutor, tool, tutee" approach is recommended. It classifies a computer application as either a tutor (technology/computer teaching the student), a tool (technology used as an aid for teaching and learning), or a tutee (student teaching the technology/computer). Major applications within each of these classifications have been described.

Computer technology is also merging with other technologies—namely, multimedia and communications—to create a variety of new instructional applications. The Internet of the 1990s is evolving into the major medium of the 21st century. New applications using these technologies are far more exciting and pedagogically more stimulating than anything that the individual technologies alone provided in the past. The potential of these merged technologies is very great and will be more evident as they improve and as educators learn how to use them.

KEY CONCEPTS AND QUESTIONS

1. Schools are investing significant resources in instructional technology. How have the schools benefited from this investment to date?

2. Instructional technology has been evolving since the 1950s and 1960s. Some computer educators consider that much of the early work has very little application in today's schools. Do you agree? If so, why? If you do not agree, provide

examples of early work in instructional technology that are commonly used in today's schools.

3. In implementing instructional technology, administrators may have several objectives. What are some of these objectives? What do you consider the most important objective for using technology in the classroom?

4. Developing a classification system for instructional technology has proved to be an elusive endeavor. Why? Are you comfortable with the "tutor, tool, tutee" classification developed by Robert Taylor? Explain. Which of the three broad types of instructional computer applications do you consider to be the most beneficial for students? Might your opinion change for different age groups?

5. Integrated learning systems are probably the most complete instructional computer applications available. If this is so, why have most schools not acquired them? Do you see any change in their acquisition in the near future? Explain.

6. Computer technology is gradually merging with video and communications technologies to provide instructional applications. Give examples and discuss the potential of the following: (a) computer and video; (b) computer and communications; and (c) computer, video, and communications.

7. Integrating technology into the curriculum is proving to be a major problem in many school districts. Why? How do you see this problem being resolved?

SUGGESTED ACTIVITIES

To complete the Suggested Activities online, go to the Companion Website at **www.prenhall.com/picciano,** then to this chapter's *Suggested Activities module.*

REFERENCES

Archer, J. (1998). The link to higher scores. *Education Week, 18*(5), 10–21.

Becker, H. J. (1994). *Analysis and trends of school use of new information technologies.* Irvine: Department of Education, University of California.

Bloom, B. S. (1956). *Taxonomy of educational objectives handbook: Cognitive domains.* New York: David McKay.

Bullough, R. V., & Beatty, L. F. (1991). *Classroom applications of microcomputers.* Upper Saddle River, NJ: Merrill/Prentice Hall.

Christensen, R., & Knezek, G. (2001). Instruments for assessing the impact of technology in education. *Computers in the Schools, 18*(2/3), 5–25.

Clark, R. (1983). Reconsidering research on learning from media. *Review of Educational Research, 53*(4), 445–459.

Clark, R. (1985). Evidence for confounding in computer-based instruction studies. *Educational Communications and Technology Journal, 33*(4), 249–262.

Clark, R. (1989). Current progress and future directions for research in instructional technology. *Educational Technology Research and Development, 37*(1), 57–66.

Cuban, L. (2000, February 23). Is spending money on technology worth it? [Electronic version]. *Education Week, 19*(24), 42.

Cuban, L. (2001). *Oversold and underused.* Cambridge, MA: Harvard University Press.

Fatemi, E. (1999). Building the digital curriculum. *Education Week, 19*(4), 5–8.

Gagné, R. M. (1977). *The conditions of learning.* New York: Holt, Rinehart & Winston.

Koumi, J. (1994). Media comparison and deployment: A practitioner's view. *British Journal of Educational Technology, 25*(1), 41–57.

Kozma, R. (1991). Learning with media. *Review of Educational Research, 61*(2), 179–211.

Kozma, R. (1994a). Will media influence learning? Reframing the debate. *Educational Technology Research and Development, 42*(2), 7–19.

Kozma, R. (1994b). A reply: Media and methods. *Educational Technology Research and Development, 42*(3), 11–14.

Kulik, J. A. (1984). Evaluating the effects of teaching with computers. In G. Campbell & G. Fein (Eds.), *Microcomputers in early education.* Reston, VA: Reston.

Kulik, J. A., Bangert, R., & Williams, G. (1983). Effects of computer-based teaching on secondary students. *Journal of Educational Psychology, 75*(1), 19–26.

Kulik, J. A., Kulik, C., & Bangert-Downs, R. (1984). Effectiveness of computer-based education in elementary schools. *Computers in Human Behavior, 1*(1), 59–74.

Kulik, J. A., Kulik, C., & Cohen, P. (1980). Effectiveness of computer-based college teaching: A meta-analysis of findings. *Review of Educational Research, 2*(2), 525–544.

Kulik, J. A., Kulik, C., & Schwab, B. (1986). The effectiveness of computer-based adult education: A meta-analysis. *Journal of Educational Computing Research, 2*(2), 235–252.

Linn, M. C. (1985). The cognitive consequences of programming instruction in classrooms. *Educational Researcher, 14*(5), 14–29.

Lockard, J. (1992). *Instructional software: Practical design and development.* Dubuque, IA: Wm. C. Brown. Retrieved March 29, 2004, from the Web site of Logo Computer Systems, Inc. (http://www.lcsi.ca/company/profile.html).

Luehrmann, A. (1980). Should the computer teach the student, or vice-versa? In R. Taylor (Ed.), *The computer in the school: Tutor, tool, tutee* (pp. 127–158). New York: Teachers College Press.

Merrill, P., Tolman, M., Christensen, L., Hammons, K., Vincent, B., & Reynolds, P. (1992). *Computers in education.* Upper Saddle River, NJ: Prentice Hall.

Papert, S. (1980). *Mindstorms: Children, computers, and powerful ideas.* New York: Basic Books.

Park, J., & Staresina, L. (2004, May 6). Tracking U.S. trends. *Education Week, 23*(35), 64–67.

Pea, R. D. (1987). The aims of software criticism: Reply to Professor Papert. *Educational Researcher, 16*(5), 4–8.

Piaget, J. (1952). *The origins of intelligence in children.* New York: Norton.

Picciano, A. G. (1991). Computers, city and suburb: A study of New York City and Westchester County public schools. *Urban Review, 23*(3), 93–109.

Quality Education Data. (1996). *Education market guide and mailing list catalog.* Denver: Quality Education Data.

Robyler, M. D., Castine, W. H., & King, F. J. (1988). Assessing the impact of computer-based instruction. *Computers in the Schools, 5*(1), 1–149.

Sheingold, K., & Hadley, M. (1990). *Accomplished teachers integrating computers into classroom practice.* New York: Bank Street College of Education, Center for Technology in Education.

Sheingold, K., Kane, J. H., & Endreweit, M. E. (1983). Microcomputer use in the schools: Developing a research agenda. *Harvard Educational Review, 53*(4), 412–432.

Simonson, M. R., & Thompson, A. D. (1997). *Educational computing foundations* (3rd ed.). Upper Saddle River, NJ: Merrill/Prentice Hall.

Taylor, R. P. (Ed.). (1980). *The computer in the school: Tutor, tool, tutee.* New York: Teachers College Press.

Thompson, A. D., Simonson, M. R., & Hargrave, C. P. (1992). *Educational technology: A review of the research.* Washington, DC: Association for Educational Communications and Technology.

Trotter, A. (1998). A question of effectiveness. *Education Week, 18*(5), 7–9.

Trotter, A. (1999). Preparing teachers for the digital age. *Education Week, 19*(4), 37–46.

U.S. Congress, Office of Technology Assessment. (1995). *Teachers and technology: Making the connection* (Report No. OTA-EHR-616). Washington, DC: U.S. Government Printing Office.

U.S. Department of Education, National Center for Education Statistics. (2000). *Internet access in U.S. public schools and classrooms: 1994–99,* NCES 2000-086. Washington, DC: U.S. Department of Education, National Center for Education Statistics.

Vockell, E., & van Deusen, R. M. (1989). *The computer and higher-order thinking skills.* Watsonville, CA: Mitchell.

Vygotsky, L. (1978). *Mind in society: The development of higher psychological processes.* Cambridge, MA: Harvard University Press.

Yancey, K. B. (2004). Using multiple technologies to teach writing. *Educational Leadership, 62*(2), 38–40.

Chapter 6

Multimedia in Education

esponding in an interview to a question about a leading soprano's singing and acting talents, James Levine (1995), the artistic director of the Metropolitan Opera in New York City, commented that good music does not need words. His point was that music alone was enough to communicate emotion and beauty between those with talent and those with the ability to appreciate it. However, when a Verdi melody is combined with words, the result is an aria that touches and appeals to many more people who can better appreciate the melody within the context of a story or event. Add actors in colorful dress, a set depicting a quaint mountain village, some graceful dancers, and the result is opera that appeals and communicates to the world.

The expansion of a libretto into an aria and an aria into an opera is an appropriate metaphor for introducing the subject of multimedia as applied to teaching and learning. Indeed, words conveyed by writing and reading alone may not be sufficient to reach all students. Combining words with images, sounds, and movement can extend the teaching/learning process and help communicate a lesson to many more students.

MULTIMEDIA DEFINED

The term *multimedia* refers to many types of communication processes, delivery systems, and events. It is a buzzword that is used in connection with entertainment, advertisement, museum exhibitions, theme parks, video games, and dozens of other areas of human endeavor. *Multimedia* adds a certain technological chic that conjures up images of color, movement, dazzling special effects, and provocative sounds. Because of the variety of ways in which the word has been used, multimedia has come to mean different things to different people.

Generically, multimedia can be defined as any combination of two or more media such as sound, images, text, animation, and video. When used with computer technology, multimedia refers to a variety of applications that combine media and that utilize CD-ROM, video, audio, DVD, and other media equipment.

In addition to this basic definition, multimedia, when used with computer equipment, also implies interactive navigational or hypermedia capabilities that can be invoked and controlled by the user. *Hypermedia* is the integration of sights, sounds, graphics, video, and other media into an associative or linked system of information storage and retrieval. It is an extension of the concept of hypertext, which links text information in an associative system. Ted Nelson, an engineer, coined the term hypertext in 1965 to describe computer-based document retrieval systems that could be used in a nonlinear fashion as opposed to the traditional linear format of other document retrieval systems such as books and microfilm.

Hypermedia allows users to navigate in a nonlinear manner from one topic to another by the use of information linkages built into the associative system. The navigational system for the entire World Wide Web is based on this concept. Linkages are usually presented in the form of active screen areas or buttons that, when clicked on by a mouse, transfer or link the user to some other material. Examples of these linkage techniques are also commonly found in electronic encyclopedias such as Microsoft's Encarta and Grolier's Multimedia Encyclopedia. For educational technology purposes, multimedia refers to computer-based systems that use associative linkages to allow users to navigate and retrieve information stored in a combination of text, sounds, graphics, video, and other forms of media.

■ MULTIMEDIA FOR MULTIPLE INTELLIGENCES (MI)

For educators, multimedia may seem like nothing more than a higher technological use of sounds and sights to stimulate instruction. Educators have been using slide projection, film, videotape, and videodisc for decades to enhance student interest. However, in addition to being a point on the media continuum, multimedia also relates to theories of brain functioning and learning theory, especially those that relate learning to sensory stimulation and multiple intelligences (Armstrong, 2000, p. 153).

Since the early 1980s, Howard Gardner, a psychologist at Harvard, has been popularizing a theory of *multiple intelligences* (see Table 6.1). He posits that intelligence has been too narrowly defined; it is not a singular entity that can be measured by standard intelligence tests but rather is composed of multiple entities. Gardner (1983) identifies eight basic or multiple intelligences that all humans possess to some degree or another:

- ■ *Linguistic intelligence*—the capacity to use words effectively, either orally or in writing (e.g., writers, poets, orators)
- ■ *Logical–mathematical intelligence*—the capacity to use numbers effectively and to reason well (e.g., mathematicians, accountants, computer programmers)
- ■ *Spatial intelligence*—the capacity to perceive the visual-spatial world accurately, including the capacity to visualize and graphically represent visual and spatial ideas (e.g., architects, designers, artists)
- ■ *Bodily-kinesthetic intelligence*—the capacity to use one's body to express ideas and feelings and the facility to use one's hands (e.g., athletes, dancers, craftspeople)
- ■ *Musical intelligence*—the capacity to perceive, discriminate, and express musical forms (e.g., musicians, composers, singers)

TABLE 6.1	Theory of Multiple Intelligences	
Intelligence	**Definition**	**Learning needs**
Linguistic	Capacity to use words effectively	Books, writing, discussion, debate
Logical-Mathematical	Capacity to use numbers effectively	Manipulatives, science puzzles
Spatial	Capacity to perceive the visual-spatial world accurately	Art, video, slides, building blocks
Bodily-Kinesthetic	Capacity to use one's body to express ideas	Movement, dance, drama, sports, hands-on learning
Musical	Capacity to perceive and express musical forms	Song, instrumental music, background music
Interpersonal	Capacity to perceive moods and feelings of others	Group activities, social gatherings
Intrapersonal	Capacity to know oneself	Self-paced learning, quiet time
Naturalistic	Capacity to perceive and understand things in the world of nature	Field trips, garden projects, animal and pet care

Source: Based on Gardner (1983, 1993, 2000).

- *Interpersonal intelligence*—the capacity to perceive and make distinctions in the moods and feelings of other people (e.g., counselors, social workers)
- *Intrapersonal intelligence*—the capacity to know one's strengths and limitations and to act according to this knowledge (e.g., psychotherapists, religious leaders)
- *Naturalistic intelligence*—the capacity to perceive and understand things of the natural world (e.g., farmers, gardeners, veterinarians)[1]

Gardner's theory has been questioned and debated, particularly whether he has really expanded the concept of intelligence or simply extended it to long-recognized talents or aptitudes. Regardless, his theory makes a good case for using multimedia and other multisensory techniques in teaching and learning. Applied to instruction, his theory supports a concern that U.S. education at all levels (primary, secondary, higher) is too linguistically oriented. Teacher talks, students listen; teacher writes, students read; students write, teacher reads; and so forth. If we accept Gardner's theory—or even if we simply accept that people have different talents, aptitudes, or modalities for learning similar to the multiple intelligences—then should we not be teaching in

[1]At the time of this writing, Gardner was considering adding a ninth intelligence, which he describes as *existential intelligence*.

a way that can tap into these multiple intelligences instead of relying on one of them while neglecting the others?

This concept has generated an extensive debate that cannot be treated fairly here. Readers interested in pursuing this topic are encouraged to read Gardner's books, especially *Frames of Mind: The Theory of Multiple Intelligences* (1983), *Multiple Intelligences: The Theory in Practice* (1993), and *Intelligence Reframed: Multiple Intelligences for the 21st Century* (2000). An excellent review of Gardner's theory can also be found in Thomas Armstrong's (2000) *Multiple Intelligences in the Classroom.* The Association for Supervision and Curriculum Development (ASCD) has also provided coverage of Gardner's ideas in its main publication, *Educational Leadership,* and maintains a Teaching for Multiple Intelligences network.

The application of the multiple intelligences (MI) theory to multimedia and other computer technologies is apparent. If materials can be developed and used that extend instruction beyond the linguistic intelligence and make greater use of visual stimulation, sounds and music, logic and mathematics, and so forth, then perhaps a more effective teaching and learning process could evolve. The literature includes many examples of multimedia technology as an outgrowth of Gardner's theory. David Thornburg (1989), who has been involved in designing provocative educational technology such as the Muppet Learning Keys and the Koala Pad, bases much of his application designs on MI theory. Thomas Armstrong (2000) also advocates using multimedia for implementing MI theory in the classroom. Researchers at the Center for Media and Learning at the City University of New York likewise have developed interactive video models for teaching history based on MI and modalities of learning (Picciano, 1993).

MULTIMEDIA LITERACY

Fred Hofstetter (1994), professor and director of the Instructional Technology Center at the University of Delaware, raised this question for educators: "Is multimedia the next literacy?" It was a serious question not only for the future, as Hofstetter implied, but for the present as well.

The question concerns the manner in which society receives its information. Essentially, since the advent of television (a multimedia technology in its own right) in the 1940s, Americans have been receiving ever-increasing amounts of their information from the moving images and sounds emanating from their TV sets. In 1991, most Americans did not read about the Gulf War in the Middle East in the morning paper; they saw it on TV in real time. Scud missiles firing, tanks rolling, soldiers running with guns, and reporters ducking for cover were flashed on television sets all over the world by the Cable News Network (CNN). In 1995, they did not read about the O. J. Simpson "trial of the century" either; it was fully covered on a daily basis by several of the major networks. People watched in real time or set their VCRs to tape portions of the trial and watched it at night. For those without VCRs, several stations devoted as much as an hour each night recapping the trial's daily events. Other major events—such as the death of Princess Diana in 1997, the impeachment proceedings of President Bill Clinton in 1998 and 1999, the recounting of election ballots in Florida during the 2000 presidential election, and the terrorist attacks on the World Trade Center and the Pentagon in 2001—have likewise been followed by hundreds of millions of people on television.

Without question, for the average American, television has evolved into the most powerful information delivery mechanism ever—supplanting newspapers, magazines, and other material. On the other hand, television can generate so much interest in a subject that viewers actually seek out additional reading. Shelby Foote, playwright and author of a trilogy on the Civil War, was an adviser for, and appeared in, the award-winning PBS documentary *The Civil War,* which was viewed by more than 40 million people. In an interview, he commented that in the 15 years before the PBS broadcast, his trilogy sold about 30,000 copies. In the first 6 months after the broadcast, his trilogy sold more than 100,000 copies (Toplin, 1996).

For young people, not only television but also other multimedia technologies have become a fact of their daily lives. A generation or two ago, music was essentially heard on the radio, the phonograph, or the cassette player, but now it is heard and seen on MTV, VH1, and other cable TV channels. Pop singers and rap music artists are not simply heard but are seen in colorful costumes and designer clothes, dancing and acting while provocative still and moving images are displayed in the background. Highly sophisticated morphing technology is routinely used in these music videos and motion pictures, too, to dazzle and capture the viewers' imaginations. These displays are dominating how young people receive information and are creating a new generation that increasingly expects and responds to multisensory delivery systems. Competing with such stimulating visual and audio presentations is becoming a challenge for educators.

This challenge has three important components. First, if the American people, especially the younger generations, are becoming a multimedia-dependent society, should schools take advantage of the technology and use it in delivering instruction? Could it be that today's students, who do not read as well and are not as literate in the traditional sense as past generations, are developing a "multimedia literacy"? If this is the case, educators should begin to capitalize on this state of affairs by channeling their students' multimedia literacy into educational activities. More teachers, for instance, are integrating and assigning documentaries and educational programs aired by PBS, the Discovery Channel, or the History Channel into their lessons.

The second component of the educator's challenge is more complicated and involves the ability of young people to discern what is real and what is fake. American society has begun to ask: What is fact and what is fiction? For instance, are the events depicted in docudramas true or false? Some of them are true and some are false. How do viewers, especially young people, discern the truth? Oliver Stone's 1991 movie *JFK* is a case in point. Parts were footage or images of the actual assassination of John F. Kennedy and related events. Other images were enactments of a script written by Hollywood fiction writers. However, given the technical superiority of the movie and its extensive treatment of the topic, many viewers, especially those born after the events in 1963, came to accept this movie's version as fact. Errol Morris, director of the 2003 Oscar-winning documentary *The Fog of War,* about former defense secretary

Robert McNamara, responded to a question about the truth of documentary film-making with this observation:

> Does it make sense to talk about a movie being true or false? I'm not sure it does. In fact, I am pretty sure it doesn't. Movies are movies. (Waxman, 2004, p. E5)

American educators must consider teaching how media, particularly multimedia, can be manipulated to display events so that fiction appears to be fact.

In addition to television and film, which are nondigital and essentially passive technologies that do not require computer interfaces, young people today are the biggest consumers of video games such as Nintendo, Sega, and others provided on CD-ROMs and DVDs. These games are highly sophisticated, interactive multimedia computer systems that take advantage of the latest digital technologies to deliver stimulating activities. Go into a neighborhood computer software store and look at the product displays; there will be sections for business software, educational software, and games. Invariably, the sections for games are generally two to three times larger than the others. Young people, especially males, are not only seeing and hearing multimedia presentations but are also actually manipulating and interacting with them to create and control outcomes. Thus, the third challenge for educators is to develop and provide beneficial content that moves multimedia beyond the action game genre.

Hofstetter, quoted at the beginning of this section, raised the issue of multimedia literacy as a requirement for basic functioning in the evolving American society. He provided examples of how everyday existence will depend on multimedia delivery systems in the form of home shopping, electronic publishing, banking, worldwide communications systems, telecommuting or working from home, and so forth. The future society that Hofstetter (2000) envisioned as needing to be multimedia literate is already here for many of the young people in our primary and secondary schools. Multimedia will dominate the world in which they will function as adults.

MULTIMEDIA SYSTEMS

In planning for multimedia applications, educators will need to consider specialized hardware and software components. The following sections provide information on some of the technical requirements for developing and implementing multimedia applications.

Basic Hardware Requirements for Multimedia

The hardware requirements for a multimedia microcomputer system are dynamic and rapidly evolving. In addition to a basic computer system with the standard input devices, central processor, and output devices, multimedia systems require additional media hardware such as CD-ROMs, DVDs, sound boards (or cards), speakers, and video boards. Furthermore, because of the tremendous amount of digital storage required for the simplest multimedia presentations, higher speed central processors and more extensive secondary storage (hard disk) are needed for most applications. High-end microcomputers meeting or exceeding these requirements are packaged as "multimedia machines" by several manufacturers including Apple, Dell, Gateway, Sony, IBM, and Compaq.

Sound and Video Hardware

Sound and video hardware differentiate multimedia from other computer systems. Sound boards that provide audio/sound capabilities to computers such as those from Creative Labs (Sound Blaster boards), Ad Lib Multimedia, and Tandberg Educational are readily available in hardware catalogs and computer stores. Major microcomputer manufacturers now include sound boards as standard components of their basic computer configurations. Likewise, video boards with full-motion video capabilities are also becoming commonplace.

If sound or video hardware needs to be acquired, educators should be aware of their technical features and capabilities. In evaluating sound features, CD (regular compact disc) audio quality has become the standard. To attain this standard, two features must be considered:

> *Bit capacity:* The amount of data that a sound board can store. The greater the bit capacity, the better (speed and sound quality) the board. For CD quality, a 16-bit sound board is minimally needed, but a 32-bit sound board is recommended.

> *Sampling rate:* As measured in kilohertz (KHz), the rate at which sound can be recorded and played back. The higher the sampling rate, the better the sound quality. The CD standard requires a 44-KHz rate or higher.

Depending on an application's requirements, other sound features to be considered include frequency modulation, wavetable synthesis capability, and musical instrument digital interface (MIDI) compatibility.

Full-motion video as established by the video and film industries is now the standard for video boards. To meet this standard, the following features must be considered:

> *Image resolution:* The clarity of detail that a video board can store for an individual image or frame. The resolution of video boards ranges from a minimum of 40,330 pixels to more than 1,0243678 pixels. The higher the resolution, the better the quality of the image. For full-motion video, the minimum resolution is 6,403,480 pixels.

> *Color capacity:* The number of colors that a video board can store in each pixel. Sixteen bits per pixel will store 32,000 to 64,000 different colors, which is more than sufficient for full-motion video. The 24- and 32-bit-per-pixel video boards now available are capable of storing millions of colors.

> *Frame rate:* The number of frames or images per second that a board can record or play back. Thirty frames per second is the full-motion standard. Slower rated boards will produce video that appears as slightly slow motion.

Depending on the applications being considered, other factors in evaluating video boards include compression formats, audio capture capabilities, video capture, and editing and playback capabilities.

An in-depth knowledge of the specifications described here is essential if users are interested in developing their own multimedia applications. In all likelihood, multimedia software packages will be acquired rather than developed, in which case users simply need to be generally familiar with the technical requirements of the packages.

Multimedia Hardware for Image, Sound, and Video Capturing

Development of multimedia applications may require, in addition to the basic hardware described earlier, specialized equipment for sound, video and image capturing, recording, and playback. A brief review of this equipment will enhance the understanding of multimedia applications.

Images, whether still or moving, are a fundamental feature of multimedia applications. Images can be in digital format and ready for processing by a computer, or they can be in analog format. Computer-generated graphics, animations, and digitized photographs are examples of images in digital format. Film, videotape, and videodisc are examples of images in nondigital or analog format. Although computer equipment is available to handle either format, educational multimedia development is significantly facilitated when all image handling is done in digital format.

For many years, optical scanners have been available to convert photographs and hard-copy documents into digital images. This equipment continues to become more reliable and is ideal for simple still-image digitization. Flatbed and handheld scanners are inexpensive and simple enough to be used by students. For those individuals who use 35mm cameras and would like high-quality digital images, film developers such as Kodak will convert 35mm film into digital format for just a little more than the cost of normal film processing. To bypass the film-developing step, affordable digital cameras are available from major manufacturers such as Kodak, Canon, and Sony. They take the photographs, store them in digital format, and import them directly to a computer for subsequent processing. Once captured in digital format, photographs can be modified, edited, or enhanced through software. In the past several years, the prices for digital cameras have come down dramatically as more manufacturers enter this market and increase competition.

For use in multimedia projects, camcorders, videotape, videodisc, CD-ROMs, and DVDs are the major video input media. Video boards are necessary computer components for using any type of video. Hardware and software are available that allow camcorders to connect directly to a computer's video board and subsequently convert the video into digital format. Most of this technology will accept camcorder input from the major manufacturers such as Canon, Sony, and Toshiba. Videocassette recorders and videodisc players can likewise be connected to a computer's video board for conversion to digital format.

A videodisc player can be controlled by a computer to play video in its original analog format. This technique is desirable if high-quality video is required or if a user is not allowed to make a copy of the video material because of copyright restrictions. Converting analog video into digital format is considered copying and is thus subject to copyright restrictions. Analog videodiscs are coming to the end of their product life cycle as the computer industry moves toward all-digital formats for image and video handling. DVD technology, which emerged in the late 1990s, is rapidly replacing analog videodisc technology.

The use of audio and sound equipment for multimedia projects is becoming commonplace in schools and media centers. The most common devices are microphones for input and speakers for output that connect directly to a sound board. The microphones and speakers used for multimedia are the same as those used with noncomputer equipment. Prices and quality range broadly for this equipment, which is available in both computer and general electronics stores. For more sophisticated sound input, such as might be required for musical instruments, MIDI equipment is available that will connect musical instruments and synthesizers to computers. MIDI equipment can be used to create, record, and play back music. Common in the professional music business for many years, MIDI equipment used to control synthesizers and instruments is also growing in popularity in education. Companies that provide MIDI equipment include Sony, Yamaha, and Roland.

ANALOG VIDEO AND DIGITAL VERSATILE DISC TECHNOLOGY

The emergence of DVD technology has added a significant new option to multimedia development. In all likelihood, the new DVD technology will be most attractive to current multimedia developers, especially those using analog videodiscs.

Videocassette

Videocassette technology, which gained considerable popularity in the 1980s, remains an important technology for instruction. It is simple to use and graphically rich. Teachers and students alike have no problem dropping a videocassette into a VCR and hitting the Play button to provide video clips on subject matter. Teachers and students also increasingly have become familiar with using camcorders for creating videocassettes for classroom projects. A good deal of pedagogically valuable material is also available on videocassette from the Public Broadcasting Service (PBS), the Discovery Channel, and other major educational software suppliers. The major limitation of videocassette technology is its noninteractive or passive nature. Viewing a videocassette in a class requires the teacher to stimulate discussions and activities. Videocassette is also a sequential medium with little or a generally clumsy Rewind/Playback facility for randomly selecting segments or clips from the larger videotape. As more advanced technologies (e.g., videodisc, CD-ROM, DVD) have evolved, the demise of videocassette has been predicted many times. However, because of its simplicity, it remains an incredibly popular technology for instructional activities.

Analog Videodisc Technology

Videodisc (or laserdisc) is an analog direct-access medium. Frames are stored on a series of concentric tracks on 12-inch or 8-inch metallic disks. Laser (light) technology is used to read the frames. Any individual frame or segment of frames can be accessed directly and played independently of any other frame. This technology has been popular for delivering instruction. Unlike digital video, videodisc may or may not be used with computer equipment, and because of its direct access capabilities, it is a much more advanced technology than videotape or other sequential media. Direct access also allows videodiscs to be integrated with computer technology to provide interactive video instruction as desired.

There are several levels of interactivity. Level I provides no actual computer interactivity, but assumes that the person using the videodisc has a handheld controller for directly accessing desired frames or chapters. The simplest controllers are similar to those used to change channels on television sets. Some textbook publishers provide bar code readers that can control a videodisc player. Frames on a videodisc are selected when the reader is passed over bar codes that have been added to the teacher's edition of a textbook. These bar codes have been prelinked to certain frames on the videodiscs to provide direct access to relevant video material that might be used as a demonstration during a lesson.

A Level II interactive system is a videodisc player with a built-in internal microprocessor. The microprocessor receives its instructions from programs that must be added onto the discs. These systems have not been very popular for several reasons. The videodiscs and players for Level II systems are quite expensive. In addition, the videodiscs are programmed specifically for a particular manufacturer's disc player. This limits their market considerably.

Level III interactivity combines a videodisc player with a standard microcomputer. The microcomputer controls the player through programs usually supplied by the videodisc vendor. Using authoring languages such as Authorware Professional or Asymetrix's ToolBook, a teacher can also develop programs to control a videodisc presentation.

In the 1990s, a number of videodisc titles were produced specifically for education in the sciences, social studies, literature, art, and music. Optical Data Corporation, in particular, produced a highly acclaimed Windows on Science series. In one of the first such actions taken by a state board of education, this series was approved in Texas in 1990 for adoption in the science curriculum for grades 1 through 6. However, the future of videodisc technology is very much in doubt because most videodisc users are rapidly moving to new DVD formats.

Digital Versatile Disc Technology

Digital versatile (or video) disc (DVD) is a small plastic disc used for the storage of digital data and is the successor to the compact disc (CD). A DVD may have as much as 26 times the storage capacity of a CD, and has better graphics and greater resolution. A DVD stores digital data as a series of microscopic pits on an otherwise polished surface. The disc is covered with a protective, transparent coating so that it can be read by a laser beam. The playback or record heads never touch the encoded portion, and the DVD is not worn out by the playing process. Because DVD players are backward compatible to existing optical technologies, they can play CD and CD-ROM discs; however, CD and CD-ROM players cannot play DVD discs.

At the time of this writing, a standard DVD format had not been established. DVDs can hold data in a number of evolving formats depending on the application. DVD formats include DVD-Video (often simply called DVD), DVD-ROM, and DVD-Audio. DVD-Video discs hold digitized movies or video programs and are played using a DVD player connected to a standard television monitor. DVD-ROM (read-only memory) discs hold computer data and are read by a DVD-ROM drive hooked up to a computer. These discs are impressed with data at the point of creation and once written cannot be erased and rewritten with new data. DVDs also include recordable variations. DVD-R (Recordable) discs can be written to sequentially but only once. DVD-RAM (random-access memory), DVD-RW, and DVD1RW (ReWritable) discs can be written to thousands of times.

The amount of content available in DVD format is growing especially for entertainment purposes. Educational content has begun to be developed and it is likely that this will grow significantly in the near future. For example, Microsoft now offers its Encarta Electronic Encyclopedia, which used to require five CD-ROMs, on one DVD. Microcomputer manufacturers have begun to offer DVD drives or combined DVD/CD-ROM drives instead of CD-ROM drives as standard equipment. Because of the backward compatibility mentioned earlier, most buyers are naturally opting for the newer DVD technology. All of this bodes well for the future of DVD.

MULTIMEDIA SOFTWARE

Authoring

Authoring languages are especially popular for doing multimedia applications. Easier to use than traditional programming languages, authoring has become the software of choice for teachers and students developing multimedia. The many authoring languages now available allow users to integrate text, images, digital and analog video, sound, and so forth, merely by selecting screen objects such as buttons, fields, and hotwords with the click of a mouse. Authoring languages such as Microsoft PowerPoint, HyperCard, HyperStudio, ToolBook, and Authorware Professional are increasingly being used by educators for instructional applications.

In acquiring authoring languages, ease of use should be of paramount importance, as will be discussed further in Chapter 10. Ease of use is relative to the skills and talents of the users, and while designed for the nontechnical individual, a good deal of training and practice is necessary for the average teacher to use this software effectively. However, these packages are easy enough to use so that even students can become proficient in developing multimedia applications. One of the most popular student assignments is to take the traditional composition or essay and make it into a multimedia project that incorporates sights and sounds with the text material. Word processing and desktop publishing software such as The Print Shop and The Newsroom incorporate pictures and graphics into their programs, so that even primary school children are capable of expanding the traditional writing assignment into something beyond simple text.

Image, Video, and Sound Editing

In addition to preparing multimedia presentations using authoring languages, image, video, and sound editing software is being used to assist in acquiring and editing visual and audio materials for inclusion into multimedia projects.

Simple image editing such as sizing and cropping a digital photograph can be easily accomplished with a wide range of software products including Adobe's Photoshop, Aldus's PhotoStyler, and Kodak's Photo-CD. Simple image editing is being directly incorporated into authoring and other multimedia software packages. More sophisticated image-editing software packages, such as North Coast Software's Photomorph, allow users to convert one image into other images using a variety of transitions such as pinpoint size reduction or expansion, color, and special effects. Photomorph can also be used to create effects on digital video files.

For video projects, video-capturing and video-editing software packages such as Adobe Premiere are needed. *Video capturing* is the term used for converting analog video as it exists on a videotape or videodisc into a digital video file. A video board is necessary to accomplish video capturing. Once captured into a digital file, the video material can be edited for subsequent multimedia projects. Likewise, sound-capturing software packages such as Creative Labs' Sound Blaster Pro allow users to capture sound either through a microphone or a MIDI device and save it as a digital file. The digital file is usually stored in a wave format that can be subsequently edited to reduce or expand portions of waves and add echo, bass, and other sound effects.

Digital Animation

Digital animation as a field grew considerably in the 1990s. No longer are simple "jerky" movements of a single figure the norm. Digital animation packages have become sophisticated enough to provide animations to multiple objects on a screen, special effects such as 3-dimensional images, and high-color resolution approaching photograph quality. Because the animation is all digital, computer processing is simplified and faster. Digital animation is also an important area for future development as major international industries in film, music video, television advertising, and video games continue to invest significant capital and human resources in advancing and perfecting digital animation technology. Disney's popular 1995 film *Toy Story* was one of the first full-length feature films to incorporate advanced digital animation techniques. Reasonably priced, high-level digital animation software products that are appropriate for use in schools today are available from companies such as Autodesk, Adobe, and Macromedia.

MULTIMEDIA FOR TEACHING AND LEARNING

In planning and implementing multimedia applications in schools, a distinction should be made between using this technology for teaching versus learning. For teaching, the emphasis is placed on the presentation of lessons, with the teacher as the center of the lesson delivery and the use of equipment. For learning, the emphasis is on the use of multimedia by students either for discovering learning, accessing information, or developing projects. For the latter, a good deal more hardware and software needs to be acquired, and an investment must be made in class time to train students to use the technology. The possibilities are endless and limited only by the teacher's imagination and creativity. Several common educational uses of multimedia are described here.

For teaching applications, software packages such as PowerPoint (Microsoft), HyperStudio (Knowledge Adventure), and Harvard Graphics (Software Publishing) provide templates or ready-to-use models for doing simple multimedia presentations. Teachers with a basic understanding of computers can learn presentation software relatively quickly, given some support by a technology coordinator or other expert. Once the software is mastered, a 50-minute multimedia lesson incorporating images, sound, animation, or video into a text outline can be completed in 1 or 2 hours. Usually, the greatest effort in developing a multimedia presentation is spent in locating appropriate images, sounds, or video. In planning presentations, a large monitor or overhead projection system is necessary so that a class can easily see the presentation.

Teachers may also wish to develop their own custom multimedia programs for use by students in a discovery learning or other pedagogical mode. More advanced authoring languages such Authorware Professional (MacroMedia) and ToolBook (Asymetrix) are ideal for these applications. Teachers will have to devote considerable time to learning these software packages, and although easier to use than other instructional programming languages, they will test the technical abilities and skills of the average teacher. Most likely, custom-designed and developed multimedia programs will require a team effort on the part of teachers and technical support staff. The time required to develop a custom multimedia program will depend on a number of factors, including the scope of the project, whether it will be incorporating digital or analog video, and the availability of video. Such projects usually require several months, if not more, for design and development.

Doing a customized multimedia project should be carefully considered, with serious planning devoted to training, design of the project, and the availability of media. This is especially true if part of the work involves doing video production. Even with the latest editing hardware and software, 30 minutes of quality video can require weeks and weeks of scripting, shooting, and editing. Readers interested in designing such a project are encouraged to refer to Simkins, Cole, Tavalin, & Means's (2002) *Increasing Student Learning Through Multimedia Projects,* Semrau and Boyer's (1994) *Using Interactive Video in Education,* or Kemp and Smellie's (1989) *Planning, Producing, and Using Instructional Media.* In addition to technical factors, teachers designing a custom project will also have to consider the abilities and learning styles of their students. Multimedia programs should not be designed for only the higher ability students, but should be easy enough for all students to use. This means that careful consideration is given to "help" features, navigational techniques, and program prompts.

For student learning, the use of commercially developed multimedia is appropriate for many learner-centered activities for studying a topic. Figure 6.1 provides a list of commercial multimedia packages that are appropriate for use in classroom activities. Electronic multimedia encyclopedias such as Microsoft's Encarta are becoming prevalent in school libraries and media centers. They incorporate sophisticated but easy-to-use search tools for finding not only text but images, sounds, and video. Custom software products dealing with a specific topic—such as A.D.A.M. The Inside Story (of

FIGURE 6.1	Popular Multimedia Software		

Program	Developer	Subject
A.D.A.M. The Inside Story	adam.com Software	Biology/health reference
Amazon Trail	The Learning Company	Social studies
American Sign Language Dictionary	Multimedia 2000	Special education
Children's World Atlas	Rand McNally	Atlas
Encarta	Microsoft	Encyclopedia
Eyewitness Series	DK Interactive Learning	Encyclopedia
Great Ocean Rescue	Tom Snyder Productions	Environment
Grolier Encyclopedia	Grolier	Encyclopedia
In My Own Voice	Sunburst	Poetry/multicultural
Imagination Express Series	Edmark Corporation	Book and movie production
Kid Pix	Broderbund	Drawing tools
Magic School Bus Series	Scholastic Software	Science
Multimedia Workshop	Knowledge Adventure	Multimedia tool/bilingual
Music Loops for Multimedia	FTC Publishing	Music clips
National Geographic CD-ROM	National Geographic	Geography/wildlife
Romeo & Juliet Center Stage	Sunburst	Drama/literature
Operation Frog	Scholastic Software	Biology
Oregon Trail	The Learning Company	Social studies
Point of View Series	Scholastic Software	Social studies
Science Court Series	Tom Snyder Productions	Science
Science Explorer Series	Riverdeep Interactive	Science
Voyage of the Mimi	Sunburst	Interdisciplinary
Who Built America?	Grolier	American history

the human body) from adam.com Software—are available for all the major subject areas. In addition to the appeal of pictures, sounds, and moving images, the benefit of using simple multimedia encyclopedias and programs is that students can begin to learn how to use this technology easily.

A more advanced level of learning applications would be for students to develop their own multimedia project. Examples include the following:

- Compiling a photo essay
- Doing a news report on an event using video
- Collecting oral histories from family members
- Doing a weather report using maps and animations
- Creating an artistic or musical piece using multimedia

Planning and implementing these applications require training students to use the necessary hardware and software. Sufficient equipment must also be available for the students to use for extended periods. Because of the amount of preparation and work involved, student multimedia projects are generally group or collaborative activities involving two or more students. One of the benefits of multimedia projects for learning is that students need to use a variety of skills, including reading and writing, in developing the project. Additionally, student-developed projects are excellent for helping children develop multimedia literacy; with guidance from teachers, students can begin to learn how media in general can be manipulated and edited to fit the message that they wish to deliver. In recent years, most of the popular multimedia authoring languages have also provided options to save files in hypertext markup language (HTML) format so that they can easily be made available and shared as pages on the World Wide Web.

MULTIMEDIA RESOURCES AND COPYRIGHTS

All of the major educational software developers mentioned in Chapter 5 have begun to market multimedia programs that would be appropriate for school use. If a multimedia program that meets a school's instructional needs is available, then certainly it should be acquired. No need exists for teachers to reinvent materials that already exist. Annual catalogs, guides, and compendia are readily available from a variety of sources. These are frequently provided free of charge to educators by journal and other publishers. Highly recommended is the *Multimedia Resource Guide* published by the Educational Software Institute of Omaha, Nebraska, and *The Multimedia Home Companion Guide for Parents and Kids* published by Warner Books, a Time-Warner Company. Keep in mind that commercial multimedia packages are subject to the same copyright stipulations that apply to other software products. Generally, programs and files including image, sound, and video files cannot be copied or used in a manner inconsistent with their original intent.

For those educators who plan to develop their own materials either for presentation or for student use, locating images, sounds, and video in digital format can be very time-consuming. The first source of multimedia materials in digital format would be the files available as part of the authoring or presentation software being used to develop the application. All of the major multimedia authoring or presentation software tools provide clip media libraries or files containing materials that can be readily incorporated into multimedia projects. In some cases, both a standard version of the package without the clip media and a deluxe or all-inclusive version of the package with the clip media files are available. The deluxe versions are generally worth the additional cost and can save hours of searching for images and sounds. Clip media libraries generally can be used freely by educators without the need to secure permissions for their use.

A second source of digital media would be electronic encyclopedias and multimedia databases. In many cases, the developers allow users to copy a photograph or image for limited use, as would be appropriate in a class presentation. Microsoft and Grolier are two of the major marketers of electronic encyclopedias that allow for a limited amount of copying of their materials, generally through a copy-and-paste mechanism.

A third source for digital multimedia materials would be commercially available clip media CD-ROMs and DVDs. Companies such as America On-Line, Aris Entertainment (Marina Del Ray, California), and Corel Corporation (Ottawa, Canada) provide clip media libraries of multimedia materials that can be freely used for educational purposes.

The Internet is a fourth source that will be discussed in more detail in the next chapter. Sites around the world make available images, sound, and video that can be accessed and copied by educators for classroom use. The Internet, in fact, will likely be the major source for all types of digitally formatted data in the not too distant future.

Local video stores such as Blockbuster Video maintain up-to-date lists and provide search services to locate titles of commercially available materials including videotape, videodisc, and DVDs. Copyright restrictions generally prohibit copying this material or converting it into other formats.

Taping television programs is also another source of analog video; however, using this material is also subject to copyright laws. Discovery Communications (The Discovery Channel) of Bethesda, Maryland, publishes a pamphlet titled "All About Copyright: Off-Air Taping Guidelines Explained," which describes the restrictions established by all the major network and cable television stations.

For more information on copyright issues, go to the *Web Links module* for this chapter on the Companion Website at **www.prenhall. com/picciano.**

In using any copyrighted materials (text, images, sound, video), educators should be aware of the restrictions on their use. Generally, but not always, educators have a fair or limited use of copyright materials as long as they are used for instructional purposes. However, even here prohibitions exist against the unauthorized use or proliferation of copies. It would be safe to say that any attempt to profit by selling or showing copyrighted materials, even for educational purposes, is generally prohibited. For educators unfamiliar with copyright issues, especially as applied to instructional multimedia, an excellent source of information is *The Multimedia Legal Handbook: A Guide from the Software Publishers Association* (1994), by Thomas J. Smedinghoff. Stanford University also maintains an excellent Internet site dedicated to copyright issues, which includes specific information on multimedia.

MEDIA DISTRIBUTION SYSTEMS

Media distribution systems integrate several media sources (videotape, videodisc, DVD, cameras, computers, etc.) and are able to distribute them to a number of output devices, usually stand-alone monitors. Figure 6.2 shows a flow diagram of such a system—developed by Dynacom, Inc., of Mishawaka, Indiana—that illustrates a router controlling and distributing media from several sources. Dynacom has since merged with Safari Systems, Inc. (Lawton, Michigan).

These systems are designed to function within a central media center operation so that, rather than media equipment (monitors, VCRs, videodiscs, DVDs, etc.) being lent out to teachers or students, the media are available for distribution over the system wherever a monitor is connected. One major benefit of these systems is that they can

FIGURE 6.2 **Media Distribution System**

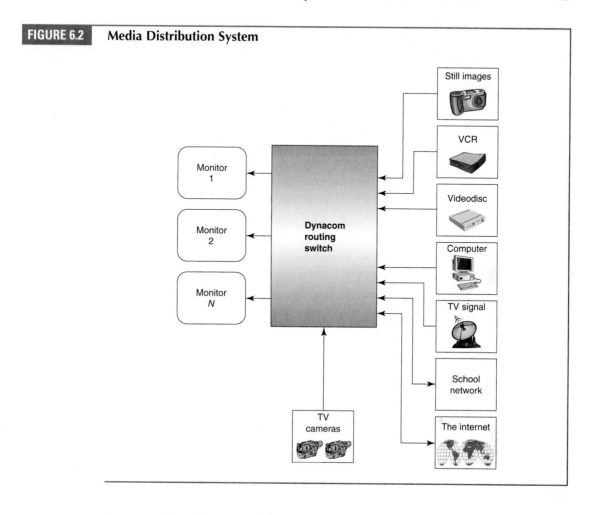

integrate all media sources, both digital and analog. Using such a system, a teacher might present a lesson that integrates several still images, video from a videodisc player, and computer data from the Internet. These systems can also be combined with distance learning facilities so that both the teacher's presentation and the media can be distributed over an entire district or to selected locations within a district.

A good deal of planning is required for these systems, particularly in wiring and setting up monitors in various locations. Some schools wire selected classrooms; others attempt to equip all classrooms. Media distribution systems are an expensive technology costing hundreds of thousands of dollars to acquire and install the basic routing equipment. However, educators who are making a major commitment to multimedia technologies may want to consider them. Whether such systems will become widely used is difficult to say. The hardware cost, along with the cost for wiring classrooms, will make them prohibitive for many school districts. In addition, media services that become available on data communications networks such as the Internet will also compete with these systems in the future.

PLACE: REDWOOD MIDDLE SCHOOL
YEAR: 2004

Redwood Middle School is located in an urban center in the northwestern part of the United States. Redwood provides a 6th to 8th grade program for approximately 500 students. The school enjoys an excellent reputation in its community, and the administrators and teachers are generally regarded as doing a good job of educating the children. Technology is apparent throughout the school, with computer equipment located in classrooms as well as in three central laboratories. The library media center maintains an excellent videotape selection and arranges for loans of portable (VCR/large monitor) workstations to teachers. The coordinator of the library media center would like to upgrade the video collection by adding DVD titles and players and has been in discussions with the Redwood site-based management (RSBM) team. An active Parent-Teacher Association has been helpful in securing additional resources for Redwood and has been particularly supportive of instructional technology.

Redwood is one of five pilot schools in the district that plans and administers much of its program under the auspices of a site-based management team. The members of the RSBM team are:

The cochairs of the PTA (one parent and one teacher)

Two teachers elected by the staff

Two parents appointed by the PTA

A representative from the school district's central office

A guidance counselor

A librarian

The assistant principal

The principal

Decisions are made as much as possible through consensus, with most issues being decided by unanimous vote. When opinions are divided, issues are generally tabled for further discussion.

A special (one-time infusion) city appropriation for the advancement of instructional technology has been made available to all the schools in the district for the 2004–2005 fiscal year. Redwood's share of these funds is $75,000. Each school is required to come up with a plan on how it would use these funds. It is October 2004, and all plans for using this appropriation must be submitted by February 2005 to secure funding in the current fiscal year.

The RSBM team has been discussing upgrading its instructional technology equipment for more than 2 years, especially with regard to multimedia applications. Several approaches have been discussed, with members of the team leaning toward multimedia systems using DVD technology. It is estimated that 15 classrooms can be upgraded for approximately $4,000 per classroom. The remaining $15,000 would be used to start a DVD collection in the library media center. However, at the first meeting in September, the school district representative suggested using the entire $75,000 appropriation for a wireless data communications system and 25 laptop computers that can be stored in a mobile cabinet for transportation throughout the school. The district representative reported that this was the way many schools were now accessing the Internet and its rich array of data resources.

At a second meeting in October 2004, the RSBM team seemed evenly split, with most of the administrative members supporting the school district representative's suggestion of the wireless/mobile laptop system, and the teachers and parents supporting the plan to upgrade the classrooms with multimedia. It appears that the team will have difficulty reaching a consensus by February 2005.

DISCUSSION QUESTIONS

1. Assume that you are the principal and have not yet committed yourself to a position on this issue. Given that you are concerned with developing a plan by February 2005 so as not to risk losing the funds, explain what your plan would be for assuring that the team will reach a consensus by the deadline. In developing your strategy, you should have a clear understanding of your own position on the technological merits of the two proposals.

2. Assuming the team makes the decision by February 2005, how do you present it to the school community? Do you have any fallback strategy for those who might not agree with the team's decision?

SUMMARY

This chapter reviews the development and use of multimedia technologies in education. Particular emphasis is put on the instructional uses of multimedia. Interest and investment in this technology are increasing, and indications are that it has appeal to both teachers and students.

Multimedia can be defined generically as any combination of two or more media such as sound, images, text, animation, and video. For educational technology purposes, multimedia refers to computer-based systems that use associative linkages to allow users to navigate and retrieve information stored in a combination of text, sounds, graphics, video, and other media.

Howard Gardner's theory of multiple intelligences establishes a theoretical framework for using multimedia in instruction. This theory relates to other widely recognized theories on learning styles and modalities of learning.

Multimedia literacy is a growing concern among educators as American society continues to depend on image technologies such as television, video, and film. Educators need to prepare children to live and function in a society that relies more on multimedia for information storage and dissemination.

Components of multimedia systems have been reviewed. Hardware components include a variety of both basic and specialized equipment. Software components include authoring languages, image handling software, and digital animation packages.

Multimedia can be used in instruction in a variety of creative and stimulating ways. Applications include teacher presentations, student projects, and discovery learning. Although teachers are encouraged to develop their own materials, many excellent educational multimedia products are available and should be considered rather than "reinvented."

In developing multimedia applications, many resources are available to educators. Educators should be aware of copyright issues and infringements when acquiring and using materials, especially video, images, and sound. The chapter concludes with a discussion of media distribution systems.

KEY CONCEPTS AND QUESTIONS

1. Multimedia technology has been evolving slowly but steadily during the past decade. How has this technology affected your daily activities? How do you see multimedia developing in the 21st century?

2. Multimedia means different things to different people. How do you define *multimedia?*

3. Multimedia is frequently used in conjunction with the application of technology for a variety of applications. Is multimedia strictly a technological phenomenon? Or does it have some theoretical basis for teaching and learning? Explain.

4. *Literacy* is a frequently used term in education and generally refers to language (reading and writing). Explain literacy in conjunction with multimedia. Does a need exist for developing multimedia literacy? Explain.

5. Multimedia can include a variety of hardware components. How are multimedia hardware components changing? Which do you consider the most beneficial for education? Why?

6. Multimedia can be used in a variety of applications. How would you differentiate multimedia applications as used by teachers for presenting lessons, as
opposed to use by students in learning?

7. Locating multimedia resources such as video, images, and sounds can be a
time-consuming activity. If you were to design a multimedia project, how would
you locate appropriate material? Do you need to be concerned about copyright
in using this material? Explain.

SUGGESTED ACTIVITIES

To complete the Suggested Activities online, go to the Companion Website
at **www.prenhall.com/picciano,** then to this chapter's *Suggested Activities
module.*

REFERENCES

Armstrong, T. (2000). *Multiple intelligences in the classroom.* Alexandria, VA: Association for Curriculum Development and Supervision.

Gardner, H. (1983). *Frames of mind: The theory of multiple intelligences.* New York:
Basic Books.

Gardner, H. (1993). *Multiple intelligences: The theory in practice.* New York: Basic Books.

Gardner, H. (2000). *Intelligence reframed: Multiple intelligences for the 21st century.*
New York: Basic Books.

Hofstetter, F. (1994, Winter). Is multimedia the next literacy? *Educator's Tech Exchange,
2*(3), 6–14.

Hofstetter, F. (2000). *Multimedia literacy* (3rd ed.). New York: McGraw-Hill.

Kemp, J. E., & Smellie, D. C. (1989). *Planning, producing, and using instructional media.*
New York: Harper & Row.

Levine, J. (1995, September 26). Interview with Charlie Rose, on *Charlie Rose* [Televi-
sion broadcast]. New York: Public Broadcasting Service.

Picciano, A. G. (1993). The Five Points: The design of multimedia model on teaching social history. *Journal of Educational Multimedia and Hypermedia, 2*(2),
129–147.

Semrau, P., & Boyer, B. A. (1994). *Using interactive video in education.* Boston: Allyn &
Bacon.

Simkins, M., Cole, K., Tavalin, F., & Means, B. (2002). *Increasing student learning
through multimedia projects.* Alexandria, VA: Association for Supervision and Curriculum Development.

Smedinghoff, T. J. (1994). *The multimedia legal handbook: A guide from the Software
Publishers Association.* New York: Wiley.

Thornburg, D. (1989). *The role of technology in teaching to the whole child: Multiple
intelligences in the classroom.* Los Altos, CA: Starsong.

Toplin, R. B. (1996, August 4). Plugged into the past. *New York Times,* section 2, pp. 1, 26.

Waxman, S. (2004, July 5). Nonfiction films turn a corner; "Fahrenheit" shows
approval of audiences and of distributors. *New York Times,* pp. E1, E5.

Chapter 7

Data Communications, the Internet, and Educational Applications

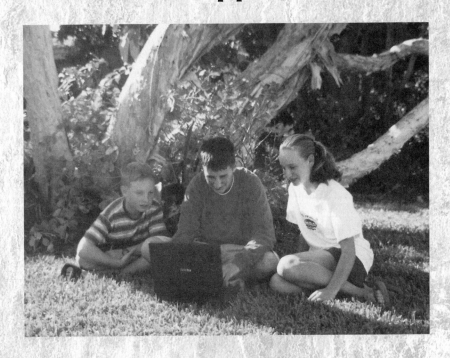

ladimir Zworykin, the "father of television," invented the iconoscope and kinescope, which became the basic technologies used for broadcasting and receiving television signals in this country. Born in Russia, he emigrated to the United States in 1919 and was hired by the Radio Corporation of America (RCA) in 1929 to do research and development in communications technology.

In the early years of the development of television, Zworykin envisioned a technology that could be useful in a free and democratic society. He struggled to receive funding for his work and had to convince others of the benefits of his new technology. In later years, even while rising to the position of vice president at RCA, he became concerned, even dismayed, at the commercialization of broadcast television. In 1962 he met President John F. Kennedy, who praised him for his contributions to this country, especially for his invention of the television. Zworykin replied wryly, "Have you seen television recently?" (Negroponte, 1995, p. 82).

In his later life, Zworykin commented frequently on the commercialization of television as a necessary evil. In an interview he gave in 1975, 8 years before his death, he expressed deep emotion over the "violence and murder" that we teach our children through television. But commercial television was driven by ratings, and the ratings ironically provided the funding for much of his own and others' research and development.

Zworykin's surprise at the direction taken by his own invention serves as an apt vignette to introduce this chapter on data communications and the Internet. The Internet is an infant medium with a potential comparable to television in terms of its societal influence. Observations and concerns have already begun to emerge regarding the content on the Internet. Those involved with its original development had no idea what the Internet would become.

Without a doubt, the Internet is evolving into the major technology within which a host of information, entertainment, and educational services are being provided. In December 1995, an education advisory council to President Bill Clinton recommended that every school in the United States be connected to the Internet. The basis for this recommendation was a carefully done, 2-year study conducted by McKinsey & Company, an international management consulting firm. The study estimated that every school in the country could establish a new 25-station computer laboratory with connections to the Internet via ordinary telephone lines for a cost of approximately $11 billion. Educators and newspaper editorials ("Connecting Every Pupil," 1995) praised this recommendation and commented that such an undertaking could "democratize education by bringing the world's best materials into the classrooms of the nation's . . . schools" (p. A20).

This recommendation is worth citing for several reasons. First, its specificity was unusual; recommendations regarding national policies for all schools in the country tend to be very general. Here, the recommendation specifies the number of work stations per school, as well as details on the nature of the application, and costs. Second, the recommendation also highlighted the importance of the Internet, not simply in terms of teaching and learning, but by characterizing its information resources as the "world's best materials." Lastly, by 2003, 98% of all schools in the United States were connected to the Internet, of which 80% had high-speed (T1, T3, or cable modem) connections (Park & Staresina, 2004).

These developments are indicative of how far communications technologies, especially as integrated with computer and video technologies, have come. The American public is aware of the extensive use that television has made of advanced communications systems to reduce the distance between audiences and live events. Major happenings—whether NASA space exploration projects, international crises, or the Olympic Games—are brought into living rooms in real time as they occur. The same advances that have been made in the television or video communications industry are now beginning to be made in the digital or computer communications industry. In the 1990s, terms such as *the Internet, the World Wide Web, cyberspace,* and *the information superhighway* became household words, whether used by government officials espousing national policy or children asking parents to subscribe to America Online so they could e-mail their friends. Data communications (i.e., the methods and media used to transfer data from one computer device to another) provide opportunities for a wide range of educational applications. Whether browsing the Internet, using a local area network in a computer lab, or accessing a database on a commercial online service, staff and students are discovering that data communications systems are becoming a major technology to support teaching and learning. In 2004, President George W. Bush promised that by 2007 affordable, high-speed access to the Internet will be available for "every corner in America" (Darman, 2004).

In this chapter, we examine data communications systems in schools, especially those provided by the Internet. Before continuing, readers are encouraged to review the material in Appendix A that covers the basic hardware components of most data communications systems.

DATA COMMUNICATIONS IN THE SCHOOLS

During the past several decades, educators have seen data communications systems and networks expand in size, sophistication, and the ability to communicate over distances. In the late 1970s and 1980s, schools began to install their first *local area networks (LANs)* (see Figure 7.1). The use of these LANs in computer laboratories, libraries, and administrative offices has become commonplace. In larger school districts, *wide area networks (WANs)* are in evidence, connecting computers and LANs that are dispersed miles apart throughout the district (see Figure 7.2). The essential concept here involves a large computer network integrating the activities of smaller computer networks. Using district-wide networks, a student in one school can determine whether a library in

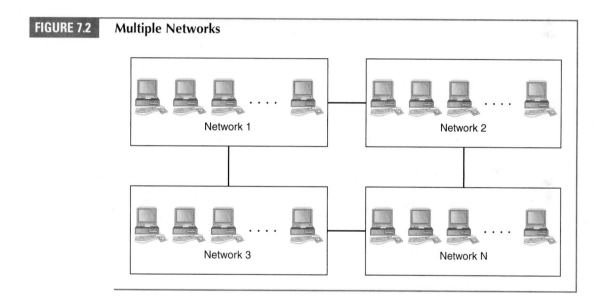

FIGURE 7.1   **Simple Local Area Network (LAN)**

Computer 1   Computer 2   Computer 3   Computer N

FIGURE 7.2   **Multiple Networks**

Network 1   Network 2   Network 3   Network N

another school has a particular book, an assistant principal can examine the transcript of a student who has just transferred from another school, or a district business manager can monitor the daily expenditures of several schools.

 The data communications technology that enables a computer in one school to communicate with a computer in another school is essentially the same, whether the schools are one mile apart or many miles apart. Once a WAN has been established in a locality, the distance between sites does not make that much difference in the ability of individual sites to communicate with one another. In the late 1980s, this concept was taken a step further, as computers in school districts began to communicate with computers on networks outside the school district. A student looking for a particular book was able to use a computer in the school's library to locate the book at a local public library or perhaps even a local college library. A superintendent using a computer in the school district office was able to transfer data on student demographics to a computer located in the state education office.

In the 1990s, data communications technologies advanced to the point where a computer on one network could easily communicate with a computer on another network hundreds or even thousands of miles away. The grants officer in a local school district office in Juneau, Alaska, could examine a database of funded programs that existed on a computer network maintained by the U.S. Department of Education in Washington, D.C. A state education department administrator in Albany, New York, could e-mail a new curriculum proposal to all 800 school district superintendents on a state-wide education network. A social studies teacher in Tulsa, Oklahoma, developing a module in cultural studies could access a database of curricular materials maintained by the National Geographic Society.

With the expansion of data communications capabilities over the past several decades, networks likewise have expanded to cover greater distances and to link with many other networks. At some point, all of this data traffic occurring on thousands of networks throughout the country and the world could pass over a common universal network.

THE INTERNET

The Internet (see Figure 7.3) is an international computer network consisting of hundreds of thousands of smaller networks that link schools, colleges, government agencies, research organizations, and private businesses through satellites and other high-speed data communications facilities. The essential function provided by the Internet is to allow users to transfer and receive data. The data can be a simple, one-line e-mail message, a complex weather map, or a huge subset of the United States 2000 census. The Internet also provides the conceptual framework for a universal computer network and is evolving into the network of networks.

A Brief History

The roots of the Internet can be traced to the U.S. Department of Defense in the 1960s. Concerned about establishing and maintaining a worldwide communications system in the event of a major disaster such as nuclear war, engineers and scientists from Rand, UCLA, and MIT designed a "doomsday" data communications system that would be decentralized and capable of functioning regardless of whether any single node or point in the network was no longer available. This design was a departure from the common centralized data communications systems that required a hub or center point to control the entire network.

In 1969, the Pentagon's Advanced Research and Projects Agency established the first node of this new network—called Advanced Research and Projects Agency Network (ARPANET)—at UCLA. Throughout the 1970s, the ARPANET grew but was used essentially by government officials, engineers, and scientists connected with research for the U.S. Department of Defense. In 1983, the military segment of ARPANET developed

FIGURE 7.3 **The Internet**

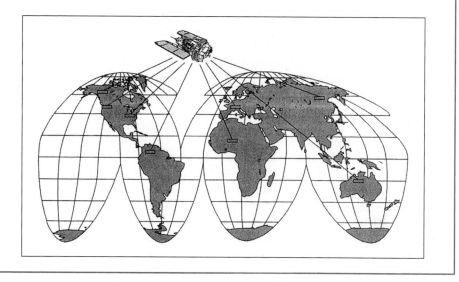

a separate network called MILNET, and access to ARPANET was expanded to include other computer networks worldwide that used its standard *protocol* or method of transferring data.

Also in the early 1980s, other international networks were being established in the higher education, government, and research communities. Because It's Time Network (BITNET) was established by the City University of New York, Yale University, and IBM to link university mainframe computers. Computer Science Network (CSNET) was funded by the U.S. National Science Foundation (NSF) to provide data communications facilities for industry, government, and university groups engaged in computer science research. Later, several U.S. agencies—namely, the NSF, the National Aeronautics and Space Agency (NASA), and the U.S. Department of Energy—funded and established networking facilities that eventually would be used to enhance the aging ARPANET system. By the late 1980s, all of these major networks were communicating with one another, either using or converting to the standard protocol established on ARPANET; hence the birth of the Internet.

The Internet Today

Since the early 1990s, the Internet community has grown exponentially. The number of users was estimated to be increasing at the rate of 20% per month, or doubling every 5 to 6 months. These numbers were strictly estimates because no one really knew at the time how many people were using the Internet. The art of estimating how many people are online throughout the world is an inexact one at best. Surveys abound, using all sorts of measurement parameters. However, from examining many of the published surveys, one educated guess has the number at 600 million people, with 180 million in the United States and Canada (Nua Internet Surveys, 2002).

This growth and popularity is understandable because joining the Internet is relatively inexpensive, voluntary, and service is equitable. The cost of using the Internet is not usage based. For example, sending an e-mail message costs the same whether the message is going a mile down the road to a neighbor or halfway around the world. Furthermore, a user incurs very few obligations by joining the Internet and can use its resources as needed. Although connecting to the Internet depends on acquiring equipment and online services, once on the Internet all users are equal. A major corporation or government agency does not receive quicker or better service than a group of 4th graders using the Internet to help with their homework.

The type of users on the Internet are changing significantly. In the late 1980s, the Internet was dominated by the nonprofit, research, university, and government sectors. Since the 1990s, many private enterprises, both small and large, joined the Internet for marketing, sales, and other commercial purposes. Likewise, private individuals are using the Internet daily for such routine activities as reading the news, checking on the weather, purchasing goods and services, or communicating with friends and relatives around the globe. Although still dominated by users in more technologically advanced countries, the number of Internet users in developing nations has also increased significantly in the past few years.

This expansion has significant implications. A major issue facing the Internet is in administration; presently, no single organization is really responsible for the Internet. Various government-sponsored arrangements and consortia exist in different countries to administer the Internet on a voluntary basis. In the United States, for instance, the NSF sponsors and funds the Internet Network Information Center (InterNIC), which maintains information, database directories, and registration services for the Internet. However, the funding for this center is not guaranteed, and the providers of the services do not accept responsibility for the accuracy of their information and services.

Interestingly, whereas data communications technology usually requires a good deal of precision in developing procedures, protocols, and access, the Internet has evolved with little planning or administrative precision. Some observers (Shirky, 1995; Stoll, 1995) have even referred to this evolution as *information anarchy* and predict that the Internet will outlive its usefulness. On the other hand, others (Ellsworth, 1994; Williams, 1995) consider this voluntary, loosely administered digital community as the very essence of freedom and equality in accessing and sharing information.

The Future of the Internet

Speculation on the future of the Internet is difficult given its dynamic nature. However, the Internet has attracted a good deal of attention, and because planning requires consideration of the future, a few comments and concerns about the Internet in the coming years are appropriate.

The Internet has been, perhaps, the most dynamic digital technology ever introduced. Computer industry analysts and software developers believe that it set "a new computing standard or platform much as the personal computer did in the 1980s," (Fisher, 1996, p. C15). In a period of a few years, hundreds of millions of people, most of whom did not even know of its existence as late as 1990, have used its services. Its growth rate in the mid-1990s, doubling the number of users approximately every 6 months, was nothing short of phenomenal.

This dynamism is stimulating for those who believe in the benefits of technology for the general populace, but it is a cause for concern as well. The Internet is a voluntary community with few rules and little formal administration. In the future, attempts will be made to impose rules and regulations, some of which will require administration and oversight. As an example, the U.S. Congress has considered censorship legislation for the Internet, particularly as it applies to child pornography and other sex-oriented material. Given the absence of mechanisms in place capable of controlling such activity, combined with the international character of the Internet, such legislation, whether warranted or not, would have limited impact. In the years to come, if the Internet continues to evolve into the network of networks, some international effort will likely be made to administer, and to some degree, control it. Whether this will be good or bad for the Internet is difficult to predict. If its growth continues, some technological administration, planning, and funding will have to be implemented. On the other hand, the same forces that provide administration and planning may also bring control, which has the potential of changing the free and voluntary access and sharing of information that has made the Internet so popular.

An issue related to administration and control is the commercialization of the Internet. The Internet evolved from the nonprofit (government, research, university) sectors. Commercial use of the Internet came afterwards; however, much of the growth in the Internet during the past several years has been fueled by commercial activities—everything from private entrepreneurs selling crafts to international corporations marketing goods and services. The Internet was designed primarily for information access and sharing, not necessarily for high-volume commercial transaction processing.

Furthermore, security on the Internet is limited. Security breaches happen regularly on many commercial networks, but the Internet is far more vulnerable to such breaches because it lacks any security oversight. The protection of common credit card transactions may require security oversight of the Internet. In fact, the possibility exists that the Internet will always be too vulnerable for high-volume commercial transaction processing typically found in banking or financial services and may have to be replaced by some other type of international commercial network that will have security controls in place.

The nature of commercial enterprise and high-volume transaction processing significantly adds to the traffic on the Internet. Most nonprofit uses of the Internet, such as information access, do not compare in volume with commercial activity in financial services, retail sales, and marketing. The Internet is already suffering from growing pains, as access and searches have slowed considerably, particularly during the prime business usage hours of 9:00 a.m. to 10:00 p.m. (Some critics have begun to refer to the World Wide Web as the "World Wide Wait.") Spamming or mass e-mailing from marketing enterprises have begun to jam e-mail inboxes. If commercialization of the Internet continues with its concomitant high-volume transaction processing, then access and search speed will continue to slow considerably, possibly changing its character and usefulness.

The basic hardware and software technology that is the foundation of the Internet was conceived in the 1970s and 1980s; the designers, however, were not envisioning a network that would meet the needs of hundreds of millions of people throughout the world. Data communications, as most technologies, evolved and improved in a steady, predictable fashion. Recently, however, the rapid growth of the Internet has fueled a significant increase in research, development, and new products meant to improve the hardware and software that all data communications systems require. The speed of modem equipment rises every year while its cost comes down. The introduction of handheld information appliances is adding a whole new dimension to accessing the Internet. Using wireless communications (satellite transmissions) and palm-size microcomputers, anybody is able to access e-mail and surf the Web literally in any place and at any time.

As we entered the early years of the new millennium, almost 158 million people in the United States used cell phones and other wireless devices (CTIA, 2003). It is only a matter of time and a bit more refinement of the technology before these people use wireless information appliances for most of their Internet activities. The future evolution of Web browser software is impossible to predict because new companies and products seem to appear almost overnight. The speed with which this technology is changing is unprecedented and generating new products with technological life cycles of no more than 1 or 2 years. The very nature of the providers of Internet access—whether public or private telephone companies, cable TV companies, satellite services, or strictly commercial Internet service providers—is not at all settled and can change significantly in the future. Such rapid change requires the most flexible of planning strategies as organizations, including schools, attempt to keep up with and adjust to newer data communications hardware and software technologies.

While considering the future of the Internet, it is most important for schools to provide experiences and opportunities for children to learn to use this rapidly evolving technology. Schools have traditionally prepared children to contribute, work, and play in the larger society—and using the Internet exemplifies the facility that will be required of individuals to technologically function in the future. Nicholas Negroponte (1995) relates a discussion that he had with the late Jerome Wiesner, then president of MIT, on considering the advances of technology and the evolution of a "digital" society. Although optimistic, Wiesner was concerned that such a society "takes jobs and may have fewer to give back" (p. 233). The Internet and/or its successors will require users in all sectors of society to continually hone their skills as they adjust to rapid advances and changes in using data communications and other technologies. Educators would be wise to include, as part of their technology planning, the establishment of goals and objectives that require students to be prepared for a digital society that will be largely dependent on a worldwide data communications system similar to, but more advanced than, the Internet of today.

An excellent reference for technology standards for students has been developed by the International Society for Technology in Education (ISTE) and is available online.

For more information on technology standards, go to the *Web Links module* for this chapter on the Companion Website at **www.prenhall. com/picciano.**

THE WORLD WIDE WEB

Terms for the Internet, such as *cyberspace* or the *information superhighway*, are designed to provide a descriptive character to this network of networks. Another term that is used in conjunction or interchangeably with the Internet is the *World Wide Web,* or simply the Web. The Web is actually a software system that introduced hypertext and multimedia capabilities to the Internet. Originally developed in the early 1990s at CERN (the European Particle Physics Laboratory in Switzerland), the Web was designed to provide hypertext and full multimedia support in a relatively easy-to-use language for physicists and other scientists using the Internet. This concept of a hypertext-based software system for the Web is generally credited to Tim Berners-Lee, currently director of the World Wide Web Consortium, who envisioned an Internet that would be much easier to use.

Hypertext, as used on the Web, is a nonsequential retrieval system for accessing data on the Internet. Rather than sequential searching, hypertext relies on linkages of data files to one another in a complex "web" of associations. Hypertext is not a new software search concept, having been routinely used in large databases for years. Electronic encyclopedias, for instance, employ hypertext searching when a particular topic or passage has links or "hotwords" that users can click on to jump to a related topic, which in turn has links to other related topics. The same approach is used on the Web to locate data files on the Internet.

Protocols and Client Servers

To understand the nature of the Web in relation to the Internet, a brief discussion of protocols, as used in data communications, is necessary. *Protocol* is a general term for a set of rules, procedures, or standards that are used in exchanging data in a data communications system. Examples of these rules would be a code or signal indicating the beginning of a message, a code or signal indicating the end of a message, or a code or signal indicating that a device is busy. Computer and communications equipment manufacturers established different protocols for exchanging data, which complicated the ability of one manufacturer's computer to communicate with another manufacturer's computer. This protocol incompatibility problem was resolved to some degree by the development of protocol conversion software that enabled computers to translate and convert data messages of other computer protocols. The Internet established a standard protocol for all its activity, called *transmission control protocol/Internet protocol* (TCP/IP). All computers using the Internet had to exchange data using TCP/IP. The Web's data transfer method or protocol, called *hypertext transfer protocol* (http), was designed to run "over" or in conjunction with the TCP/IP, the standard Internet protocol. Many other protocols have also been designed to run in conjunction with TCP/IP on the Internet; however, because of its hypertext and multimedia capabilities, the Web has become the most popular.

Because of its hypertext facilities, the Web is also an excellent software system to run on a client-server data communications system, which is how the Internet functions. In the early days of data communications, the standard network model was for a central computer to control all the activity on a network and also function as the central depository for data files and programs. The client-server data communications model does not require a central depository or controlling computer. The basis for the Internet and its predecessor, ARPANET, was to distribute or share control broadly among the networked computers.

In a client-server model, computers essentially perform two major functions. The client or end-user function makes a request or query for data to a server. The server function, performed by one of many computers sharing network control, processes the request and returns the results to the client. Many computers, not just one, can function as servers and can locate data on a network. Furthermore, servers can forward requests to other servers and create a chain reaction to process the original client's data request.

Uniform Resource Locator (URL)

Within the client-server environment of the Web, the uniform resource locator is the standard method of accessing the location of information resources on the Web. *Uniform resource locators* (URLs) are electronic addresses that identify a unique location of a data file. URLs serve the exact same function as an address in the U.S. Postal Service. If a letter is to be delivered in a timely fashion, an envelope is generally addressed with the recipient's name on the first line, the house number and street on the second line, and the city, state, and Zip code on the third. The standard for addressing envelopes is well known and works well. The standard format for entering a URL address is as follows:

protocol://host/path/file

where

protocol is the method of transferring data from one computer to another (i.e., http)

host is the name of the host computer

path is the name of the directory on the host computer

file is the name of a file in the directory

For example, the following URL uses the hypertext transfer protocol (http) to access a file that contains an index of education resources at the College of Chemistry at the University of California, Berkeley:

http://www.cchem.berkeley.edu/Education/index.html

where

http is the protocol

www.cchem.berkeley.edu is the host computer name

Education is the path or directory

index.html is the file name

For new users of the Web, the format of URLs may seem complicated. However, after frequent use they become second nature. Software browsers that provide the software facilities for locating information on the Web also provide URL address lists that can simply be clicked on to access the data file at the desired host computer or site.

The most commonly used protocol on the Web is *http*. Other less frequently used protocols are:

ftp	file transfer protocol
gopher	database and communications software system for searching for data in files
Wais	wide area information system

For more information about popular sites on the Web, go to the *Web Links module* for this chapter on the Companion Website at **www.prenhall. com/picciano.**

The host name on many URLs will contain a suffix designating a type of organization. In the previous example, *edu* represents an educational institution. Other commonly used suffixes include these:

com	commercial enterprise
gov	government agency
mil	military agency
net	network service
org	nonprofit organization

These suffixes are not required but are considered good form conventions when establishing a host name.

Web Browsers and Search Engines

Searching for data and information on the Web using URLs requires software browsers. The most popular browsers—Netscape and Internet Explorer—are available in versions for both Windows and Macintosh computers. It is quite possible that by the time this book is in print, new software browsers will be in use. However, the basic concept and nature of Web browsing is expected to remain the same.

Browsing software is used to access data files that are generally displayed as "pages" on the Web. Figure 7.4 is a sample page from the Netscape Web browsing software. Web browsers generally provide a series of pull-down menus or navigation buttons that allow users to navigate or "surf" the Web. The location where a user starts a Web browsing session is referred to as the user's home page. Besides standard features such as save, copy, paste, and help, common basic navigational functions of browsers include the following:

Back	Returns to the previous page
Forward	Goes to the next page
Reload	Reloads the current page
Home	Returns to the user's home page
Search	Transfers the user to a search engine
Print	Prints the current page
Security	Provides security information
Stop	Stops the current operation
Bookmark	Stores/lists frequently used URLs

Web browsers allow users to enter URLs in some designated areas to access the page of the requested data file. Depending on the overall traffic on the Internet, the

FIGURE 7.4   **Sample Web Page**

number of users requesting data from the same host computer, and the speed of the data communications line being used to make the request, requests are usually processed in a matter of seconds. If too much traffic exists or if the host does not respond to a request, a message is displayed within some reasonable period of time, giving the user the option of continuing or canceling the request. For readers who have not had much experience using a Web browser, one of the Suggested Activities accompanying this chapter on the Companion Website provides practice in navigating to various sites on the Web.

Web browsers rely on software called *hypertext markup language* (HTML) to establish and convert data files. "Filter" or conversion programs are available that will convert documents produced by word processing or some other software into an HTML or Web page document. However, other software languages—such as Java and JavaScript, developed by Sun MicroSystems—have been introduced that are enhancing the way data are established and displayed on the Internet. Java adds a great deal more programmability and multimedia capabilities to data files on the Web.

Without assistance, locating and accessing data on the Web can be a formidable task. An electronic card catalog of all of the Web's holdings does not exist and never will, given its dynamic and loosely administered nature. Users can easily spend hours trying to locate some particular data or information. Web browsers provide keyword search capabilities that work similarly to other database query languages. In addition, another type of software, referred to as a *search engine,* has evolved that provides keyword search facilities. Search engines are available at URLs on the Web and can save users a significant amount of time in attempting to identify URLs that contain the information being sought. Several popular search engines are Google, Lycos, AltaVista, and Yahoo!—and their respective URLs are listed in the Web Links module found on the Companion Website. Users should be aware that much of the data searched by these engines has been voluntarily submitted by other users or is gathered using various algorithms. By no means do search engines conduct complete searches of all the data resources on the Web.

COMMERCIAL ONLINE SERVICES

Schools can connect to the Internet in several ways. They establish their own Internet connection via a SLIP (serial line Internet protocol); they can connect via an online service provided by a local nonprofit organization such as a college, university, or government agency; or they can subscribe to a commercial online service. When contemplating connecting to the Internet, educators should consider commercial providers, especially if other nonprofit online services are not available or if the technical expertise needed to establish and maintain an Internet connection is limited in the school district. The commercial online services provide technical support and are very effective in getting new users connected to the Internet. In addition to Internet service, they also provide access to online newspapers, home shopping, financial reports, and so forth. They charge monthly rates based on usage of their services; basic rates for individual subscriptions start at about $10 per month and increase depending on usage and connect time. With increasingly heavy usage, flat-rate fees for unlimited access are highly desirable. America Online (2004), for instance, implemented a flat rate of approximately $20 per month for unlimited access to the Internet. However, the competition among commercial online service providers is keen and prices are expected to decrease. Group rates for organizations such as schools need to be negotiated.

If commercial providers are not required for a school's connection to the Internet, educators may still want to become familiar with them for their own professional development and to understand what their students are likely using in their homes. The major commercial providers have not ignored education as part of their menu of services. On the contrary, educational services such as professional homework assistance, educational databases, and standard reference materials are available. Educational discussion groups sponsored by the National

Education Association, the United Federation of Teachers, the National Principal's Center, and the Association for Supervision and Curriculum Development are also available via these services and are excellent forums for communicating with other professionals on national issues.

The Internet has been described in this chapter as a dynamic, free, and voluntary community. Commercial activity is growing significantly, which means that commercial providers will likely have a more significant role in defining the Internet in the years to come. Based on such speculation, major corporate entities in the telephone, computer, and television industries have been developing strategies to provide Internet services and are willing to make significant financial investments to corner a substantial part of this market.

APPLICATIONS ON THE INTERNET

The Internet is a dynamic communications and information resource. Information of all sorts is constantly being added, deleted, and most importantly, shared among millions of people. For educators, the Internet can provide a pedagogically valuable array of skill activities such as writing, reading, and research, as well as a content-rich resource for culture, science, current events, and so forth. The list of possibilities and specific applications is endless, but most of these activities fall into several broad categories.

Global electronic mail (e-mail) is the most popular activity on the Internet. Although e-mail has existed for a little more than three decades, the Internet has made it available to the masses worldwide, making it just as easy to send or receive messages over thousands of miles as for a couple of miles. Teachers and students are establishing pen pal correspondence with others all over the globe. Furthermore, any delay in sending and receiving messages is limited only to the time it takes to collect, organize, and write one's thoughts; there is no waiting period of days or weeks while paper letters are hand delivered.

The Internet does not provide the e-mail software itself, but works through URLs to route messages that have been composed and stored on local e-mail software systems. A school or school district that has established a local e-mail system should continue to use that system and integrate it for use on the Internet.

Group e-mail including discussion groups, newsgroups, or listservers (or listservs for short) extend the e-mail concept beyond the individual. Rather than sending mail to individuals, it is sent to groups of individuals or is posted to an electronic bulletin board for members of a group to read and respond as they wish. The messages stay on the electronic bulletin board for a given period of time. Generally, these groups identify a topic of common interest to all their members.

Electronic bulletin boards exist for all levels of education and in all subject areas. Activity-related bulletin boards on a host of topics sponsored by state education departments, professional societies, museums, and libraries are regularly being established. In addition to supporting discussion groups on the Internet, electronic bulletin boards are also being used by educators on local and commercial computer networks to discuss locally important issues.

Live conferencing takes the discussion group concept and organizes it into a real-time activity. The Internet provides a software system known as Internet Relay Chat (IRC), commonly known as *chat*. On the Internet, text-based "chat areas" or "chat rooms" are available on a host of topics. Live conferencing differs from discussion groups in that the discussion is live and text messages are posted as they are written and answered.

Organizing a real-time discussion group requires familiarity with the IRC software, which can be complicated for the average person using the Internet. However, with a commercial online service such as America Online, software facilities for setting up a chat area are easy to use. Administrators and teachers in particular might use this feature to carry out informal conferences, eliminating the necessity of traveling many miles. The nature of live conferencing may also take on another dimension, as live audio and video facilities are advanced for use on the Internet. This topic will be discussed more fully later in this chapter, in the section titled "The Internet and Distance Learning."

File transferring (or FTP, file transfer protocol) refers to the transfer and receiving of data files on the Internet. These files can include text, pictures, sound, and video. File transfer can occur in several ways, depending on how a user is connected to the Internet. In some cases, FTP is automatically included as a feature of the e-mail software system in which users send and receive files as attachments to a specific message. In other cases, files are made available for all members of the Internet community to access by invoking specific FTP software. The acts of sending and receiving data files are generally referred to as *uploading* and *downloading,* respectively. The Internet community is generous in what it allows users to access, especially for educational purposes. The National Aeronautics and Space Administration (NASA), for example, makes data resources available on many of its active space exploration projects, and the U.S. Weather Service updates data files on weather conditions throughout the world on a timely basis.

In downloading and uploading files, users should be sure to have virus protection software to scan files that are made available to the public. Also, when accessing data files—especially images, sound, and video—users should be aware of any copyright restrictions associated with the further use of the data. The copyright guidelines discussed in Chapter 6 also apply to materials downloaded from the Internet.

Through a software feature known as Telnet, a user on one computer can literally connect to and use the resources of another computer. As an example, rather than downloading a single file from NASA's central computer system, a user might actually be able to connect to and use all the resources available on NASA's computer. Though theoretically possible, most computers on the Internet do not allow outside users to access their computer facilities directly for practical and security reasons. Permission is required along with establishing proper sign-on procedures with user IDs and passwords.

Information navigation—also known as "Net surfing," "cruising," and "Web browsing"—is very popular. Using Web browsing software such as Netscape or

Internet Explorer, users are making their information available to all other members of the Internet community. At the same time, by using these relatively simple navigational software tools, a vast amount of pedagogically valuable instructional information is readily available. Students and teachers can spend hours looking up pages of pertinent information on a topic and not even touch the surface of all that is available on the Internet. Reference materials, maps, art collections, frog dissection simulation software, the Periodic Table of Elements, the White House, and the U.S. Congress are all available with a click of a mouse. Never in the history of humankind has such an extensive collection of informational resources been so readily available. However, users need to be educated and need to practice browsing the Web to use it efficiently. Once proficiency is developed in browsing the Web, the informational rewards can be abundant.

MULTIMEDIA AND THE WEB

Most educational applications on the World Wide Web rely extensively on text (e-mail, discussion groups, bulletin boards, etc.) for instruction and communication. In the early 1990s, the usefulness of extending this discussion to other media such as audio or video would have been questionable because the Internet did not handle media beyond text very well. Now multimedia applications on the Web are becoming commonplace. In teaching and learning, a picture can indeed be worth a thousand words. Full-motion video, capable of transmitting thousands of pictures accompanied by an audio track in minutes, can perhaps be worth much more. However, while pedagogically important, producing high-quality multimedia material for the Web is not yet easy for the average computer user and can be expensive in terms of cost and, especially, people's time. Nonetheless, the potential of multimedia for Web-based learning activities cannot be ignored.

Five Levels of Digital Media

There are essentially five levels of digital media: text, still images, animation, audio, and full-motion video. A brief review of these will be helpful as part of this discussion on the use of multimedia on the Web.

Text (letters of the alphabet, numbers, special characters) is handled very efficiently in any digital form whether on stand-alone or networked computers or the Internet. By far, the most popular applications on computer equipment worldwide are text-based and include word processing, e-mail, and database/data file manipulation.

Still images and photographs likewise are also handled well in digital format. Standard word processors such as Microsoft Word or Lotus WordPerfect have made adding an image or photograph to a text document a routine, click-the-menu item. Internet service providers such as America Online or CompuServe encourage subscribers to attach a photograph to their e-mail messages. Digital cameras, which were a rarity and quite expensive several years ago, can now be purchased for less than $100. These cameras attach to a computer or produce images on a floppy disk for immediate use in any digital-based application. Today, Kodak and other major camera companies routinely develop a roll of 35mm film into digital format on a CD-ROM for approximately the same price as standard 4-by-6 snapshots. Still images and photographs have become standard accompaniments to text on digital applications and are important enhancements to Web-based learning.

Animations are still images to which motion has been added. As a field, digital animation grew considerably in the 1990s. Major film producers such as Disney and Lucasfilm depend on digital animations for special effects. In 1997, the highly acclaimed movie *Titanic* relied almost exclusively on digital animation for the sequences in which the doomed luxury liner was seen cruising the Atlantic. In the summer of 2004, the immensely popular animation movie *Shrek* led all movies in total revenues. For the average individual, developing high-quality animation is not easy and requires many hours of editing and refining the images and sequencing flow. On the other hand, with some technical assistance and expertise, developing a good animation can significantly enhance a presentation, including a class lesson. Animations have been used very successfully to add meaning to complex processes in many subject areas, especially in the sciences. For students, viewing an animation on a stand-alone or locally networked computer is relatively simple. Downloading or "playing" an animation from the Web can be effective, assuming sufficient modem speeds and other communications facilities are available.

Digital audio and sound files without images are also becoming easier to develop. An inexpensive microphone (less than $20) can be attached to an input jack on the back of most computers and a lecture or presentation can be converted into digital form. If done in an acoustically controlled environment with more sophisticated recording equipment, the quality of a digitally produced sound file can be superb. Playing the sound file of a lecture on a stand-alone or locally networked computer is easy and can be more effective than reading a comparable amount of text. To enhance understanding, instructional applications can combine the two (text and audio). On the Web, "streaming" technologies such as those used with RealAudio applications have significantly improved the quality and timing of audio transmissions. Downloading or "playing" audio files from the Internet can be effective, provided sufficient modem speeds and other communications facilities are available.

Thirty frames of still images per second accompanied by a sound track is the recognized standard for full-motion video digital or analog productions. Fewer than 30 frames per second provides a "jerky" and poor-quality video, with the accompanying audio frequently out of synchronization with the images. Producing high-quality full-motion video in digital format, while becoming easier, is beyond the technical expertise and ability of the average computer user; technical support staffs that spend many days editing the digital video footage are needed to produce an acceptable product. Playing digital video on a stand-alone or a locally networked computer works well, and although streaming technologies are also being used with video on the Web, they need further development to be effective for those applications that require high quality. Full-motion video requires extensive digital storage running into hundreds of millions if not billions of bytes or more. Students and other users attempting to download or play large video files need substantial computer capability (disk space, processor speed, and input-output transfer rate) as well as high-speed modem and communications capabilities. This is sometimes beyond the capability of the average home computer user.

Designing Multimedia for Web-Based Learning

In developing multimedia for Web-based learning applications, teachers and technical assistants should start by considering student access to the Internet. The effective transmission of sound, animation, and full-motion video on the Internet depends on computer hardware and communications capabilities. If the goal of the application is to provide learning opportunities to students in their homes, then teachers should carefully consider the extent to which multimedia can be effectively used, because student access will likely be through slow-speed modems or communications facilities. Providing a good deal of multimedia content requiring students to download large media files may be frustrating if hardware capability or transmission speeds are not available in the home environment or unaffordable to the targeted population. On the other hand, where teachers control students' computer environments, such as in a school's computer laboratory with high-speed mode access, then Web-based multimedia applications can be very successful. If the student computer environment cannot be controlled, then teachers should use multimedia carefully.

In developing multimedia materials for the Web, teachers must strive for high quality. A video that has the look or feel of amateurism will not be effective in any learning environment. Given the superb media quality that students are accustomed to viewing on television, in films, and in video games, educators have found it difficult to compete. In traditional classrooms, instructors rely on materials such as videocassettes, videodiscs, or DVDs that they have purchased or rented from commercial or other professional producers. Delivering these same materials over the Web, even locally to a school's computer laboratory, may be impossible because they may not be available in digital form. To copy them for use on a computer network may be a serious infringement of copyright laws.

Given the issues of student access to technology, technical support requirements, and difficulties involved in producing or obtaining high-quality multimedia materials, teachers should consider providing substantive Web-based animation, audio, or video material only if it in fact adds to the instructional value of an activity—not merely to add pizzazz or technological glitz to the course content. Certain subject matter is significantly enhanced when multimedia illustrations, animation, or video are added to the presentation. The sciences make extensive use of computer simulations to conduct experiments and should seek to continue to do so in Web-based applications. High-quality documentaries such as those produced by educational television, National Geographic, or the Annenberg Project can add significant pedagogical value to a class presentation. Teachers will have to consider the costs and benefits carefully as they attempt to provide content and learning experiences on the Web comparable to those provided in the traditional classroom.

Digital Videoconferencing

Point-to-point videoconferencing using analog television transmitters and receivers has been available for many years. This analog format, however, does not work on the World Wide Web. Most point-to-point analog video conferencing systems operate in dedicated spaces or distance learning classrooms in which students attend at specific times. Digital videoconferencing systems using the Internet, on the other hand, have the potential of operating at any place and any time, but will need some maturation before they are used extensively in people's homes. In addition to modem speed and other communications limitations, digital videoconferencing systems can be expensive and will require high-end technical support services. Currently, digital videoconferencing systems are working best in LAN environments where all elements of transmission, communications, and end-user equipment can be controlled and maintained by technical staff. These systems are also being used to connect dedicated sites—such as two schools in the same or nearby district—with compatible equipment, and where technical staff are available to maintain the hardware and software.

On the Web, digital videoconferencing is being used to replace synchronous chat areas in which students and/or instructors establish some specific time to be available to each other to answer questions or to collaborate on a project. Rather than being limited to text messages, digital videoconferencing allows participants to see and speak to each other in a more efficient and personal manner.

Web-based videoconferencing technology is evolving rapidly. The popular CUSeeMe technology developed at Cornell University, and now available as a commercial product from White Pine Software, has advanced beyond the postage stamp sized jerky image of several years ago. Streaming audio techniques have advanced to include streaming video capable of providing relatively high-quality images in synchronization with the audio track. RealAudio, RealVideo, RealSystem G2 (RealNetworks, Inc.), NetShow (Microsoft), and QuickTime (Apple) are examples of highly rated streaming video software packages. Access to sufficient computer and communications resources is a must. While the standard microcomputer capable of transmitting and receiving high-quality video is available and affordable for many students, the same is not true for communications facilities in students' homes, where slower speed telephone lines are still the norm. A case in point involved Comcast, a major American cable company that established a Web site in 1998, to provide "quality" video clips produced by major film companies from around the world. In reviewing this site in 1999, Peter Nichols, a *New York Times* film critic, commented that although each clip pushed the boundaries of the technology, poor picture quality caused by a slow-speed modem on the receiving end hindered the most creative efforts of these Web site developers. Nichols further mentioned the need for image smoothing, larger frames, and the elimination of streaming interruptions that may make a "shambles" of the picture. Since 1999, streaming video technology has improved significantly and a number of Web sites provide the services that Nichols appropriately criticized. As communications technology advances, digital videoconferencing and video streaming whether used in real-time (synchronous) or anytime (asynchronous) activities will play a more significant role in Web-based instruction.

THE INTERNET AND EDUCATION

In developing Internet applications for education, administrators should consider how to integrate the Internet with other data communications facilities in a school district. The Internet does not necessarily replace existing facilities such as LANs, WANs, or access to commercial online services, but it should be used to enhance them. Schools have begun to establish *intranets,* which are LANs or WANs that use Internet software tools such as Web browsers. Also referred to as mini-Internets, intranets are useful for controlling access to sensitive data, reducing data traffic, and speeding access to frequently used data files. An intranet depends on local software systems (e-mail, file servers, databases, etc.) to accomplish much of its activity. Some of these local software packages may be easier to use than those that exist on the Internet.

Global E-Mail

Global e-mail applications have educational value mainly because they require and aid in the development of basic skills such as reading, writing, and researching. In addition, they can literally be conducted around the world so that electronic cultural exchanges take place with minimal cost or effort. Once a school has access to e-mail, implementing provocative e-mail applications is relatively easy. Examples of e-mail applications abound in the professional literature, including these:

- *Local news reporters:* Have students assume the role of local news reporters and have them swap news stories with students in other locales.
- *Local weatherpersons:* This activity is the same as the previous one, but asks students to report on weather conditions. Expand on this same theme and trace weather patterns (rainfall, snowfall, days hotter than 90°) over the course of a semester or academic year.
- *Conduct surveys:* Conduct surveys with a number of schools around the country or world on a variety of topics (important people, favorite singer, most important event in the 20th century, most important event of the current year).
- *Problem solvers:* Develop a problem (mathematical, scientific, riddle) and solicit opinions for its solution.
- *Story starters:* A very popular activity is to start a story and have others add to it to see how long the story can become.

Organizations such as NASA's K-12 Project and the National Geographic Society's Kids Network provide ideas and limited assistance in helping teachers develop e-mail activities. Several sites on the Internet, such as KidLink, are set up specifically to facilitate worldwide communications among students through e-mail and discussion groups.

Information Navigation

Navigating the Web for information is becoming one of the more popular applications. Students as well as teachers and the general public do it just for fun. Internet cafes are opening up around the country, providing a social environment in which people hang out and surf the Web. For a modest fee, one sits at a computer workstation with a companion or two and looks at interesting sites for hours. They may take a break, sip espresso, and then go back to the workstation for more Net surfing.

For more information about educationally oriented Web sites, go to the *Web Links module* for this chapter on the Companion Website at **www.prenhall. com/picciano**.

Schools are already providing this type of environment—minus the espresso—in school computer labs and libraries. Navigating the Web can be a significant "time-sink" and is especially enjoyable when valuable informational experiences result. Educators should develop activities such as Webquests that encourage both fun and more serious uses of the Internet. Ideas for navigating the Web for educational activities should be predicated upon the age of the navigators, subject area, and skill level. Visiting the numerous Web sites that contain resources and activities related to education demonstrates the value of the Web. Administrators might find interesting information on school policy at the Council of Great City Schools Web site or become acquainted with new grant programs in the NSF database. Teachers can get lesson plans and other teaching ideas from the Galaxy directory or the Texas Education Network. For students, Ask Jeeves is both fun and educational, the KidLink site is excellent for participating in international discussion groups, and the University of Arizona site provides many useful resources for high school students engaged in space research projects.

Several educationally oriented Web sites relate to specific subject areas and disciplines. If a particular subject area is not listed, readers are encouraged to use a search engine such as Yahoo! where, in addition to keyword searching, a list of subject categories is provided. Generally, when looking for information on broad subject areas such as history, biology, or mathematics, so much information will be provided that it will take hours to read and consider. Searching for resources on the Internet is like using an electronic card catalog or database: Users need to practice to hone and narrow a request for information. One benefit of using a Web browser for this activity is that users can easily collect useful URLs and store them electronically on address lists. For new users, allow time for practice, and provide instruction on using address lists or bookmarks to save URLs. As with other applications of instructional technology, particularly for new or intermediate learners, collaborative activities should be encouraged.

For more information on screening Internet materials, go to the *Web Links module* for this chapter on the Companion Website at **www.prenhall. com/picciano**.

In developing Internet navigating applications for students, educators must take on some responsibility for screening the materials that students might accidentally or purposefully come across. The Internet is a free and voluntary community with little oversight. Some of the material is unsuitable for children, including child pornography and hate group activity. Children need to be educated about the world around them; however, schools have some obligation to protect children from material that might be harmful. Presently, adults (teachers, parents, paraprofessionals) may simply have to provide guidance and be alert to damaging uses of the Internet. Software—such as Cybersitter and Net Nanny—has been developed that will assist schools and other organizations in screening some of the material that is delivered from the Internet on their networks.

Creating Web Sites

The development of Web sites is growing in popularity as an educational activity. Developing a Web site is not as complicated as one might assume but requires becoming familiar with a programming language such as HTML or an HTML authoring or filtering program. Dozens of Web authoring programs have been developed that make creating and editing Web pages no more difficult than using a word processing program. Thousands of schools have already begun creating their own Web sites. To develop a Web site, a school either has to have its own server with a direct connection to the Internet, generally referred to as a *serial line Internet protocol* (SLIP), or, if connected via commercial or public online service, it must obtain permission from the provider to develop a Web site. Many commercial providers make this service available for free, but some will charge a modest fee.

Developing a school Web site is a stimulating and educationally valuable activity; however, schools must think seriously about how they want themselves portrayed to the Internet community. The major purposes of the Internet are communication and information sharing. When establishing a Web site, schools become information providers and should provide useful information about their students, academic programs, and related activities. Suggestions for developing a Web site abound. For instance:

For more information on developing Web sites, go to the *Web Links module* for this chapter on the Companion Website at **www.prenhall. com/picciano.**

- Avoid too much clutter per page, which can make it difficult for readers to access important information.
- Avoid "electronic vanity plate" syndrome via extensive photographs of one or two individuals.
- Highlight the school, not the computer systems or software.
- Keep current events current.
- Assume that many computers in students' homes have limited-speed modems, so use graphics in moderation or allow for text-only access options.

For more information, Exworthy Educational Resources maintains an excellent Web site that provides ideas, templates, and examples of Web sites of schools from around the world.

Individuals or small groups—a class, an individual teacher, a student, or group of students doing a class project—can develop their own Web sites. As the Internet continues to evolve, providing information on a Web site is becoming a routine activity for all educators and students.

Course Management Software (CMS)

Up until a few years ago, teachers wishing to develop a Web site for their classes would have had to use hypertext markup language (HTML) as their software base for creating all Web pages. Figure 7.5 is an example of the HTML language for a sample

| **FIGURE 7.5** | **HTML Code for the Course Home Page in Figure 7.6** |

```
<<!DOCTYPE HTML PUBLIC "-//SQ//DTD HTML 2.0 1 all extensions//EN" "hmpro3.dtd">
<HTML>
<HEAD>
<TITLE>ED722 - Fall 1998</TITLE></HEAD>
<BODY
BGCOLOR = "#FFFFFF" TEXT = "#0000A0" LINK = "0000FF" BACKGROUND = ">webback.jpg"
VLINK = "FF0000"
<P ALIGN = "CENTER"><IMG SRC = "hunter.gif" ALIGN = "MIDDLE"></P>
ALIGN = "CENTER"><B>Thomas Hunter High School</B></P>
<H2><A NAME = "Return"></A>American Government</H2>
<H3><B>Instructor: Lynne Jones,          </B><A
HREF = "mailto:antho13926@aol.com"> E-mail address: ljones@hunter.edu </A></H3>
<H3><B>Course Description</B></H3>
<P><B><FONT SIZE = "11">This course is designed to provide an overview of the American
government system. Major issues such as how it evolved, its strengths, and its weaknesses will
be presented and discussed. It is also designed to provide students with an appreciation of the
American system of government as compared to others' systems that exist in the world today.
Key aspects of the American system such as its democratic foundation, representative govern-
ment, and separation of powers will be emphasized. </FONT></B>
</P>
<H3><B>Below are the resources and information you need to participate in the course. If this
is the first time you are accessing this Web page, please select &quot; Getting Started /Help
Desk. &quot;</B></H3>
<P></P>
<TABLE
WIDTH =" BORDER = "7" ALIGN = "CENTER" CELLPADDING = "20" CELLSPACING = "20"
BGCOLOR = "C0C0C0">
<TR ALIGN = "LEFT" VALIGN = "TOP">
<TD>NOWRAP = "NoWrap"><IMG SRC = "bullet.gif"><A HREF =
"a722cout.html"></A><B>Course Outline</B></TD>
<TD><IMG SRC = "bullet.gif"><A HREF = "a722read.html"></A><B>Reading List</B></TD>
<TD><IMG SRC = "bullet.gif"><A HREF = "a722conf.html"></A><B>Student
Assignments/Evaluation</B></TD></TR>
<TR ALIGN = "LEFT" VALIGN = "TOP">
<TD NOWRAP = "NoWrap"><IMG SRC = "bullet.gif"><A HREF =
"a722conf.html"</A><B>Topic
Presentations</B></TD>
<TD NOWRAP = "NoWrap"><IMG SRC = "bullet.gif"><A HREF =
"a722link.html"></A><B>Web
Resources</B></TD>
<TD><IMG SRC = "bullet.gif"><A HREF = "a722supp.html"></A><B>Library & amp; Media
Resources</B></TD></TR>
```

(continued)

| FIGURE 7.5 | *continued* |

```
<TR ALIGN = "LEFT" VALIGN = "TOP"
<TD NOWRAP = "NoWrap"><IMG SRC = "bullet.gif"><A HREF =
"a722week.html"></A><B>Communications
Center</B></TD>
<TD><IMG SRC = "bullet.gif"><A
HREF = "http://listserv.cuny.edu/archives/ADSUP-722.HTML"></A><B>Archives</B></TD>
<TD NOWRAP = "SNoWrap"><IMG SRC = "bullet.gif"><A HREF =
"a722pics.html"></A><B>Getting
Started/Help Desk</B></TD></TR></TABLE>
<$><B>Figure 7.6- Sample Course Home Page </B></P></BODY></HTML>
```

course Web page (see Figure 7.6). HTML is not a difficult language to use, but because of its cryptic style that makes use of various special characters, tags, and two-character instruction codes, it may prove difficult to the average teacher. In the past, teachers who wanted to teach on the Web either learned this language to produce the Web content or would be provided with the technical assistance to do so.

Web developers now have the option of using an HTML filter, authoring, or conversion software program such as Netscape's Composer, Microsoft's FrontPage, or Softquad's Hot Metal Pro to develop HTML documents. These filters generally provide a menu-driven, relatively easy-to-use interface for developing Web pages in HTML. They are continually evolving so that even sophisticated routines such as those generally provided by more advanced software languages such as Java and JavaScript are now becoming available by pointing and clicking on a menu. Learning to develop relatively straightforward Web pages is now no more difficult than learning an advanced feature on standard word processing software packages. In fact, the latest version of Microsoft Word allows the user to automatically save any word processing document in HTML format. Even electronic presentation software packages such as Microsoft's PowerPoint, which are designed to integrate images, text, sound, and animation into digital slide shows, have "Save as HTML" features for automatically converting these shows into Web pages. The point here is that developing HTML documents is becoming relatively easy and with a little bit of guidance requires about the same technical skill as using a standard word processing program.

More recently, a number of course management software (CMS) (also referred to as learning management software, or LMS) packages designed specifically for teaching on the Web have become available. Table 7.1 is a list of some popular CMS products. These CMS packages provide a complete set of software tools for creating Web-based course materials, including Web sites, electronic bulletin boards, e-mail systems, test generators, chat areas, and multimedia facilities. Almost all of these packages provide a course template that makes developing Web-based course materials no more difficult than filling in the blanks and

FIGURE 7.6	**Sample Course Home Page**

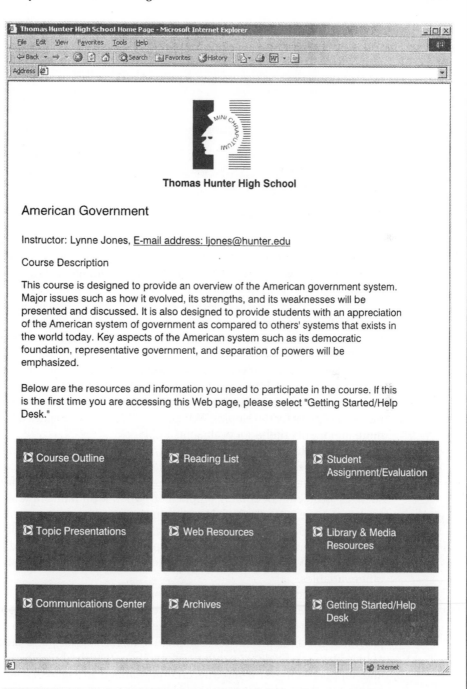

TABLE 7.1	Popular Course Management Software Systems

Product	Vendor
Authorware	Macromedia, Inc.
Blackboard/Course Info	Blackboard, Inc.
IconAuthor	Aimtech, Inc.
IntraLearn	IntraLearn Software Corporation
The Lotus Virtual Classroom	Lotus Development Corporation
Toolbook	Asymetrix, Inc.
TopClass	WBT Systems, Inc.
Web Course in a Box	madDuck Technologies
WebCt	WebCT, Inc.

selecting menu options. CMS packages are frequently used to enhance lessons and materials presented in traditional classrooms. Students at home can continue to discuss a lesson via e-mail or chat rooms, participate in a collaborative project, review reading and other materials, or ask a teacher a question about an assignment. CMS packages are also being used to develop entire Web-based, distance learning instructional modules and courses, which will be discussed further in Chapter 8.

Although CMS software makes developing a course Web site easier, evaluating these systems for adoption can be time-consuming and, in some cases, difficult. McCollum (1997) describes the situation as a "new industry that offers faculty a dizzying array of tools for developing Web courses." Figure 7.7 provides a list of some of the more important criteria for evaluating a CMS.

Most of the general criteria in Figure 7.7 will be subjective in nature depending on the evaluator's experience and level of expertise and cannot easily be quantified or reduced to a yes/no issue. Even a relatively straightforward criterion such as cost can become complicated when evaluating a CMS. Some of the packages have complex pricing structures that depend on a variety of factors including several levels of site licensing, the number of servers allowed to house the CMS, the number of course developers, the number of students who will be enrolled, the maximum number of developers and/or students at any one time, and other variables.

In selecting a CMS, good practice suggests establishment of a school district-wide committee or task force that includes teachers, technical support staff, and students. A district-wide approach is suggested, so that a common Web interface can be provided to facilitate teacher training, technical support, and student access to course materials. Evaluation criteria should be established on which all faculty users and support staff can agree. The criteria outlined in Figure 7.7 are good starting points, but local committees should determine and prioritize those that will best meet their needs in the long run. Ease of use, training and staff development

FIGURE 7.7	**Criteria for Evaluating Course Management Software Packages**

General criteria
Cost (total including ownership, site licensing, maintenance)
Ease of administrative management (stability, reliability, performance)
Ease of use (faculty and students)
Level of vendor support
Software platforms supported (Windows, UNIX, Macintosh)
Standards-based
Training opportunities

Features/capabilities provided
Chat (synchronous discussions)
Conversion tools (i.e., from word processing files)
Desktop videoconferencing
Discussion groups
Electronic mail
Grading
Indexing of course material by instructor, major, field, course name
Individualized student assignments
Multimedia support
Related resources
Sharing materials across courses
Standard design with flexible customization
Student progress reporting
Template development tools
Test generator

requirements, and software stability and reliability may be more important in certain environments than more advanced technical features or capabilities.

In adopting a CMS for a district, evaluators should also keep in mind that they are dealing with a rapidly evolving technology. CMS and other software systems that support applications on the Internet are being pioneered by small companies where competition is fierce and unpredictable. To remain competitive, software products are being upgraded and enhanced with new features every few months. Although desirable with respect to improving product capability, this rapid change can be unsettling for long-range course planning where design, development, and evaluation can take several years. Web-based course designers and planners have to be prepared to be flexible and open to new products and/or changes in existing products.

The Internet and Distance Learning

With the expansion of the Internet into people's homes and places of business, distance learning is becoming more popular in the United States. Early distance learning projects employed passive analog communications such as one-way tele-vision and radio. In the 1980s, two-way analog communications using videoconfer-encing technologies began to dominate distance learning applications. Today, data communications facilities as provided by the Internet and other large networks are beginning to redefine distance learning. Initiatives such as the Georgia Statewide Academic and Medical System (GSAMS) and the Iowa Communications Network (ICN) are making excellent use of data communications networks in providing highly interactive distance learning activities.

The Internet is a fully interactive, digital technology that will eventually rede-fine distance learning in several ways. First, students will no longer have to group themselves together into a common classroom or space to participate. Internet technology is such that students can actively participate in a lesson from any place (schools, day care centers, business establishments, homes) with a connected com-puter. Second, students will no longer necessarily have to participate at the same time. In digital format, lessons can be delivered and stored, and then called up by students as needed. Interactivity is achieved asynchronously through electronic bulletin boards, discussion groups, and e-mail. Third, instruction delivery will be an integration of several resources from which students can customize their lesson. Multiple resources may already exist, but students need to budget their time and schedule their learning in a sequential mode, such as (1) attend a lecture, (2) go to the library, (3) collect thoughts, (4) write a paper, (5) receive teacher comments, and so on. On the Internet, students may have at their immediate disposal a resource that includes the teacher as well as other instructional materials such as videos, computer simulations, and reference works. A student could possibly inte-grate the sequence by listening to the teacher for awhile, consulting a reference work, looking at a simulation, sending an e-mail message, and then once again listening to the teacher. In the not too distant future, new digital facilities such as video on demand and split-screen monitors will allow students to do several of these tasks simultaneously.

Advances are being made in communications technology such as wire-less digital communications, digital subscriber lines (DSL), cable modems, integrated service digital network (ISDN), and other high-speed transmission rates. In the future, much of what can be done with text on the Internet will be done routinely with live or real-time digital videoconferencing. Educators, especially those already investing in distance learning applications, should keep abreast of these and other developments that will have a significant impact on the potential of the Internet as a distance learning medium. This will be discussed further in Chapter 8.

SUMMARY

This chapter reviews the state of data communications as applied to education—specifically, the evolution of the Internet in terms of its applicability for instructional activities. Important concepts associated with global communications, information access, and new learning technologies are considered.

Data communications have been evolving and expanding for almost five decades. In the 1990s, this evolution resulted in the Internet, or network of networks. It is a truly global network that expanded rapidly in the 1990s and now reaches hundreds of millions of people worldwide. Every indication is that the Internet will continue to evolve and become a major component of computer and communications applications in all areas of endeavor, including education.

A critical catalyst for the Internet's evolution was the development of the World Wide Web, a hypertext- and multimedia-based software system for establishing and sharing information resources. Through user-friendly Web browser software, individuals and groups throughout the world can access and share information on a system with standard protocols.

The major applications of the Internet are global e-mail, discussion groups, live conferencing, file transfer, direct access to other computer systems, and information navigation—all of which can be adapted for instructional activities. A list of Internet resources helps readers become more familiar with basic activities. More detailed examples of Internet-based instructional activities for e-mail, information navigation, and information sharing are also presented.

Increasingly, course management software (CMS) packages are being used to develop Web-based course materials. Titles of some popular CMS packages, as well as evaluation criteria, are presented in the chapter.

The chapter concludes with a brief examination of and speculation on the role that the Internet will play in defining and expanding the possibilities for distance learning applications. Future advances in digital video communications will significantly expand present concepts of distance learning.

KEY CONCEPTS AND QUESTIONS

1. Data communications have evolved steadily for almost five decades. How has this evolution affected your daily activities? How do you see this evolution continuing over the next 10 years?

2. The Internet is a relatively new phenomenon. How do you explain its popularity and growth from the 1990s to the present? Will this popularity and growth continue? Explain.

3. Many terms such as cyberspace, information superhighway, and the Web are used interchangeably to refer to the Internet. How do you explain the World Wide Web in relation to the Internet? Why has the Web become such an important aspect of the popularity of the Internet?

4. Applications on the Internet are almost endless and depend on users' imagination and creativity. How do you categorize the major Internet applications? Are they adaptable for instructional and other educational uses? Explain. In

developing a plan for using the Internet in an instructional program, what applications would you consider first? Why?

5. Distance learning has had limited applications in education. How do you see distance learning evolving or changing? What role, if any, will the Internet play in changing or redefining distance learning? Explain.

SUGGESTED ACTIVITIES

To complete the Suggested Activities online, go to the Companion Website at **www.prenhall.com/picciano,** then to this chapter's *Suggested Activities module.*

REFERENCES

America Online. (2004). America Online corporate home page (http://corp.aol.com/index.shtml).

Connecting every pupil to the world. (1995, December 28). *New York Times,* p. A20.

CTIA. (2003). CTIA's annualized wireless industry survey results. Retrieved April 2, 2004, from the Web site of the Cellular Telecommunications & Internet Association (http://files.ctia.org/img/survey/2003_endyear/752x571/Annual_Table_Dec_2003.jpg).

Darman, J. (2004, May 14). Broadband in every pot. *MSNBC News/Newsweek.* Retrieved April 2, 2004, from the MSNBC Web site (http://www.msnbc.msn.com/id/4980129/site/newsweek).

Ellsworth, J. H. (1994). *Education on the Internet.* Indianapolis: Macmillan Computer.

Fisher, L. M. (1996, January 2). Surfing the Internet sets the agenda for software. *New York Times,* p. C15.

McCollum, K. (1997, October 21). Colleges sort through vast store of tools for designing Web courses. *Chronicle of Higher Education.* Retrieved April 12, 2004, online (http://chronicle.com/data/internet.dir/itdata/1997/10/t97102101.htm).

Negroponte, N. (1995). *Being digital.* New York: Knopf.

Nichols, P.M. (1999, January 17). The newest wave: Made-for-the-Internet movies. *New York Times,* p. AR27.

Nua Internet Surveys. (2002). *How many online?* Retrieved April 1, 2004, from the Web site of Nua.com (http://www.nua.com/surveys/how_many_online/).

Park, J., & Staresina, L. (2004, May 6). Tracking U.S. trends. *Education Week, 23*(35), 64–67.

Shirky, C. (1995). *Voices from the Net.* Emeryville, CA: Ziff-Davis.

Stoll, C. (1995). *Silicon snake oil: Second thoughts about the information superhighway.* New York: Doubleday.

Williams, B. (1995). *The Internet for teachers.* Foster City, CA: IDG Books Worldwide.

Zworykin, V. (1975, July 4). Interview conducted by M. Heyer and A. Pinsky [Broadcast by the Radio Corporation of America, Inc.]. IEEE History Center, Rutgers University, New Brunswick, NJ. Retrieved April 5, 2004, from the Web site of the IEEE History Center (http://www.ieee.org/organizations/history_center/oral_histories/transcripts/zworykin21.html).

Chapter 8

Distance Learning

I n April 1997, educators from 22 countries met in Salzburg, Austria, to attend a 9-day seminar, the focus of which was planning and implementing distance learning projects for teaching English as a foreign language in their countries. Participants shared the experiences of their homelands. In Iceland, radio transmission and the Internet were being used to provide instruction to fishermen who spend weeks at sea. In Indonesia, television was being used to provide basic language literacy to inhabitants of the hundreds of islands that make up this country. In Pakistan, a combination of mail and satellite television was being considered to improve English language skills in villages in the remote northern mountain provinces. These images of great distances, geographic obstacles, and scattered populations are frequently invoked as the basic rationale for distance learning programs or courses. At this same seminar, participants from Great Britain and the United States also described programs for students in large metropolitan areas such as London or New York City who take courses "at a distance" within a mile or two of their schools for the convenience of studying in their homes or places of business.

Educators throughout the world, whether in rural or urban areas, are increasingly considering developing distance learning as part of their academic programs. For rural and isolated communities, distance learning can be the vehicle to conquer geography and space between teachers and students. In populous metropolitan areas, distance learning is sometimes seen as a mechanism for fitting education into the busy lives of older students who struggle to find the time to balance careers, family responsibilities, and schooling.

Distance learning through the mail, radio, and television has an extensive history, but newer technologies such as digital communications and networking now make it much easier for educators to provide some form of distance learning for their students. Conquering space and time—a daunting venture in the not too distant past—is becoming more commonplace as computers, communications, and video technologies are being used to bring learning to virtually any place on earth at anytime. The implications of the newer digital and communications technologies for education are extensive and are being recounted in journals, newspapers, and books every day. Neil Rudenstine (1997), former president of Harvard University, observed that the Internet and other electronic networks allow communications to take place at all hours and across distances and permit a significant extension of the scope, continuity, and even the quality of certain forms of instructional interaction. Indeed, these technologies are having an enormous influence on traditional education while redefining our concept of distance learning.

In this chapter, we examine distance learning from several perspectives, including the postsecondary level. The rationale is that many school districts have collaborated with colleges and universities, or as participants in regional and state consortia for developing and delivering distance learning to adult as well as K-12 students.

DISTANCE LEARNING DEFINED

Distance education, distance teaching, distance learning, open learning, distributed learning, asynchronous learning, telelearning, and blended learning are some of the terms used to describe an educational process in which the teacher and students are physically separated.

Distance education is the term that has most commonly been used for several decades. As an all-inclusive term, *distance education* has served well to define the physical separation of teaching and learning. However, in recent years, the term *distance learning* has become popular, particularly in the United States, to define this separation. Although used interchangeably with *distance education*, *distance learning* puts an emphasis on the "learner." Indeed, the concept of student-centered learning has become popular for all forms of education, distance or otherwise, but is especially appropriate when students need to take on greater responsibility for their learning, as is the case when doing so from a distance.

Within this definition, distance learning can take on many different forms. Figure 8.1, Figure 8.2, and Figure 8.3 illustrate three common forms of distance learning. While all fall within the definition of distance learning, they have very different components and characteristics.

The intent here is not to cover all the various possibilities, but to emphasize that distance learning can take on many different forms to meet different needs. The possibilities are extensive and will likely increase in the future, especially as digital technology continues to expand and integrate with other technologies.

DISTANCE LEARNING TECHNOLOGIES: AN OVERVIEW

The U.S. Department of Education (2003) reported that 56% (3,077,000 course enrollments) of all postsecondary institutions offered some type of distance learning courses. Table 8.1 provides data on the distance learning hardware technologies being used by these institutions and under consideration for use. The first column of percentages indicates that the most commonly used technologies in institutions offering distance learning courses are the Internet using asynchronous communications (90%), two-way interactive video (51%), the Internet using synchronous communications (43%), and one-way prerecorded video (41%). In looking at the

FIGURE 8.1   **Broadcast Television**

A teacher delivering a live lecture over a television network into student homes is a distance learning format that provides for communication by teacher to student, via video technology, synchronously (at the same time), from one to many delivery points. This form allows the teacher to conduct the class for hundreds of students. Students do not interact immediately with the instructor, but can ask questions using telephone, mail, or e-mail.

Source: Distance Learning: Making Connections Across Virtual Space and Time, by Anthony G. Picciano, © 2001. Reprinted by permission of Pearson Education, Inc., Upper Saddle River, NJ.

FIGURE 8.2   **Two-Way Videoconferencing**

A college professor teaching a course on a college campus that is also being videoconferenced to a class at a local high school is a format that provides for interaction of teacher to student, and student to teacher, via video technology, synchronously, in a point-to-point, two-way delivery mode. Students can interact immediately and ask questions of the professor, and he can reply.

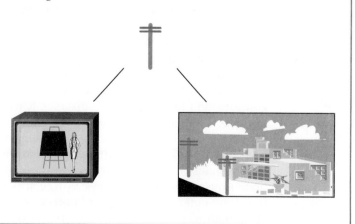

Source: Distance Learning: Making Connections Across Virtual Space and Time, by Anthony G. Picciano, © 2001. Reprinted by permission of Pearson Education, Inc., Upper Saddle River, NJ.

FIGURE 8.3	**Asynchronous Learning Network**

A teacher using the World Wide
Web and group e-mail software to
teach an Internet-based course is a
form that provides for interaction
of teacher to learner and learner to
teacher, via computer technology,
asynchronously (at different times),
in a multipoint delivery mode.
Students and the instructor
continually interact, but rarely
at the same time.

Source: Distance Learning: Making Connections Across Virtual Space and Time, by Anthony G. Picciano, © 2001. Reprinted
by permission of Pearson Education, Inc., Upper Saddle River, NJ.

percentages for the second column, the future plans of these institutions include a
substantial use of Internet technologies (88% and 64%), two-way interactive video
(43%), and CD-ROM (39%). These data indicate that the trend is to use more digital,
computer-based technologies, especially the Internet, for delivering distance
learning in the future.

Perhaps the most important aspect of the data in Table 8.1 is the indication
that within institutions, multiple technologies are currently used and are under
consideration for future use in distance learning applications. No single technology is considered the "best" technology for distance learning. To the contrary, the
data suggest that different technologies may be more or less appropriate depending on the application. While the trend to digital, computer-based technologies
predominates, it is not all-inclusive—and many institutions are planning to continue to use other technologies as well. It is likely that in many of these institutions, computer networking for Internet access has been established for reasons
other than distance learning. Why not also use it for distance learning applications? Table 8.2 compares the advantages and limitations of various distance
learning technologies.

TABLE 8.1	Technology Used in Higher Education to Deliver Distance Learning Courses

Percent of higher education institutions currently offering distance education courses, showing technology currently being used to deliver the courses and future (next 3 years) distance learning technology plans.

Hardware technology	Current technology being used	Future technology plans
Two-way interactive video with two-way audio	51	43
One-way video with two-way audio	11	12
One-way live video	8	11
One-way prerecorded video	41	22
Two-way audio	9	9
One-way audio (e.g., radio)	11	12
Internet using synchronous communications	43	64
Internet using asynchronous communications	90	88
CD-ROM package	29	39
Multimode packages	19	35
Other	3	5

Source: U.S. Department of Education, National Center for Education Statistics (2003). From information in the NCES Postsecondary Education Quick Information System, "Survey on Distance Education at Higher Education Institutions, 2000–2001" (tables 10 and 12). Sample based on mailing to 1,599 postsecondary institutions in the United States, the District of Columbia, and Puerto Rico, with 1,500 returns (94% response rate).

PRINT TECHNOLOGIES

By far the most commonly used technology in distance learning—and in all education, for that matter—is print. Textbooks, journals, newspapers, syllabi, tutorials, assignments, tests, and papers commonly consist of printed materials. While the demise of the printed word has been predicted as a result of the growth of mass media and the evolution of the electronic age (Birkerts, 1994), in education the printed word continues to be alive and well. It will be a number of years before the standard textbook is replaced completely by another form. By the same token, educational planners should also be aware that electronic textbooks on CD-ROM or DVD, online journals, and Web-based syllabi are also becoming more common and are particularly suitable for distance learning. A number of states (e.g., Maine, Texas, Virginia) have piloted programs that replaced printed textbooks with electronic ones on laptop computers ("Texas May Drop Texts," 1997). The major benefit is that this is a way of keeping up

TABLE 8.2	Comparison of Distance Learning Technologies	
Technology	**Advantages**	**Limitations**
Print		
Textbooks	Easy to use	Noninteractive
Study guides	Familiar	Dependent on learner reading skills
Syllabi	Spontaneous	Passive/self-directed
Assignments	Inexpensive	
Workbooks	Portable	
	Self-paced	
Audio		
Audiocassette	Easy to use	Noninteractive
	Portable	Passive/self-directed
	Inexpensive	Requires printed study guides
	Self-paced	Nongraphic
Radio	Mass distribution	Noninteractive
	Easy to use (student)	Requires printed study guides
		Nongraphic
Audioconferencing	Interactive	Nongraphic
	Immediacy	Development time
		Requires printed study guides
Audiographics	Interactive	Requires printed study guides
	Immediacy	Limited graphics
Video		
Videocassette	Easy to use (student)	Noninteractive
	Self-paced	Passive/self-directed
	Graphic	Requires printed study guides
Television	Mass distribution	Noninteractive
	Graphic	Requires printed study guides
	Easy to use (student)	Development time
		Expensive
Videoconferencing	Interactive	Development time
	Graphic	Expensive
	Immediacy	Complex technology
Computer (digital)		
Packaged software (CD-ROM, network)	Interactive (limited)	Development time
	Multimedia	Expensive
	Self-paced	Complex
Synchronous/network (videoconferencing)	Interactive	Development time
	Multimedia	Expensive
	Immediacy	Complex
	Participative	
Asynchronous/network	Interactive	Development time
	Graphics (limited)	Complex
	Self-paced	Expensive
		Student access to technology
		Rapidly evolving technology

with rapidly changing information and of alleviating the problem of replacing aging textbooks, which costs school districts hundred of millions of dollars every year.

Print material enhanced and integrated with electronic technology will play a significant role in distance learning for the foreseeable future. A few years ago, the typical correspondence course that relied entirely on printed materials such as a self-study guide and tutorial is just as likely today to include a videocassette, a CD-ROM, a DVD, or access to a Web site. This movement and evolution away from printed material will continue, and perhaps accelerate, as more people in the general population gain access to electronic technologies.

AUDIO TECHNOLOGIES

Audio technologies rely on the spoken word and sound for instruction. Audio was the next logical evolution of distance learning technology. Similar to print, it is familiar and—depending on the nature of the application—relatively easy to use. The major drawback of all audio technologies is that graphics are either not possible or generally limited. Most audio technologies also require that substantial additional material be provided in the form of study guides to provide additional content.

Audiocassettes

Audiocassettes have been used extensively in distance learning programs throughout the world. From the student perspective, audiocassettes are very convenient, portable, and inexpensive. Students can listen to an audiocassette in any room of a house, in a car, or on vacation. Once an audiotape has been developed (mastered), it can be reproduced for mass distribution at relatively modest cost.

The main limitation of audiocassette technology is its noninteractive and passive nature. This requires a good deal of student self-direction and discipline to complete courses. Alternative communication methods either using mail or telephone are also necessary to enable students to ask questions of instructors, and interactivity among students using this technology is not commonplace. Graphics cannot be delivered via audiocassettes and therefore additional, and in some cases substantial, study guides are necessary as accompaniments to the audio material.

Radio

Radio has been used successfully as a mass distribution distance learning technology for decades. Although still used in some parts of the United States, most broadcast radio distance learning applications were replaced by television in the 1940s and 1950s, but in developing countries where access to video technology is limited, broadcast radio continues to be used. As a noninteractive technology, radio also requires other communications technologies to enable students to ask questions. Where telephone and other forms of communications are limited, teaching assistants are sometimes made available. And like audiocassettes, radio requires substantial printed study guides to be used effectively.

Audioconferencing

Audioconferencing overcomes one major limitation of other audio technologies by providing interactive capabilities between instructor and student and between student and student. Of the various teleconferencing technologies, audioconferencing is the least expensive and generally most reliable. Audioconferencing technology uses some type of telephone message-handling equipment, generally referred to as a "bridge" that connects the various sites or parties simultaneously. A dedicated audioconferencing network can be established, or existing telephone lines can be used to connect sites.

Popular opinion holds that audioconferencing will eventually be replaced by videoconferencing, but audioconferencing will continue to be used for many years. Most distance learning programs that presently use this technology have plans for expanding its use in the future. Because of the expense and complexity of videoconferencing technology, audioconferencing is viewed as a cost-effective method of providing interactivity for distance learning.

Audiographics

The major limitation of a basic audioconferencing network is the lack of graphics capability. However, this situation has begun to change as graphics capabilities are being added to audioconferencing networks. Audiographics is essentially an audioconference system with some limited graphics capability, usually in the form of an electronic blackboard capable of transmitting and receiving images and illustrations at sending and receiving sites, respectively. Computers, document cameras, and other image-capable technologies have been used successfully in audiographics applications. An instructor uses the electronic blackboard or document camera as he or she would in a traditional classroom. However, the notes, illustrations, or drawings are automatically transmitted via the audio connection to similar equipment at the receiving site so that students can see them as the instructor makes a presentation.

Audiographics capability significantly improves on the complete lack of graphics found in the basic audioconferencing network, but it should be noted that these systems are not as visually stimulating as full video capability. Because audiographics requires more substantial transmission capability (bandwidth) to transmit high-quality images in real time, distance learning programs prefer videoconferencing technology.

VIDEO TECHNOLOGIES

The power of the image has become well recognized in education at all levels. In distance learning, many successful programs have relied on some form of video to deliver or at least enhance course materials. Videocassettes and educational television have been important vehicles for providing high-quality distance learning materials and activities for decades. In recent years, interactive video technologies delivering high-quality, stimulating class materials have emerged that also allow learners to interact and participate in discussions and activities. The new interactive video technologies are presently complex and expensive but nonetheless have established themselves as major distance learning delivery systems, especially in the United States.

Videocassettes

As the popularity of the videocassette recorder (VCR) grew in the United States and other developed countries in the 1980s, so did its popularity for distance learning. Videocassettes are easy to use, self-paced, and graphically rich. When accompanied by well-designed study guides, videocassettes can be very effective in delivering distance learning. The quality of the instructional video on cassettes is important. It should include stimulating graphics, illustrations, and simulations—not simply a recorded lecture.

The Open University of the United Kingdom has integrated videocassettes into its programs using material produced by the British Broadcasting Corporation (BBC). In the United States, the Annenberg Foundation, in cooperation with the Corporation for Public Broadcasting (CPB), initiated a grant program in 1981 to fund the development of high-quality video materials that can be used by colleges and high schools to enhance instruction in a traditional classroom. When used in conjunction with study guides, much of this material is also appropriate for distance learning programs. These materials can be purchased or rented for modest fees. As a result, schools can begin a distance learning program with high-quality videocassette materials relatively quickly. Without the availability of this material, production costs for some schools would probably be prohibitive. Since its inception, hundreds of thousands of students all over the world have received credit for courses using video materials produced by the Annenberg Foundation/CPB project.

The major limitation of videocassette technology is its noninteractive nature, which requires a good deal of student self-direction and discipline to complete courses. Alternative communication methods using either mail or telephone are necessary to enable students to ask questions of instructors, and interactivity among students using this technology is rare. It is expensive for schools to develop their own materials, facilities, and equipment for editing and mastering videotape, and requires the assistance of a trained technical support staff. Without such support, even a simple taping of a lecture may result in a poor-quality and instructionally ineffective videotape. With the advent of DVD technology in the late 1990s, distance learning providers began to convert videotape material to this newer technology.

Television

Without question, television has evolved into the most effective mass communication system ever, supplanting newspapers, magazines, and other materials. Television has become a fact of daily life. Major news stories such as the Gulf War, the O. J. Simpson trial, the funeral of Princess Diana, and the impeachment of President Bill Clinton were more likely to be seen on television than read about in the newspapers. Hundreds of millions of people view television daily throughout the world. As a result, for education and especially for distance learning, television has emerged as a very important delivery mechanism.

In China, the Central Chinese Radio and Television University (*Guangbo dianshi daxue,* or Dianda for short) provides programs for 50 universities serving approximately 850,000 students per year. Dianda uses an extensive network of regional television stations, television education centers, and tutoring groups to deliver and support its educational programs. In the United States, the Public Broadcasting System (PBS)—through its Adult Learning Service and Going the Distance program—has provided distance learning opportunities for hundreds of thousands of adult students. Since its inception in 1981, the Adult Learning Service has enrolled more than 5 million students. The Going the Distance program is specifically designed to help colleges and universities develop entire distance learning degree programs using the services of PBS. The Going the Distance project was launched in 1994 with 60 colleges and 22 public television systems and has evolved to include the participation of more than 200 colleges in 43 states supported by 69 public television systems (Public Broadcasting Service, 2004).

Television, like videocassettes, is most effective in distance learning when accompanied by well-designed study guides. As a passive medium, television requires support systems that enable students to ask questions using telephone, mail, or other communications systems. Although most distance learning television is broadcast—that is, sent over the airwaves for anyone with an antenna to receive—some schools also use "narrowcast" transmission for limited distribution to a region or locality of approximately 20–25 miles. Narrowcast for distance learning, also referred to as Instructional Television Fixed Service (ITFS), requires a microwave transmitter and a transmission studio. Special receiver antennae are required by the students to access the microwave transmission. ITFS is especially effective in rural and less crowded airwave spaces where interference is at a minimum. ITFS can also relay transmissions or "feed" from other sources such as satellite or cable television systems, thereby expanding the programming available.

The use of television for distance learning has a secure future; however, the technologies used for transmission are evolving rapidly. In the 20th century, broadcasting over the airwaves using transmitters and antennae for reception dominated television in most countries. But satellite and cable television services that can significantly improve and integrate television transmissions with other technologies such as telephone and computer are evolving. Direct satellite services are now available for the modest cost of a small (18-inch diameter) satellite dish. Cable television and telephone companies are presently investing millions of dollars in providing fiber-optic, broadband services to people's homes. It is difficult to predict which television technology, if any, will emerge as the dominant technology of the 21st century, but it is safe to say that distance learning will benefit significantly from an integrated system capable of delivering video, telephone, and computer services via one transmitting and receiving technology.

Videoconferencing

Videoconferencing (or teleconferencing) technology provides all the benefits of television, and in addition allows the audience or students to interact in real time with the instructor and other students. Videoconferencing approximates the traditional classroom more than any other distance learning technology. Instructors conduct classes, students can see the instructor, instructors can see students, and students can ask questions of the instructor or each other. When accompanied by electronic blackboards and other imaging systems, instructors can use illustrations, write notes, and use images or video to enhance their class presentations. Videoconferencing is most frequently being used in a two-way interactive mode, but technology is evolving so that multiple sites can also participate. Using digital technology, videoconferencing is also now available on desktop computers so that a session may include individuals in many different locations. The delivery technologies being used for videoconferencing include high-speed telephone systems, satellite (wireless), cable, and dedicated fiber-optic networks.

In the United States, according to the data provided by the National Center for Educational Statistics (NCES) (see Table 8.1), interactive videoconferencing has emerged as one of the most popular forms of distance learning technology. Many statewide systems (e.g., Oklahoma, Iowa, Wisconsin, Maryland, Florida) support videoconferencing links for a variety of educational, medical, and other nonprofit agencies. The Georgia Statewide Academic and Medical System (GSAMS) is a videoconferencing system that connects most of the state's colleges, school districts, and hospitals. GSAMS is especially effective in bringing distance learning programs to health care and medical professionals who regularly need to update their skills and knowledge of current medical practices and techniques. PBS's Adult Satellite Service operates one of the largest satellite-based video-conferencing networks for higher education. Videoconferencing is also being provided by private corporations such as the Distance Learning Network in Pennsylvania. Many of these networks specialize in professional training for adult and continuing education as well as degree-credit programs in conjunction with educational institutions.

Compared to other distance learning technologies, videoconferencing is an expensive, complex, and evolving technology that will test the administrative and technical expertise of most educational institutions. Those institutions that have been developing this technology for years and have grown with it are in a much better position to upgrade, expand, and move ahead as videoconferencing technologies evolve. Those institutions just beginning to use this technology will probably find it daunting and may rely on others (consultants, private providers, and consortia) for services. States and other regional entities that have established and provided technical support for videoconferencing networks have been most helpful in assisting schools to start cost-effective distance learning programs. Unfortunately, videoconferencing systems have experienced growing pains and have not always been reliable. In traditional face-to-face learning, sessions are rarely canceled due to technical difficulties. In real-time videoconferencing sessions, prudent planning requires that backup and alternative activities be provided in the event the system fails or technical difficulties are encountered. For large or widely dispersed student audiences, the instructor will likely have to have the assistance of facilitators to help in answering questions or assisting with technical difficulties.

▊ COMPUTER TECHNOLOGIES

Computer or digital technologies incorporate most of the capabilities of print, audio, and video, and in addition allow for a certain degree of user control. Computer technologies have made significant progress during the second half of the 20th century. In the United States and other developed countries, an increasing number of students of all ages have access to computer technology in their homes as well as in their schools. A computer, which as late as the 1970s consisted of a large, room-size gray electronic box, now fits in an attaché case or book bag. Complexity still exists, but the mystique of computer technology is evaporating as more people use computers in everyday activities. In distance learning applications, this has had, and will continue to have, important ramifications.

Packaged Software

Packaged computer software used in distance learning is similar in content to material provided in audio and video technologies. Learning modules, specific skills, and entire courses are offered or packaged on CD-ROM, DVD, or increasingly at an Internet or World Wide Web site. In addition to text, sound, and images, these packaged programs provide for a good deal of student control and interaction. Study guides may be provided but frequently are built into the digital content. Many of the techniques used for packaged software include programmed instruction, self-paced learning, and student testing and prescription. As discussed in Chapter 5, most of these techniques were developed over the past 30 years via technology referred to as computer-assisted instruction (CAI) and computer-based education (CBE).

Good examples of packaged software are video materials developed by the Annenberg Foundation/CPB project that have been converted into CD-ROM format. A reader might ask: Why not simply convert everything? The answer is that the conversion from videotape material into a packaged CD-ROM or other computer medium involves not simply the conversion of the video portion but also the development of control programs that guide and assist the student in using the video material. These are labor-intensive activities usually requiring the expertise of high-salaried software specialists and instructional designers. Frequently, the investment of money and time for the conversion may be worthwhile only for the more popular titles.

Designing and developing original packaged software for distance learning programs will require a team of specialists (content, software, graphics). Such an investment is typically only considered by large, comprehensive distance learning programs and institutions.

Synchronous Networks/Videoconferencing

In addition to packaged software, distance learning is also available in several different forms on computer networks including the Internet. These activities can be *synchronous* (that is, instruction happening at a specific time), or they can be *asynchronous* (instruction happening at any time).

Increasingly, synchronous distance learning via computer networks involves digital videoconferencing. The benefits and limitations of this approach are similar to those discussed earlier, in the section on video technologies. One major difference is that students participate while sitting at a computer workstation rather than as part of a class viewing a large monitor of an instructor presenting material at a distant site. Rather than pushing a button on a microphone to ask a question, a student might key in the question in text mode and receive a prompt text reply. Videoconferencing using standard video technologies almost always assumes that an instructor is leading the presentation, whereas with computer technology the presentation may be "led" by a packaged software program with the instructor acting more as a facilitator available to answer a question or help a student having some other difficulty.

Synchronous computer conferencing without packaged software—which depends on an instructor to present, control, and interact with the students—is similar to other audioconferencing or videoconferencing techniques. However, with large and widely dispersed student audiences, the instructor will likely need the assistance of facilitators to help answer questions or assist with technical difficulties. This can become costly. As a result, schools and other organizations using computer networks for distance learning are beginning to consider less costly asynchronous approaches.

Asynchronous Computer Networks

Perhaps the most significant development in distance learning is the use of asynchronous learning networks. An asynchronous learning network (ALN) is generally defined as using computer networking technology to provide instruction at any place and any time. An instructor provides a file of instructional materials that students can access remotely from any computer workstation that has a modem or other communications capability. Interaction, discussion, and questions are handled through group software systems and course management software (e.g., Blackboard/Courseinfo, Top-Class, WebCT) that provide e-mail, electronic bulletin board, threaded discussions, and other communications facilities. With the emergence of the Internet, ALNs are increasingly relying on the World Wide Web for part or all of their networking features.

In an example of an asynchronous learning session, an instructor introduces a topic or provides a file of materials that students can read or otherwise use for some activity at a Web site, say on a Sunday evening. The instructor might supplement the materials by posing key questions on an electronic bulletin board or other group e-mail system that all students in the class are able to access. Students access this material at any time during the week and can post comments to the electronic bulletin board for the entire class to see, and may ask questions directly of the instructor or of other students through regular e-mail. An assessment or review of the material and the week's instructional activity (discussions, questions, etc.) is conducted on Saturday. The cycle begins again on the following Sunday evening with a new topic. In this example of asynchronous learning, the instructor and students did not communicate synchronously—that is, at the same time—but instead accessed all materials or asked questions from computer workstations in their homes, at a school, or in their places of business.

Many schools in the United States and developed countries have begun to use ALNs for distance learning. Course modules, entire courses, entire programs, and entire "virtual" schools are relying on ALN techniques. The major benefit of ALNs is that they are very convenient for students, especially adults who may work full-time, have family responsibilities, and are attempting to improve their professional skills or complete an academic program. The major limitations of ALNs are that instructors and faculty must have access to networking technology in their schools and beyond. Schools that have already invested in a modern computer networking infrastructure that provides ready access to the Internet are more easily able to support this approach. Likewise, students wishing to enroll in ALN courses generally must have access to the Internet either in their homes or workplaces or both in order to participate effectively.

■ BLENDING TECHNOLOGIES

A wide variety of technologies are available for distance learning. Each of these technologies has certain benefits and certain limitations, and as indicated earlier, a "best" technology does not yet exist for distance learning. Educators should attempt to use the technology that will best meet their goals, that is most readily available, and that will be educationally sound as well as cost effective. The data in Table 8.1 indicates that Internet-based computer and video technologies will be used more extensively in the future for distance learning. But even within these technologies, various options are available.

In selecting a technology for distance learning, educators should assume that they may blend technologies to provide the optimal approach. Although one technology may be the primary means chosen to deliver instruction for a particular distance learning course, other technologies or even face-to-face instruction may be more appropriate for some other aspect of the program. For example, interaction and communication between student and instructor is a major consideration. E-mail is increasingly viewed as an excellent and cost-effective method of improving interaction and communication—among distance learning participants and even in traditional classrooms. If access to e-mail or the Internet is not available, however, standard telephones and fax machines provide another easy-to-use communication technology for faculty and students. Students who encounter problems might be encouraged to telephone a teacher, tutor, or adviser. Students might be able to fax written assignments rather than mail them. Educators need not take a purist attitude and commit to the idea that all distance learning must be conducted via a single technology. On the contrary, common sense and good planning dictate that the most effective technologies be used, and in combination if necessary. Naturally, other factors, such as costs, need to be considered.

Many of the technologies discussed above are evolving. In planning distance learning programs, it's most important that educators remain flexible in their selection of a technology. Using several technologies may seem costly, but in the long run may protect against major shifts or advances in technological approaches. Change, and in some cases rapid change, is becoming a dominating characteristic of many of the newer video and digital technologies. The Internet is being used by hundreds of millions of people from every walk of life on every continent. Internets II and III are already evolving. Flexibility with cognizance of major trends will best serve planning activities for distance learning.

DESIGNING INSTRUCTIONAL MATERIALS: A COMPARISON OF DISTANCE LEARNING TECHNOLOGIES

Figures 8.4, 8.5, and 8.6 are examples of distance learning materials appropriate for three different delivery systems: the printed study guide, the interactive videoconference, and asynchronous learning using the Internet and World Wide Web. All three use the same general content that encompasses the U.S. Supreme Court's landmark 1954 decision, *Brown v. Board of Education of Topeka, Kansas,* its aftermath, and its relevance to modern American society. This content is commonly used in American history, sociology, political science, cultural studies, education, and constitutional law courses at the secondary and postsecondary education levels. Each example concludes with the same written assignment. Although the content and student assignment are the same, the materials and presentations have been customized to suit the benefits and limitations of the technology used.

In reviewing the three examples, readers should compare the benefits and limitations of each of the distance learning methods. All three methods provide for routine communication and interaction between the instructor and student, but the same cannot be said for student-to-student interaction. In the printed study guide example, student-to-student interaction would be rare. The use of high-quality media such as a video documentary is highly desirable in all learning, distance or otherwise, but may not be possible or cost-effective depending on the technology used. Of the three examples, video is provided only in the interactive videoconference. In terms of student convenience in taking classes, the printed study guide and asynchronous learning are better suited for students to learn at their own pace or according to their daily schedules.

The Printed Study Guide

Figure 8.4 provides a sample lesson from a printed study guide that could be used for a learning module on the *Brown* decision. The material presented here is abridged but should serve to give the reader a sense of the nature of printed study guides. Assume that this printed study guide is used by students individually and not as part of a group learning activity. The design of printed study guides is a skill that develops through experience and repetition. Derek Rowntree (1996), a professor of educational development at the Open University (Great Britain), has an excellent guide for preparing such materials that is highly recommended for further study. He covers extensively the organization of such guides (e.g., writing style, graphics, fonts). His fundamental precept is that the guide should meet the needs of the intended student body. Student reading levels and comprehension are critical factors in the development of a good study guide.

By its very nature, the printed study guide relies on text to communicate the content to the student. It is organized in paragraph form but makes extensive use of enumerations, bullets, or different font sizes and styles to highlight important comments. The writing style is succinct and to the point. Paragraphs tend to be shorter than in textbooks and other text-based instructional materials. Each guide, lesson, or lesson component

FIGURE 8.4   **Excerpt of a Sample Lesson from a Printed Study Guide**   This excerpt is part of a larger instructional unit on the U.S. Supreme Court's *Brown v. Board of Education* decision in 1954.

Lesson Objectives:
1. To study the checks and balances system in the American governmental system.
2. To analyze how a democracy responds to crisis.
3. To explain events before and after the Brown v. Board of Education Decision.

Key Questions:
1. Why is the *Brown v. Board of Education* decision regarded as one of the most significant decisions of the U.S. Supreme Court in the 20th century?
2. What was the reaction to the *Brown* decision on the part of various segments of American society?
3. What has been the effect of the *Brown* decision on American society in general?

Synopsis of the Case:
In the early 1950s, de jure (by law) segregation in public schools was well-established in seventeen states and Washington, D.C. In Topeka, Kansas, a black third-grader named Linda Brown had to walk one mile through a rail-road switch yard to get to her black elementary school, even though a white elementary school was only seven blocks away. Linda's father, Oliver Brown, tried to enroll her in the white elementary school, but the principal of the school refused. Brown went to McKinley Burnett, the head of Topeka's branch of the National Association for the Advancement of Colored People (NAACP), and asked for help. Other black parents joined Brown, and, in 1951, the NAACP requested an injunction that would forbid the segregation of Topeka's public schools.

The U.S. District Court for the District of Kansas heard Brown's case from June 25–26, 1951. At the trial, the NAACP argued that segregated schools sent the message to black children that they were inferior to whites; therefore, the schools were inherently unequal. . . .

The Board of Education's defense was that, because segregation in Topeka and elsewhere pervaded many other aspects of life, segregated schools simply prepared black children for the segregation they would face during adulthood. The board also argued that segregated schools were not necessarily harmful to black children; great African Americans such as Frederick Douglass, Booker T. Washington, and George Washington Carver had overcome segregated schools to achieve what they achieved. The request for an injunction put the court in a difficult position. On the one hand, the judges agreed with the expert witnesses; in their decision, they wrote: "Segregation of white and colored children in public schools has a detrimental effect upon the colored children. . . . A sense of inferiority affects the motivation of a child to learn."

On the other hand, the precedent of *Plessy v. Ferguson* (1896) allowed for "separate but equal" public facilities including school systems for blacks and whites, and no Supreme Court ruling had overturned *Plessy* yet. Because of the precedent of *Plessy*, the court felt "compelled" to rule in favor of the Board of Education.

Brown and the NAACP appealed to the Supreme Court on October 1, 1951, and their case was combined with other cases that challenged school segregation in South Carolina, Virginia, Delaware, and the District of Columbia. The Supreme Court first heard the case on December 9, 1952, but failed to reach a decision. In the reargument, heard from December 7–8, 1953, the Court requested that both sides discuss "the circumstances surrounding the adoption of the Fourteenth Amendment in 1868."

On May 17, 1954, Chief Justice Earl Warren read the decision of the unanimous Court: (*Brown I*) "We come then to the question presented: Does segregation of children in public schools solely on the basis of race, even though the physical facilities and other "tangible" factors may be equal, deprive the children of the minority group of equal educational opportunities? We believe that it does. . . . We conclude that in the field of public education the doctrine of 'separate but equal' has no place. Separate educational facilities are inherently unequal. Therefore, we hold that the plaintiffs and others similarly situated for whom the actions have been brought are, by reason of the segregation complained of, deprived of the equal protection of the laws guaranteed by the Fourteenth Amendment."

(continued)

FIGURE 8.4 *continued*

With this decision, the Supreme Court struck down the "separate but equal" doctrine of *Plessy* and ruled in favor of the plaintiffs. One year later, the Supreme Court issued its implementation decree ordering all segregated school systems to desegregate (*Brown II*).

Major Personalities:
Oliver Brown – father of Linda Brown . . .
Thurgood Marshall – lead attorney for the case for the NAACP Legal Defense Fund . . .
John W. Davis – lead attorney for the defense . . .
Kenneth Clark – social scientist and expert witness in the case . . .
Charles Houston – dean of Howard University's Law School . . .
Earl Warren – Chief Justice of the U.S. Supreme Court . . .

Aftermath of the *Brown* Decision:
Integration of Central High School in Little Rock, Arkansas (1950s) . . .
School decentralization and community power in New York City (1960s) . . .
Busing as a remedy for segregated schools in Boston (1970s) . . .

Legacy of the *Brown* Decision:
Provided the legal foundation for the American civil rights movement . . .
Catalyst for federal legislative initiatives and entitlement programs . . .
Established the legal precedent for other groups on constitutional issues of equality . . .

Reading Assignments:
Carter, R. L. (1995). The unending struggle for equal educational opportunity. *Teachers College Record, 96*(4), 619–626.
Kluger, Richard (1976). *Simple justice: The history of Brown v. Board of Education and black America's struggle for equality.* New York: Alfred A. Knopf. (Selected Chapters)
Miller, L. P. (1995). Tracking the progress of Brown. *Teachers College Record, 96*(4), 609–613.

Writing Assignment:
On the occasion of the anniversary of *Brown v. Board of Education, The Nation* conducted interviews with a number of activists and scholars on the relevance of the decision to present-day America. Ben Chavis, civil rights activist and former head of the NAACP, and Jack Greenberg, an attorney who assisted Thurgood Marshall in preparing the case in 1954, and professor emeritus at Columbia University's School of Law, gave the following responses to the question, "Does *Brown* Still Matter?":

"In many cases access to schools has been achieved while access to knowledge has not. African-Americans and Latinos are disproportionately isolated in underfunded school systems and substandard schools. Wealthier school systems provide their mostly white students with experienced teachers, modern technology, better facilities and lower student/teacher ratios"—Ben Chavis

"There is now a large black middle class and substantial black political power (forty members of Congress, many mayors) as a result of a civil rights revolution, of which *Brown* was one of the main progenitors. This political and economic power is a direct consequence of *Brown*'s perceptions and requirements."—Jack Greenberg

After studying the *Brown v. Board of Education* decision, do you tend to agree more with Chavis or Greenberg? Prepare a brief (1,200 words) paper explaining your position and cite examples either from your personal experiences or publicized current events to support it.

If you have any questions, do not hesitate to contact your instructor.

has a beginning, middle, and end. The beginning usually identifies the learning objectives and key questions to be explored. The middle presents the material in text form—but where appropriate, illustrations and pictures are added to provide visual clues for the learner. Increasingly, video materials are being developed and provided along with the printed guide. The end of the lesson directs the student to further study or formal assignments. Self-evaluation, if being used, should be both formative and summative, and should provide the learner with enough feedback to determine whether he or she can proceed to the next section or should review the current lesson again.

In looking at the sample in Figure 8.4, objectives and key questions are clearly stated at the beginning of the lesson. A synopsis of the case (in abridged form here) and other pertinent elements of the lesson (major personalities, aftermath, legacy) follow. The example concludes with both reading and writing assignments and encouragement to contact "your instructor" should the student have any questions.

The Interactive Videoconference

Figure 8.5 provides an excerpt from a script for a 3-hour interactive videoconference in which an instructor will teach to both a local and a distant student audience. Scripting is highly recommended in developing any type of conference (audio, video, one-way, two-way, multipoint). The conference should be carefully organized according to a time schedule so that the parties at all sites have a clear understanding of the sequence of a lesson's activities. In addition to helping an instructor organize his or her lesson, the script is used extensively by site facilitators to prepare for and assist in the delivery of the conference.

For the oral delivery in an interactive videoconference, an instructor can adapt much of his or her own traditional teaching style to the lesson. However, encouraging the students to ask questions, particularly at the remote site(s), is critical. A major advantage of interactive videoconferencing is its inherent interactivity, and instructors should plan their lessons accordingly. Study and observation of videoconferences indicate that the students at the local sites are frequently able to read the body language and energy of the instructor better than those at the remote sites, especially at the beginning of a course. It is not unusual to see students at a local site asking more questions than do students at the remote sites. A good script will identify specific periods for questions from all sites. Instructors should also be comfortable with camera angles and positioning and to the extent possible look into the camera. Another advantage of interactive videoconferencing facilities is the ability to incorporate media such as videotape, videodisc, slides, and document cameras. Where appropriate, instructors are encouraged to use media to enhance their basic oral delivery.

The script excerpted in Figure 8.5 starts with a testing of all technology, especially audio and video connections. Site facilitators or teaching assistants should be familiar with the session's activities. A backup plan is highly recommended in case a connection is lost or some other technical difficulty occurs. The session starts promptly at 1:30 p.m. with a welcome, another brief test of audio and video quality, and the taking of attendance. The instructor proceeds to introduce the topic orally, pretty much as he or she would in a traditional class. The script allocates frequent and specific times for questions to ensure that the students at the remote site(s) are

FIGURE 8.5	**Excerpt of a Script for a Two-Way Interactive Videoconference**

This excerpt is part of a script of a lesson on the U.S. Supreme Court's *Brown v. Board of Education* decision in 1954.

1:00 p.m. - Prepare audio-visual setup for today's session.
Test interactive video connection for audio and video quality.
Test instructor and student microphones.
Discuss with teaching assistants at the remote and local sites that they have received back-up material and understand lesson and procedures for today.

1:30 p.m. - Interactive video session starts.
Welcome the students at both sites and verify that they can see and hear you.
Take attendance.

1:40 p.m. - Begin the lesson.
Orally present the synopsis of the U.S. Supreme Court's *Brown v. Board of Education* decision from prepared notes.*

2:00 p.m. - Ask for questions from each of the sites.

2:10 p.m. - Orally present background of major personalities involved with the decision from prepared notes.*

2:30 p.m. - Ask for questions from each of the sites.

2:40 p.m. - Break

2:50 p.m. - Welcome the students back.
Provide a brief summary of the material/discussion during the first half of this session.

3:00 p.m. - Show a series of video clips from the award-winning documentary *Eyes on the Prize* from videodisc player. These clips will include the following:
Additional background on the *Brown* Decision;
Footage of the integration of Central High School in Little Rock, Arkansas, in the 1950s;
Footage of the school decentralization movement in New York City in the 1960s;
Footage of the school busing issue in Boston in the 1970s.

3:40 p.m. - Highlight pertinent comments/scenes made in the video clips.

4:00 p.m. - Ask for questions from both of the sites.

4:15 p.m. - Distribute/announce/refer students to the reading and writing assignments.*

4:20 p.m. - Ask if there are any questions with the assignment.

4:30 p.m. - Interactive video session ends.

Note: Prepared notes, reading and writing assignments are the same as those used in Figure 8.4.

encouraged and have the opportunity to interact. In a videoconference of 2 or more hours, at least one break is recommended. The example script also makes use of videodisc material to illustrate and support the oral presentation. PBS markets the highly acclaimed *Eyes on the Prize* documentary series of the civil rights movement in the United States in both videotape and videodisc formats. In this particular situation where several video clips are being used, videodisc with its rapid direct accessing capability is the recommended choice.

Distributing prepared notes on the topic is generally the prerogative of the instructor. Some instructors in traditional classes make their notes available; others do not. The same is true in distance learning lessons. Minimally, it is assumed that teaching assistants and site facilitators have received a copy of the instructor's notes. For this particular script, assume that the notes are similar to those in the printed study guide that are presented in abridged form in Figure 8.4.

The lesson concludes with the same reading and writing assignments that were required in the printed study guide. The reading assignments are generally provided as part of the entire schedule of assignments in the course syllabus. It may be helpful to students to have writing assignments scheduled in advance, but some instructors prefer to distribute writing assignments as needed.

Asynchronous Learning Using the Internet and World Wide Web

Figure 8.6 provides the outline for an asynchronous learning class using the Internet and the World Wide Web. Instructional activities described in this outline rely on Internet-based facilities such as e-mail, Web pages, and electronic bulletin boards. Students participate from their homes, places of business, or wherever they have access to the Internet, within given parameters, convenient for them. A good course management software (CMS) package, as discussed in Chapter 7, will facilitate developing many of these materials for the Web.

In this example, the course is organized according to weekly discussion topics. The discussion commences on Sunday evening on an electronic bulletin board and formally concludes on Saturday morning. Additional material is also provided at a class Web site. Several students are selected each week to serve as facilitators of instruction and are reminded on Friday of this assignment via e-mail. Student facilitators are expected to be especially active in making comments, in responding to questions, and in moving the discussion along for the week. In asynchronous learning, open-ended questions are very effective in allowing students to express themselves and are highly recommended. In the example outline, each scheduled posting by the instructor concludes with an open-ended question. In addition to the bulletin board, students are encouraged to contact the instructor directly via individual e-mail if need be throughout the session. In the absence of face-to-face contact, positive feedback and reinforcement techniques such as frequent compliments or references to students are desirable.

In this particular outline, the discussion continues for a week and ends with the instructor providing a summary of the week's discussion and posting his or her notes on the class Web site. At the Web site, students can also find the reading and writing assignments. In this example, the reading assignment includes material provided on the Web at another site from a symposium that was held on the *Brown v. Board of Education* decision. Where possible, using the information resources of the Web is highly recommended for asynchronous, Internet-based learning. Students in these classes are familiar with the Web and generally can access Web-based materials. Unfortunately,

FIGURE 8.6 **Excerpt of an Outline for an Asynchronous Learning Class** This excerpt is part of an outline for an asynchronous learning session on the U.S. Supreme Court's *Brown v. Board of Education* decision in 1954.

This class is conducted entirely in asynchronous mode over the Internet. Students access all material remotely via e-mail and the World Wide Web from their homes or in their places of business. Each session lasts 1 week beginning on Sunday evening and ending on Saturday morning.

Friday - Remind student facilitators via e-mail for the coming week's discussion that they should have read all the material and are familiar with key questions.*

Sunday - Initiate week's discussion on the class electronic bulletin board by introducing the topic and concluding with the following open-ended question:
"Why is the *Brown v. Board of Education* decision regarded as one of the most significant decisions of the U.S. Supreme Court in the 20th century?"
Refer students to a synopsis and major personalities of the case that is available at the class Web site.
Remind students that if they have any questions, feel free to e-mail the instructor at any time.

Monday - Monitor student comments and questions on the electronic bulletin board and individual e-mail.

Tuesday - Compliment students who made exceptionally good postings to the electronic bulletin board over the past 48 hours. Review the wording of the *Brown* decision (*Brown I*) and the implementation decree (*Brown II*).
Conclude with an open-ended question:
"What did the *Brown* decision mean to those states that had established de jure segregated school systems? How did these states attempt to implement the *Brown* decision?"
Remind students that if they have any questions, feel free to e-mail the instructor at any time.

Wednesday - Monitor student comments and questions on the electronic bulletin board and individual e-mail.

Thursday - Compliment and refer to students who made exceptionally good postings to the electronic bulletin board over the past 48 hours.
Briefly review the discussion for the week.
Emphasize that the *Brown* decision did not just affect the states that had established de jure segregated school systems, but that it ended up affecting the entire country. Provide examples in New York City in the 1960s and Boston in the 1970s.
Conclude with an open-ended question:
"What has been the effect of the *Brown* decision on American society in general?"
Remind students that if they have any questions, feel free to e-mail the instructor at any time.

Friday - Monitor student comments and questions on the electronic bulletin board and individual e-mail.

Saturday - Compliment and refer to students who made exceptionally good postings to the electronic bulletin board during the past week.
Indicate that a summary of this week's discussion and further information from the instructor's notes** will be available at the class's Web site by 4:00 p.m. this (Saturday) evening.
Refer students to the class Web site to a written assignment.**
Thank student facilitators for their contribution to this week's discussion.
Wish everybody a Happy Weekend!

Note: Reading assignment includes material available at a Web site maintained by Woodstock Techological Center at Georgetown University that held a symposium in 1994 commemorating the 40th Anniversary of the *Brown* decision.
**Note:* Instructor notes and written assignment are the same as in Figure 8.4.

depending upon the topic and content, quality reading and other instructional materials are not always available online. While the book and journal publishers are moving toward providing access to some of their materials on the Web, too frequently user fees are required that may be prohibitive for students. An instructor might be tempted to scan in an excerpt from a particularly useful article and post it at a Web site; however, if the material is copyrighted, permission will have to be secured. The writing assignment in this example is the same as in the previous examples and can be submitted by fax, e-mail, or regular mail depending on the preferences of the instructor.

DESIGNING PROGRAMS FOR DISTANCE LEARNERS

Academic programs are designed with a consideration of the basic characteristics of students, including their age, interests, skill levels, academic preparedness, and career goals. With respect to distance learning, these same characteristics must be considered.

Much of the literature suggests that older students and adults are the primary targets and enrollees in distance learning programs. For example, distance learning institutions around the world patterned on the British Open University model were established essentially for adult populations. Keegan reports that the average distance learning student in the Open University of the United Kingdom is 30 to 55 years of age with a "diverse accumulation of experiences" (1996, p. 150).

In the United States, many adult distance learning students are between the ages of 25 and 50, two thirds are female, and most are married and work full-time. Data collected by the National Center for Education Statistics (U.S. Department of Education, 2003) show that distance learning programs are predominantly directed to adults in undergraduate, graduate, and continuing education programs. The NCES further reports that these programs are targeted to certain types of individuals—specifically, to professionals seeking recertification and workers seeking skills for updating or retraining.

In recent years, however, a growing number of distance learning programs have been directed to primary and secondary school students. Large-scale literacy programs in developing countries with geographically remote or dispersed populations have been established for younger students as well as for adults. In the United States, rural school districts unable to offer courses to fulfill graduation requirements to small student populations have relied for many years on distance learning programs offered by other districts, colleges, or statewide consortia. The National Center for Education Statistics estimated that approximately one-third of all school districts were offering some form of distance learning to their students. Most of these districts were located in the rural areas in the Southeast and central areas of the country (Setzer & Lewis, 2005). Distance learning is also increasingly being viewed as an important instructional component for students who, by necessity or by choice, are being educated in their homes. Major distance learning initiatives—such as the U.S. Department of Education's Star Schools (see Figure 8.7) created in 1988—have been established for primary and secondary school populations. More than 1.6 million students annually enroll in Star Schools, although in many cases, Star School programs enhance and do not necessarily replace existing traditional classroom instruction.

FIGURE 8.7	**Star Schools**

Star Schools

What is the Star Schools Program?
The Star Schools Program provides quality, cost-effective instruction through distance learning to more than 1.6 million learners annually in 50 states and U.S. territories. Although the program began with small rural schools in 1988, it is now equally valuable to schools in large urban areas.

Projects offer Instructional modules, video field trips, enrichment activities, and semester-long and year-long courses. Through Star Schools, students can question astronauts about the principles of physics. Japanese- and German-language students can talk with native speakers and visit Japan and Germany through live and Interactive teleconferences. For most students served, distance learning is their only access to science, math, foreign language, and advanced placement courses.

How do Star Schools projects work?
To deliver services, projects use many distance education technologies, including the Internet, satellite delivery systems, open broadcasts, cable, fiber optics, microcomputers, digital compression, interactive videodiscs, facsimile machines, and the ordinary telephone.

What services are available from Star Schools projects?
Through Star Schools projects, schools have access to instructional programming, including hands-on science and mathematics, general mathematics, algebra, calculus, physics, advanced placement courses, and workplace skills. Foreign language offerings include Russian, Japanese, Swahill, Arabic, Spanish, and Mandarin Chinese. Instructional programs serve K-12 students, including limited English-proficient students and disabled students.

Who operates Star Schools projects?
The U.S. Department of Education awards grants to telecommunications partnerships to operate Star Schools projects. Partnerships include local school districts, state departments of education, public broadcasting entities, and other public and private organizations.

Source: U.S. Department of Education (http://www.ed.gov/programs/starschools/index.html).

Many states have established "virtual" primary or secondary schools using the Internet for course delivery. According to an *Education Week* survey, 21 states had formally established a virtual school and 13 had approved a charter virtual school (Park & Staresina, 2004). The purposes of virtual primary and high schools vary, but essentially they are designed to provide online alternatives to traditional primary and high schools. The Kentucky Virtual High School, for example, is aimed in large part at students in small, rural school districts that suffer from a shortage of teachers qualified to teach upper-level math, science, and foreign language courses. Originally the Florida High School offered only a few core high school courses such as algebra and English; however, now it offers all the courses necessary for a student to earn a high school diploma. Most of the students enrolled are public high school students, but a substantial minority are home-schooled students (Mendels, 1999). Perhaps the most extensive virtual venture may be the Virtual High School, or VHS, financed in part through a U.S. Department of Education grant and operated by the nonprofit Concord Consortium in

---

FIGURE 8.8   **The Virtual High School**

The Virtual High School (VHS) - Concord Consortium

The VHS (Virtual High School) project is a collaborative of high schools from around the country. In exchange for contributing a small amount of teaching time, a school in the collaborative can offer its students NetCourses ranging from advanced academic courses to technical and specialized courses. Schools donate computers, Internet connectivity, and staff time. Each school also provides a VHS site coordinator who is responsible for project management and support of teachers and students at their local school. The VHS grant provides training, software, and technical and administrative support. Each school can enroll up to 20 students for each course a teacher contributes. Quality of teaching is maintained by requiring each teacher to successfully complete the Teachers Learning Conference, a graduate-level NetCourse designed to give participants exposure to the best educational strategies and technologies for NetCourse teaching. As the Virtual High School gains popularity, schools can contribute more teachers, enroll more students, and help make a wider variety of courses available to the student body.

Funding for the Virtual High School comes primarily from a 5-year Technology Challenge Grant awarded to Hudson Public Schools in October 1996 by the U.S. Department of Education. The Concord Consortium, a nonprofit educational research and development organization, assisted with the design and implementation of the project. School year 1996–97 was a start-up year for VHS; classes for students were first offered by VHS during the 1997–98 school year when 29 Internet-based, credit-bearing courses were offered to about 500 students in 27 schools located in 10 states. There were more than 100 schools participating in the project by 2001.

Source: Retrieved from the Web site of the Concord Consortium (http://vhs.concord.org).

Concord, Massachusetts (see Figure 8.8). It is operated as a cooperative, with schools in 26 states and a number of countries agreeing to design and teach Internet-based courses in exchange for their students being able to participate. The VHS has won international recognition for the quality of its programs including the 2001 Stockholm Challenge Award for Global Excellence in Information Technology.

In addition to programs funded by government and individual school districts, for-profit ventures are also targeting distance learning students. Companies such as Kaplan Education, K-12, and Apex Learning are aggressively pursuing primary and high school students for specialized courses and educational needs. Apex Learning is a Seattle-based company originally established as a demonstration project by Paul Allen, the cofounder of Microsoft. The company provides courses that rely on the interactivity and accessibility of the Internet as well as the experience of master teachers and content specialists. Apex Learning's current programming includes Advanced Placement online courses in several subject areas and the AP Exam review. The subject areas include calculus, statistics, U.S government and politics, microeconomics, macroeconomics, U.S. history, and English language and composition. Apex Learning was honored with a *Technology & Learning* Software Award of Excellence for its calculus and U.S. government and politics courses and for its CramCentral Web site. *Technology & Learning* is a leading education technology magazine for K-12 educators.

DISTANCE LEARNING: SOME ISSUES

Distance learning is increasingly being viewed as an important alternative to traditional in-class instruction. In the 1990s, the Internet and digital networks almost doubled the number of students taking distance learning courses. Data collected by the U.S. Department of Education (2003) suggests that growth in distance learning will continue for the foreseeable future. Figure 8.9 lists some of the providers of distance learning programs for primary and secondary schools.

FIGURE 8.9   **A Sample of Primary and Secondary School Distance Learning Providers**

- *Adventure Learning Network* - organization that sponsors online curriculum-based programs for kids, emphasizing the environment and ocean ecology.
- *Alice Springs School of the Air* - distance education school specializing in correspondence materials and electronic communications for primary school aged students in rural areas of Australia.
- *Aphelion* - offers "School Without Walls" an Internet-based education program or gifted and talented students.
- *Arts and Sciences Teleconferencing Service* - credit courses via satellite from Oklaloma State University.
- *AZ Home Academy* - a private correspondence school for grades 1 through 8 featuring a basic middle grades curriculum.
- *Babbage Net School* - alternative high school offering online, interactive courses in English, math, science, social studies, and other subjects.
- *California Distance Learning Program* - K-8 public school distance learning program emphasizing the needs of the whole child, including academic, social, emotional, and developmental needs.
- *Christa McAuliffe Academy* - nationally accredited private school that provides K-12 distance learning via the internet.
- *CyberSchool* - high school credit classes over the Internet, sponsored by Eugene, Oregon, Public Schools, District 4J.
- *Domus Preparatory School* - offering live Latin, Greek, logic, rhetoric, and great books tutorials to private, public, and homeschool students.
- *Eldorado Academy* - specializing in distance learning and home schooling on the Internet for grades K-12.
- *Escondido Tutorial Service* - offers classical Christian education to home-based learners via the Internet.
- *Florida High Schools, The* - meets all of the Florida Sunshine State Standards.
- *Fraser Valley Distance Education School* - courses for home-based learners of all ages in Canada.
- *Home Study International* - a Seventh-Day Adventist distance education provider, offering accredited and nonaccredited programs for pre-K to grade 12; also certified, transferable college courses.
- *Indiana University, Bloomington - Division of Extended Studies* - accredited college and high school courses offered using distance learning, Internet, e-mail, video, CD-ROM, and correspondence.
- *Iowa Digital Education Association* - offers K-12 and postsecondary courses through the Internet.
- *Laurel Springs School* - dedicated to providing online and home schooling to K-12 children.
- *Louisiana State University* - offers continuing education and distance learning courses to university and high school students.
- *North Carolina School of Science and Mathematics* - offers high school courses, student enrichment programs, and teacher workshops over the North Carolina Information Highway (NCIH).

(continued)

FIGURE 8.9   *continued*

- *North Dakota Division of Independent Study* - fully accredited provider of high school and middle school distance education classes; students can enroll in over 150 classes.
- *NorthStar Academy* - private Christian online school offering grade 7-12 programs that meet Canadian or U.S. requirements.
- *Phoenix Special Programs & Academies* - allows youths and adults to accelerate, remediate, of graduate from high schools.
- *Project DIANE (Diversified Information & Assistance Network)* - nonprofit video teleconference consortium with cooperative programs in education, community outreach, and economic development.
- *Satellite Educational Resources Consortium (SERC)* - combines resources of state and local departments of education with public broadcasting to design, produce, and deliver educational programs.
- *Schola Classical Tutorials* - offers tutorials using a classical liberal arts curriculum: Latin, Greek, classical books rhetoric, and logic.
- *Spanish via Satellite* - offers Spanish I and II on satellite TV through Kansas State University and participating school districts.
- *Summit Christian Academy* - combines distance learning and home schooling with a Christian curriculum.
- *TEAMS Distance Learning* - satellite distance learning provider of instruction for the elementary grades; also providing online resources for parents, teachers, and students.
- *Toronto Virtual School* - an online learning service making the math and science curriculum for grades 8 to OAC available in lesson units with interactive exercises and tests.
- *Utah Education Network* - organization of public and higher education that represents higher, public, and vocational education; provides educational television, telecourses, and online teaching.
- *Virginia Satellite Educational Network (VSEN)* - K-12, advanced placement, foreign language courses, and staff development programs available nationwide.
- *Virtual School for the Gifted* - provides courses aimed specifically at gifted students.
- *Willoway CyberSchool* - private online middle school that uses video cameras to enhance Internet instruction.

As educators evaluate the appropriateness of distance learning for their students, several major issues—including instructional quality, for-profit enterprises, student access to technology, scalability, and social interaction and development—need to be considered.

First, the issue of instructional quality in distance learning has and will continue to be closely scrutinized. Most of the research literature finds well-delivered distance learning in various forms on a par with traditional face-to-face instruction, but skepticism will continue. In an extensive review of the research literature completed for the Association for Educational Communications and Technology and the Research Institute for Studies in Education at Iowa State University, Hanson and colleagues (1997) concluded that distance learning can be just as effective as traditional education with regard to learner outcomes such as performance and student completion. There was little difference based on gender or age other than the fact that attrition occurs more frequently for students over the age of 25. Academic preparation was determined to be an important factor. Students who had achieved higher levels of education, with higher grade point averages, or who had already successfully completed a distance learning course were more likely to succeed. Successful distance learners also tended to be abstract learners who possess an internal locus of control and who are self-directed and persistent in achieving their goals. Motivational factors such as having higher educational or career goals and objectives were also mentioned as important determinants of success. The Sloan Consortium, in a national survey of chief academic officers at colleges and universities, reported that the majority (61%) believe that the learning outcomes for online distance learning was at least equal to and possibly superior to face-to-face instruction; 77% believe that it will be at least as equal to and possibly superior within three years (Allen & Seaman, 2004).

Second, the issue of instructional quality also relates to the number of for-profit digital schools that have emerged in recent years. Apex Learning is one of the award-winning for-profit distance learning providers. However, of the 600 students in 28 states who enrolled in at least one of the company's online Advanced Placement courses in 1999, two thirds did not complete enough of the course work to take the final exam (Steinberg, 2000). Apex Learning is a legitimate, conscientious company trying to provide a valuable service and has been candid in reporting its results, both successes and problems. However, some for-profit distance learning providers are little more than "digital diploma mills." George Connick, in a publication titled *The Distance Learner's Guide* (1999), clearly alerts prospective students "to beware of diploma mills" and unscrupulous distance learning providers. Although a small minority, low- or no-quality schools will cast a shadow on others. Distance learning providers and regional accrediting agencies will need to be scrupulous in assuring the quality of courses and programs offered and publicizing the same to prospective students.

Third, the issue of student access to technology was discussed in Chapter 3 but deserves consideration with respect to distance learning mainly because online technology has become the main delivery mechanism. In the United States, concern has existed regarding the "digital divide" and the evolution of a nation of information haves and have-nots. Although the digital and communications technology industries offer excellent products for reasonable cost, distance learning providers, particularly those supported by public resources, need to be mindful that these products do not exist in many poorer people's homes. Developing academic programs that are not accessible to a large—and often the most needy—segment of a student population will rightfully be questioned.

Fourth, the issue of scalability is becoming more important as schools and colleges experiment with new distance learning technology and attempt to broaden the scope or scale of programs. Many teachers in schools with little experience in distance learning have begun to experiment by offering one or two courses in selected programs. This is desirable and worthwhile experimentation. However, some concerns exist. For example, Park & Starasina (2004) report that 10 states have found it necessary to require that teachers of online courses receive formal training in online instruction. In expanding programs, distance learning providers have learned that other issues, particularly related to student and academic support services (staff development, counseling, tutoring, library, etc.), will need to be addressed and provided for. Failure to do so will leave institutions, faculty, and students vulnerable to a number of logistical and policy problems that will be more difficult to resolve after the program has commenced. These problems, in turn, will lead to negative perceptions of the quality of the programs and will hinder their future development.

Lastly, given the complexity of the educational enterprise, educational policy makers and planners should ensure that distance learning programs take into consideration all of their learners' needs. Magellan University, for example, operates out of 600 square feet of office space in Tucson, Arizona. William R. Noyes, with 26 years at the University of Arizona as a professor and administrator, started Magellan University in 1996 with $1 million provided for the most part by Research Corporation Technologies. Magellan has directed most of its courses to adults over the age of 25, in areas such as basic mathematics, engineering, and technology systems design. It enrolled its first students in 1998 and eventually hopes to have an enrollment of 12,000. Noyes carefully considers the academic quality and rigor of the program at Magellan. By design, class size is small, tutors are always available, and writing is an important component of all courses. However, in comparing Magellan to a traditional university, Noyes favors the conventional university setting for an 18-year-old, because of the social interaction and "the breadth of the educational experience" (Christman, 1998). His point is that care must be taken that distance learning is not seen as the quick, easy, or inexpensive way to provide all the education needs for all students.

CASE STUDY

PLACE: CLIFTON HIGH SCHOOL
YEAR: 2005

Clifton High School is a small rural high school located in the farmbelt of the United States. The enrollment at Clifton is approximately 550 students. Clifton's academic programs are excellent and it has a good deal of support from the community. One ongoing issue has been attracting and hiring teachers— particularly in the sciences, mathematics, and foreign languages. Fortunately, in the 1990s a statewide distance learning consortium was established and housed at the state's University Center. The consortium is subsidized by the state, and for a nominal fee Clifton may enroll any of its students in the program, which is based on interactive video technology delivered over the state's fiber-optic network. Clifton enrolls approximately 50 to 75 students per year in consortium courses, especially in advanced placement subjects, mathematics, and foreign languages.

Decisions involving new distance learning courses and programs should involve administrators, faculty, and students to assure that such offerings are appropriate and well prepared. Administrators, elected officials, and corporate sponsors cannot simply embrace the new technology as a way of servicing many or all students at reduced costs. The classroom has been evolving for centuries and will continue to do so. Where distance learning technology is appropriate and can be effective, it should be used. If it is not effective, it should be adjusted or abandoned. Finding the proper fit of academic program, student need, and instructional tools is the essence of good educational planning. Noyes's insight is essential to the successful planning and development of quality distance learning programs. Schools are not only places where teachers teach and students learn. The bottom line cannot simply be how well students performed on a test or how many were accepted by good colleges and universities. The place called *school* is a microcosm of society where values are transferred and people, especially the young, are developed. Learning is not simply knowing how to do one or two things well, but involves understanding where one's knowledge fits in the broader context of life.

Sandra Parks, the principal at Clifton, has been concerned about the science program. She has had trouble recruiting qualified science teachers, especially in physics and chemistry. Even if she could hire two science teachers, she is not sure she has a full teaching program for them. In recent years, a number of her students have been taking science courses via distance learning (interactive video) provided by the state's University Center. Although the lecture and discussion portions of these courses are appropriate, the laboratory experiences have been problematic. Students can view the laboratory exercises that are demonstrated at the University Center's site but they cannot participate in a hands-on fashion. Ms. Parks sees the distance learning program in the sciences as "better than no science courses" and as very cost-effective given the fact the state subsidizes them—however, she is convinced that students learn science by doing, not simply by watching. She has approached the University Center's distance learning coordinator regarding whether the science offerings could be improved with some type of hands-on activity at Clifton High School. The coordinator has indicated that he would be more than happy to have several of his science faculty meet and discuss this with Clifton faculty, but that he could not

Continued on next page

possibly afford to send his faculty to Clifton. Ms. Parks has also recently seen advertisements in *Education Week* for a new Internet-based distance learning program offered by a for-profit company on the West Coast. The program includes several science courses provided on DVD-based instructional software packages that are designed to simulate laboratory experiments. Students not only are able to view graphically rich experiments but can actually manipulate variables and hence change outcomes and results. These DVD software packages are to be used in conjunction with asynchronous Internet-based courses taught by highly qualified high school science teachers.

SUMMARY

This chapter introduces the topic of distance learning. Distance learning has an extensive history, including mail, radio, and television, but newer technologies such as digital communications and networking have begun to emerge that make it much easier for educators to provide some form of distance learning to their students. However, distance learning means different things to different people and can take many forms. This discussion includes an analysis and comparison of the various technologies. In selecting a technology for distance learning, educators should assume that they may pick and choose or blend technologies to provide the best approach.

The chapter also includes a presentation on design considerations for developing distance learning materials for three different delivery systems: the print study guide, the interactive video conference, and Internet-based asynchronous learning. This is followed by a section on identifying who distance learners are and the programs that are being established to meet their needs.

The chapter concludes with a discussion of emerging issues including instructional quality, for-profit enterprises, student access to technology, scalability, and social interaction and development.

KEY CONCEPTS AND QUESTIONS

1. Distance learning means different things to different people. How do you define distance learning?

2. Distance learning can use several different delivery technologies. Identify and compare several different distance learning delivery technologies. What do you see as the future of these technologies?

3. Distance learning seems to be growing in popularity, especially in adult learning programs. What do you see as the growth of distance learning in primary schools? And high schools?

DISCUSSION QUESTIONS

1. Assume you are Ms. Parks. Review your two alternatives for improving Clifton's science program and develop a plan for improvement. Consider carefully all options, costs, and academic issues as well as who should be involved with developing your plan.

2. Are there other alternatives besides the two described in the case study that are appropriate for Clifton High School?

4. The terms *synchronous* and *asynchronous* distance learning are referred to several times in this chapter. Define and compare the two approaches. Especially identify the pedagogical benefits of each.

5. Many educators do not see distance learning as ever replacing the teacher in the classroom. Do you believe that distance learning technologies will ever substantially replace teachers in K-12 classrooms? If so, under what circumstances would this occur or be appropriate?

6. Many issues have arisen as a result of the expansion of distance learning in the United States. Identify and compare some of these issues. Are they significant issues in your school or district?

SUGGESTED ACTIVITIES

To complete the Suggested Activities online, go to the Companion Website at **www.prenhall.com/picciano,** then to this chapter's *Suggested Activities* module.

REFERENCES

Allen, I. E., & Seaman, J. (2004). *Entering the mainstream: The quality and extent of online education in the United States, 2003 and 2004.* Needham, MA: Sloan Consortium.

Birkerts, S. (1994). *The Gutenberg elegies.* Boston: Faber & Faber.

Christman, B. (1998). Information revolution fills space between the ears: Magellan abandons bricks and mortar. Originally retrieved from the Web site of Magellan University, no longer available online.

Connick, G. P. (Ed.). (1999). *The distance learner's guide.* Upper Saddle River, NJ: Prentice Hall.

Hanson, D., Maushak, N. J., Schlosser, C. A., Anderson, M. L., Sorenson, C., & Simonson, M. (1997). *Distance education: Review of the literature* (2nd ed.). Washington, DC: Association for Educational Communications and Technology.

Keegan, D. (1996). *Foundations of distance education* (3rd ed.). London: Routledge.

Mendels, P. (1999, October 13). Kentucky reaches for high school students with Internet courses. *New York Times*, p. B10.

Park, J., & Staresina, L. (2004, May 6). Tracking U.S. trends. *Education Week, 23*(35), 64–67.

Public Broadcasting Service. (2004). PBS Adult Learning Service Web site. (http://www.pbs.org/als/about_als/index.html).

Rowntree, D. (1996). *Preparing materials for open, distance, and flexible learning.* London: Kogan Page.

Rudenstine, N. (1997, February 21). The Internet and education: a close fit. *Chronicle of Higher Education, 37*–38.

Setzer, J. C., & Lewis, L. (2005). Distance education courses for public elementary and secondary students: 2003-03 (NCES 2005-10). U. S. Department of Education. Washington, DC: National Center for Education Statistics.

Steinberg, J. (2000, July 7). As teacher in the classroom, Internet needs fine-tuning. *New York Times*, pp. A1–A12.

Texas may drop texts for laptops. (1997, November 19). *New York Times*, p. B11.

U.S. Department of Education, National Center for Education Statistics. (2003). *Distance education at degree-granting postsecondary education institutions, 2000–2001,* NCES 2003-017. Washington, DC: U.S. Department of Education, National Center for Education Statistics.

Section III

PLANNING AND IMPLEMENTATION

Chapter 9

Hardware Planning
and Evaluation

The components of every application include hardware, software, staffing, facilities, and finances, each of which is crucial to the eventual outcome and effectiveness. Planning the application, therefore, must involve an integrated approach to planning all the components. Detailed evaluations and specifications should be developed for each component that brings the overall application together rather than fragmenting it.

The concept of integrating components such as hardware and software or hardware and facilities is critical, particularly as related to the selection and evaluation of hardware, because too often in the past there was overemphasis on the acquisition of hardware alone. A common assumption was that once the hardware was acquired, the other components (software, staff development, facilities renovation, etc.) would follow. This unfortunately did not always happen, and, as a result, some schools invested in hardware but did not always realize the benefits they expected.

This chapter presents the major criteria for evaluating the hardware component, concluding with an examination of some of the special hardware considerations for administrative and instructional applications.

HARDWARE PLANNING FOR THE LONG RANGE

Planning for computer hardware requires planning for the long range. The life cycle of most computing equipment is 5 to 7 years, but it is not unusual to see equipment used longer. In fact, many schools continue to use computer hardware until the equipment literally no longer works. As a result, when acquiring hardware, decision makers should be aware that this equipment may be used for a long time and evaluate it accordingly.

The durability of hardware also tempts administrators and others to look at their available hardware, which may have been acquired for one purpose, and to consider using it for other purposes. This is desirable as long as the hardware is appropriate, not too old, and can meet the needs of the application. However, the normal modus operandi should not be one of searching for applications for underutilized hardware, which reflects poor planning and an overemphasis on hardware. Rather, planning for hardware should be integrated with the other components of an application. If available hardware is appropriate, then it should be used. Otherwise, new hardware should be considered.

In buying hardware, most schools find themselves making decisions from two different perspectives: acquiring new hardware for new applications, and replacing hardware for existing applications. In acquiring new hardware for new applications, the purchasing pattern is more varied, with buyers attempting to select the best equipment to meet the needs of the application. When replacing hardware for existing applications, the pattern reveals a tendency to continue with the same manufacturer and platform, simply upgrading to a newer model with greater capacity or speed. The various reasons for this include familiarity with the equipment and concern about retraining and conversion costs, particularly if larger computer systems are involved.

This approach is similar to the way people purchase most personal equipment, such as home appliances or automobiles. If they have had a good experience with a particular manufacturer, they go back to that manufacturer and buy a newer model when the old one needs replacing. There is one significant difference when it comes to computers, though. Once someone knows how to drive a car, for example, he or she is able to drive a new car of almost any manufacturer with relative ease. With computers, the "driving" is performed via software, and changing the hardware manufacturer may require changing the software, which in many cases means learning to "drive" all over again. The reason for this is that software standards generally do not exist, and software that drives one manufacturer's machine will not necessarily drive another. This is especially true for large mainframe systems and servers, and less so for microcomputers.

Organizations with mainframe systems have shown a reluctance to change hardware manufacturers even if a better performing and less expensive piece of hardware is available, because they do not want to change or convert the software. In years past, manufacturers of large computers—such as Unisys, Control Data Corporation, and Honeywell—knew this very well. Proposals from these companies to customers who already had an IBM computer included additional software conversion factors for actually doing or assisting the customer in doing the conversion. Because such software conversions were people-intensive and therefore expensive, these companies were not able to compete effectively with IBM. The same was true if IBM made a proposal to a customer who already had a Control Data Corporation or Unisys computer. However, because IBM had such a large share of the mainframe market, the other manufacturers usually found themselves in the more disadvantaged position.

With microcomputers, the situation is somewhat different. Although several companies dominate the market, hundreds of microcomputer manufacturers exist, which makes for very keen competition. Many of these manufacturers have designed their products to be compatible with the dominant manufacturers and to use the same software. Another interesting phenomenon unique to microcomputers is the fact that much of the software being used, including the operating systems, is not being provided solely by the hardware manufacturers. The term *software platform* is used for this foundation software (operating system and other fundamental programs of a computer system). Software companies such as

Microsoft Corporation (DOS/Windows) are providing software that runs on a wide variety of microcomputers and is not entirely machine-dependent. These factors have combined to create a more dynamic hardware acquisition pattern than exists with mainframe computer systems.

The issue of manufacturer dependence will be discussed further in the next section, which deals with various hardware evaluation criteria. The selection of a manufacturer in any equipment acquisition is important; with computers, especially mainframe systems and servers, it becomes critical because it frequently commits a user to a continuing relationship.

■ HARDWARE EVALUATION CRITERIA

Evaluating hardware can be a complicated process. For school districts with large mainframe computer systems, acquiring hardware means the investment of millions of dollars for many years with a particular vendor. As an example, Palm Beach County, Florida, a school district of approximately 100,000 students, completed a $20 million district automation project that connected all of the district's schools and administrative offices in a wide area network (WAN). The planning, evaluation, and selection of hardware took several years and involved awarding contracts to four major hardware vendors. This type of expenditure is not uncommon for larger districts with dozens of schools and tens of thousands of students. However, all districts, both large and small, are finding that they are committing more and more of their equipment budgets to computer technology. Making such large investments requires the careful development of specifications and evaluation of equipment. In the public sector, administrators will likely use competitive bidding procedures that may require identifying a formalized evaluation procedure to prospective bidders.

Opinions regarding evaluation criteria vary significantly. One survey of administrators identified 19 different factors used in evaluating hardware (Ferrante, Hayman, Carlson, & Phillips, 1988, p. 36). On the other hand, some administrators simply ask, "How much does it cost?" Figure 9.1 identifies seven important factors for evaluating and selecting computer hardware:

1. *Performance:* How well does the hardware work?
2. *Compatibility:* Does the hardware work with other equipment?
3. *Modularity/expandability:* Can the hardware grow as applications grow?
4. *Ergonomics:* Is the hardware designed with people in mind?
5. *Software availability:* Is the software you wish to use currently available?
6. *Vendor:* What is the reputation of the manufacturer in terms of technical support, maintenance, and industry position?
7. *Cost:* What are the costs?

| FIGURE 9.1 | **Major Hardware Evaluation Factors** |

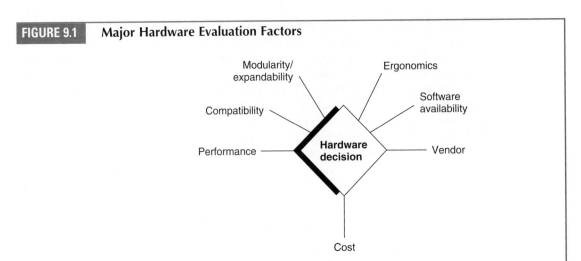

A serious hardware evaluation will take each of these factors into account when comparing different products. As much as possible, quantitative assessments should be developed. Certain factors such as capacity, speed, and costs are easily quantified. However, other factors such as ergonomics or software availability lend themselves better to qualitative assessments.

Site visits or field tests should be part of every acquisition, particularly when purchasing new models. Perhaps the most revealing activities in evaluating hardware are visits to comparable schools or districts that are using the hardware and running similar applications. In addition, popular vendors of both large and small hardware systems are generally most cooperative in demonstrating their products. For larger systems, vendors will also assist in conducting benchmark tests of typical applications. A *benchmark test* consists of running the same computer program on several different machines and comparing speed, response time, hardware resource requirements, and other factors. For microcomputer systems, local retail businesses are most accommodating in providing demonstrations. Trade journals and consultants should also be employed. Commercial research services such as the Gartner Group of Stamford, Connecticut, and San Jose, California, (http://www.gartner.com) do periodic hardware evaluation reports and ratings based on national surveys. While expensive, they can be valuable starting points in assessing the performance and customer satisfaction with various products.

In conducting an evaluation, one approach is to provide a hardware checklist or evaluation form to assist evaluators. However, the factors that go into a hardware evaluation can be very complex, especially for larger and more expensive systems. Hardware evaluations are not easily reduced to a simple checklist and should have substantial qualitative as well as quantitative backup material. However, Figure 9.2 provides a checklist that one district used to summarize and compare hardware evaluation ratings. The most appropriate use of a checklist like this would be as part of an evaluation summary and a discussion among administrators and teachers.

FIGURE 9.2	**Hardware Evaluation Summary Checklist**

North Central School District No. 1

Hardware description (Type of equipment; identify three manufacturers or models evaluated)

Manufacturer/model 1 _____

Manufacturer/model 2 _____

Manufacturer/model 3 _____

	Ratings		
Evalution criteria	*1*	*2*	*3*
Performance (capacity, speed)	_____	_____	_____
Compatibility	_____	_____	_____
Modularity/expandability	_____	_____	_____
Ergonomics	_____	_____	_____
Software availability	_____	_____	_____
Vendor	_____	_____	_____
Costs	_____	_____	_____
Final ratings	_____	_____	_____

All of the evaluation criteria identified here are important for an effective evaluation, but in some circumstances one or more factors may carry more weight than others. A brief review of each of these factors will help clarify their general importance in the evaluation process.

Performance

Most hardware performance indicators attempt to assess capacity, speed, or quality of output. Table 9.1 provides some of the common performance criteria in evaluating major computer hardware components.

Large mainframe manufacturers generally customize their central processing units (CPUs), and an in-depth evaluation requires a good deal of technical expertise. For microcomputers, the most commonly used CPU components are provided by Motorola, Inc., (for Apple computers) and Intel Corporation (for DOS/Windows computers). Several major attributes of all CPUs can be understood by many nontechnical people. For example, CPUs are frequently compared based on the capacity of the primary storage units as measured in bytes. Generally, the more primary storage a CPU has, the more processing that can be accomplished, assuming other factors such as software and other hardware components are equal.

In terms of processing capacity, one of the most important factors in evaluating a CPU is the size of the data path within the CPU itself. These are usually established in 8-bit increments (8, 16, 32, 64, etc.), each designed to carry instructions or data from one CPU subunit to another. A 32-bit data path can carry twice as many instructions or data in the same time as a 16-bit data path; a 64-bit data path can carry twice as many as a 32-bit data path, and four times as many as a 16-bit data path. Theoretically, the size of

TABLE 9.1	Performance Criteria of Major Hardware Components

Component	Criteria
CPU	Capacity of the primary storage unit as measured in millions (megabytes) or billions (gigabytes) of bytes
	Size of data paths within the CPU as measured in bits (8, 16, 32, 64, etc.)
	Machine cycle time as measured in millions (megahertz) or billions (gigahertz) of cycles per second
	Number of input and output devices that can be connected to the CPU
Magnetic disk	Capacity as measured in megabytes, gigabytes, or terabytes
Video display	Quality of visual image as measured by resolution and color capability
Printer	Print technology (laser, ink-jet, etc.)
	Quality of print image (text and graphics)
	Speed as measured by characters per minute, pages per minute, or lines per minute
Modem	Speed as measured by kilobits per second

the data path should directly relate to processing speed. In practice, however, although larger data paths are without a doubt faster, a direct proportion of speed to size is not realized because of software and waiting for other hardware components such as input and output devices.

Evaluating the speed of a CPU can be confusing because different terminology and measures are used. The term *megaflop* (MFLOP) is used to compare the processing speeds of different types of computers. A megaflop is defined as a million mathematical calculations per second. This is similar to the commonly used acronym MIPS, which designates a million instructions per second. However, in comparing CPUs, probably the most common speed measure is megahertz (MHz), which is a million machine cycles per second. A machine cycle is defined as the number of electronic pulses that a CPU can generate as controlled or timed by its own internal clock. A machine cycle can be compared to a traffic light that goes through a timed sequence of red, yellow, and green signals. When the timing sequence changes (speeds up or slows down), the lights change accordingly. In the case of a CPU, the time pulses control the execution of instructions, so that the more pulses that can be generated, the faster the CPU operates.

Performance of various input and output devices is also frequently measured in terms of capacity or speed. Storage capacity of magnetic disk equipment is measured in megabytes (millions of bytes), gigabytes (billions of bytes), and terabytes (trillions of bytes). The most important speed measure for magnetic disks and most input/output devices is transfer rate, which is simply the speed of moving data from the device to the CPU as measured in millions of bits per second.

These various measures may seem a bit confusing, or perhaps even alarming, because they involve speeds and numbers that are impossible for most people to conceptualize. However, in evaluations, the relative speeds and capacities are more important than the absolute. A 240-MHz machine is twice as fast as a 120-MHz machine, which is twice as fast as a 60-MHz machine.

For devices such as video displays and printers, the quality of the output is as important as speed. As an example, many users prefer the quality of a laser printer even though it might be slower than other types of printers. Readers may wish to review Appendix A, which compares the characteristics of various output devices.

Reliability and durability are important factors but are sometimes overlooked because they cannot be measured with the same precision as other performance criteria. Evaluation of these factors is best handled by contacting other users or research services, such as Datapro Research Group (1995). Computer operations managers frequently keep logs of hardware downtime and are willing to share this information with colleagues. In evaluating durability, keep in mind that usage variables may exist that might not apply in all situations. For example, keyboards in a primary school computer lab used frequently by many young children might not last as long as keyboards used occasionally by adults. In evaluating reliability and durability, the best approach is to seek information from similar environments.

Compatibility

Compatibility is a common term in technology but is used two different ways—referring either to the capability of one device to work well with another device, or the capability of one device to work the same way as another device. An important element of compatibility is whether the hardware manufacturer supports *open system architecture*, which essentially means that all hardware specifications are made public so that third party manufacturers can develop components that are in fact compatible. Many smaller hardware manufacturers market their products based on their compatibility (to work well) with other equipment. Manufacturers of peripheral equipment such as disk drives or printers will always identify their products' compatibility with various central processing units. For example, Hewlett-Packard makes laser printers that are fully compatible with IBM PC and Apple Macintosh microcomputers. As more school districts have become involved in designing WANs or LANs, it has become critical for them to know whether the various hardware components (CPUs, printers, disk devices, etc.) of these networks are compatible and can connect to one another.

The ability to meet compatibility criteria is easy to judge because no relative measures are involved. The equipment is either compatible or not. Qualified compatibility, percentage compatibility, or other "gray area" compatibility should not be accepted. The vendor should be able to demonstrate to a customer's satisfaction the complete compatibility of the equipment.

For a computing device to work the same way as another means that it will execute a program in the exact same fashion. A good example is the number of manufacturers that sell "IBM-compatible" equipment. This is critical for any applications that are expected to share the same programs, such as a common database system or an instructional local area network. Generally, the hardware products from a common vendor will execute programs in the same way. Historically this was not always the case. As an example, Apple Computer marketed two popular microcomputers in the 1980s—Apple IIs and Macintoshes—that were not compatible or were incapable of running the same programs.

In plans for technology at the district level, compatibility is frequently considered as an overall policy issue and one that is not left to individual schools. Many districts establish compatibility guidelines that restrict the types of equipment that can be purchased. It is an excellent discussion item for any planning committee because it leads naturally into long-range thinking about hardware.

Modularity/Expandability

Modularity and expandability are also very important factors for long-range planning. Some hardware analysts consider these to be two different factors that should be evaluated separately. However, the importance of modularity frequently manifests itself when considering expansion, and therefore these two features can be evaluated together. *Modularity* refers to the interchangeability of components or parts of a hardware system. For example, can RAMs or ROMs easily be replaced in a CPU, or can several different types of devices be used or interchanged on an input/output port? *Expandability* is the ability of computer hardware to grow or expand as new applications are developed or as old applications become larger.

The evaluation of modularity and expandability is critical, especially in the acquisition of mainframe computer systems. Because of the costs involved, computer operations managers tend to develop equipment plans that stagger the replacement of certain components of a large hardware system at set intervals. A simplified example of the replacement cycle for a mainframe computer might be as follows:

Component	Replacement cycle
CPUs	Years 1 & 2
Data communications controllers	Year 3
Secondary storage devices	Years 3 & 4
Input/output devices	Years 5, 6, & 7

At the end of 7 years, the cycle repeats itself depending on application growth, financial condition, and available technology. As a result, mainframe systems are acquired as a series of upgrades rather than as onetime, total system replacement. It would be impossible to function in this mode unless the equipment was both modular and expandable.

Modularity and expandability should also be considered in acquiring microcomputer systems. For example, as with large systems, users should know how many and which type of input and output units can be attached or whether the primary storage can be expanded. Information on these issues is readily available from manufacturers and retailers. However, these factors are not quite as critical because at some point the entire microcomputer system will be replaced.

Modularity and expandability depend to a certain extent on the currency of the equipment's technology. Technology is constantly evolving. To expand, newly purchased equipment should not reflect old technology being phased out or considered "dead-ended." By the same token, some new technology is experimental and may not catch on or may quickly be replaced by newer technology. This is not a common problem, but even the major manufacturers have had to discontinue products (e.g., IBM PC Junior and Apple Lisa) because of changes in technology, design problems, or customer apathy. Information is readily available from user groups and trade journals on the nature of the technology being used on most major manufacturers' equipment. If serious doubts exist about the technology of equipment under consideration or if information is difficult to come by, this might indicate a problem and should be evaluated accordingly.

Ergonomics

Ergonomics describes hardware features directly related to whether the equipment is user-friendly. Is it pleasant to use? Is it easy to use? Most manufacturers of hardware—particularly items like keyboards, video displays, and other widely used devices—do consider the people who have to use their equipment. For example, the basic color patterns for most computer equipment are soft, pleasing to the eye, and blend into office and classroom environments.

For administrative applications, the feel of a keyboard is very important to staff who may be using the equipment for many hours at a time. Some of the early microcomputers used what was known as a "chiclet" keyboard, so named because the keys were small plastic pegs that looked and felt like Chiclet chewing gum. Although fine for occasional use, they were a problem for many typists. Their feel was different from a standard typewriter keyboard, and their spacing was more compact, which caused coordination problems. Although they are still available on some portable computers, they have been replaced on desktop microcomputers by the standard keyboard. Several manufacturers also offer keyboards that are designed to reduce stress to ligaments and muscle tissue in the wrists and lower arms. These may be more appropriate, especially for secretaries and other staff who use a computer for long periods of time.

For instructional applications, various ergonomic features such as video display resolution, color, and sound capability can add significantly to lessons and presentations. However, the potential of these features is generally realized only through appropriate graphics and audio software. Other ergonomic features and options important for instruction include the availability of special hardware features for younger children, such as the enlarged Muppet keyboard and voice synthesizers, Braille keyboards, and large video screens for special education students.

Software Availability

In evaluating hardware, it is most desirable to identify the software that will meet the needs of an application. A determination can then be made as to whether the identified software can run on the hardware being evaluated. This principle may seem obvious, but situations abound in which schools have acquired equipment without consideration of software. Administrators or teachers then search for applications that in some cases cannot be found or do not exist.

Such situations are typically more of a problem with small manufacturers but can also arise with the major manufacturers. A good example of this occurred when the Apple Macintosh microcomputer was first introduced in 1985. In terms of most hardware evaluation criteria such as performance, ergonomics, and vendor, the Macintosh rated very highly. However, very little software was available for it. Although the Macintosh provided a very advanced authoring language in Hyper-Card, none of the popular software products developed by independent software companies could run on it. As a result, many schools that had invested significant resources into Apple II microcomputers were slow to acquire the newer Macintoshes. Although many instructional software developers caught up with Macintosh hardware technology in the early 1990s, software availability is still an issue, especially when one considers the number of software products available for DOS/Windows machines.

Vendor

For more information on vendor performance, go to the *Web Links module* for this chapter on the Companion Website at **www.prenhall. com/picciano**.

A hardware investment is usually long-term. Through the purchase of hardware, schools are also buying into a long-term relationship with a vendor. This is particularly true for mainframe systems but exists to a certain degree for all hardware acquisitions. The vendor should be evaluated in terms of reputation, technical support, training, hardware maintenance, and industry position.

Most schools find themselves in situations in which they have already had experience with one or two manufacturers. These experiences are valuable and provide the best information regarding a vendor's performance. Additional information is easily obtained from services such as CNET, journals such as *Technological Horizons in Education,* and buyers' guides such as ZDNet. However, the computing industry is dynamic; many new companies have entered it, and many have left. School administrators should be open to, and aware of, some of these dynamics.

IBM has been a dominant manufacturer of mainframe, minicomputer, and microcomputer equipment for decades. Its reputation for technical support, maintenance, and software availability, among other things, is excellent. For certain segments, especially in private businesses and corporations, IBM has cornered in excess of 70% of the world market. However, IBM struggled in the 1980s and 1990s to keep up with the competition in the microcomputer market and failed to maintain its base as customers switched from larger to smaller computer systems. As a result, relatively new companies such as Dell, Compaq (now a division of Hewlett-Packard), and Gateway became the dominant manufacturers of microcomputer systems. In December, 2004, IBM announced the sale of its entire PC division to a Chinese manufacturer (Lenova) of microcomputers.

In the primary and secondary school instructional microcomputer market, the market share picture is different. Apple Computer had dominated this market for many years. The foundation of Apple's success was based on the wide acceptance of the Apple II microcomputers, which were first introduced in the late 1970s, followed by the introduction of the Macintosh in the 1980s. Apple is a classic example of the dynamics of the computer industry and how a new company that began in 1976 can become a major player in a short time. In the 1980s, Apple was clearly a leader in microcomputer design and manufacturing. In the 1990s, because of increasing competition from new companies, Apple struggled to maintain its leading position and began to lose its market share, even in the primary and secondary schools. Estimates indicate that Apple's share of the total microcomputer market is approximately 3 percent (Dvorak, 2004) while maintaining about a 25 percent share of the education market (Trotter, 2002).

Since the 1960s, many well-known companies such as RCA, General Electric, Osborne, and Coleco have either merged, declared bankruptcy, or left the industry (see Figure 9.3 for a timeline of Amiga computer products). Now hundreds of companies provide computer hardware products.

FIGURE 9.3   **The Dynamics of a Computer Manufacturing Company**

1987 - Commodore International introduces Amiga A2000 and A500 machines.

1992 - Commodore introduces more powerful A4000 and A1200 machines.

1994 - Commodore International files for bankruptcy.

1995 - Escon A. G., a German computer retailer, takes over the Amiga line.

1996 - Escon files for bankruptcy.

1997 - Gateway takes over the Amiga line.

1999 - Gateway drops plans for the Amiga and sells Amiga assets to Bill McEwen (Gateway executive).

2000 - Amiga, Inc., is established by Bill McEwen and announces plan for a new line of Amigas.

Cost

School administrators understand the importance of costs as a factor in all equipment acquisitions, including computer hardware. Defining costs for hardware can be complex and involves initial acquisition, yearly maintenance, lease purchases, and a host of other possible arrangements. School administrators, particularly in public bidding situations, find the competition very keen. Many of the smaller companies provide very attractive proposals that can result in substantial savings. Needless to say, all proposals, regardless of the source, need to be very carefully reviewed and evaluated. (Financing computer applications, including hardware costs, is given full treatment in Chapter 13.)

SPECIAL CONSIDERATIONS FOR ADMINISTRATIVE APPLICATIONS

In evaluating hardware for administrative applications, several special considerations need to be mentioned. Because an objective of many administrative applications is developing information resources, certain hardware evaluation criteria such as compatibility and modularity/expandability become critical to ensuring that all equipment can contribute, connect, and grow together. Information needs to flow smoothly up, down, and across the school organization; any present or future incompatibility of hardware can seriously jeopardize this. As a result, school districts tend to establish central district control in developing hardware evaluation guidelines for administrative applications. In many cases, this might mean hardware standardization policies, district-wide procurement plans, or direct approval procedures by a district coordinator.

In school districts with large administrative computer operations, administrators generally do best by relying on their technical staffs. The technology for large systems is very sophisticated, and a trained staff is probably in the best position to conduct in-depth hardware evaluations and to recommend acquisition policies.

Administrative applications such as budgeting, personnel, and inventory control and the hardware used for them are almost identical to those in private industry and public agencies. Administrators and teachers involved with evaluating hardware for administrative applications should take advantage of the extensive data resources available in the private sector in addition to those in the educational sector. Many of the trends that have developed in administrative applications—such as data communications, optical disc storage, and laser printers—had their first applications in private industry.

Hardware manufacturers are increasingly designing all equipment to support and function in the client-server environment on which Internet technology is based. In large districts where schools are geographically dispersed, a wide area network likely is, or will be, put in place to integrate these schools and to connect the network to the Internet. Planning and upgrading data communications services to function effectively in the dynamic world of the Internet continues to be one of the more complex areas of technology. If necessary, consultants should be considered, especially when designing something new or making a major upgrade to an existing data communications system.

SPECIAL CONSIDERATIONS FOR INSTRUCTIONAL APPLICATIONS

Evaluating hardware for instructional applications has evolved differently from administrative applications because many school districts have allowed more control and flexibility at the school level. To a degree, this is the result of differences in the hardware available for different subjects and grade levels. Hardware that is appropriate for teaching basic skills in the early grades may not have been appropriate for teaching business in the high schools or for doing desktop publishing. Districts will frequently provide guidelines for teachers to recommend equipment that they think will work best in their classrooms. As a result, some diversity of equipment, particularly with microcomputers, can be expected. However, administrators should also be careful to avoid a "technology of Babel" situation in which the district acquires many different machines that cannot communicate with one another.

Software availability is probably the most significant factor in evaluating hardware for instructional applications because, in many cases, teachers tend to identify software first and even consider it a far more important decision than the hardware. Teachers need to be aware of the hardware requirements of any software they are considering. All instructional software developers identify their products' hardware requirements. In addition, certain software packages used to control special-purpose devices such as voice synthesizers, scientific probes, DVDs, and videodiscs may work only with particular equipment.

Data communications capability has become increasingly more important as school districts seek to establish and maintain high-speed and reliable connections to the Internet. To plan for the development or expansion of a school district's data communications system to support instructional applications, a major hardware consideration is connecting local computer systems into local area (LAN) and wide area (WAN) networks first, and then connecting these to the Internet via a common communications interface. There can be many variations of this basic approach of computers connecting to LANs, LANs connecting to WANs, and WANs connecting to the Internet. Wireless networks (WLANs) also are becoming increasingly popular. Many benefits will derive from a well-planned network, but it is also a more complex technology than a stand-alone environment. If the expertise does not exist within a district, administrators should consider using consultant services in designing and evaluating the hardware required for a network.

C A S E   S T U D Y

PLACE: APPLETON   YEAR: 2004

Appleton is a small, suburban school district located in the Midwest with
a population of 3,000 students. It operates one high school, two middle
schools, and three primary schools. The school population decreased in the
1980s but has stabilized and has been increasing slightly since 1995. The
tax base for the school district has been very good mainly because of the relo-
cation of a large corporation into the district in 1990. The district considers
technology important to the instructional program. A district-wide planning
committee, established in 1985, has been most supportive of acquiring
microcomputer equipment at all grade levels. The student-per-microcomputer
ratio for the district is 5.8:1, with the distribution of instructional equipment
as follows:

High school - 210 units as follows:
160 Windows/PC compatibles including Dell, Gateway, and IBM
50 Apple Macintoshes

Middle schools - 150 units as follows:
100 Windows/PC compatibles including Dell, Gateway, and IBM
50 Apple Macintoshes

Primary schools - 160 units as follows:
85 Windows/PC compatibles including Compaq, Dell, and Gateway
75 Apple Macintoshes

A basic hardware acquisition policy of the district has been to make sure that
in every school there are both Windows and Apple Macintosh microcomputers.
While much of the equipment is distributed to individual classrooms, each school
has at least two central computer laboratories: one for Windows/PC machines and
one for Apple Macintosh machines. In recent years, with the exception of the art

SUMMARY

This chapter describes the major factors in evaluating computer hardware. Because
this equipment will be retained for many years, it is critical to approach hardware
selection as a long-term investment requiring careful evaluation.

classes, there has been significantly decreased use of the central Apple Macintosh laboratories in all the schools.

An issue facing the district as it continues to acquire technology is whether to standardize its equipment for instructional applications. The factors involved are varied. First, much of the equipment currently in use, particularly in the middle and primary schools, was acquired in the late 1990s and needs to be replaced because the costs of repairs are increasing significantly. Second, the principals in the high school and two middle schools would like to close their Apple Macintosh central laboratories, standardize with only Windows/PC compatible machines preferably from one manufacturer, and distribute more equipment to individual classrooms. Third, the principals in the primary schools have indicated that they would like to close all their central computer laboratories and distribute more equipment into individual classrooms. They also indicated that they would like to continue to have a combination of both Windows/PC and Apple Macintosh machines. Fourth, it should be mentioned that for administrative applications, the district has purchased only Windows/PC microcomputers that are used for local school building applications, district-wide applications, and as communications terminals to a state-wide database system.

DISCUSSION QUESTIONS

1. Assume that you are the superintendent and have been asked by the board of education to develop a preliminary 3-year proposal for the district's planning committee to replace computer hardware for instructional applications. What are some of your options/priorities?

2. What is your position on central laboratories versus putting more equipment into the classrooms?

3. Lastly, what are the benefits and costs of the principals' recommendations concerning eliminating (in the high school and middle schools) or at least reducing significantly (in the primary schools) the use of Apple Macintosh equipment?

The major criteria to be considered when acquiring computer hardware are performance, compatibility, modularity/expandability, ergonomics, software availability, vendor (support, maintenance, industry position), and cost. Although some of these factors may be considered more important than others, none of them should be ignored when acquiring equipment.

In selecting and evaluating hardware, administrators need to be aware that the policies of a district might be different for administrative and instructional applications. Administrative applications tend to be controlled centrally at the district level to ensure compatibility and an easy flow of information across the administrative structure. Instructional applications frequently result in more diversity of equipment, mainly because of different subject and grade-level needs. Software availability, which may limit the acquisition of hardware to particular manufacturers or models, is especially critical in instructional applications.

KEY CONCEPTS AND QUESTIONS

1. Evaluating and selecting hardware requires a serious consideration of long-range implications. Why? What are the characteristics of hardware acquisition and use that tend to make schools dependent on particular machines or manufacturers for many years?

2. In evaluating hardware, the major factors are performance, compatibility, modularity/expandability, ergonomics, software availability, vendor, and cost. Are any of these factors more important than the others? If so, why or under what conditions?

3. Performance simply refers to how well a piece of equipment works in terms of capacity and speed. What are some of the specific performance criteria used in evaluating computer hardware? Which do you consider the most important?

4. In evaluating hardware, many administrators consider compatibility with other equipment a most critical factor. Why? Is compatibility a universal factor that is always important, or can it be more or less important depending on the application?

5. Software availability might be considered the major factor in acquiring hardware. In fact, in many districts, it is common to identify the software to be used before acquiring hardware. What are some circumstances or situations in which the software might be the most important factor in selecting hardware?

6. As with most expensive equipment acquisitions (e.g., school buses, maintenance vehicles, air conditioners), the vendor or manufacturer is a major consideration. Is this any different with computer hardware? Is it more or less the case? Why?

7. Administrative and instructional applications are different. Do these differences affect the way in which hardware is evaluated for them? Should a district establish acquisition policies that recognize these differences? Explain.

SUGGESTED ACTIVITIES

To complete the Suggested Activities online, go to the Companion Website at **www.prenhall.com/picciano,** then to this chapter's *Suggested Activities module.*

REFERENCES

Datapro Research Group. (1995). *Management of microcomputer systems* (Vols. 1 & 2). Delran, NJ: McGraw-Hill.

Dvorak, J. C. (2004, December 28). Grim Macintosh market share forebodes crisis. *PC Magazine.* Retrieved online (http://www.pcmag.com/article2/0,1759,1745930,00.asp).

Ferrante, R., Hayman, J., Carlson, M. S., & Phillips, H. (1988). *Planning for microcomputers in higher education: Strategies for the next generation* (ASHE-ERIC Higher Education Report No. 7). Washington, DC: Association for the Study of Higher Education.

Meltzer, K. H. (1990). The district automation project. *Technical Horizons in Education Journal, 18*(4), 84–85.

Trotter, A. (2002, May 15). Apple struggles to regain share of school market. *Education Week.* Retrieved online (http://www.edweek.org/ew/articles/2002/05/15/36apple.h21.html).

Chapter 10

Software Selection and Evaluation

Hardware, with its flickering lights, buzzing circuits, and colorful screens, may seem like the exciting component of computer technology, but among many computer professionals, software is where the action is. A computer cannot perform a single function unless a software program has been developed to provide instructions for the hardware. Some programs can be easily written with several basic commands, whereas more complex programs may require hundreds of thousands of instructions. Programmers who are involved in such large-scale software development are among the most talented and creative in the computer industry. Their completed work can engender feelings of accomplishment similar to those of an artist who has just completed a painting or a chef who has prepared a magnificent meal.

On the other hand, when something goes wrong, when a computer bug occurs, feelings of accomplishment can quickly fade. If a program is critical to an operation, a great deal of stress and frustration develop that evoke mental images of other, more appealing lines of work. These feelings last until the bug is found and corrected, and a sense of accomplishment returns, beginning the cycle again, waiting for the next bug to emerge.

With the proliferation of computing technology over the past decade or two, this scenario occurs at many levels—perhaps involving a team of software engineers correcting the transmission of data from a NASA satellite, a staff of computer programmers in a state education department implementing an electronic educational exchange and bulletin board, a secretary experimenting with new features of the latest version of a word processing package, a high school class creating a home page on the Web, or a group of 4th graders completing their first newsletter with a desktop publishing program. Software surely is where the action is, where things happen, and where feelings of joy and frustration come and go in relation to successes and problems.

Selecting the software that teachers, administrators, and students will be using may therefore be the most important technical decision made in implementing computer applications. The topic of this chapter is the selection and evaluation of computer software. Commonly used evaluation criteria that are appropriate for both administrative and instructional applications are examined.

DECISIONS, DECISIONS, DECISIONS

Tom Snyder Productions, one of the more successful instructional software development companies, markets a series of excellent simulation programs titled Decisions, Decisions. These simulation programs require students to make frequent decisions regarding real-life phenomena. Depending on the decision selected, new situations are created, each requiring the students to make additional decisions. The series title provides an *almost* adequate description of the real-life activity of evaluating and selecting software: "Decisions, Decisions, and More Decisions" may be more appropriate. With tens of thousands of software products available, the possibilities are mind-boggling. Even after a software package has been selected, new versions of it quickly appear—requiring yet another decision. Software updates, modifications, and new releases are commonplace in computing life. The number and types of decisions related to software have grown considerably in the past 20 years.

Although the fundamental nature of software has not changed over the past several decades, its acquisition, people-interface formats, and implementation have changed radically. Throughout the 1970s, all computer installations required a well-trained software staff to develop application programs using high-level languages such as COBOL, FORTRAN, or PL/1, provided by the hardware manufacturer. Today, in large computer installations, a good deal of application program development still exists, but programmers are also making much greater use of software development tools such as database management systems, communications control software, and HTML filters that significantly reduce the number of high-level language instructions. In some cases, these software tools are provided by the hardware manufacturers, but more likely they are supplied by software development firms.

In traditional large mainframe applications, users are very dependent on the programming staff for support, documentation, maintenance, and modification of the software. A major application such as a student record-keeping system or a financial management system can have a useful life cycle of 15 years or more. As a result, users and programmers must have good working relationships and procedures for regularly maintaining and upgrading these systems. Clear lines of responsibility may be drawn, with the users identifying needs and improvements, and the programming staff modifying the software. In the most successful situations, the overall software decisions are shared between the users and the technical staff.

The movement to microcomputer technology has changed the technician-user relationship. The vast majority of microcomputer users do not program in a high-level language but instead purchase software packages for word processing, spreadsheets, desktop publishing, and a host of other applications. Most of these packages require only a basic understanding of how to load a CD-ROM or a disk and to respond to a series of menus, prompts, and alternatives. With good documentation and minimal technical support, users are expected to be able to master enough of the features of these packages to do most of what they wish to accomplish. Not unexpectedly, the degree of user success in these environments varies. User aptitude and experience are factors, but the choice of appropriate software is also a critical and determining factor.

The Internet and World Wide Web have also significantly changed the way software is developed and acquired. With so many companies, schools, and individuals using the Internet, many companies have had to reconsider how their software products can be used in a networked environment. As a result, many of them are now providing Web versions and interfaces to be used on the Internet or on local intranets.

In some cases, stand alone software products are being completely redeveloped as Web products.

For most administrative users, the major applications and appropriate software programs center on database, spreadsheet, word processing, desktop publishing, and office automation applications. Although many packages exist for these applications, several major vendors—such as Microsoft and Lotus—are beginning to dominate the market. For instructional microcomputer users, the number of applications and appropriate software packages is becoming almost unlimited. Depending on subject, grade level, and student interests and abilities, thousands of software packages exist, and the number keeps increasing every day. Presently, hundreds of companies are marketing educational software products. In addition, there are unknown numbers of programmers working in colleges, school districts, and state agencies who have developed packages, most of which are available free of charge, for use in primary and secondary schools.

School districts have begun to establish instructional software evaluation teams to sort through and evaluate all that is available. Large school systems such as those in Chicago and New York City employ full-time staffs whose major responsibilities involve evaluating and selecting software for use in their schools. Some states have established effective state-wide software evaluation services that publish or provide online databases of their software reviews along with suggestions for developing lesson plans. Despite this centralization, more and more instructional software evaluation is being done at the school level. Frequently, it is an opinion-driven activity, with people liking or disliking certain products based on their knowledge, experiences, or teaching philosophies. Technology coordinators may have the greatest influence in evaluating and selecting software for use in the schools, but committees or teams of teachers and other professionals are increasingly involved in evaluating software as they would any other curricular or academic materials. Involving end users in software selection may seem obvious, but stories abound of teachers and others questioning the value of software products acquired by somebody else.

Regardless of the process by which software is selected in a district or school, administrators have a responsibility to ensure that the software is appropriate for its intended use. Although administrators need not be involved in every software evaluation activity, they should establish procedures to ensure that the appropriate technical and application (administrative or instructional) criteria are considered.

SOFTWARE EVALUATION CRITERIA

The most important factor in evaluating and selecting software is determining how well it meets the application's needs. For example, a word processing package might be evaluated in terms of text manipulation features, spell checking capabilities, and the number of type fonts supported, whereas a database package might be evaluated in terms of file handling capabilities such as data merging, query language, and sort features. These evaluation factors can be extensive. In a report issued by the U.S.

| FIGURE 10.1 | Major Software Evaluation Factors |

For a listing of these 200 instructional software evaluation factors, see *Appendix C,* which is found on the Companion Website, at **www.prenhall. com/picciano.**

Congress's Office of Technology Assessment (1988), a survey of regional educational software evaluation agencies identified more than 200 factors being used to evaluate instructional software. All of the factors for every school application will not be reviewed here; however, several major evaluation criteria (see Figure 10.1) are common to all computer software packages, as follows:

1. *Efficiency:* How well are the programs written?
2. *Ease of use:* How easy is the software to use?
3. *Documentation:* What is the quality and quantity of the documentation?
4. *Hardware requirements:* What hardware is needed to run the software?
5. *Vendor:* What is the reputation of the developer in terms of support, maintenance, and industry position?
6. *Cost:* How much does it cost?

These factors should be considered in the evaluation and selection of every software product. As is the case in judging hardware, one or more of these factors may be more important than the others, depending on individual circumstances and applications. Together with a determination of how well the software meets the needs of a particular application, they form the basis for evaluating all types of software.

Efficiency

Most software efficiency measures relate to the speed with which a program executes. Overall response times, data access or search time, and sort time all relate to the operational speed of a program and are easily quantified. For software packages that are to run on mainframe systems, technical staff are needed to evaluate efficiency. For microcomputer software, users with some assistance from technical

For more
information
about
professional
software
research firms,
go to the *Web
Links module* for
this chapter on
the Companion
Website at
**www.prenhall.
com/picciano.**

staff can evaluate basic speed measures such as response time and access time. Response time measures how quickly a program responds with the desired computer activity once a request has been made. It can refer to fetching a record from a database, answering a Help inquiry, or performing a calculation. Data access or search time refers specifically to locating data on a disk file. It directly relates to the number of records on the database and, more importantly, to the manner in which they are stored.

In evaluating data access times, the same disk equipment must be used when comparing software, because the speed of the disk hardware can greatly influence access times. In fact, the term *access time* is also used to measure the speed of disk equipment itself in fetching records, and this factor must be neutralized. For large record keeping applications involving thousands or tens of thousands of records, *sort time* or the time required to sequence or merge data is also frequently used to test the efficiency of file handling software.

Professional software research firms such as the InfoWorld Test Center generally use a method of measuring software efficiency called the benchmark test. Benchmark tests can be developed by technical staff in any organization, including schools. As described in Chapter 9, these tests consist of identifying tasks that the software being evaluated would be expected to perform, which are then executed on different software packages and measured in terms of speed. For example, in evaluating a sort feature of a database program, an appropriate benchmark test might be to sort the typical number of student records that might exist in a school's student files.

Benchmark tests are easy to perform but, again, it is essential to make sure that the hardware, data files, and any other factors that can influence speed are identical. Hardware characteristics, even within a family of computers, are very different, and software will perform differently depending on these characteristics. For example, a software benchmark test that compares two programs by running one on an Apple G3 iMac 350-MHz computer and the other on a G3 iMac 500-MHz is not valid because the inherent CPU speed of the iMac 500 is much greater than that of the iMac 350. The same would be true if the first program were run on an Intel Pentium III 500-MHz computer and the other on an Intel Pentium III 900-MHz computer.

Efficiency also relates to how well a program is written in terms of structure, logic flow, programming language, and so forth. When the source code (high-level language instructions) is available, it is desirable to have the technical staff evaluate the quality of the programs. This is generally a subjective evaluation dependent on the staff's knowledge and expertise. In cases in which only the object code (machine language instructions) is provided, this type of evaluation is not possible.

Ease of Use

The software evaluation factor of ascending importance in the past few years is ease of use. With machines being placed in offices, libraries, classrooms, and teacher prep rooms, their utilization depends significantly on how easy the software is to use. This factor relates directly or perhaps inversely to the level of knowledge of the intended users. Software that is to be used by a professional technical staff may be more difficult to use and may require a certain amount of training. Software that is to be used by occasional or beginning users such as students should be as user-friendly as possible. Menu-driven screens, online Help features, and good supporting documentation are characteristics of user-friendly software and should be evaluated accordingly. These are generally subjectively evaluated, although they can be reduced to a quantified individual or group rating.

In evaluating ease of use, seeking input from the target users is very desirable. Secretaries may be the best choice for evaluating a desktop publishing package, accountants for an electronic spreadsheet program, teachers for computer-managed instruction, and students for instructional software. This approach is an obvious example of involving users at various levels in a school in technology planning and implementation activities. Not only is their opinion important to the decision maker, but their involvement enhances the environment required for moving ahead with technology.

Documentation

The importance of documentation in software evaluation is consistently recognized regardless of the type of computer being used, the nature of the applications, or the level of expertise of the target users. The critical questions that should be clearly answered in the documentation are: What does the software do? How does it do it? and How do you use it?.

Documentation standards have grown considerably since the proliferation of microcomputers; therefore, good documentation is to be expected and should be evaluated most rigorously. In recent years, the documentation manual has been supplemented or replaced by user-friendly Help files. Product updates, frequently asked questions (FAQs), and troubleshooting services also are provided on the software vendor's Web site. Software designed to execute on mainframe computer systems and most administrative software tend to be well documented, mainly because of the competition but also because this kind of software has matured. Word processing, spreadsheet, and database packages from the major vendors come with a good deal of high-quality documentation. These vendors have learned that to be competitive in these markets, they must have comprehensive, easy-to-understand manuals, and intuitive, online Help features.

For instructional software, however, the quality and quantity of documentation varies. Some instructional software comes with little more than a CD-ROM and one or two pages of installation instructions. On the other hand, the more established companies will provide a complete set of installation and operating instructions. The best instructional software documentation will also include curricular materials and suggestions for integrating the package into classroom activities. Tom Snyder Productions, Sunburst.com, and the Learning Company are some of the major instructional software developers that have been attentive to providing good documentation with their products.

One of the exceptions to good documentation standards is software that may be available at little or no cost from software exchanges and individuals. It frequently may not have high-quality documentation, but this is to be expected given that the software is usually provided for free or just a nominal fee.

Hardware Requirements

This evaluation factor is the corollary to the software availability criterion used in evaluating hardware. Just as any hardware purchased must have available software, software being evaluated, likewise, may have specific hardware requirements. Generally, the hardware requirements for software are:

Specific computer manufacturer/model/platform or CPU

Minimum primary storage capacity

Minimum magnetic disk space

Specialized input/output devices

This information, along with any other specialized hardware requirement, is readily available from the software supplier.

Most major software developers provide products for all major software platforms, but some smaller companies only market for a specific machine. Because it has the largest share of the market, DOS/Windows is usually the preferred platform for these companies.

All software programs have some minimum primary storage requirements. For very popular software products reissued periodically as newer versions, purchasers should try to determine future primary storage requirements. For example, in the 1990s, earlier versions (2.0 and 3.0) of Lotus 1-2-3 spreadsheet software required 512,000 to 1 million bytes of primary storage. The recent version (9.5) required 8 million to 32 million bytes with voice input technology. Users might question why the need for additional storage. However, the software developers are attempting to provide additional options and capabilities to make their products more attractive and competitive. It is highly recommended that extra primary storage space exist on all computing equipment so that this particular requirement can be easily met when evaluating software.

Any software packages that perform some type of file handling will require disk space. As with primary storage, the basic rule is that whatever is needed presently will surely increase in the future. A standard computing adage is "You can never have enough disk space." You should remember this when evaluating the hardware requirements of software, especially for applications using large databases and multimedia files.

Many software products also identify certain specialized input/output or other peripheral equipment to use all of their features and options. For example, many software packages for microcomputers provide deluxe versions that require DVD drives. Many packages providing color images and graphs may require certain levels of screen resolution on video display equipment. Some instructional software packages used in science, music, or art may require certain quality sound boards, custom probe, synthesizer, or other specialized input equipment. When these packages are evaluated, this information is generally available and must be considered when selecting software. Failure to do so may result in acquiring software that will not run as planned on the school's hardware or, in the worst cases, not run at all.

In some situations, such as in selecting an integrated learning system, both hardware and software are evaluated together. This is a very desirable situation and streamlines evaluation activities considerably. In general, when the hardware and software can be planned and acquired together, one can expect a smoother implementation of the application.

Vendor

All of the vendor characteristics that apply to hardware evaluation—such as support, maintenance, industry position, and reputation—also apply to software. However, given that there are thousands of software companies, evaluating this factor becomes a more difficult undertaking. Some of these companies consist of one full-time employee; others employ thousands. Microsoft Corporation, one of the world's largest software suppliers, has tens of thousands of support staff employees. As with many acquisitions, it is important to know with whom you are dealing, particularly if you expect to establish a long-term relationship. In an industry as dynamic as software development, those companies with proven track records should be considered over other companies that may be here today and gone tomorrow.

For more information about software suppliers, go to the *Web Links module* for this chapter on the Companion Website at **www.prenhall. com/picciano.**

Track record cannot be considered in isolation, however, because many software companies specialize and develop expertise in limited applications. Companies that are the leaders in administrative software such as databases or spreadsheets may have very little expertise in instructional software such as simulations or interactive video programs. As a result, the evaluation of software vendors may require some in-depth exploration.

Software reviews, journal articles, and industry research services such as the Gartner Research Group, CNET, InfoWorld Test Center, and ZDNet are all excellent sources of information regarding vendors. *Technology & Learning* (formerly *Classroom Computer Learning*) includes a software review column in each issue and devotes at least one issue to the best instructional software products of the year. Anyone involved with software evaluation, be they administrators or teachers, should use sources such as these to become familiar with the major software suppliers.

Cost

Costs for software vary significantly. On large computer systems, some comprehensive contracts—including software, certain levels of on-site support services, and training—can easily involve millions of dollars over several years. Integrated learning systems that combine software, hardware, and curriculum can easily cost in excess of a million dollars for a large school system. Some course management software (CMS) providers may charge a modest flat fee for the basic software license but might also require additional per-user (e.g., student) fees that can become quite expensive depending upon the usage. In undertaking evaluations involving software of this magnitude, school districts must be careful and deliberate in making their selections.

On the other side of the spectrum, some instructional software programs for microcomputer applications cost less than $50. Where in the World Is Carmen Sandiego?, Broderbund Corporation's award-winning program, normally retails for $49.99 and on sale can be purchased for less than $20. Such inexpensive programs may be purchased simply for experimental purposes or as part of a software library without immediate application, which is desirable because it builds expertise and technical knowledge within a school. However, this approach should not constitute the modus operandi. Whether performed by an individual or, more desirably, by a team, software that is to be used regularly in a classroom should be reviewed and evaluated for both technical and instructional features. Simply because a software product might be inexpensive is not sufficient reason to relax or eliminate evaluation activities.

One of the most cost-effective approaches in acquiring software is the procurement of a site license. A site license allows the purchaser to use a software product for a number of users or computers. For example, Broderbund sells its award-winning Science Court series for primary school science classes. In 2004 a single copy of the program cost $799; 10 copies cost $4,000; and an unlimited site license cost $9,900. If a district planned to make extensive use of this program, the site license would be far more cost-effective than purchasing individual copies or even multiples of 10.

Chapter 13 provides a thorough treatment on finances and cost factors in acquiring technology. Readers are encouraged to review the material there.

ADMINISTRATIVE SOFTWARE EVALUATION FACTORS

Critical to software evaluation is a determination as to how well the software meets the specific needs of the application through the various features provided. Reviewing all the existing administrative applications software is not possible here, but Figures 10.2, 10.3, and 10.4 list some of the more important evaluation features for the three most popular applications: word processing, electronic spreadsheets, and databases. These features can be considered regardless of whether the specific software product is stand-alone or part of an integrated package such as Microsoft Office.

Microsoft Word and WordPerfect are the most popular word processing software packages in use today. Originally developed for the DOS/Windows machines, versions are also available for Macintosh computers. Both packages also measure up well against most of the features identified in Figure 10.2. Furthermore, they are regularly upgraded, with versions providing new features issued every year.

Figure 10.3 identifies some of the features to look for in electronic spreadsheet programs. Lotus 1-2-3, Microsoft's Excel, and Borland International's Quattro Pro are among the most popular packages. All of the products provide the standard spreadsheet cell and mathematical features. As spreadsheets advance in sophistication, more importance is being placed on graphics, charts, data presentation facilities, and integration with other software (word processing, database) applications.

| FIGURE 10.2 | **Features of Word Processing Software** |

Number and type of fonts
Number of type styles (boldface, underline, shadow, etc.)
Footnoting
Wordwrap
Menu-driven
Lengthwise printing
Print preview
Graphics integration
ASCII file conversion
Conversion of other word processing files
Multiple document processing
   (work on more than one document at a time)
Multiple column controls
Spelling checker (how many words?)
Thesaurus
Document security
Grammar checker

| FIGURE 10.3 | **Features of Electronic Spreadsheet Software** |

Number of rows and columns
Editing features
Copy features
Lengthwise printing
Multiple spreadsheet processing
Menu-driven
Spreadsheet merging
Spreadsheet security
Graphics integration
Database integration
Types and dimensions of charts (line, bar, pie, etc.)
Types of statistical functions supported
   Basic (summaries, averages, percentages)
   Advanced (standard deviations, correlations, analysis of variance)

| FIGURE 10.4 | **Features of Database Software** |

Database structure (relational, flat file, etc.)
File security
Report generator program features
Statistical reporting features
Query language capabilities
Database restructuring
Sort/merge
   Speed
   Options (ascending, descending, levels)
Data-sharing features
Conversion of other database files
File merge capabilities (electronic spreadsheet,
   word processing, address labels)

The most important administrative software evaluation decision is the selection of a database management package (see Figure 10.4). Although it is not unusual to experiment with different word processing and spreadsheet programs, most organizations, including schools, will standardize their database software and, once established, will be reluctant to change it. One of the most important features of database software relates to data and file sharing in both local and wide area networks. Given the inherent complexity of networked systems, administrators should rely on the expertise of the technical staff when evaluating the networking capabilities of database software. For many years, Ashton-Tate's dBASE had been the industry leader for database management software for microcomputer systems. However, other database products such as Access (Microsoft), Paradox (Borland), Approach (Lotus), FOCUS (Information Builders), and FileMaker Pro (FileMaker, Inc.) have become more popular. For mixed (mainframe and microcomputer) environments, products such as Oracle (Oracle, Inc.) and FOCUS (Information Builders) are often more appropriate.

Many school systems employ technical staff to develop customized programs for various administrative applications. Using high-level languages such as COBOL or PL/1, programming staffs have developed and continue to maintain extensive administrative applications for record keeping and data reporting. In these situations, school administrators make their most important decisions regarding technology when hiring their personnel and should defer to them on most matters of software development. Administrators should be involved in establishing major priorities and in ensuring that a good working relationship exists between the technical staff and the end users. Custom software developed by a district's staff should also be evaluated according to criteria established jointly by the technical staff and the end users. These criteria may vary significantly depending on the nature of the software; however, they should concentrate on the specific needs of the application.

INSTRUCTIONAL SOFTWARE EVALUATION FACTORS

Like their administrative counterparts, different instructional applications will have different needs and will require specific software features to meet these needs. As examples, a game simulation program such as Broderbund's Where in the World Is Carmen Sandiego? would be evaluated differently from an instructional tool such as the Learning Company's Student Writing and Research Center. A programming language such as Logo would be evaluated differently from a desktop publishing program such as Adobe's Pagemaker.

Please see the *Web Links module* found on the Companion Website, at **www.prenhall. com/picciano.**

As mentioned earlier in the chapter, the U.S. Congress's Office of Technology Assessment (1988), in a national survey, identified more than 200 factors that could be used in evaluating instructional software. Many of these factors relate to pedagogical and instructional quality considerations (e.g., content, motivation, creativity). Some factors (e.g., simulations, probeware) relate only to a particular type of software. Other factors include the qualifying phrase "where appropriate" to signify that they are not always to be considered. Appendix C, which is found on the Companion Website, provides a good reference for developing a software evaluation policy in a school district, provided administrators and teachers remain flexible and establish a manageable number of criteria.

Many school districts have adopted an instructional software evaluation form or checklist that highlights some of the more important criteria. The form approach does not necessarily provide the mechanism for a thorough evaluation and will not include the hundreds of factors identified. However, the form or checklist does have value; otherwise, it would not be employed in so many districts and schools. A software checklist, for instance, ensures a record of the opinions of the staff involved in doing the evaluation of some proposed software.

Because major software developers will provide preview copies of programs to a school free of charge and without any obligation to purchase, it is not necessary to purchase a product to do an evaluation. After previewing the software, the evaluators meet and discuss its strengths and weaknesses. Providing a common evaluation form helps focus the discussion.

The criteria can be identified in an open-ended or a check-off format. However, because the nature of these evaluations is subjective, the open-ended format may be more appropriate. It is also relatively simple to provide detailed explanations of the open-ended items in a supplementary manual of procedures for doing software evaluation. Figure 10.5 is an example of an evaluation form combining both the check-off and open-ended approaches. An evaluation form helps define the evaluation procedure itself, and administrators and teachers should work together to develop what they feel will work best in their schools.

The process of designing an instructional software evaluation form and procedure will provide many insights into the role of technology in the classroom and into many other curricular issues. Software evaluation should be a rigorous activity comparable to other important curricular and academic decisions. In addition to basic software evaluation criteria, the form in Figure 10.5 devotes an entire page to criteria associated with instructional quality.

| **FIGURE 10.5** | **Instructional Software Evaluation Form** |

North Central School District No. 1

Title:_____

    Company/vendor:_____

    Subject matter:_____

    Grade level:_____

    Cost:_____

        (Attach additional supporting information if necessary)

Type: Tutor: Simulation_____   Tutorial_____   Drill/practice_____   Game_____

      Tool: Word processing_____   Spreadsheet_____   Database_____   Other_____

      Tutee: Specify language/title_____

      Other/hybrid:_____

    Computer system:_____

    Special hardware requirements:_____

    Internet-based/enhanced:_____

Objectives:

Program description:

Efficiency:

Documentation:

Ease of use:

Evaluation
    Grade (0=lowest; 9=highest)

General characteristics		*Instructional quality*	
Efficiency:	_____	Content:	_____
Documentation:	_____	Pedagogical features:	_____

(continued)

| FIGURE 10.5 | *continued* |

Ease of use: ———   Motivational: ———
Company/vendor: ———   Creativity: ———
                                                         Feedback: ———
                                                         Evaluation and record keeping: ———
                                                         Audio/visuals/graphics: ———
                                                         Flexibility: ———

Overall rating: ____

Instructional quality (Comments)
Content:

Pedagogical features:

Motivational:

Creativity:

C A S E   S T U D Y

PLACE: METRO HIGH SCHOOL
YEAR: 2004

Administered centrally by a city board of education, Metro High School is
an inner-city, public high school with 2,500 students. It is a comprehensive high
school offering college preparatory and business programs. The school population has been increasing, particularly among Latino students. The school is

continued

Feedback:

Evaluation and record keeping:

Audio/visuals/graphics:

Flexibility:

Reviewer's name:_____ Date:_____

For further information on instructional software evaluation, readers are encouraged to review Chapter 5, which includes lists of popular software titles and instructional software developers.

considered by the board of education and the community to be a good school with a dedicated administrative and teaching staff. Metro High has been very fortunate in securing funds from the central board of education for computer technology. It has approximately 340 microcomputers in the school and a computer science program that has received a good deal of acclaim from the central board of education and parents. The computers are primarily housed in 13 centralized laboratories. However, in 1998, after various recommendations and discussions with the faculty, a decision was made to place some equipment into individual classrooms. As of 2001, all laboratories and classrooms were wired to the Internet.

Continued on next page

The former technology coordinator for 25 years retired in 2002. In the early 1980s, he was instrumental in developing the computer science program and actively sought funds from the businesses in the city and the administration for equipment. The principal depended upon him for making most of the decisions regarding the acquisition of hardware and software for the school. An acting technology coordinator, Mr. Carlos Ortiz, a mathematics teacher, was appointed in 2003 and appears to be doing a fine job.

Most of Metro High's technology resources (hardware, software, staff) are devoted to supporting the computer science program, which consists of four half-year courses as follows:

CSC 101: Introduction to Computers
Introduces students to fundamental hardware concepts and provides a beginning programming experience in BASIC

CSC 102: Computer Tools
Introduces students to four major software tools: word processing, electronic spreadsheets, databases, and a presentation authoring package

CSC 103: Internet and World Wide Web Technology I
A first course in the basics of data communications, Internet, and hypertext markup language (HTML) programming

CSC 104: Internet and World Wide Web Technology II
A more advanced course in Internet technology, including Web page design and introduction to Java scripting for the more serious student

All students in Metro High are required to take CSC 101 unless they can pass a computer proficiency test. All business students are required to take CSC 101, 102, and 103. CSC 104 is an optional course, with enough students enrolling so that at least one section of 104 is offered every semester. As a result, 90% of the students who graduate from Metro High have taken at least one computer science course, and a little more than 50% have taken two courses.

SUMMARY

This chapter describes the major criteria used in evaluating computer software. Because software directs or instructs the hardware, many professionals consider software to be the most important component of a computer application. Evaluating software therefore should be a rigorous activity involving both technical staff and end users.

A major issue facing the school is how to integrate computer technology into the curriculum. Several faculty from the social studies, language arts, and science departments have indicated that they need more support from the administration for hardware and software. In 2000, this same group of faculty was instrumental, after several years of discussions and meetings with the former technology coordinator, in having computers relocated from the centralized facilities into their regular classrooms. But although equipment was moved to the classrooms, it frequently consisted of older models. Furthermore, no provisions were ever made for acquiring software.

In a discussion with the principal and the assistant principal for instruction, Mr. Ortiz has suggested that the computer science program be reduced and funds reallocated to supporting and integrating technology into the regular classrooms. He specifically suggested that CSC 101, 103, and 104 be eliminated and that a course similar to CSC 102 be required of all students. He also suggested that five of the central computer laboratories be dismantled and equipment be redistributed to regular classrooms. Finally, he suggested that technology budgets be provided for all the academic departments to acquire software to integrate into their own courses.

The principal is not sure what to do and has asked the assistant principal to review the situation and give her a report with recommendations as to whether or not to support Mr. Ortiz's plan.

DISCUSSION QUESTIONS

1. Assume that you are the assistant principal. What recommendations do you think you would make?
2. What additional information or data might you need?
3. Who would you involve in helping to develop your recommendations?
4. Lastly, how would you deal with Mr. Ortiz's suggestion to establish software acquisition budgets in each department?

Several factors are common to most software packages and should always be considered when doing evaluations: efficiency, ease of use, documentation, hardware requirements, vendor, and cost. Evaluators should also examine the specific features of software packages in terms of how well they meet the needs of the planned application.

Administrative software such as word processing, electronic spreadsheets, and database management systems each have unique features. Evaluators should be familiar with these features when evaluating and comparing software packages.

The number of instructional software programs has increased significantly since the late 1970s. The sheer number of appropriate packages has made software evaluation a major undertaking. Because it frequently involves other curricular issues, evaluating instructional software requires a good deal of time and care. Evaluation teams should be familiar with the many factors that can be considered in evaluating the instructional quality of a software package. Evaluation procedures should be developed that best meet the needs of a school district and that allow for a good interaction of technical and pedagogical considerations.

KEY CONCEPTS AND QUESTIONS

1. Many computer professionals think that software is where the action is. Why? Compared with hardware, which do you consider the more important component in planning and implementing computer applications? Why?

2. In evaluating software, the major factors are efficiency, ease of use, documentation, hardware requirements, vendor, and cost. Are any of these factors more important than the others? Why? And under what conditions?

3. Efficiency refers to how well a program is written. What are some of the specific efficiency measures used in evaluating software? How would you test some of these measures while doing an evaluation?

4. With the introduction of microcomputers, people are using equipment for a variety of applications. Because so many people have become familiar with computer equipment, has this reduced or increased the need to produce software that is relatively easy to use? Explain. Who are the best individuals in a school to determine if a software package is user-friendly?

5. Of the major software evaluation criteria, some computer professionals consider documentation the most important factor. What questions does the documentation have to answer? As a software evaluation factor, is documentation more or less important depending on the nature of the application or the type of equipment being used? Explain.

6. The relationship between hardware and software is critical in implementing computer applications. In terms of software evaluation, provide examples illustrating the importance of this relationship.

7. Many instructional software programs have become very inexpensive. If this is so, is it necessary to establish extensive software evaluation procedures? Or can a school district simply allocate funds each year and let a technology coordinator select a number of packages for each school's software library? Explain.

SUGGESTED ACTIVITIES

To complete the Suggested Activities online, go to the Companion Website at **www.prenhall.com/picciano,** then to this chapter's *Suggested Activities module.*

REFERENCES

U.S. Congress, Office of Technology Assessment. (1988). *Power on! New tools for teaching and learning* (Report No. OTA-SET-379). Washington, DC: U.S. Government Printing Office.

Chapter 11

Staff Development

A n important ingredient for implementing change, improvement, and innovation in education is a knowledgeable and vibrant staff. Studies and research (Fullan & Pomfret, 1977; Huberman & Miles, 1984; Joyce, 1990; Joyce, Murphy, Showers, & Murphy, 1989; Joyce & Showers, 1988; Knapp & Glenn, 1996; Pink, 1989; Sheingold & Hadley, 1990) have consistently supported this concept. Regardless of the nature of change—whether it be introducing a new teaching technique or implementing a major new administrative policy—individuals involved must understand and to a degree accept what is expected and what is going to be done. Neglecting to develop this understanding among the people who ultimately will most influence success or failure will likely jeopardize the implementation of any new project.

In this chapter, staff development is examined as it relates to implementing technology in our schools. Although all school personnel should be participating in staff development activities, particular emphasis is placed on teacher development, because using technology in the classroom has become and will continue to be a critical need in most schools.

A LONG WAY TO GO

All schools in the country have acquired some computer equipment, and every indication is that the hardware acquisition trend that began in the late 1970s and grew significantly in the 1980s and 1990s is continuing in the 21st century. Using surveys and field visits, governmental agencies, industry analysts, and academic researchers have monitored the number of computers purchased, the types of components acquired, and the dollars schools have expended (Becker, 1994; Fatemi, 1999; Park & Staresina, 2004; Quality Education Data, 1996; U.S. Congress, 1995; U.S. Department of Education, 2000). These activities have helped administrators to make decisions to acquire equipment, develop facilities and infrastructure, and support technology services in their schools.

Data and surveys also report that this equipment is not being fully used. There have been anecdotes of microcomputers remaining unpacked in locked closets or sitting in the back of a classroom where they are rarely turned on because the teacher does not know how to use them. Studies and observations (Becker, 1994; Goodson, 1991; Northrup & Little, 1996; Park & Staresina, 2004; Trotter, 1999; U.S Congress, 1995) consistently report that the majority of teachers are not making extensive use of technology. They suggest a situation in which hardware and software were being acquired at an escalating rate in the schools, and yet many teachers appeared not to know how or were otherwise not using them. In a national survey conducted for *Education Week* in 2004, many teachers considered themselves beginners in the use of technology in their classes. Furthermore, in a national survey of 4th grade students, only 63% reported using a computer at least once a week in school. In 8th grade mathematics courses, only 32% of the students reported using a computer at least once a week (Park & Staresina, 2004).

If administrators are to develop strategies for correcting a serious imbalance between computer acquisition and technical knowledge, some background information on the causes would be helpful. One fundamental reason for the imbalance is that some of today's teachers, especially those trained before the early 1990s and before the proliferation of microcomputers, were not exposed to technology as part of their preservice teacher training programs. As a result, they did not include it as part of their teaching repertoire and have been slow to do so. Schools of education as well as state education departments (which are responsible for certifying teachers) generally had not required competency in technology as part of a teacher certification program.

This situation began to change in the 1990s, and the problem is alleviating as state agencies and schools of education have come to recognize the importance of a technologically literate teacher corps. Twenty-two state education departments require technology training for certification of teachers (Park & Staresina, 2004). Most teacher preparation programs have developed and are requiring methods courses in educational technology in their programs. These courses typically include the following:

- Basic operations, including use of hardware, software, and simple programs such as word processing
- Information technology, including use of the Internet, database searching programs, and simple presentation authoring tools
- Evaluation of instructional software
- Pedagogical issues, such as integrating technology into the curriculum and lesson planning
- Values and ethical issues, such as appropriateness of information resources, copyright, censorship, and plagiarism

School administrators are finding that new teachers and recent graduates of teacher preparation programs are more familiar with technology but need ongoing training to keep their skills honed.

A more difficult problem is an attitudinal one. Many teachers are not convinced of the benefits of using computer technology. Some teachers feel threatened by technology and see it as impersonal and an infringement on their ability to maintain control of their classroom environments. Educators have observed that the natural evolution of technology is such that it changes the nature of teaching. In schools that use technology extensively, teachers, in addition to their teaching role, must also adopt a techno-managerial role in providing instruction. In environments where advanced computer-assisted instruction techniques such as integrated learning systems are in operation, teachers are required to spend more time monitoring student progress and prescribing appropriate curriculum materials rather than teaching the subject matter.

In planning staff development activities, administrators should be prepared to deal with these attitudinal issues. Assuming that attitudinal concerns will go away simply by exposing teachers to the benefits of technology is a fallacy. Educators need to convey also that computer technology, although becoming an important tool in the teaching process, is not a substitute for caring, talented human beings.

One of the most important reasons that teachers do not use technology is that it is not always easy to implement in the regular classroom. In schools where teachers have received training, many other problems such as the lack of enough hardware, poor support services, or inappropriate software have hindered teachers' ability to use technology effectively in the classroom (Trotter, 1999). Administrators and teachers find they spend a good deal of time on solving basic logistical and technological problems associated with implementing effective technology applications. Even in school districts where training and staff development activities are provided, teachers need to continue to invest time and effort to feel comfortable using computer technology routinely in their classrooms.

Sheingold and Hadley (1990), in a national study of teachers who were identified as experienced and accomplished in integrating technology into their teaching, found that it took several years of practice to master computer-based teaching approaches. Although these teachers were supportive of staff development programs that have enabled them to use computer technology, they also cautioned against one-shot approaches or quick fixes. A major recommendation of this study was that there should be ample support and time for teachers not only to learn how to use technology but also to plan carefully for its use in the classroom. This may even require fundamental changes in the way teachers teach.

THE STAFF DEVELOPMENT PLANNING MODEL

Figure 11.1 is a schematic for a staff development planning model that can be integrated with the general planning for technology model discussed in Chapter 2. A basic assumption is that staff development is a product of the larger technology planning model. The major components of the staff development planning model consist of:

- Staff development (integrating staff development with other planning activities)
- Assessing needs (identifying the staff development needs of a district or school)

FIGURE 11.1   **Staff Development Planning Model**

- Designing a program that meets the needs of both district and school
- Providing incentives for staff to participate
- Implementing the program
- Evaluation and review

This model forms the framework for most of the discussion in the remainder of this chapter.

WHO LEARNS?

In planning staff development activities, the critical question is: Who learns? The simplest and broadest answer is: Everybody—administrators, teachers, clerical staff, and so forth. However, a more specific answer to the question should be related directly to a district's planning objectives.

Assessing staff development needs is a logical outgrowth of the computer applications that a district or school wishes to implement. In addition to identifying hardware and software, planning computer applications should also inherently determine the users and developers of these applications and identify the targets for staff development. If a district is planning to implement a new financial management system, it would be appropriate to assess the needs of financial managers, accountants, and clerical staff in using databases, query languages, or electronic spreadsheet software packages. If a district is planning to begin using word processing as a tool for teaching writing in the elementary school curriculum, it would be appropriate to assess the needs of the elementary school teachers in using word processing software. Once identified, the personnel (administrators, teachers, or clerical staff who will be using the actual applications) should be included in the process of determining needs and designing appropriate staff development activities.

Staff development should relate to a planning objective and, in the case of technology, to a computer application. Although some school districts adopt staff development as a planning objective in and of itself, this should be the exception and not the rule. Planning that continually identifies staff development as an objective without relating it to an application is indicative of a planning integration problem and should be reviewed. Just as hardware and software should relate to the applications a district wishes to implement, the staff likewise should be trained to implement or use these same applications.

The importance of principals, superintendents, and other leaders participating in staff development activities should not be underestimated. The example set when a school leader participates in staff development or when she or he begins to use some new technology is extremely powerful. A clear and direct message is sent that will be picked up by staff and others that developing staff and implementing technology are important.

High-level administrators who appear technologically illiterate or provide staff development activities for others but consistently avoid participation themselves send the opposite message. Many administrators rely heavily on some other person(s) to buffer them from technology. Such situations are very common and also unfortunate. These administrators would love to use the available technology but "just have not had enough time to learn it." In their schools, you will find that many of their teachers and other staff "have not had enough time to learn it," either. Readers may want to refer to Appendix B, which identifies the competencies required for educational administrators to be leaders in planning, developing, and implementing technology in their schools and districts.

DIFFERENT ALTERNATIVES FOR DIFFERENT NEEDS

Designing a staff development program should be done in a systematic way so that the proposed program relates closely to the district's overall technology plan. Simply offering several workshops each year that may or may not be relevant to a district's goals and objectives will not be effective. A major requirement in planning a staff development program is conducting a needs analysis to identify what the district needs to do. If a district has not provided very much staff development in the past, comprehensive analysis may be in order. If a district has been active in providing staff development and is experienced in using technology, then the analysis can be targeted to specific applications and educational objectives.

Doing a comprehensive needs analysis for the purpose of designing a staff development program for technology requires an in-depth examination of all existing and proposed computer applications, both administrative and instructional—followed by an evaluation of all staff (administrative, teaching, clerical, etc.) in terms of their technical knowledge and their abilities to develop, implement, or use these applications. The needs that are identified become the targets of the staff development plan.

Although some districts are able to do comprehensive needs analyses, most limit them to specific school populations, categories of applications, or specific applications. For example, doing a needs analysis and designing a training program for all 4th to 6th grade schoolteachers in the use of digital video technology involves a category of application for a specific school population, whereas a needs analysis and training program for 4th to 6th grade teachers in the use of Tom Snyder Productions' Science Court CD-ROM series involves a specific application for a more specific school population. Some districts may start with broad training of many teachers or staff and work to more specific applications; others might experiment with a smaller group and, if successful, expand the program for larger groups and categories of applications. Both approaches can and do work. Which approach should be taken is best determined by the district as part of its overall planning activities.

When identifying and targeting staff development to specific applications, planners should keep in mind that the common or unifying goal should always be to build and expand on the accumulated mass of technical knowledge and expertise (see Figure 11.2) in the district. As districts attempt to do more, a correspondingly larger accumulated mass of technical knowledge is required. An interesting characteristic of technical knowledge is that it grows almost naturally as a district implements more technology. Diane Ravitch (1992) referred to this phenomenon by describing educational technology

---

FIGURE 11.2   **Accumulating Mass of Technical Knowledge/Expertise**

School district

Schools/departments

Accumulating knowledge

---

as difficult and costly to initiate, but once established it has a "relentless forward momentum" (p. 7). Therefore, the more teachers and other staff use technology, the more they learn and the more capable they become of expanding to newer technologies.

As a result of staff development, a threshold or level of technical confidence is reached in most organizations that acts as a driving force from within for further technological enhancement and development. Many staff members will learn a great deal on their own through contacts with colleagues both inside and outside the school or district.

DESIGNING AND IMPLEMENTING EFFECTIVE STAFF DEVELOPMENT PROGRAMS

Designing and putting into practice effective staff development programs is a complex undertaking. The input of the target groups is most important and will provide many suggestions for the nature of the development activities. As much as possible, programs should be designed that provide some variety of activities (lectures, demonstrations, discussions, hands-on workshops, Web-based activities, etc.) and that take place over

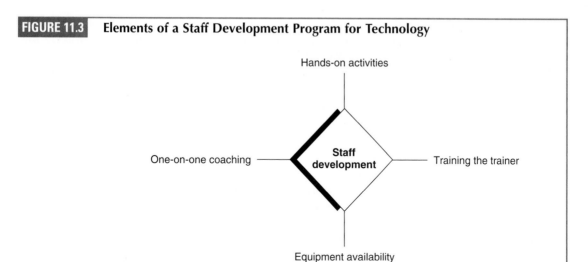

FIGURE 11.3   **Elements of a Staff Development Program for Technology**

an extended period of time to allow participants to practice and experiment. Staff development programs also require resources, and budgets need to be allocated as part of the design and implementation.

School districts use a wide-ranging assortment of staff development activities. Workshops (on- and off-site), large conferences, small seminars, World Wide Web courses, electronic bulletin boards, and user group activities abound. The most effective common elements (see Figure 11.3) for technology training are hands-on activities, one-on-one coaching, training the trainer, and equipment availability.

Hands-On Activities

A fundamental tenet of staff development for technology is the concept that you learn by doing; therefore, a portion of any technical training program should include hands-on activities. Participants can listen to and read about technology, but not until they use it will they develop an understanding. Consider how you learn to type. A teacher may lecture on how to type or a student can read about typing, but until the student actually types, he or she really cannot develop the skill of typing. The same is true with computer technology. To understand computer technology, you need to use hardware and to experiment with software, and the more you practice, the greater your proficiency. This holds true whether the target populations are high-level engineers and computer scientists, teachers, secretaries, students, or principals.

One-on-One Coaching

Individualized training or coaching is another characteristic of many staff development programs. If a district has support staff who can function as individualized trainers or coaches, they should be used. If not, then coaching should be provided by outside experts or consultants. Regardless of who provides the individualized training, short (1 or 2 hours), one-on-one coaching sessions are more effective than longer, large-group activities. A common format is a large-group, information delivery session followed by much smaller coaching sessions in which participants can practice or experiment with the assistance of a coach who customizes the training to individual needs. A variation of this format is to have participants enroll in a Web-based course, followed by smaller coaching sessions that are in person, made available through electronic bulletin boards, or a combination of both.

Training the Trainer

A certain amount of outside expertise and consulting is required for many staff development activities, but relying extensively on external trainers can become costly over the long term. A popular approach is to have outside consultants train a cadre of trainers who in turn will train large numbers of the staff. This "train the trainer" approach can be most effective in developing a core group of in-house experts who become actively engaged in sharing their knowledge with others.

A cadre of trainers can be a critical component that drives the entire staff development activity for a school or district. Such a group can begin with computer teachers, media specialists, and representatives from every department or grade level who have shown a particular interest in technology.

Deciding whether to convert numbers of present employees into full-time trainers depends upon the size of the district and the number of people to be trained. Large districts with thousands of employees would probably find that a group of full-time trainers would be less expensive than the large-scale use of outside consultants. Small districts might make training a part-time or add-on responsibility (for extra compensation) for existing full-time staff who have an aptitude for technology training.

Using existing staff versus outside consultants for training can also provide many attitudinal benefits. Teachers, for instance, might relate better to colleagues who are a few steps ahead of them in using technology in the classroom. A sense of "If they can do it, so can I" frequently develops. This approach also can be very effective in fostering a team or "We are in this together" attitude. It helps build an esprit de corps among the teaching staff that begins in the technology area and carries over into other areas of the school, such as implementing collaborative learning, reviewing a writing program, or expanding the teaching of process skills in science instruction. Given the many problems involved with integrating technology into the curriculum, training a group of trainers may be one of the most effective ways of resolving them.

Teachers Need Equipment, Too!

The design of a staff development program that includes hands-on activities implies that equipment, software, and other facilities are available for the participants' use. Along with other factors such as costs and travel arrangements, access to equipment becomes a critical consideration. Frequently, the number of participants may be limited by the availability of equipment.

Administrators understand the need to acquire equipment for instruction and student use, and providing this same equipment for teachers to learn and to use is also a necessity. Whereas secretaries and other administrative staff are routinely given equipment to take advantage of standard office automation applications such as e-mail, word processing, or electronic spreadsheets, teachers frequently are the last group to receive equipment from the district and in some cases are even expected to acquire it on their own. Given the premise that one learns technology by doing, attempts to integrate technology into the classroom are likely to fail if teachers are not able to practice, to experiment, and "to do computing."

The most common approach to resolving this problem is to set aside a teachers' area (laboratory, library, media center, lounge, study room, etc.) where equipment is provided exclusively for teachers' use. This approach is effective because it provides access to equipment and also allows for the informal exchange of information and ideas among peers. Teachers can work together on common computer applications, and a good deal of technology sharing can occur. For this reason, schools that have progressed and moved away from central computer laboratories and provide equipment for individual teacher use should also consider offering or maintaining a small central training area for teachers.

Some school districts have begun to adopt policies that aim at supplying every teacher with a portable laptop microcomputer. Though costly, this may be the best approach for providing teachers with access to equipment and ultimately for using technology in instruction. The Shoreline School District in Seattle, Washington, was among the first to adopt such a policy in 1989, providing a laptop for each of the district's 600 teachers (Schlumpf, 1991). Although the district owns the equipment, teachers are free to take the computers home. Administrators report that not only has this approach been effective in terms of staff development and the use of technology, but it also has unleashed a mass of creativity and has given the teachers a sense of technological empowerment. Other districts implementing a "computer for every teacher" policy have reported similar results (Buckley, 1995).

Before long every teacher will likely have a computer on her or his desk and one at home. Some administrators and teachers have doubts that this will happen, but a simple look at the desks of stockbrokers, insurance salespersons, department store cashiers, attorneys, and others suggests otherwise.

Incentives

Staff development programs should also consider providing incentives for teachers and others to ensure active participation. Both intrinsic and extrinsic rewards need to be considered for staff who become substantially involved with developing other staff and implementing technology in their schools. Professional growth, stimulating involvement with instructional innovations, experimentation with different teaching styles, and other intrinsic rewards may be the most important reasons that teachers become involved with technology. However, because of the time and effort involved, particularly in districts that have fallen behind technologically, more extrinsic incentives such as extra compensation, release time, or gifts of equipment are also needed.

Staff should be compensated for attending workshops, seminars, and other activities conducted in the summer or on weekends. Tuition reimbursements or sabbatical leaves should be considered for teachers who upgrade their skills by taking college courses. Teachers who agree to be trainers should receive extra compensation for assuming additional responsibilities. Those involved with developing a major new curriculum using technology or some other innovation should be provided with release time to evaluate and plan their materials carefully. Faculty involved with evaluating software (which if done properly can take many hours of viewing, discussing, and reviewing) should be compensated. Recognizing faculty who make a major contribution to staff development, in the form of a cash award or a gift of a laptop computer, can be a very strong inducement for others to participate.

The possibilities for providing incentives are extensive, and administrators should be attuned to offering incentives that would be most appropriate for the staff involved and for the nature of the contribution. In developing an incentive program, administrators may have to conform to existing employee compensation policies within the district. Schools that have advanced technologically develop a culture that lends itself more to incentives involving recognition and professional acknowledgment. Schools that have to catch up with technology or are planning major leaps forward should consider more direct rewards such as extra compensation and release time. Regardless, administrators should be able to identify incentives to which a school staff will respond, and provisions for them should be made accordingly.

Evaluation and Review

As with any other technology planning activity, staff development should be evaluated and reviewed. Participants in workshops or demonstrations should evaluate the effectiveness of these activities, and offer suggestions for improvements. Simple evaluation questionnaires distributed and collected at the end of a staff development activity are common practice. Depending on financial resources, external evaluators might also be considered. Because a major purpose of staff development is to have teachers and others using technology in their classrooms or offices, evaluation should also provide for some follow-up to determine whether participants have in fact been able to transfer their training to actual application.

Evaluation and review activities should not be considered the end of staff development. As with other planning activities, evaluation should naturally start the process of assessing needs and designing new staff development programs.

A Continuous Process

Planning a staff development program for technology should be a continuous process, primarily because technology is constantly changing and new equipment and software are regularly being introduced. Mechanisms should be in place for evaluating and sorting out new technology to determine appropriateness in a district. Some individuals must be provided with the resources to visit other schools or attend vendor meetings and specialized workshops that enable them to keep up with the technology. Determining who these individuals are is best decided as part of an overall planning activity. Obviously, computer coordinators and trainers are the most likely candidates; however, teachers who show an interest in or have an aptitude for technology should also be included.

The need for continual staff development will become apparent as planners review and evaluate their activities. Whether it be the evaluation of a single workshop or an entire year's program, the most common suggestions and requests from participants tend to be for additional staff development opportunities and activities. Besides the enjoyment they have in attending such activities, the staff members quickly recognize their need to learn and advance, advance and learn. As planners look at the broader staff development picture, they will see different individuals functioning at different levels along a skills or competencies continuum. The essence of their staff development planning will be to keep all these individuals moving along this continuum.

One inexpensive and effective approach to continuing staff development activities is to set up an electronic bulletin board. Such a bulletin board is dedicated to initiating issues and questions regarding the use of technology in a school or district. Trainers and staff development participants can share their work, ideas, or techniques with others and solicit feedback. Electronic bulletin boards are most effective as vehicles for follow-up activities to a staff development program or activity. In certain situations where participants already possess a degree of technological skill, they can be used in place of face-to-face activities.

■ RESOURCES

For more information on staff development program planning, go to the *Web Links module* for this chapter on the Companion Website at **www.prenhall. com/picciano**.

Although the emphasis in this chapter has been on developing and using in-house staff as much as possible, outside expertise and consultants should also be considered, particularly if a new or inherently complex technology is being considered.

Consultants abound in every state and most urban centers because the need for technical training is broad-based and exists in all types of commercial enterprises and public agencies. Before contracting with any consultants—whether private individuals, state agencies, or divisions of large corporations—administrators should do a careful review of their expertise and track record in providing the type of training or development that the district or school is seeking. Local colleges and universities, particularly if they have a school of education, generally are helpful resources for providing staff development expertise. Professional organizations and collective bargaining unions also have begun to offer staff development programs aimed at the use of technology in schools. Most states fund some type of assistance to school districts in the use of technology. User groups based on vendor hardware, special interests, common software, or subject matter are excellent sources of information and can be extremely valuable in helping keep school personnel current on technological developments.

Vendors know their products better than anybody else, and if they provide training services, which in many cases may be free or at a discount for customers, school districts would be wise to take advantage of them. Major technology corporations such as Apple, Microsoft, and IBM provide a wide range of training services and facilities. Major educational software suppliers such as Broderbund, Sunburst, and Tom Snyder Productions provide many excellent curriculum materials to help teachers use technology in the classroom. Vendors who specialize in particular products—such as Optical Data Corporation (video) and Novell, Inc. (local area networks)—have extensive expertise that they routinely provide to their customers and potential customers. In acquiring computer products, a vendor's background and reputation regarding support services, including training, should always be considered. Additional cost may be warranted if the staff's ability to use the product is facilitated.

C A S E   S T U D Y

PLACE: LEARNING TOWN   YEAR: 2003

Learning Town is an urban school district in the farm belt. It has 41,100 students and operates 75 schools. The board of education created a planning committee in 1985 that regularly establishes a broad set of goals for the district. The planning committee relies heavily on subcommittees to study issues at length and make recommendations, most of which it accepts. In terms of instructional technology, the board of education has been supportive. In 1991, a major procurement was made to equip the schools with microcomputers. Since then, the board has regularly allocated funds to allow each school to make incremental improvements in equipment and software. As a result, all of the schools have computer laboratories, a variety of software, and at least one computer coordinator. The overall student-per-microcomputer ratio is 5:1. Most schools have placed equipment in individual classrooms; however, each school still maintains one or more centralized computer facilities.

Last year a proposal was made to the board of education by the chair of the Middle School Principals' Association that the district consider making a major new thrust in the use of technology as a teaching tool. She recommended that the district make an investment in digital video technology and that each classroom be equipped with a teacher workstation that would consist of a microcomputer, a DVD player, and a large-screen projection system. Such a workstation would allow teachers to take advantage of new multimedia materials combining sound, pictures, and the programming power of the computer. Teachers would be able to use authoring languages such as HyperStudio and PowerPoint to enhance classroom presentations. Each school would also acquire digital camera equipment so that teachers could make and edit their own instructional video materials. She concluded her presentation with the success stories of two of the schools in the district that have begun using interactive digital video technology on a limited basis.

An ad hoc subcommittee of the district-wide planning committee has met six times in the past 5 months to study the feasibility of implementing this proposal. Members of the central administration have been supportive, providing a variety of data

SUMMARY

In this chapter, staff development is examined as a critical component for implementing technology in a school district. National estimates and other indications are that most schools have a long way to go to train their staffs, particularly teachers, in the use of technology. The reasons for this involve lack and analyses for the subcommittee members. Initial hardware costs for each workstation have been estimated at approximately $6,000. Costs for digital cameras, editing software, and supplies would vary depending on the size and level of the school.

The subcommittee appears split in terms of recommending this proposal to the planning committee. Whereas some members view interactive digital video as an exciting and stimulating instructional technology, others do not feel that the district should invest in it at this time. Specifically, some members are concerned that classroom instruction and effort would be better spent on basic subject matter and after-school tutoring sessions to ensure that students do well on state proficiency tests. The subcommittee has nearly completed its work for the year and would like to either recommend this proposal or table it for reconsideration next year. Also, the chairperson of the subcommittee has just received a memorandum from one of the committee members who represents the Teachers' Association. It indicates that the Teachers' Association discussed this proposal at its last two meetings and is very supportive. However, it stated that most of the teachers were not familiar with using digital video technology and would need training especially in developing and editing their own video materials. The head of the subcommittee, a supporter of the proposal, has asked the superintendent to do a quick analysis of the training needs of the district regarding the proposal before the next, and last, meeting of the year, which will be in 2 weeks.

DISCUSSION QUESTIONS

1. Analyze this case study assuming that you are the superintendent. What course of action do you take?

2. While you respect the divergent opinions of the subcommittee members, you would like to see the subcommittee recommend the proposal to the planning committee rather than table it until next year. However, you also recognize that the Teachers' Association has raised an important issue, and you do not have any data at this time to provide to the subcommittee. If your decision is to do a quick analysis, what information would you need?

of preservice training, attitudinal concerns, and lack of support services, which together have made it difficult for many teachers to use technology effectively.

Planning a staff development program should be integrated with other planning activities and should relate to the objectives that a district hopes to achieve. The key elements of a staff development planning model include assessing needs, designing programs for specific applications, providing incentives, and doing a review and evaluation. In designing a program, a unifying goal is the expansion of the mass of technical knowledge and expertise that exists in a school district. Staff development techniques proving to be most successful include hands-on activities, one-on-one coaching, in-house trainers, and ready access to equipment. Because of the time and effort required to implement new technology, administrators should be prepared to provide incentives such as extra compensation, release time, and recognition awards for staff who actively participate and make significant contributions to staff development activities.

Staff development is a continuous process. Technology changes and so do the people who use it. Planning staff development requires a long-term commitment that aims to upgrade technical skills gradually and continually rather than on a short-term or one-shot basis.

KEY CONCEPTS AND QUESTIONS

1. Staff development for technology has been a major issue in the nation's schools for many years. Why? What are the factors that have made staff development such an important issue? Is it likely to be resolved in the near future? Explain.

2. Staff development should be integrated with other planning activities. Why? What planning objectives should be considered in designing a staff development program for technology? Who are the personnel within a school district who should participate in staff development?

3. Identifying the needs of a school district for staff development should be a careful and well-planned activity. What are some of the critical questions to be answered in a needs analysis?

4. As a district develops its technical resources and capabilities, a mass of knowledge and expertise develops. How does this mass of technical knowledge relate to staff development?

5. Designing a staff development program for technology can consist of many different activities. What are some of the common characteristics of a staff development program? Why are they effective?

6. Equipment availability for participants in staff development is important for the success of a program. Why? What does it provide? Is it essentially a short-term or long-term requirement? Explain.

7. Staff development is described as a long-term, continuous process. If this is so, why do so many staff development activities consist of relatively brief workshops and seminars?

SUGGESTED ACTIVITIES

To complete the Suggested Activities online, go to the Companion Website at **www.prenhall.com/picciano,** then to this chapter's *Suggested Activities module.*

REFERENCES

Becker, H. J. (1994). *Analysis and trends of school use of new information technologies.* Irvine: University of California.

Buckley, R. B. (1995). What happens when funding is not an issue? *Educational Leadership, 53*(2), 64–66.

Fatemi, E. (1999). Building the digital curriculum. *Education Week, 19*(4), 5–8.

Fullan, M., & Pomfret, A. (1977). Research on curriculum and instruction implementation. *Review of Educational Research, 47*(5), 335–397.

Goodson, B. (Ed.). (1991). *Teachers and technology: Staff development for tomorrow's schools.* Alexandria, VA: National School Boards Association.

Huberman, M., & Miles, M. (1984). *Innovation up close.* New York: Plenum.

Joyce, B. (Ed.). (1990). *Changing school culture through staff development.* Alexandria, VA: Association for Supervision and Curriculum Development.

Joyce, B., Murphy, C., Showers, B., & Murphy, J. (1989, March). *Reconstructing the workplace: School renewal as cultural change.* Paper presented at the annual meeting of the American Educational Research Association, San Francisco.

Joyce, B., & Showers, B. (1988). *Student achievement through staff development.* New York: Longman.

Knapp, L. R., & Glenn, A. D. (1996). *Restructuring schools with technology.* Boston: Allyn & Bacon.

Northrup, P. T., & Little, W. (1996). Establishing instructional technology benchmarks for teacher preparation programs. *Journal of Teacher Education, 47*(3), 213–222.

Park, J., & Staresina, L. (2004, May 6). Tracking U.S. trends. *Education Week, 23*(35), 64–67.

Pink, W. (1989, March). *Effective development for urban school improvement.* Paper presented at the annual meeting of the American Educational Research Association, San Francisco.

Quality Education Data. (1996). *Education market guide & mailing list catalog, 1996 & 1997.* Denver: Quality Education Data.

Ravitch, D. (1992). TECHNOS interview. *TECHNOS Quarterly for Education and Technology, 1*(3), 4–7.

Schlumpf, J. F. (1991). Empowering K–12 teachers. *Technological Horizons in Education Journal, 18*(9), 81–82.

Sheingold, K., & Hadley, M. (1990). *Accomplished teachers: Integrating computers into classroom practice.* New York: Bank Street College of Education, Center for Technology in Education.

Trotter, A. (1999). Preparing teachers for the digital age. *Education Week, 19*(4), 37–46.

U.S. Congress, Office of Technology Assessment. (1995). *Teachers and technology making the connection* (Report No. OTA-EHR-616). Washington, DC: U.S. Government Printing Office.

U.S. Department of Education, National Center for Education Statistics. (2000). *Internet access in U.S. public schools and classrooms: 1994–99,* NCES 2000–086. Washington, DC: U.S. Department of Education, National Center for Education Statistics.

Chapter 12

Managing Facilities

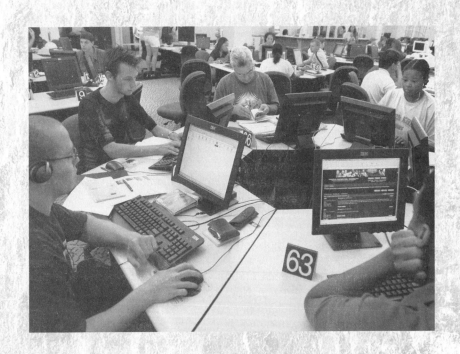

An important aspect of planning and implementing for technology is the establishment and management of facilities, an area that generally did not receive enough attention in the early days of computer acquisition. Schools purchased equipment and housed it as best they could. Classrooms were converted into laboratories overnight by simply putting microcomputers on available desks, running additional electrical cables, and assigning release time to one of the teachers (whoever was most interested in technology) to "manage" the facility. This approach enabled schools to get their programs started, but soon they ran into many problems as computer acquisitions increased, more space was needed, and the management of equipment, software, and training became a full-time job. In this chapter, the planning and management of technology facilities is examined, including space utilization, personnel, policies, procedures, and security.

GETTING BIGGER

As late as the 1930s, airplanes were regarded with a certain awe, much like the way people view a space shuttle today. However, now airplane travel is routine and among the safest ways to travel. In the next 20 to 30 years, space travel, maybe as provided by a space shuttle, will also become more routine, and its mystique will disappear. So too with computers; the mystique behind computer technology is gone because computer equipment has become so commonplace. The days of huge blue and gray boxes in temperature-controlled computer centers have given way to the nearly ubiquitous presence of microcomputers. Cash machines, personal digital assistants (PDAs), checkout counters, exercise equipment, and video games are some examples of computers that we see and use in everyday life. In schools, too, we are beginning to come across computers just about everywhere: in laboratories, classrooms, and libraries; on the desks of secretaries and administrators; and slung over shoulders in student book bags.

Because of their convenient size and propensity to become smaller, microcomputers are fitting into almost any available space. However, although computer equipment has become remarkably smaller in the past 30 years, the number of machines has increased dramatically, and so has the job of managing them. School administrators should be planning for computers to exist nearly anywhere in their buildings. At the same time, they need to establish the proper support services to assure that this equipment is being used effectively.

STAFFING AND ADMINISTRATION

Though getting easier to use, computer technology will require more management in the foreseeable future for both administrative and instructional applications. More resources and support will likely be needed to help in planning hardware, software, and physical environments; to provide maintenance; to establish data communications systems; to distribute and maintain documentation; and to assist in training. This will be true regardless of where equipment is located. However, the nature of the resources and support will change depending on the applications and the location of equipment.

For administrative applications, the need to establish highly efficient information systems tends to support a strong centralized approach. Major databases are implemented and maintained centrally by well-trained technical staff and distributed as needed throughout the district. This operation is housed in a central computer facility whose size depends on the size of the district in terms of both enrollment and geography. The informational resources are distributed throughout the district through a data communications network. Secretaries and administrators use microcomputers both to access database information and to perform tool applications such as word processing, e-mail, and electronic spreadsheets. This approach is not unique to schools but is common in businesses and governmental agencies and has been evolving over the past 40 years.

The staff requirements to manage these applications depend on the size and geographic distribution of a district. Larger districts with tens of thousands of students will need larger and more technically sophisticated staffs to develop and maintain systems and to distribute them over data communications networks than will smaller districts with 2,000 or 3,000 students. The staffing for administrative applications in schools has been evolving similarly to other noneducational environments such as private businesses and governmental agencies. Typically, a staff of computer programmers, computer operators, data communications specialists, and other technicians is established at a central location. In districts governed by municipalities, a certain amount of support may be provided by local governments, particularly for financial and payroll applications. The staffing and management for administrative applications is better understood and in many districts has matured as the applications have developed.

For instructional applications, the use of computing technology is still an evolving phenomenon, becoming more widely used in the early 1980s as microcomputer technology became available and again in the 1990s as the Internet grew in popularity. The nature of instructional applications is somewhat different from administrative applications. Whereas administrators need efficient and accurate information flow, teachers and students need variety, stimulation, and ease of use in their applications. Administrators find rewards in using computers because they reduce manual efforts and produce accurate and timely reports for use inside and outside the school. Teachers and students, on the other hand, require pedagogically appropriate software designed more to meet individual needs. The applications needed for language arts, for example, are frequently different from those needed for science and mathematics or the fine arts.

These requirements tend to support a more decentralized environment unique to educational institutions. The staff to support these applications needs to be not only technically knowledgeable but also pedagogically knowledgeable. The key to effectiveness is being able to integrate technology into the regular curriculum. In the 1980s, schools generally established centralized laboratories mainly because of the limited amount of equipment on hand and because there was a tendency to follow the administrative approach, with which most district administrators were more familiar. Centralized facilities will continue to play an important role in supporting instructional applications, but the general thinking is that more equipment has to be placed in the regular classrooms to be effective. The staff needed to support these facilities includes technology teachers who have received both pedagogical and technical training. In addition to teaching responsibilities, they also frequently function as coordinators for technology in each school and work with regular classroom teachers. Their main roles are to help other teachers use technology and provide basic technology instruction for the students. As equipment continues to be acquired for instruction, schools increasingly will need at least one staff member who will serve to coordinate technology activities. Schools with an extensive amount of equipment (i.e., several hundred microcomputers) may have several staff members coordinating activities.

To manage technology facilities throughout the district, school superintendents must decide on an appropriate administrative structure. Two common organizational models (see Figure 12.1) for managing administrative and instructional technology are: one central administration managing both activities (Model A in the figure), or separate administrations for administrative and instructional technology (Model B). Either model works.

The single administration model (Model A) can provide significant economies in terms of technical knowledge and maintenance services. Certain applications that require good student record keeping, such as computer-managed instruction, might be easier to establish if both administrative and instructional technology report through the same administrator. Data communications systems for applications such as Internet access also are better planned and implemented from a single administrative source. However, the director in this model needs to make sure that both administrative and instructional technology are equitably provided for in terms of philosophy and share of resources. Hardware, software, and training decisions may be very different for administrative and instructional applications, and an effective administrator has to develop different procedures and processes for the two areas.

Organizational Model B, which separates the administration of services into two separate entities, generally will produce more philosophically appropriate applications and will ensure a more equitable distribution of resources. On the other hand, certain economies may not be realized, particularly for basic hardware acquisitions and maintenance. Regardless of the model being used, a district administrator or superintendent will attempt to make sure that economies are realized where appropriate while allowing differences in philosophy, staffing, and approaches to occur. Planning and policy committees for the two activities would remain separate and have different participants. Committees for instructional applications need to have

FIGURE 12.1   **Organizational Charts**

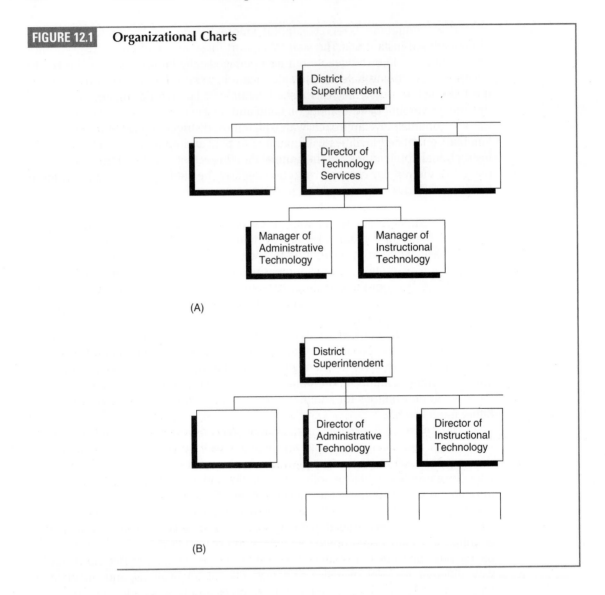

(A)

(B)

greater participation at the building level to ensure that various academic departments and disciplines are represented. Committees for administrative applications
need to involve administrative and clerical staff for analyzing the system and for using
the centralized applications effectively. Budgeting for the two areas should be kept
separate mainly because the sources of funds generally are quite different. Administrative technology usually relies on the local school district operating budget for
funds, whereas instructional technology can pursue a variety of funding sources
including not only the operating budget but gifts and grants, special state appropria-
tions, and so forth.

CENTRAL LABORATORIES

A major issue in facilities planning and management is the establishment of centralized laboratories for instructional applications. If a school district had the funds to purchase an unlimited amount of equipment, make it available throughout the day, and provide assistance to and train all the teachers, such a district would locate technology where learning occurs—in the classrooms. Computers would routinely be available as tools to be used as needed by teachers and students. However, school districts do not have unlimited funds; therefore, alternative locations for computer equipment must be considered.

Centralizing computers is appropriate when the supply of equipment and the supply of technically trained teachers is limited. The familiar approach of moving students to a central laboratory for several periods per week is effective given limited resources, but it is not ideal. In addition to disrupting the schedules of both students and teachers, a central facility tends to separate computers from the learning that goes on in the regular classroom. On the other hand, many teachers are not yet able to use computer equipment effectively in their instruction. In this case, the centralization at least guarantees that students will have some computer experience, and it especially benefits those students who are more interested in or better able to use computer technology. The solution is to compromise and provide for some mix of centralized and decentralized facilities depending on the amount of equipment available and the technical training of the teaching staff.

The location of central computer facilities can be a significant decision. The choices are typically between developing a dedicated central computer laboratory or becoming part of another centralized instructional support center such as a library or media facility. Either approach works and essentially depends on the skills and knowledge of the personnel supervising the areas. If library and media staff are knowledgeable about the technology, then housing a computer facility as part of these centers is appropriate. If they are not knowledgeable, then the tendency has been to set up a separate computer laboratory.

Other organizations such as colleges and universities have had to make similar decisions. The major tendency there has been to establish dedicated computer centers rather than integrate them as part of a library or other instructional support activity. Instructional computing in colleges evolved differently from that in primary and secondary schools. Higher education, particularly research universities and schools of engineering, were at the forefront in the early years of computing in the 1950s and 1960s when computer centers were all centralized and staffed by highly trained technicians and faculty from the science and technology departments. Primary and secondary schools did not become involved with computing until the late 1970s and 1980s with the introduction of microcomputers, which physically did not require a central facility and could be housed almost anyplace. These could be operated by most teachers interested enough in using the equipment in their lessons. Colleges in the past 10 years have been making major strides in distributing equipment very widely throughout their campuses, and microcomputers can now be seen in dormitories, libraries, and hallways as well as in classrooms. In the 1990s, colleges and universities started examining the organizational structure of information services. Computer centers, library services, and media services in particular are now being examined in terms of greater organizational integration.

Primary and secondary schools, likewise, should be focusing on how to distribute and integrate computers into everyday instruction by physically locating equipment where teaching and learning occurs. Where centralization is necessary because of equipment or staff limitations, locating computers where staff can assist teachers and students makes good sense. However, an increasingly popular alternative to the central computer facility is the mobile/portable laboratory or central lab on wheels. A cart equipped with slots for up to 30 laptop computers can be wheeled almost anyplace in the school building. This eliminates the need to move the children to the lab and brings the technology to them in the classroom. These carts are also equipped with wireless communications devices so that all of the laptops have immediate access to the Internet without a need to wire them individually to a local or wide area network. Most of the major computer manufacturers (e.g., Apple, Gateway, Hewlett-Packard) market complete mobile labs that include the cart, laptop computers with wireless adaptor cards, and a wireless access point or transceiver.

■ PHYSICAL ENVIRONMENT

The physical environment in which computer equipment is located, regardless of whether it is centralized or not, is very important and should be well planned. Ergonomics, floor layouts, furniture, electrical precautions, and security requirements are critical. School districts in which some degree of administrative computing exists probably have technical staff who can be helpful in planning the facilities. However, there are certain factors in designing space for children and learning that are not the same as designing work spaces for adults.

Facilities for Administrative Applications

For administrative applications, expertise in designing the physical environments is frequently available both inside and outside the district. In establishing or expanding a central mainframe computer facility, usually the technical staff, with assistance from a computer vendor, is able to design an efficient and pleasant work environment.

In facilities for office staff, computer workstations should be comfortable and blend into the office environment. Desks and chairs with adjustable heights are readily available and help make it easier for staff to use their keyboards. Wall space should be used to reduce the amount of electrical cable and wires that have to be distributed onto areas where people walk. Even when covered by floor strips, cables can be serious tripping hazards. For administrators or secretaries who are expected to spend a great deal of time using a workstation, glare on a video screen can be annoying and lead to eyestrain. Situating workstations to minimize glare is a common practice, and using polarized video shields is also effective. Most districts may call on the expertise of their professional computer and architectural staffs to design pleasant and safe workstation layouts to provide comfortable work environments.

Administrative applications (office automation, database, Internet access, etc.) are increasingly relying heavily on a high-speed data communications network. Careful planning should be done at the district level in developing the physical requirements of such a network.

Facilities for Instructional Applications

For instructional applications, the physical layout should be conducive to learning and meeting the requirements of children of different ages, sizes, and understanding. For a central laboratory or a computer classroom, the location of workstations should be carefully evaluated.

Figures 12.2, 12.3, and 12.4 provide several floor plans for a 20-station computer facility. These figures assume that each station has at least a keyboard and video monitor resting on top of the processor equipped with a disk drive, as is typical for Apple Macintosh and DOS/Windows machines. Additional equipment, such as printers, video players, CD-ROMs, and DVDs, can be added as needed. Most of these peripherals can also be shared and stacked one on top of another to use the available space efficiently. Local area networks also fit into this basic workstation configuration without any problem.

The row design (Figure 12.2) is a common layout for a computer facility and represents an efficient use of floor space. It is conducive to teaching, with the teacher in the front of the class delivering lessons and instructions. However, a drawback involves the distribution of electrical wires and computer cables, which can become tripping hazards if not hidden or entrenched in conduits. In computer instruction, a good deal of time is needed for hands-on use of the equipment by students. Most teachers during this time move from workstation to workstation, providing advice and helping children with their computer work. Teachers may also encourage other students to look at what one of their peers has accomplished for both demonstration and recognition. This is especially true in the younger grades. For both teachers and students, this configuration tends to create barriers that inhibit free movement around the room.

Figure 12.3 illustrates a cluster design with four student workstations grouped together. It makes efficient use of available floor space and reduces some of the tripping and mobility problems by locating most of the computer cables in the back of the equipment away from where teachers or students might walk. The cluster design provides open spaces for teachers and students that are effective for group and collaborative learning environments, especially if large tables are used for the workstations. If this floor plan is used in an instructional resource room where students are expected to work alone, a recommendation is that carrels be used for the workstations.

| **FIGURE 12.2** | **Floor Plan for 20 Workstations: Rows** |

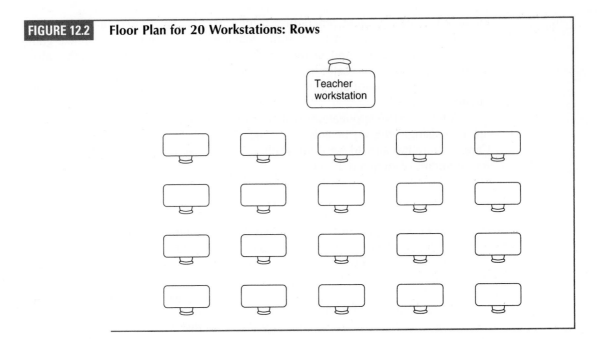

| **FIGURE 12.3** | **Floor Plan for 20 Workstations: Clusters** |

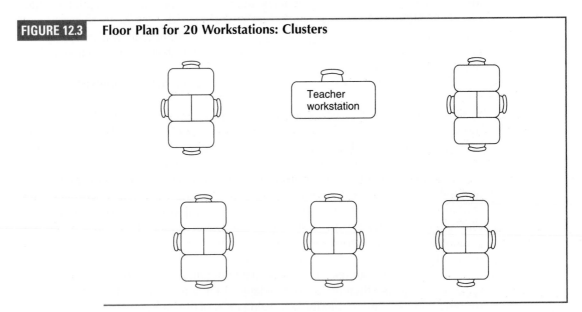

Figure 12.4 depicts a horseshoe design that places workstations along the walls of the room. This approach is the least efficient in terms of the use of floor space, but it may be the most conducive to teaching and encouraging free movement. In this configuration, all wiring and cables are located along walls away from walking areas. Teachers can choose to be either in the front or right in the middle of the class. Students will never

FIGURE 12.4   **Floor Plan for 20 Workstations: Horseshoe**

have to have their backs to the teacher, and they can easily and safely move about the room. Variations of the horseshoe approach are used in some schools to allow students to work in teams, with each station providing equipment and chairs for two or more students.

Regardless of the configuration, some consideration should also be given to furniture that will be comfortable, useful, and conducive to learning. Large open work tables allow for greater sharing and group activity, whereas carrels are more appropriate for individual activity. Light colors are more cheerful than dark colors and blend better with the equipment, most of which is beige, gray, or white. Glare, especially natural light coming in from windows, can be a serious distraction for students using video monitors. In planning the placement of monitors, some evaluation should be done as to whether certain stations would have a glare problem. One solution for this might be the installation of vertical blinds, which are very effective in shutting out natural light.

Physical planning for the teacher's workstation also requires special consideration and should be designed to maximize learning. Large monitors (i.e., 36 inches) and video projection systems increasingly are becoming the standard demonstration vehicles for computer-based lessons. Many products are available, and improvements in resolution and image quality are being made every day. In general, a large monitor provides better image quality than an overhead projection system, but it is also more expensive. Light switches or controls should allow teachers to dim all or part of the room so that students can view a monitor free from glare. If an instructor likes to move about a great deal while teaching, consideration should be given to situating the keyboard on a high stand rather than on a standard-height desk, so that commands and other keyboard operations can be executed while standing up rather than bending over. Simple overhead projectors and whiteboards using dry markers should be provided rather than chalkboards, which generate dust—a potential problem for the equipment.

In designing spaces for standard classrooms where only a limited amount of equipment is provided, many of the considerations mentioned still are appropriate. If two to five workstations are to be provided, consider setting them up in a computer corner to take advantage of the wall space for wiring and cables. In classrooms with only one computer, give consideration to providing a large monitor so that several children can participate and view what is happening. This can be especially effective when used in conjunction with group or cooperative learning exercises where the large images can make an activity come to life. For readers wishing additional information on teaching with limited equipment in a classroom, *Great Teaching in the One-Computer Classroom* (Dockterman, 1998) provides many useful suggestions.

DATA COMMUNICATIONS FACILITIES AND INFORMATION INFRASTRUCTURE

As discussed in Chapter 7, technology is becoming increasingly dependent upon data communications facilities for teaching and learning. Internet access, local area networks (LANs), wireless local area networks (WLANS), and wide area networks (WANs) are becoming common wherever computing is taking place. As a result, administrators should consider developing an overall planning and support mechanism for providing "connectivity" throughout a district for both administrative and instructional applications. Such plans should consider not only the local school needs but may be integrated with a larger community's or municipality's planning and requirements. These plans can take into consideration all aspects of information processing including telephone, fax, video, and computer. Other key factors such as the geographic distribution, size of population, and the reliance on public or private telephone and cable systems should be evaluated and understood.

Of all the areas of information technology, planning and implementing a data communications network combining computer, telephone, and video technology is probably the most complex. Even districts with experienced staff frequently require the services of consultants in planning a new data communications system or making major revisions to an existing one. Investing funds to hire a good consultant for this planning is generally very worthwhile. Such planning can take into consideration the cooperation of local utilities and businesses, especially telephone, cable television, and other technology-based enterprises.

In the 1980s, planning and implementing communications systems usually focused on the wiring of buildings and rooms to be able to receive digital transmissions. Modern communications systems require a far more careful analysis and design. Carlitz, Lentz, and MacIlroy (1995) recommend a "layered" approach that considers data communications networks in three basic layers:

1. The physical layer
2. The protocol layer
3. The application layer

The physical layer contains all aspects of the media and devices through which data or signals will pass. Discussions regarding physical transmissions using copper wire, fiber optics, or wireless transmission are critical. Whereas school districts can control to some degree the physical medium within their buildings and campuses, outside connections are totally dependent on local utility providers—hence the need to involve these providers in planning this aspect of the system.

An example of an issue discussed within this layer would be bandwidth. The frequency with which signals can be transmitted and received directly affects the speed of a network and is dependent on the medium. Lower bandwidth, as is available over standard telephone lines, is fine for simple data transmission, and many existing networks use telephone lines for their outside connections. However, applications requiring high speeds, such as video transmission, will need much larger bandwidth than that provided through standard telephone connections. Identifying how higher bandwidth can be provided at a reasonable cost is a serious issue that is and will continue to be discussed in many school districts and communities.

The protocol layer refers to the rules or standards that enable one device to send signals to other devices on a network and to receive signals from them. Although the Internet has provided an overall standard protocol (see Chapter 7), most LANs and WANs are using machine and/or manufacturer designed protocols for local signal processing. In the past, planning the protocol layer would involve determining whether and how the protocol from one LAN or WAN would interact with the protocol from another LAN or WAN. This has begun to change as more schools adopt the Internet and its derivative protocols as the standard for their networks, especially for WANs. Schools are developing Internet-based protocol networks—or intranets—within their districts. Because of the extensive communications systems using several different protocols already in place, school districts cannot change these quickly and will generally have to plan and implement such changes in phases over a number of years.

The application layer refers to all the existing and foreseeable applications that are expected to run on computers connected to the networks. At this third layer, it is especially important to identify how data are to be transferred from one network to another and from one program to another. School districts might adopt basic tool applications (e.g., word processing, e-mail, spreadsheet, virus protection, database) and may establish popular software packages such as Lotus Notes or Microsoft Office as the district standards for use on the network, thereby assuring easy transfer of data. Some applications, however, such as multimedia and digital video, are still evolving as software technologies and generally accepted standard packages and formats are more difficult to establish throughout a district.

Because of the phenomenal growth of the Internet in the 1990s, all organizations, including school districts, are rethinking their data communications systems. Schools, private corporations, and government agencies at all levels are examining their information infrastructures to determine whether they are poised to use the evolving resources on the Internet. This type of facilities planning will be the focus of district-wide planning discussions for many years to come.

The vast majority of all data communications systems in schools rely extensively on cables or hard wires to connect computing equipment in LANs and WANs. However, in the past few years, schools have begun to invest in wireless local area networks or WLANs. Park & Staresina (2004), in a national survey of school districts, report that 27% of them have established at least one WLAN. Conceptually a WLAN is the same as a LAN without the connecting cables or wires (see Figure 12.5) and instead uses high-frequency radio waves to send and receive data signals.

While there are several variations, in a typical WLAN configuration, a transceiver device, called an *access point,* connects to the school's wired network backbone from a fixed location using standard cabling. A *backbone* is a large data transmission line that carries data gathered from smaller lines that interconnect with it. Generally all LANs are connected to a network backbone in order to access the Internet and other wide area networks. The access point receives and transmits data between the WLAN and the wired network backbone. A single access point can support a number of users. Users access the wireless LAN through WLAN adapters, installed as PC cards in laptop or desktop computers or integrated within personal digital assistants (PDAs) and other handheld devices.

FIGURE 12.5   **Wireless Local Area Network (WLAN)**

Laptop

Desktop

Wireless →

Access point →
(transceiver)

Cabled to the network →

Wired network backbone

The benefits of WLANs are their flexibility, mobility, and ease of use. They also may be especially cost-effective in older school buildings where coaxial cables or fiber optics are not available or may be expensive to install. The drawbacks of WLANs are that they are not as fast, secure, or reliable as cable LANs. Also there are no communications or signal standards for WLANs although Wi-Fi—Institute of Electrical and Electronics Engineers (IEEE) Wireless Standard 802.11b—is emerging as the most commonly used. In planning data communications infrastructure, school administrators should be considering both cable and wireless options.

HARDWARE MAINTENANCE

As more equipment is acquired, maintaining it in good working order becomes a bigger and more complex job. The three major components of hardware maintenance are repairs, preventive maintenance, and upgrading.

Making Repairs

Computer hardware, because it has mostly electronic components rather than mechanical parts, is not prone to breakdowns. This is especially true of the main processor components but less true of printer and disk devices, which do have mechanical and moving parts. However, when repairs are needed they have to be performed by someone with the appropriate knowledge and training. For mainframe computer systems, a district should have a comprehensive service contract with an outside vendor that provides for quick response by field engineers to correct any hardware problems. Generally these contracts also offer a certain number of preventive maintenance visits involving testing, cleaning, and making minor repairs to the equipment. Most major mainframe manufacturers are responsive in accordance with the stipulations of their service contracts and do a good job of keeping their equipment functioning.

Also available are third party repair companies whose service contracts are usually less expensive than those provided by the manufacturer. The services from these companies vary significantly. Before entering into a contract with a third party vendor, carefully evaluate the company's service record, particularly with other organizations in the immediate geographic area. The qualifications of local repair personnel, response times, the availability of parts, and attention to preventive maintenance schedules are critical evaluation criteria.

Large mainframe computer systems and servers that are providing networking services throughout a school district are expected to be functioning every day. Administrators, teachers, and other staff who use such systems expect them to always be available; when they are not, the day's planned activities can be seriously disrupted. Extensive downtime due to repairs can be costly in terms of human resources, and good operations management should be able to keep it to a minimum.

For microcomputer systems, several options for handling repairs are available. First, service contracts similar to those used for large mainframe computers are available from both manufacturers and third party vendors. This tends to be the most reliable, but also the most costly, approach.

Second, because microcomputer systems are much simpler in their design than large mainframe computers, school districts are also developing their own hardware maintenance staffs. The size of these staffs depends upon the number of machines that need to be maintained. Major manufacturers such as Dell, Compaq, Apple, and IBM will train staff and provide various diagnostic tools to help identify and locate hardware problems. Less expensive parts can be kept on hand to make repairs, and more expensive parts can be ordered and generally received within 24 to 48 hours from manufacturers. Several extra backup computers can also be kept on hand and substituted during repairs. Serious problems beyond the skills of a district's staff may require packing the problem computer and bringing it to a manufacturer's local outlet for repairs. As more and more microcomputers are being acquired, the trend in school districts is increasingly to do their own repairs.

A third alternative is a combination of the two options already cited, with the district handling certain (usually simpler) repairs and an outside service company, either the manufacturer or an independent, addressing more complex problems.

Providing Preventive Maintenance

Regardless of the approach a district takes in handling repairs, attention should always be given to preventive maintenance. The old adage that an ounce of prevention is worth a pound of cure is appropriate for computer hardware. Documented procedures should be in place for equipment maintenance. These include daily routines and periodic examinations.

Students should be taught to respect the equipment and should be involved with its care. Basic rules such as no eating or drinking anywhere around computer equipment should be strictly enforced. Dust covers should be used and kept in place, especially for equipment such as printers with mechanical and moving parts. School districts may draw on their own high school students to help in doing repairs and in providing periodic preventive maintenance services such as cleaning and testing equipment. This is especially true if the school district has vocational programs in electrical or mechanical technology.

Upgrading

Hardware upgrades and replacement plans are also important as school districts become more dependent on computer technology. After awhile, computer equipment needs to be replaced because of extensive repairs or obsolescence. Hardware replacement plans should be in place that assume a 5- to 7-year life cycle for equipment, depending on use and function (see Chapter 9). For mainframe computer systems that are critical to administrative functioning, upgrades are especially necessary to keep up with current software and available technology. Microcomputer systems, especially those used by students, may need to be replaced because of wear and tear and accidents that can occur in an instructional environment.

Regardless, equipment will need to be replaced on some regular basis. Administrators need to be aware of the replacement schedule so that budgets and resources can be secured and disruption of services minimized.

SOFTWARE MAINTENANCE AND DISTRIBUTION

Computer software, like hardware, needs to be maintained. Depending on the nature of the computer applications, the manner in which software maintenance is provided can vary significantly. Large administrative software systems require a great deal of maintenance. In large administrative computer centers, a substantial portion of the programming staff will be dedicated to software system maintenance. Studies indicate that the human resources devoted to software maintenance exceed those devoted to new software development.

Maintenance involves correcting problems, modifying the software because of changes in policies or procedures, or upgrading it to take advantage of newer technology. School districts are particularly cognizant of making modifications due to changes in policies because they are dependent on various governmental bodies for funding. These bodies tend to increase their demands for data and accountability as they establish new programs or make additional budget allocations.

A current trend in instructional software is to acquire proprietary products—from companies such as Broderbund and Tom Snyder Productions—that cannot be modified by teachers or academic support staff. Assuming users know how to run the programs, most instructional software will operate without problems, and generally it is not subject to changes in policies or procedures.

When software manufacturers do upgrade their software, they will generally supply a completely new version of the package to replace the old, either free of charge or for a reduced fee. As a result, maintenance is not as significant a problem for these products. On the other hand, software distribution and lending is requiring more attention as software packages are used by more students and teachers. Questions of centralization and decentralization arise. Some control may be maintained by having a central software library that might be located in the school's library; software may be borrowed in the same fashion as books. In addition, a central software library can provide basic services such as testing newly acquired software; cataloging, securing, or making backup copies; and establishing standard software documentation manuals. Because so much instructional software is customized for specific subjects, departments will also acquire it for the use of their own teachers and students. This reduces the amount of software that can be shared throughout a school and leaves most of the responsibility for software maintenance to the individual departments.

Both centralized and decentralized approaches are used in the schools. As with hardware, the trend again is to adopt a decentralized approach, with departments and teachers acquiring software specifically for their classes much like other instructional supplies and materials. A compromise approach may be to have a central library for software that can be distributed throughout the school while allowing departments to keep a limited number of specialized packages.

Particularly effective in solving software distribution problems is the use of networks (LANs or WANs) in which a software library is kept on a central file server (with high-capacity disk equipment), with users throughout a school or district being able to access the software they need through the network. This is a major benefit of using networking to distribute computer services, both hardware and software, throughout a school.

In managing software distribution, school districts should adopt certain policies to protect their software and ensure compliance with vendor contracts and other legal stipulations. Software and files that are used regularly need to have current backup copies. For administrative software, this should be done routinely on a cyclical basis (daily, weekly, etc.), with backup copies kept in protected areas such as a magnetic tape or disk vault. Instructional software likewise should be backed up if the vendor allows copying the software. In many cases, this is not true, and a backup copy of the software needs to be purchased, usually at a nominal price.

There is a temptation to make copies or at least to try to make copies of software even when a vendor prohibits it. This is against the law and should not be encouraged. Federal laws and regulations afford considerable protection to software vendors for their products. School district administrators should acknowledge these regulations and should make sure that their students, teachers, and other staff are aware of them by prominently posting notices in computer areas against illegally making copies of software.

As mentioned in Chapter 10, software vendors generally will make available site licensing arrangements or quantity discounts to address the need for additional copies. Site licenses allow customers to make unlimited copies of packages. Modified site licenses allow customers to make some specified number of backup copies. Generally, they are very attractively priced, and school districts intending to use a particular software package extensively should acquire a site license.

Some vendors do not provide site licenses but instead offer quantity discounts in the form of "lab packs." These are discounts for purchases of certain quantities, usually the number that would be needed for a single class. In addition to price discounts, vendors such as Tom Snyder Productions and Logo Computer Systems encourage the acquisition of lab packs by including curricular material that may be helpful to teachers in preparing their lessons.

POLICIES, PROCEDURES, AND DOCUMENTATION

Written policies, procedures, and documentation are critical to the effective use of computer technology. Unfortunately, too often their importance is realized only when a problem, breach, or violation has occurred that forces administrators to wonder why a policy did not exist for the situation.

Policies

Policy issues have been raised throughout this book. For example, in Chapter 3 a number of policy issues were raised regarding equity issues such as gender, student access, and special education populations; in Chapter 6 copyright issues were presented in the context of multimedia; and in Chapter 7 there was a discussion on policy responsibilities of school districts in protecting students from prurient and other undesirable material on the World Wide Web. Almost any aspect of technology can generate important policy issues that administrators should consider.

It is not the intent here to cover policy issues in depth, mainly because they can be lengthy discussions with many ramifications depending on local situations, culture, and mores. However, some of the major technology policy issues that school districts should be considering include the following:

- Equity issues (gender, socioeconomics, special education)
- Student access to technology at school, especially after school hours
- Student home use of technology
- Loaning of equipment (e.g., laptop computers) and loaner responsibilities
- Use of school technology resources for personal activities
- Internet etiquette
- Appropriate use of school e-mail systems
- Protecting students from questionable material (pornography, hate-group activity) on the World Wide Web
- Ethical issues (plagiarism and the World Wide Web)
- Copyright and fair use
- Intellectual property
- Hardware standardization
- Access to student records (grades, addresses, telephone)
- Access to personnel records (salaries, addresses, e-mail)
- Freedom of Information Act policies

For more information on policy issues, go to the *Web Links module* for this chapter on the Companion Website at **www.prenhall. com/picciano.**

For readers wishing more information on policy issues, the following Web sites may be helpful:

- EDvancenet, a partnership formed by the Consortium for School Networking (CoSN), the National School Boards Foundation, and MCI WorldCom that was created to address education technology in the context of major policy issues
- Responsible Netizen, an initiative of the Center for Safe and Responsible Internet Use, aimed at assisting schools and other organizations to develop policies with

regard to the "safe, responsible, legal, and ethical" uses of the Internet and other information technologies

■ Stanford University Libraries' Web site on copyright and fair use, a most useful and up-to-date resource on this very complex issue

Once a school has developed new policies or revised existing ones, disseminating them becomes paramount. Posting in public places such as libraries and computer laboratories is helpful. Establishing a Web site with an updated collection of technology (and other school district) policies can be a most effective form of communication.

Procedures

Procedures are the overall manner of doing things. They are frequently developed in conjunction with policies and form the framework within which an organizational entity operates. Procedures should be developed for all the basic operations that can occur in a computer facility. Examples of procedures include activities such as the following:

■ Backing up files and software
■ Using facilities (access, hours of operation, priorities)
■ Scheduling preventive maintenance
■ Evaluating software
■ Testing software
■ Distributing and lending software
■ Distributing and lending hardware

Procedures should be well communicated so that everyone using the facilities knows them. A procedures manual or Web site that is regularly updated, reviewed, and distributed to users of computer facilities can be very effective in this regard.

Documentation

Documentation refers to applications and describes how to use specific computer programs or sets of programs. All applications, administrative and instructional, require some documentation. Organizations that do not devote enough attention to documentation are vulnerable if key staff persons who know a great deal about the software applications leave. Written documentation must be maintained and made easily accessible for every program used in a school. For simple instructional software packages, it may consist only of the documentation that the vendor supplies. Teachers who use computers occasionally need documentation to understand how to use the software. The best software packages will not result in the best applications if teachers do not understand how to use them. The reverse is also sometimes true; that is, some mediocre software packages result in successful applications mainly because good documentation was provided and teachers understood how to use them.

For complex administrative applications, the standard operating procedure should require up-to-date, detailed descriptions and maintenance histories of all the programs that comprise the software system. For major administrative applications, the basic documentation for each program should include:

- Program specifications and design
- Program description
- Logic flowcharts
- Operations documentation
- Samples of output and input formats
- Maintenance documentation and history

In addition, user manuals for the overall application have to be developed for administrators and staff who are expected to maintain and use it. User manuals may be supplemented by online Help facilities that assist users in "navigating" through a computer application. Online Help is very useful but should not replace a written document; it may be stored in a text editor file.

School administrators should not underestimate the importance of documentation when dealing with computer technology. Computer center staffs are more conscientious in developing documentation than are other departments, mainly because of their training and because they understand the vulnerability should key staff persons who know a software application leave. However, technical staff will also admit that more documentation is needed. In decentralized environments, procedures for monitoring documentation are rare and difficult to implement. Furthermore, with instructional applications, the wide variety of available software packages from many different sources makes it difficult to require documentation standards. As a result, documentation tends to be inconsistent and, in some cases, poorly done or nonexistent. Regardless of the degree of centralization or decentralization in a district or school, administrators should develop a minimum documentation standard and require it for all computer applications.

SECURITY

Computer security refers to procedures for protecting software and sensitive data files. Issues of security are of growing importance to schools as well as many other organizations. In corporate America, there have been many cases of unauthorized access via computer to customer bases, research and development test results, and financial accounts. Two well-publicized cases (O'Brien, 1989) involved major thefts from Wells Fargo ($21 million) and Security Pacific Bank ($10.2 million). Federal laws such as the Computer Fraud and Abuse Act of 1986 provide severe penalties for persons convicted of computer crime.

Schools do not maintain data subject to regular, high-volume financial transaction processing as is common in banks and brokerage houses. However, a school's payroll or accounts payable files can be vulnerable to abuse if security procedures are lax. Other files, such as student records, must also be protected. They contain sensitive information about individuals and must not be readily available except as needed for legitimate educational purposes.

Data security minimally involves establishing password protection to access a computer system. Additionally, it entails devising access codes that allow certain individuals to access particular files and data. All commercially available database management software packages routinely provide password and access code protection and should be used as standard operating procedures. Written policies should be developed citing which offices and individuals have the authority or need to access specific data. These policies also establish the degree of access—that is, whether an individual can simply view data or change or update data.

In developing and monitoring data security, school administrators should be particularly concerned with students. Although a more common problem at the college level, there have been many cases of high school computer hackers with the talent to break through a password system to access student data such as grades and test scores. Just one or two such individuals can cause havoc to the integrity of data files. A solitary breach of the security system may require major review and verification of the violated data files to determine the extent of the damage. This process can take a great deal of staff time; more important, it can also leave users feeling insecure and wondering about the integrity of the data files.

In recent years, another form of unauthorized access to data files has emerged in the form of computer "viruses" that are designed to spread from one central processing unit to another. Whereas some viruses are harmless and simply generate annoying messages on a video screen, others are destructive and designed to erase data files, especially disk directories and operating system files. The concern for the destructive power of a computer virus was evident in 1992, when headlines worldwide reported the spread of the Michelangelo virus designed to attack on the anniversary of Michelangelo's birth (March 6). Since then every few months computer viruses are regularly reported in the news media.

To protect against viruses, software products—referred to as "antiviruses" or "vaccines"—are available that will scan a disk for a virus. Antiviruses are prudent investments for all computer operations but especially in network environments in which viruses can easily spread from one computer to another. The Norton AntiVirus from Symantec and Virex from Microcom are two popular products.

In addition to data security, some schools, especially those in high-crime areas, should plan to expend resources on physically securing computer equipment and protecting it from theft and vandalism. As computer equipment becomes smaller, lighter, and more easily disposed of, this need increases. A variety of measures can be taken to secure computer equipment. Anchor pads, which bolt the main computer components to a desk or table, are commonly used and are effective in most areas.

Electronic security systems for doors and windows can also be used in centralized computer facilities and likewise are effective.

Security also becomes a more serious problem when distributing equipment throughout a school and into the classrooms. Anchor pads should be used in the classrooms; they may be the most cost-effective security measure. Electronic security systems can become very expensive depending on the physical distribution of equipment and the accesses to a school building, which for fire code and ergonomic reasons tend to have many more doors and windows than other facilities.

In planning computer facilities, security issues should not be underestimated. To ignore them leaves a school or district vulnerable and subject to major setbacks in computer development should a breach in security occur.

THE HELPING PLACE

One of the most important responsibilities for those who manage computer facilities is to develop the proper school-wide attitude to technology. The external elements (e.g., hardware maintenance, room organization, security), if done well, will contribute to a school's overall success in using technology. Critical to this success will be the development of a positive attitude or a computer culture that is supportive and nonthreatening to the teachers and staff who are expected to use the technology.

The concept is not a new one and should be familiar to many administrators and teachers. In some schools, "helping places" have been established to provide support services to students. They may be extensions of a guidance office or a tutoring program and are usually friendly places staffed by teachers who smile easily, have positive dispositions, and will go out of their way to help a student with a problem. Computer facilities likewise should be helping places. In addition to the popular "What if?" questions, staff should be available to answer the "What happened?" and "How can I do it?" questions. Given the wide disparity in training and understanding that exists regarding computer technology, computer center staff needs to be oriented to respond to simple as well as complex questions.

Technology educators (Sheingold, 1991) have espoused establishing computer environments in which children have free and open access to equipment so that it becomes a basic and routinely used tool for learning. This concept also applies to teachers, secretaries, and clerical staff who are called on to use technology systems. Furthermore, they need access not only to equipment but, just as important, to the expertise and knowledge necessary to use it. Managers of computer facilities need to provide both equipment and expertise in a friendly, helpful manner.

Formal staff training sessions are a good beginning, but continuous, ongoing support services are what will make for a positive technology culture. Hotlines or help phones, staffed by knowledgeable personnel, are extremely effective for answering questions. User groups that meet regularly in person or on electronic bulletin boards

CASE STUDY

PLACE: WATSON MIDDLE SCHOOL
YEAR: 2005

The Watson Middle School is an alternative program for bilingual students. It shares facilities with an elementary school located in an inner-city neighborhood in a large metropolitan center. The program was started in 1991 with 100 students. It has grown consistently and is regarded as a major success in the district. The current population is 300 students.

Watson is administered by a director, Marion Halo, who reports directly to a district superintendent. Thirteen teachers are assigned to the school. Ms. Halo, who started the school, feels very strongly that the success of the program can be attributed to its small size. Though very supportive of the district establishing similar programs in other schools, she does not feel the program should grow any further at Watson.

Ms. Halo has been very supportive of technology and established a central computer laboratory when the school first opened. Presently it houses 25 microcomputers. A high-speed Internet connection was added to the lab in 1996. One teacher who previously taught mathematics has served as the computer coordinator and has done an excellent job. In 1999, as part of a capital project, the central laboratory was renovated and additional computers were acquired and distributed into individual classrooms. The entire building (including the classrooms) was rewired for high-speed Internet connections. Each classroom has at least three computers with several (e.g., science) classrooms having as many as five. Most but not all teachers make good use of the available technology.

are helpful in establishing relationships among users and technical staff. Newsletters providing suggestions and hints for using hardware and software are effective communication vehicles for keeping staff informed. These are all excellent examples of ways to establish a positive computer culture in a school or district. In the final analysis, however, the most important element for building such a culture will be the positive attitude of the people providing these services.

During the last several years, funds for technology have been scarce; however, a special budget allocation has been requested for next year. The district superintendent has contacted Ms. Halo and has asked for a proposal for $75,000 for upgrading Watson's technology facilities by June 1, 2005. To prepare the proposal, Ms. Halo has met several times with the technology coordinator as well as with her teaching staff to discuss possibilities. Her coordinator indicated that most of the existing equipment is 6 years old and a number of the microcomputers in the school, especially those in the central lab, are in need of replacement. He has also suggested that three mobile presentation systems be purchased that would include a multimedia equipped microcomputer, a DVD/CD drive, and a projection system. The teachers would like more and newer equipment in their classrooms. They have also asked for their own laptop computers that they could use in class and be allowed to take home with them. Ms. Halo has attended two meetings called by the superintendent where technology proposals were discussed. At these discussions, the superintendent appeared to be particularly supportive of several of her colleagues' (principals and directors at other schools) interest in acquiring mobile laboratories equipped with laptop computers and wireless communications.

DISCUSSION QUESTIONS

1. It is May 1, 2005. Assume that you are Ms. Halo. Which of these options do you think you would like to support?

2. What additional information do you think you need to finalize your decision?

SUMMARY

In this chapter, the basic elements of planning and managing computer facilities are presented. Space utilization, personnel considerations, security, and hardware and software maintenance are examined. As more and more equipment is acquired, the task of managing it grows, too. Increasingly, school districts are establishing larger technical support groups to support technology in their schools.

Several major issues such as the centralization and locations of computer support facilities are examined. The evolution of the Internet and the demand for more extensive data communications systems is specifically identified as a major issue in facilities planning. Documentation and security are also discussed. The chapter concludes with a call for establishing a positive computer culture in the school directed not just to students but to teachers and other staff as well.

KEY CONCEPTS AND QUESTIONS

1. Computer equipment is becoming increasingly easy to use, but managing computer facilities in schools is becoming more complex. Is this situation likely to change in the near future? Does it depend on the nature of the applications? Explain.

2. Various organizational models exist in school districts for managing computer facilities. Which model do you think is most appropriate? Why?

3. Centralized computer facilities are common in many schools. What are some of the major considerations in managing centralized versus decentralized facilities?

4. Ergonomic factors in the design of computer facilities are critical for the comfort and safety of users (teachers, students, and staff) in schools. What do you consider some of the most important ergonomic considerations? Do they change depending on the users? Explain.

5. With the proliferation of microcomputers throughout the schools, maintenance of hardware and software is becoming more difficult. Why? Is it simply a matter of more equipment and software requiring more maintenance? Explain.

6. The concept of developing a positive culture in a school or any organization is a recurring theme in many discussions about leadership and administrative style. Borrowing from this theme, what are some of the techniques that can be developed to promote a positive computer culture in a school?

SUGGESTED ACTIVITIES

To complete the Suggested Activities online, go to the Companion Website at **www.prenhall.com/picciano,** then to this chapter's *Suggested Activities module.*

REFERENCES

Carlitz, R. D., Lentz, M., & MacIlroy, A. (1995). Standards for school networking. *Technological Horizons in Education Journal, 22*(9), 71–74.

Dockterman, D. A. (1998). *Great teaching in the one-computer classroom* (5th ed.). Cambridge, MA: Tom Snyder Productions.

O'Brien, J. A. (1989). *Computer concepts and applications.* Homewood, IL: Irwin.

Park, J., & Staresina, L. (2004, May 6). Tracking U.S. trends. *Education Week, 23*(35), 64–67.

Sheingold, K. (1991). Restructuring for learning with technology: The potential for synergy. *Phi Delta Kappan, 73*(1), 17–27.

Chapter 13

Financial Planning

revious chapters of Section III emphasized the need for planning the hardware, software, and people components of proposals to implement technology programs in a school or district. However, proposals cannot become realities without the financial resources necessary to initiate them and maintain them. In this chapter, the financial side of planning is examined, with emphasis on evaluating costs for technology and on seeking funds to support it. Several of the ideas and approaches discussed in previous chapters are considered again from a cost perspective.

TECHNOLOGY CAN BE EXPENSIVE

As late as 1980, the spending for computer technology in education was negligible. Becker (1994) was among the first researchers to track the acquisition of technology in K-12 education. He conducted a series of national surveys in the 1980s and early 1990s and concluded that America's schools were acquiring approximately 300,000 to 400,000 microcomputers per year. Becker predicted that this trend would maintain itself, if not accelerate, well into the 21st century. Several years earlier, the U.S. Congress's Office of Technology Assessment (OTA) issued a comprehensive report estimating that as much as 32% of the average school district's instructional materials budget would be devoted to computer technology by the year 2000 (U.S. Congress, 1988). This represented an expenditure of approximately $4 billion per year for the country's 15,000-plus school districts. Quality Education Data (QED) (1991) supported the OTA estimate. Based on actual 1990 expenditures of $1.4 billion for instructional technology, QED projected an increase of $800 million through the 1994–1995 school year, or $2.2 billion. A further projection of the QED figures through the year 2000 would generate estimated expenditures of almost $4.5 billion. These estimates all have proven to be too low. QED (1996) later reported that the actual expenditures for instructional technology by the nation's schools had already exceeded $4 billion by 1995. School expenditures for technology for the year 2001–2002 have been estimated at close to $6 billion (McCabe & Skinner, 2003).

However, this acceleration in spending may have begun to change. *Education Week* reported that because of "tight state budgets" for the first time in many years, school district spending on technology dropped by about 24% between the 2001–2002 and 2002–2003 school years (Park & Staresina, 2004).

These computer expenditures represent what has been occurring rather than what is needed. In fact, the case has been made that schools are not doing enough in terms of their investment in technology. A panel on educational technology, in a report to President Bill Clinton, found that the yearly expenditures for instructional technology in K-12 schools were much too low. The panel gathered data from six national studies, each of which recommended yearly expenditures for instructional technology that ranged from a low of $6 billion to a high of $28 billion. After careful review and analysis, the panel recommended that approximately 5% of all K-12 education spending, or $13 billion annually, should be used for instructional technology if education is to catch up with other segments of the country (Shaw, 1997).

School administrators will need to plan wisely to meet the funding requirements of technology and to make sure that they have the resources to maintain technology-based programs. In some years, they may "hold the line" or reduce expenditures because of some budgetary problems, but these measures tend to be temporary, and the long-range, overall pattern is to increase funding. This pattern of increased expenditures for technology is not unique to the field of education. It is typical in private corporations, governmental agencies, and most other organizations that have been using technology since the 1960s, well before technology became popular in schools. Once a technology-based program is established, the normal cycle has been to expand and provide additional services and to upgrade it with newer technology when necessary.

■ THE COST-EFFECTIVENESS OF TECHNOLOGY

A common assumption is that computers can be cost-effective and save money in the long run. This complicated issue greatly interests many people, including administrators, school board members, teachers, union representatives, and taxpayers. The simple and popular notion that machines can replace people and thereby save money in an instructional setting, however, has yet to be proved. This idea was often promulgated by technology salespersons as a marketing or sales strategy. In the automobile industry, telephone communications, banking, and printing, jobs have been lost to automation. It is likely that savings can be achieved in educational administration, school district communication, and record-keeping applications; however, cases in which technology has replaced teachers or significantly reduced instructional expenditures are rare.

Many teachers and administrators do see the computer as making them more effective in their daily activities. Albert Shanker, the late president of the American Federation of Teachers, spoke and wrote extensively on the potential benefits of computer technology in the classroom and saw it as a tool to be integrated into the learning process by the teacher. Early on, he indicated that the installation of computer equipment in the nation's classrooms should be education's top priority (Shanker, 1989). The National Education Association (NEA) regularly releases reports and statements declaring that computer technology holds great promise for enriching classroom instruction and management. As early as 1989, the NEA recommended that a computer be installed on the desk of every teacher (National Education Association, 1989). This has not happened yet, but the recommendation indicated the positive attitude of the nation's major teacher organization to technology in the classroom.

Although many educators are enthusiastic about the technology, the cost-effectiveness is open to debate. The basic question is: Are the funds expended on technology worth the improvement in learning when compared to costs of other types of instructional delivery? A number of studies and reports have found that technology can have a beneficial effect on student achievement (Archer, 1998; Educational Testing Service, 1999; Schacter, 1999; Shaw, 1997; U.S. Congress, 1988; Waxman, Connell, & Gray, 2002; Wenglinsky, 1998). However, reports or studies that examine the cost of technology as compared to other instructional costs and student achievement are quite rare. One example was a series of studies conducted by Levin and Meister (1986) comparing four cost-effective strategies: computer-assisted instruction, peer tutoring, increased instructional time, and reduced class size. They concluded that peer tutoring was the most cost-effective approach in terms of improved reading and mathematics scores on standardized tests. Computer-assisted instruction was the second most cost-effective strategy, followed by reduced class size, and increased instructional time. These studies were challenged by Niemiec, Blackwell, and Walberg (1986), who in reviewing Levin and Meister's methodology concluded that computer-assisted instruction was more cost-effective than peer tutoring.

The debate on the cost-effectiveness of technology will probably continue for some time. Technology is used mainly as an enhancement to existing instructional delivery rather than as a replacement. Even in large-scale deployment of instructional technology, such as an integrated learning system (ILS), teachers are still needed to manage the environment. As a result, technology has in fact been adding to instructional costs. The methodological control and rigor in cost-benefit studies needed to isolate technology costs and at the same time control for other costs in determining the effects of each on student outcomes is very difficult to achieve, so that this issue will continue to be discussed and debated for quite some time.

A TIME LINE FOR FINANCIAL PLANNING

With the introduction of microcomputers in the late 1970s, a major breakthrough was realized in the costs for computer technology, comparable to the introduction of the Model T automobile by Henry Ford, which made a car affordable for practically every American family. Before the Model T, cars were viewed mainly as luxury items affordable only to somewhat wealthy people. Within a few decades after its introduction, and even with the depression of the 1930s and World War II in the 1940s, cars became indispensable, and the multicar family has now become commonplace. We now see the same situation with microcomputers.

The major catalyst for this phenomenon was the cost, not the need. In the 1960s and 1970s, computers were not items that the average person felt they needed in order to live from day to day. As late as 1977, Ken Olsen, the president of Digital Equipment Corporation, the leading manufacturer of minicomputers, stated publicly that there was no need for any individual to have a microcomputer in his or her home (Stoll, 1995). As a matter of fact, with the exception of some video games and very rudimentary home applications such as balancing a checkbook, calculating mortgage payments, and estimating a grocery bill, there were very few applications for the average person. In the late 1970s, most people purchased microcomputers because the cost, typically about $1,000, was attractive. Large quantities of computers were purchased, and this trend has continued into the present. In the meantime, computer vendors and software firms caught up with the availability of hardware by developing tens of thousands of computer programs to meet all kinds of interests and needs. Although basic applications such as word processing, e-mail, Internet access, and electronic games tend to be the most common home uses today, microcomputers routinely touch our daily lives in the form of cash machines, checkout counters, and telephone information services.

Primary and secondary schools were among the last organizations to become dependent on computer technology. With the introduction of microcomputers, this began to change, mostly because schools were able to afford to purchase this equipment. Furthermore, the trend is clear: Computer equipment is becoming indispensable mostly for administrative applications in many schools, just as it has in many other individual and organizational activities. Educational applications have been developed and will continue to be developed to meet the demands of the education market. Administrators will be devoting more and more of their budgets to computer technology even though the unit cost of a microcomputer has been decreasing.

To understand this situation better, review Table 13.1, which provides a time line of the trends in digital technology with their respective costs from 1940 through the early 21st century. In the second half of the 20th century, digital computing steadily progressed by providing greater capacity at lower cost and in smaller sizes. As a result, more and more people have been able to acquire computing equipment. In the 21st century, this progression is leading toward an inexpensive, palm-size information appliance that will use wireless commmunications (satellite transmissions) to allow

TABLE 13.1   Digital Technology Time Line, 1940–2010

	1940→	1950→	1960→	1970→	1980→	1990→	2000→	2010→
	Premainframe		**Mainframe**		**Minicomputer**		**Microcomputer**	**Post-microcomputer**
Machine	Experimental machines such as ENIAC		IBM 700, 360, 4300 Series		Digital Equipment PDP Series		PC Macintosh	Digital information appliances
Cost	Unaffordable		Affordable to large businesses		Affordable to large and small businesses		Affordable to individuals	Inexpensive—individuals will own several
Size	Large room		Room		Large desk		Desktop laptop	Palm-size
Distribution	One in existence		Thousands sold		Hundreds of thousands sold		Hundreds of millions sold	Billions will be sold

anyone, anywhere, to look up a bank statement, compose and forward e-mail, view a television program, or call mom. Furthermore, these devices will be so inexpensive that every household will own several. If there is any doubt, just consider how Americans have moved from one piece of furniture containing a television in the living room to a TV in every room. Or from one telephone on the wall to a telephone in every room, a portable for the patio, and a cellular in the car or in a pocketbook.

The convergence of computer, communications, and audio/video technologies resulting in inexpensive, portable information devices will have a major impact on all aspects of information-related activities, including education. Communication at all levels will be more convenient and will allow teachers to teach and students to learn via technology more gracefully than ever before.

In examining costs, computing equipment has evolved from the expensive mainframe computers of the 1960s, to the minicomputers of the 1970s, to the relatively inexpensive microcomputers of the 1990s as characterized by Macintosh and DOS/Windows machines. The 1990s also saw the introduction of handheld data organizers and other super-lightweight microcomputers. Through the early part of the 21st century, microcomputers will continue to evolve, especially with advances in data storage capabilities and developments in magnetic disk, CD-ROM, and DVD technologies that will provide virtually unlimited online storage with both read and write features. In addition, video technology in the form of DVDs will be more widely used. Digital video delivered on the Internet will compete with television as the primary visual mass medium. Internet access and networking capability via high-speed modems had phenomenal growth in the 1990s and will continue to increase. Educational workstations that combine computing, video, and networking will be more prevalent, and all components (computer, video, and data communications) will be available from a single manufacturer. The vast majority of students will own their digital appliances by 2010, and the student-per-computer device ratio will be 1:1.

In terms of cost, the unit price of computer hardware has fallen dramatically from the typical $1 million large mainframe systems of the 1960s to the under-$1,000 microcomputer systems of today. Although unit prices of microcomputers were stable—even decreasing—throughout the 1980s and 1990s, performance (speed, primary storage, and secondary storage capacities) continued to expand and improve. In the 1990s, the typical microcomputer system ranged between $1,000 and $2,500 depending on options such as CD-ROMS, printers, and other peripheral equipment. Handheld and other limited application microcomputers that sold for as little as $300 were introduced. By 2010, small, portable digital appliances using wireless communications will dominate the market. The cellular phone, a Sony Walkman with video capability, and Internet access will be provided on a single device that will cost under $100, or will be given away for free as part of the incentive for contracting with communications service providers.

The cost for software has also begun to decrease, with many basic packages available for free on the Internet. Educational software will range from $20 for simple programs to as much as hundreds of thousands of dollars for integrated learning systems that provide extensive content and curriculum databases. The Internet will continue to grow as the major source of software and media. Interactive video packages, introduced in the late 1980s, will be easier to use and more generally available in 2010, especially if the cost for producing these materials can be reduced.

The people needed to support the computer technology will continue to be the crucial factor in providing technology-based education in the schools. The highly paid programmers of the 1980s and 1990s increasingly are being replaced by computer networking engineers whose main jobs are to install and maintain data communications facilities in classrooms, administrative offices, libraries, and so forth. Teacher education programs in colleges have expanded and are now providing specializations in computer education that combine technical training with teaching and learning. Many teacher education programs and state certification agencies have begun to require all new teachers to be technologically literate and to take course work in educational technology. By the year 2010, all schools will depend on technology teachers to assist regular teachers, the vast majority of whom will already have a basic proficiency in using technology. Staff development will continue to be needed to maintain technology skills and to integrate new software products into everyday teaching and learning.

With this time line providing the necessary background and a glimpse of the future direction of the costs for technology, let us consider a budgeting process for funding technology.

■ THE BUDGET WORKSHEET

Financial planning supports the overall planning processes of a school district. It should not dominate the process but be integrated as needed. As with many aspects of administration, a proper balance must be achieved so that those doing the educational planning are not stifled by budget considerations—and at the same time are cognizant of the costs of what they are proposing to do.

In planning for technology, the first step is to develop a planning process that yields worthwhile proposals for possible implementation. Each of these proposals should include a budget worksheet identifying the major costs associated with the application (see Figure 13.1). Information is required for the major components (hardware, software, personnel, etc.) of each technology planning proposal.

This worksheet serves several purposes. First, it requires those making a proposal to identify the necessary costs for implementation. Although this may be a routine procedure in some schools, administrators frequently face situations in which the cost of a project or proposal has not been carefully determined. A common example in many technology proposals is that emphasis is placed on hardware costs alone, which frequently may account for only a fraction of the total cost. The use of a budget worksheet requires an examination of all the costs associated with the proposal.

Second, the worksheet initiates important information-gathering activity for those making a proposal. Collecting information on costs requires administrators, teachers, library media personnel, and other staff to seek out vendors, salespersons, suppliers, and others who can provide important information not only about costs but also about new models of hardware, educational discounts, and demonstration opportunities. The inclusion on the budget worksheet of the name of a person in the district who functions as a technology coordinator is also very helpful. Such a person can be an important source of information about what already exists in the district

FIGURE 13.1 **1-Year Budget Worksheet for a Technology-Related Planning Proposal**

North Central School District No. 1

Please complete all sections as best as you can. Include the costs for consultants within the categories of hardware, software, personnel, and so forth. Attach additional pages if necessary. If you need help in completing this worksheet, feel free to contact Jane Dawson (Technology Coordinator) at 916-443-8445.

Name: _____

Department: _____

School: _____

Description of the project
-
-

Hardware (Identify the type of equipment and its cost.)　　　Subtotal $ _____
-
-

Software (Identify the software needed and its cost.)　　　Subtotal $ _____
-
-

Personnel (Identify any staff requirements including
training and release time for curriculum development.)　　　Subtotal $ _____
-
-

Repairs/upgrades (Estimate any projected costs for repairs　　　Subtotal $ _____
and upgrades to equipment.)
-
-

Supplies (Estimate the annual costs for supplies.)　　　Subtotal $ _____
-
-

Facilities (Identify where equipment is to be located and
any special requirements for electricity, security, etc.
Also include any requests for new furniture.)　　　Subtotal $ _____
-
-

Grand Total $ _____

and can bring together individuals who may have common purposes—which is especially effective in larger school districts where interaction between schools may be limited. Such an individual can also be effective in encouraging teachers and other staff to share equipment and facilities.

Third, the use of a budget worksheet makes it easier to coordinate the costs of all proposals into one overall financial plan. With the cost information readily available, summarizing and approximating all costs is much easier for determining the total budget request. This, in turn, can be compared to the existing or projected availability of funds, and the process of evaluating funding can begin.

A BUDGET MODEL

In developing an overall financial plan, much time is spent in determining the component costs of the various proposals. The budget worksheet is helpful in providing the approximate costs for all the requests. However, administrators will need to refine these requests because rarely are there enough resources to fund all proposals. As part of this refinement, administrators will ask teachers and administrators to reduce or sometimes to expand their requests and very frequently to pool or share resources. With technology, the pooling of resources to acquire hardware, software, supplies, and so forth can result in substantial economies. Essentially, this was one of the most important reasons that schools centralized rather than decentralized computer facilities when they first began new computer-based education programs.

In developing the overall financial plan, administrators should make sure the proposals presented have accurately projected all the various costs for implementing a plan and have considered sharing and other means to achieve the greatest benefit from available resources. For applications that may be implemented over several years, the costs should be projected accordingly (see Figure 13.2).

Table 13.2 illustrates a budget model of an overall financial plan that might be used to fund a school technology program. The major cost categories of hardware, software, and personnel comprise 72% of the total, with other items such as staff training, repairs/upgrades, supplies/furniture, and miscellaneous categories accounting for the remaining 28%. These percentages are meant to provide a general direction and can vary depending on the computer applications being supported and other local conditions.

An important element of Table 13.2 is the fact that budgets for all costs, not just hardware, are clearly identified. This is a major issue for which many administrators do not plan. In an article titled "Technology's Real Costs," Fitzgerald (1999) suggested that schools use a Total Cost of Ownership (TCO) approach. TCO is commonly used in the business sector to represent the total cost of installing, operating, and maintaining technology. Essentially, a yearly calculation is made per hardware unit (computer workstation) for all of the costs (software, support, repairs, upgrades, etc.). Fitzgerald (1999) referred to one study of 400 school districts that calculated the TCO for a school with 75 networked computer workstations as $2,251 per workstation per year. This is more than double the purchase price (approximately $1,000) of each computer hardware component.

North Central School District No. 1

Please complete all sections as best as you can. Include the costs for consultants within the categories of hardware, software, personnel, and so forth. Attach additional pages if necessary. If you need help in completing this worksheet, feel free to contact Jane Dawson (Technology Coordinator) at 916-443-8445.

Name: _____

Department: _____

School: _____

Description of the Project

-
-

	Year 1	Year 2	Year 3
Hardware (Identify the type of equipment and its cost.) • •	Subtotal $———	Subtotal $———	Subtotal $———
Software (Identify the software needed and its cost.) • •	Subtotal $———	Subtotal $———	Subtotal $———
Personnel (Identify any staff requirements including training and release time for curriculum development.) • •	Subtotal $———	Subtotal $———	Subtotal $———
Repairs/upgrades (Estimate any projected costs for repairs and upgrades to equipment.) • •	Subtotal $———	Subtotal $———	Subtotal $———
Supplies (Estimate the annual cost for supplies.) • •	Subtotal $———	Subtotal $———	Subtotal $———
Facilities (Identify where equipment is to be located and any special requirements for electricity, security, etc. Also include any requests for new furniture.) •	Subtotal $———	Subtotal $———	Subtotal $———
Year Totals	Total $———	Total $———	Total $———

Grand Total (All Years) $———————

TABLE 13.2	Budget Model for a School Technology Program

Component	Percentage
Hardware	35
Software	10
Personnel	27
Training	7
Repairs/upgrades	9
Supplies/furniture	6
Miscellaneous	6
Total	**100%**

SPECIAL CONSIDERATIONS OF BUDGETING FOR COMPUTER APPLICATIONS

Although budgeting for computer applications, whether administrative or instructional, is similar to other budgeting exercises, administrators should be aware of several special considerations unique to technology.

Opting for Centralized or Decentralized Computer Facilities

The decision to centralize or decentralize computer facilities has significant budgetary ramifications. As discussed in Chapter 12, a centralized computer laboratory can be far more efficient than decentralized facilities. Sharing technical support—whether it be the expertise of laboratory personnel, backup maintenance equipment, or a software library—is much easier to accomplish in a central facility. Other considerations such as physical security, accidental breakage, and renovation costs also contribute to the efficiency of central facilities.

On the other hand, the trend has been toward decentralization, with more and more equipment being acquired and placed where the activity occurs. For administrative applications, microcomputers are placed on the desks of administrators and secretaries. Likewise, for instructional applications, microcomputers are more and more often being placed on the desks of students and teachers. Decentralization is desirable to resolve problems of ready access to the equipment, to integrate computing with other instructional activities, and to avoid the logistics of scheduling and moving children to the central laboratories. Administrators should be planning for a more decentralized computing environment than presently exists in most schools.

That is not to say that the concept of sharing resources should be entirely abandoned. A common hardware maintenance contract for all equipment is far more economical than having each computer location handle repairs on an individual or as-needed basis. The sharing of software through site licenses is very cost-effective. The use of networks at the building level to share software, data, and documentation can also be very efficient. Some centralization also can and should continue to exist for certain applications, and the movement toward decentralization should not be viewed as completely incompatible with centralized facilities. Such a combination of centralized and decentralized facilities sharing certain resources is commonly described as a *distributed system*. Schools are moving in the direction of distributed systems. Typically, they are centrally coordinated, and hardware and software is shared via computer networks.

Hiring a Consultant

Routinely used in the fields of education, consultants are readily available for assisting in the design or implementation of technology applications. School districts that have been late in developing computer facilities, and are just beginning to invest significant resources, should consider the use of consultants to help avoid common pitfalls and costly mistakes. In the budget model provided, consultant costs are not specifically identified but should be included within specific budget categories such as hardware, software, and personnel.

Technical expertise is becoming more specialized, so a consultant who is very effective in recommending and guiding a district in one aspect of technology may not be as effective in another. For example, an expert in the hardware and data communications requirements of a wireless local area network may not be effective in helping launch a comprehensive teacher training program. As districts or schools do more, internal expertise develops and accumulates, which lessens the need for outside consultants.

However, even in districts where a good deal of expertise exists, administrators should not rule out the need for consulting services, particularly if considering some new or inherently complex technology. For example, integrating voice and data communications in a wide area network is not a simple task, and many school districts, regardless of their staffs' expertise, would probably seek outside technical advice to help them plan and implement such a project. In some states such as California, Kentucky, Minnesota, New York, and Texas, educational cooperatives and technical centers are supported by the state education departments and may be good starting points for seeking assistance.

Standardizing on a Common Vendor

The question of standardizing on some common hardware vendor and thereby realizing efficiencies in terms of quantity acquisitions, software development, hardware maintenance, or staff training should be addressed. Before the microcomputer explosion, school districts and most other organizations attempted to standardize on a common hardware vendor for these purposes. However, with the advent of microcomputer technology, this has changed. For administrative applications, the tendency is still to acquire compatible equipment, if not a common vendor. The use of common hardware will allow for the sharing of software and, most importantly, the sharing of common databases (e.g., student, personnel, scheduling) for various administrative applications within the school. In addition, in large urban school districts and districts governed by municipalities, schools may have to acquire equipment that is compatible with the local government's administrative systems so that common data systems such as financial accounting, census, and payroll can easily be used.

For instructional applications, this is not necessarily the trend. A variety of equipment is being used in the classrooms, and every indication is that this will continue in the future. Apple Computer, Compaq, Dell, and IBM, among other firms, are all providing excellent pieces of equipment. School administrators should allow for variety as long as it can be justified because of the needs of the proposed application. If the proposed application requires specialized software that is only available for a particular model of computer, then this might be a justifiable reason for acquiring that equipment. For instance, some excellent educational software packages using digital video are written in specific authoring languages that are only available on Apple Macintosh computers. The school should be able to get this software and the requisite Macintosh hardware even though the standard in the building or district happens to be DOS/Windows computers.

Hardware First, Other Needs Later?

A common practice in acquiring computer equipment is to buy as much hardware as possible up front and plan to take care of the other costs later on. This approach is becoming more common as competition among hardware vendors grows, and significant savings may be realized by taking advantage of special, limited-time discounts. Buying equipment first is acceptable as long as the equipment meets the needs of an overall plan and funds for the other costs will be provided. However, given the up-and-down budget cycles in some states and school districts, this is not always the case. Unfortunately, some administrators find themselves with equipment that is not fully used because the proper software is not available, teachers have not been trained, or electrical upgrades in the computer facilities have not been completed. The recommended planning approach for an application should include all the component costs, not just hardware.

Choosing a Purchasing Plan

Purchasing plans vary with the vendor and type of equipment. The choice of a plan was much more significant before the introduction of microcomputers, when the purchase prices of large mainframe and minicomputers were substantial. School districts and most other organizations wanted to spread out costs over a period of time. Spreading costs through a lease-purchase agreement rather than paying full price, for example, is still recommended for districts making large acquisitions such as installing a new data communications system or deploying a large-scale integrated learning system.

The main reason for this approach is to reduce the budget impact in any one given year and to spread out the costs over several fiscal years. Another reason to build a base budget is that it will be much easier to replace or upgrade equipment without having to request funds for a major new acquisition every 5 to 7 years. The yearly lease-purchase allocation can simply be continued with small percentage increases for upgrading or adding on to the original configuration. Regarding the acquisition of microcomputers, the vast majority of educational users purchase this equipment outright. However, administrators should also build an equipment replacement plan into their base budget to make sure that they can replace units that will become damaged or obsolete.

SOURCES OF FUNDS

Once a number of worthwhile planning proposals have been received and consolidated into an overall financial plan, an examination of the sources that will finance the plan is now required. The four major funding sources are the school district budget, bond issues, governmental entities, and gifts and grants.

The School District Budget

The school district budget generally is the primary source of funds for implementing technology applications. If not already in place, two base budgets for technology need to be established: one that will support administrative applications, and a second that will support instructional applications.

Administrative applications are almost always supported entirely by a school district's tax levy budget. In general, boards of education are cognizant of the need for timely and accurate data and the efficiency of office operations utilizing basic computer technology; hence, they tend to be supportive of providing funds for administrative applications. School boards also tend to be very demanding in terms of receiving data about their school districts, and they are receptive to technology that improves their information delivery systems. In some cases, other governmental agencies may provide funds because of a special initiative (e.g., the U.S. government's E-Rate program) or a mandatory reporting requirement that exists outside the school.

Instructional applications, on the other hand, because there are perceptions that funds can be provided from a variety of other sources, may require more negotiation and justification to be funded fully by the school district's tax levy budget. This situation varies significantly depending on the wealth, tax base, and financial personality of a district.

Both budgets, administrative and instructional, should have an established minimum base within the district's budget because all technology applications require some ongoing cost items, such as maintenance, supplies, and upgrades. How much is needed for a base budget depends entirely on the goals and objectives that a district has identified in an overall technology plan. There are no fixed percentages of a total budget for funding technology-related programs. Estimates indicate that the average school district is devoting about one third of its instructional materials budget for technology-related items such as hardware, software, and direct computer repairs. This will likely increase and recommendations/projections are that they will at least double (Shaw, 1997).

Besides the basic material costs (hardware, software, supplies), additional budget allocations will be needed for personnel costs, training, facilities, and infrastructure.

In seeking funds from boards of education for instructional applications, school administrators should consider drawing support from parents, many of whom want their children learning about and using computer technology. Many parents use computer equipment in their jobs and see computer literacy and competence as important for career success. They can be very helpful in securing budgetary approvals from elected school officials.

Bond Issues

Bond issues for the purpose of some major capital improvement, such as the construction or renovation of a school building, can be an important source of funds, because equipping and furnishing the building is generally an accepted part of the project. These funds, sometimes quite substantial, provide a school district with an infusion of dollars to launch major new technology programs. Of course, many districts are not necessarily building new facilities, and capital construction funds may not be available. If this is the case, administrators might ask the board of education or the governing board of the municipality to consider a special bond issue for developing a new information infrastructure, making major equipment purchases and upgrades for the entire district—including those schools that are not targeted for any capital improvements in the near future.

If a school district does acquire a significant amount of new equipment as a result of a bond issue, the necessary funds to maintain this equipment in the future should immediately be built into the operating budget. The understanding should be that bond or capital funds will be used for significant and not simply incremental acquisitions. In general, a school district should not rely on bonds for equipment and other needs that normally should be provided for in an operating budget.

Governmental Entities

Governmental entities at the federal, state, and local levels may also be the source of funds for instructional computing programs. Although subject to changing political and financial climates, various governmental agencies have demonstrated interest in technology and responded accordingly. State education departments throughout the country are increasingly providing support for technological improvements. Federal programs administered by the U.S. Department of Education and the National Science Foundation have provided funds to acquire computer equipment for educational programs, usually directed for specific populations and purposes. The Elementary and Secondary Education Act, reauthorized as No Child Left Behind, has had several provisions for assisting schools to acquire technology. The E-Rate is a federally managed program that provides significant discounts on telecommunications technologies to schools in low-income areas. Discounts of as much as 90% are available based on the percentage of students in a school who participate in the federal school lunch program. The E-Rate is administered through the Universal Service Fund, which is funded by fees charged to all telephone users.

All levels of government are aware of pressure from the business community, which has been influential in calling attention to the need for a well-educated and well-trained workforce. For example, the New York City Partnership, an organization of business and civic leaders, issued a report in 1989 indicating that New York City's position as a world financial center was threatened because of a shortage of workers with technical skills. The report went on to cite the theoretical loss of tens of thousands of jobs, recommending that the state consider revising its curricula to ensure that all students develop computer and other job readiness skills as part of their basic educational programs. In part, because of the importance of technology and information services to their economies, both New York City and New York State have set aside special budget items to be used to support technology-related instructional programs.

Several excellent sources of information regarding federal grants and funding include the following:

For more information on federal grants and funding, go to the *Web Links module* for this chapter on the Companion Website at **www.prenhall.com/picciano.**

- The Federal Register, Office of the Federal Register, National Archives and Records Administration, Washington, DC 20408.

- *Education Daily,* Capital Publications, Inc., 1101 King St., Alexandria, VA 22313-2053.

- The Benton Foundation (excellent Web site for information on the U.S. government's E-Rate program), 1625 K St. N.W., 11th Floor, Washington, DC 20006.

Gifts and Grants

Gifts and grants can also be a significant source of funds to implement computer applications. A certain aggressiveness on the part of administrators is required to seek out potential donors, foundations, and other grant agencies, but the rewards can be quite substantial. Individuals, parent-teacher organizations, small local businesses, and international corporations contribute hundreds of millions of dollars each year for improvements in schools, and technology has particularly benefited from this generosity.

One of the first substantial gifts for technology occurred in the state of Mississippi in 1990 when two businessmen—Richard Riordan and Richard Dowling—donated $7 million for a 5-year program to improve reading and writing skills. The gift required that the state contribute $6 million to the program, which entailed establishing IBM's Writing to Read computer program in kindergartens and 1st grades in all public schools.

This gift exemplified several common characteristics of gift giving and grantsmanship directed to education. First, the gift required a matching contribution. Many donors—individuals as well as foundations—prefer to give to those who are willing to invest some of their own resources in a project as evidence of its need and validity. Second, the gift required that a certain program be implemented. Attaching certain conditions to a gift or grant is not uncommon. Third, the donation was targeted specifically for technology, which is indicative of the belief by an increasing number of businesspeople in the benefits of technology.

In recent years, several major foundations have concentrated on supporting large-scale education projects with technology as their central theme. The Bill and Melinda Gates Foundation, the Carnegie Foundation, and the Open Society Institute awarded $30 million in grants in December 2000 to improve New York City high schools. Smaller schools and instructional technology were integral components of these grants. In November 2000, the Bill and Melinda Gates Foundation awarded $36.9 million to California, part of which was used to create small high-tech high schools. The Bill and Melinda Gates Foundation has also had a special focus on school leadership and the use of technology. Major grants this foundation has awarded in this area include:

New Jersey: $5.1 million to upgrade the technology skills of principals and supervisors

Mississippi: $1.1 million to establish a Technology Academy for School Leaders

Illinois: $2.25 million to bring technology into the mainstream of school administration

Texas Association of School Administrators: $6.25 million to broaden its Technology Leadership Academy

Further information on these grants is available at the Bill and Melinda Gates Foundation Web site (http://www.gatesfoundation.org).

CASE STUDY

PLACE: MOUNT HOPE SCHOOL DISTRICT
YEAR: 2003

The Mount Hope School District is located in a suburban city in the northern Midwest section of the United States. It operates 37 schools for 33,000 students and is considered a model school system within the region in terms of student performance, innovative teaching, and a progressive administration. An active planning process involving teachers, parents, and local businesspeople has been instrumental in helping Mount Hope achieve this distinction.

Mount Hope has been most active in providing and using technological tools for instruction. A carefully developed technology plan has evolved from the district's planning process that has kept the city in the forefront. The current inventory

Although not all donors are willing to give millions of dollars to education, many businesspeople are willing to make more modest donations to their school districts or localities. Banks, insurance companies, and department stores are enormous users of computer information systems and need to employ local people to operate these systems. They may be willing to make donations to ensure that their future employees are familiar with technology. Three excellent sources for information on grants from private corporations and foundations are:

For more information on grants from private corporations and foundations, go to the *Web Links module* for this chapter on the Companion Website at **www.prenhall. com/picciano.**

■ The Foundation Center, 79 Fifth Ave., Third Floor, New York, NY 10003-3076.

■ The Grantsmanship Center, P.O. Box 17220, Los Angeles, CA 90017-0220.

■ Education World Grants Center Web site

No discussion of gifts and grants to schools would be complete without mention of the work and generosity of parent-teacher associations throughout the country. In the area of technology, many school districts have received gifts of computer equipment from these associations. Imaginative fund-raisers such as bake sales, craft fairs, and collecting grocery market receipts have been used to acquire modest amounts of equipment. Administrators should encourage these activities because, in addition to acquiring funds, they also generate interest and enthusiasm for computer education.

includes approximately 4,600 microcomputers being used in the schools for instructional purposes. In the primary and middle schools, the microcomputers are a mix of Apple Macintoshes and Intel-based DOS/Windows (Dell, IBM) machines, whereas in the high schools IBM and Dell dominate. Since 1995, the district adopted a hardware acquisition policy that established three vendors (Apple, IBM, Dell) as the standard machines for the district.

Possibly the most important element of Mount Hope's success in terms of technology education has been the emphasis on involving teachers in the planning process, especially in selecting software and other educational materials. A district-wide technology planning committee has 8 members, 2 of whom are teachers. Another district committee, the software review committee, has 12 members, 8 of whom are teachers or technology coordinators. This committee prides itself on putting the needs of students first, and it diligently reviews all software packages before approving their use in the classroom.

Continued on next page

The economic base in Mount Hope in 1997 received a needed boost when a major developer of business software for DOS/Windows microcomputers, 1st-ONE, Inc., established its national headquarters in the town. With 1st-ONE have come the development of other very desirable support companies, increased tax revenue, and well-paying jobs. On May 1, 2003, the president of the company announced a new venture to develop educational software. The company was also entering into an agreement with Top-Hardware Products, a manufacturer of DOS/Windows micro-computers, to market jointly some of their products.

On June 15, 2003, the president of the Mount Hope board of education, who is a vice president at the Mount Hope Bank and Trust Company, received a phone call from the president of 1st-ONE indicating that the company was considering making a large donation to the school district over the next 3 years in the form of new equipment and software with a market value of $3 million. The equipment would be DOS/Windows machines supplied by Top-Hardware Products. Each microcomputer would also come with several new educational software products that 1st-ONE had just developed and was beginning to market.

On June 16, the president of the board of education mentioned at an executive work session that 1st-ONE would like to offer the school district a most generous gift of computer equipment and software. Three of the board members were ecstatic about the president's announcement, but others expressed some reservation about the nature of the gift. In response to several questions from these board members, the superintendent indicated that he knew very little about either 1st-ONE

SUMMARY

This chapter presents the background and several issues associated with financial planning for computer applications. Technology can be expensive, and even more so if not planned properly. Cost considerations for an entire computer application should be identified and go well beyond the direct hardware and software costs. Trend data indicate that although the unit cost for computer technology has decreased, the overall expenditure for computer technology is increasing each year in both primary and secondary schools.

A review of the literature on the cost-effectiveness of computer-based education leads to inconclusive results. Most of the major reviews of the effectiveness of computer technology in education tend to ignore the questions of cost. Regardless, schools are well on their way to implementing new systems and expanding existing ones.

A procedure for gathering budget information using a budget worksheet should be integrated into the overall computer technology planning process within a school district. A composite funding model suggesting percentage distributions of the various educational software or Top-Hardware Products, but that he would be happy to discuss both with his staff and the chairpersons of the district's technology committees and report back to the board at its next meeting, which was in one week.

On June 17, the superintendent asked his assistant to schedule a meeting the next day with his staff and the chairpersons of the district's technology committees. At 11:00, he received a telephone call from a reporter for the *Mount Hope Gazette* inquiring about a gift that 1st-ONE was about to make to the school district. The superintendent told her that it was too premature to make any comments. In the afternoon edition of the *Gazette,* on the front page of the business section, the headline "1st-ONE to Donate $3,000,000 to Mount Hope Schools" appeared.

DISCUSSION QUESTIONS

1. Assuming that you are the superintendent, what are your concerns about the headline?
2. What actions do you consider taking?
3. How do you prepare for your upcoming meetings with the chairpersons of the district's planning committees and with the board of education? Please keep in mind that at this time you do not have any information about the quality of the hardware or software.

costs associated with computer applications has been presented. However, school districts will likely fund according to their own goals and financial abilities. Several major issues associated with computer technology costs such as centralization, shared resources, single vendor procurement, and use of consultants are presented, with suggestions for possible courses of action.

In funding computer technology, school districts should establish base budgets and seek the support of their boards of education. Administrators should also be aggressive in seeking funds from other sources such as local businesses, governmental agencies, parent-teacher groups, and individuals who might be interested in providing funds for computer technology.

KEY CONCEPTS AND QUESTIONS

1. Financial planning for technology requires an understanding of changes in component costs that have occurred over time. Identify some of these changes, explaining how they have affected financial planning for educational technology.

2. Financial planning for technology requires a consideration of all the component costs of an application. What are the major component costs of a computer application? Are some more important than others? Explain.

3. Centralization and decentralization of computer resources is a recurring issue in education. Review this issue from a financial perspective for administrative applications. Do the same for instructional applications.

4. School administrators have been struggling with the standardization of hardware for many years. What are some of the factors that administrators should consider when establishing a policy regarding hardware standardization?

5. Securing resources for technology is a critical part of financial planning. What are some of the common sources of funds? On which should an administrator most rely? Why?

6. Financial planning, like planning in general, is an ongoing activity requiring a good deal of careful analysis. How might an administrator involve others, including teachers, in financial planning for technology?

SUGGESTED ACTIVITIES

To complete the Suggested Activities online, go to the Companion Website at **www.prenhall.com/picciano,** then to this chapter's *Suggested Activities module.*

REFERENCES

Archer, J. (1998). The link to higher scores. *Education Week, 18*(5), 10–21.

Becker, H. J. (1994). *Analysis and trends of school use of new information technologies.* Irvine: Department of Education, University of California.

Educational Testing Service. (1999). *Computers and classrooms: The status of technology in U.S. schools.* Retrieved January 30, 2005, from the ETS Web site (http://www.ets.org/pub/res/compclss.pdf).

Fitzgerald, S. (1999, September). Technology's real costs. *Electronic School.* Retrieved online from the Web site of the National School Boards Association (http:// www.electronic-school.com/199909/0999sbot.html).

Levin, H., & Meister, G. (1986). Is CAI cost-effective? *Phi Delta Kappan, 67*(10), 745–749.

McCabe, M., & Skinner, R. A. (2003, May 8). Analyzing the tech effect. *Education Week, 22*(35), 50–52.

National Education Association. (1989, July). *Report of the NEA special committee on educational technology.* Paper presented at the 127th annual meeting of the National Education Association, Washington, DC.

Niemiec, R., Blackwell, M., & Walberg, H. (1986). CAI can be doubly effective. *Phi Delta Kappan, 67*(10), 750–751.

Park, J., & Staresina, L. (2004, May 6). Tracking U.S. trends. *Education Week, 23*(35), 64–67.

Quality Education Data. (1991). *Technology in the schools: 1990–1991 school year.* Denver: Quality Education Data.

Quality Education Data. (1996). *Education market guide and mailing list catalog, 1996–1997.* Denver: Quality Education Data.

Schacter, J. (1999). *The impact of technology on student achievement.* Santa Monica, CA: Milken Exchange on Education Technology. Retrieved online January 30, 2005 (http://www.mff.org/pubs/ME161.pdf).

Shanker, A. (1989, December 24). Technology holds the key. *New York Times,* E7.

Shaw, D. E. (1997). *Report to the president on the use of technology to strengthen K-12 education in the United States.* Washington, DC: Panel on Educational Technology. Retrieved online (http://www.ostp.gov/PCAST/k-12ed.html).

Stoll, C. (1995). *Silicon snake oil: Second thoughts on the information superhighway.* New York: Doubleday.

U.S. Congress, Office of Technology Assessment. (1988). *Power on! New tools for teaching and learning* (Report No. OTA-SET-379). Washington, DC: U.S. Government Printing Office.

Waxman, H. C., Connell, M. L., & Gray, J. (2002). *A quantitative synthesis of recent research on the effects of teaching and learning with technology on student outcomes.* Naperville, IL: North Central Regional Educational Laboratory. Retrieved from the Web site of North Central Regional Educational Laboratory (http://www.ncrel.org/tech/effects/).

Wenglinsky, H. (1998). *Does it compute? Policy information report of the Educational Testing Service.* Princeton, NJ: Educational Testing Service. Retrieved online January 30, 2005 (http://ftp.ets.org/pub/res/technolog.pdf).

EPILOGUE

At a national computing conference held in June 1992, Dr. Robert D. Ballard, a senior scientist at the Woods Hole Oceanographic Institute, delivered a paper titled "Living the Dream," in which he described the development of a new project that he termed "telepresence." Using computers, satellite telecommunications, fiber optics, and robotics, this project allowed scientists on land to experience deep-sea explorations by manipulating a robotic system, named the ARGO/JASON, by remote control. Using deep-sea image technology, scientists in their offices and laboratories saw everything that they could see if they were actually on the ocean floor (Ballard, 2000, p. 221).

Ballard compared it to other events in his life, which included substantiating theories involving plate tectonics and continental drift, discovering mountains higher than Mt. Everest, seeing canyons deeper than the Grand Canyon, and locating the RMS Titanic located 12,460 feet deep in the North Atlantic Ocean. Ballard also stated that one of his major goals was to share these experiences with children. Through an initial series of "downlink" sites across the United States, in the most ambitious ARGO/JASON undertaking ever, 600,000 students were able to watch a deep-sea exploration of active volcanoes just off the Galápagos Islands. Ballard indicated that the highlight of this event was when young children at the remote sites actually took turns steering and manipulating the arms of the deep-sea robots. He said that seeing the expressions of wonder and excitement on the faces of these children was a joy incomparable to any other (Ballard, 1992).

What started as an experiment in 1989 has reached several million children, and Ballard has received national awards for his innovative approach to bringing "real-life" science into classrooms around the world. When asked about the future of his work, Ballard quoted his grandmother, who told him, "Great is the person who plants a tree, not knowing whether he will sit in its shade." When he started, he was not sure whether the JASON project would be a success but was willing to take a chance on something in which he believed. He was confident, however, that through hard work and by assembling good people who shared in his dream, the JASON project would touch the lives of children for many years to come.

Planning for technology has been the basic emphasis of this book, and fundamental to planning is thinking about and developing strategies for the future based upon an understanding of the past and the present. The background, history, and current issues associated with the developments in the use of technology in education have been examined and discussed. With 100,000 schools in the United States at various stages of technological development, one school's present might be another's future—or, conversely, one school's present might be another's past. Planning for the future, therefore, may mean different things to different readers. What is important is that the women and men of vision in our schools think about, plan for, and take chances to develop and implement programs that will touch the lives of their children for years to come. In this new millennium, regardless of one's political, sociological, or educational philosophy, technology should not be something separate from but should be a part of every school administrator's vision. It need not be the centerpiece of that vision, but it undoubtedly has a role to play in the future of every school.

REFERENCES

Ballard, R. D. (1992, June). *Living the dream.* Paper presented at the IBM Academic Computing Conference, San Diego, CA.

Ballard, R. D., with Hively, W. (2000). *The eternal darkness: A personal history of deep sea exploration.* Princeton, NJ: Princeton University Press.

APPENDIX A

Basic Concepts of Computer Technology

Computer science, like other disciplines, has developed a language of its own. *Hardware, software, client-server, icons, LAN, WLAN, bytes, DVDs, modems, RAMs,* and *ROMs* are just some of the terms that are heard in everyday school affairs. These are common words for the technologically trained but can evoke insecurity and frustration among even the most experienced school administrators. When faced with making major decisions such as purchasing new computer equipment for the science laboratories, upgrading Internet access in a library, or acquiring a database management system for student records, administrators must quickly learn as much of the technology as they can, relying extensively on the advice and recommendations of others. An administrator should not become the top technician in a school to manage technology. However, an acquaintance with commonly used terms as well as an overall conceptual understanding of computer systems will help administrators plan for and incorporate technology into schools.

■ THE CONCEPT OF *SYSTEM* AS A STARTING POINT

The starting point for the conceptual understanding of computer technology is that it is a system. A *system* is defined as a group of interrelated parts that are assembled to achieve some common goal or end. The three basic parts of any system are input, process, and output (see Figure A.1). Specifically, a computer is a system of interrelated input, processing, and output devices that are assembled for the processing of data (characters and numbers). This is true whether we are talking about a single microcomputer located on a secretary's desk or a national network of large

FIGURE A.1	Basic System Design

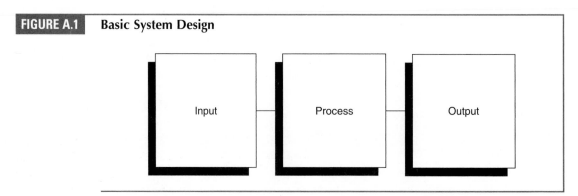

304

FIGURE A.2   **Microcomputer System Configuration**

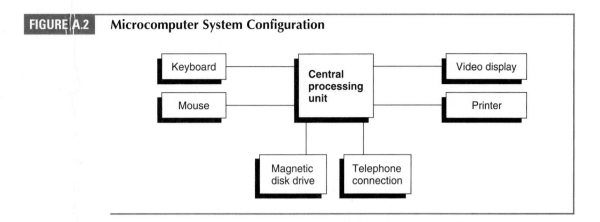

FIGURE A.3   **Large Computer System Configuration**

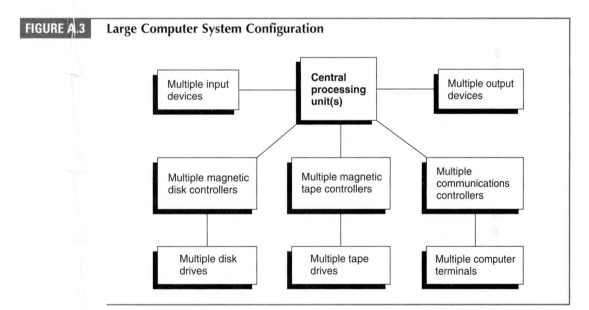

mainframe computers that might consist of thousands of devices connected by telephones or satellites. The major difference is in the number of devices, not the basic operating concept.

The minimum configuration of a computer system is best exemplified by the common microcomputer, which consists of at least a keyboard or mouse for input, a central processing unit for process, and a video monitor or printer for output. In addition, it usually has a secondary storage device such as a magnetic disk drive for storing data and instructions and a single communications interface or modem for establishing a telephone link (see Figure A.2). Larger computer systems are simply variations of this same basic microcomputer configuration. The major differences are that the larger systems are capable of having many input and output devices, multiple processors, and several additional secondary storage and other special-function devices (see Figure A.3).

An important characteristic of systems is that multiple systems can interact with one another. Some systems can function within other systems as subsystems. This interactive quality also applies to computer technology. A microcomputer on a secretary's desk is a system unto itself with input, processing, and output devices, and it can also be used to connect to a larger computer system that, for example, might be housed at a district office. Under this circumstance, the microcomputer functions as a part of the larger system or as a subsystem.

HARDWARE AND SOFTWARE

In the preceding discussion, the references are to the physical devices that comprise a basic part of any computer system. However, all computer systems must include two fundamental components: hardware and software. Hardware is the physical component—such as keyboards, video monitors, and disk drives. It also includes the wiring, circuit boards, and cabinetry that we can see and touch. Software is the nonphysical component or instructional component that directs the hardware. It consists of computer programs or sets of instructions communicated to the physical devices via electronic media such as magnetic disks and tapes. Critical to an understanding of computer technology is the fact that the physical devices are unable to perform any task without being directed to do so by software (computer programs).

The nonphysical aspect of software is sometimes difficult to understand for people who are not technically trained. Even trained technicians tend to refer to the computer as making the decisions and generating instructions. This is not the case.

To clarify this point, a comparison may be helpful. Imagine one person giving another person directions on how to get to the Grand Canyon from Chicago. The basic instructions might go something like this:

Take Airport car service to O'Hare International Airport.

Board American Airlines flight 999.

Fly to Phoenix.

Rent a car.

Drive north on Route 17.

Decide to go to either the North or South Rim of the Grand Canyon.

If going to the South Rim, drive north on Route 64.

Check in at the Bright Angel Lodge.

Enjoy!

To make sure that the traveler does not get lost or forget a point, the directions might be written on a piece of paper. In this example, the plane, car, and roads represent the computer hardware; they are the physical things that enable the traveler to get from one place to another. The directions are similar to computer software; they instruct the traveler in using the hardware to get to a destination—in this case, the Grand Canyon. These directions are not something physical; they are a logical plan of instructions that provide guidance to the traveler. Computer software is composed of the many logical plans of instructions called computer programs that guide physical devices to achieve a desired result. The piece of paper on which the directions to the Grand Canyon are written is similar to computer media such as magnetic disks and CD-ROMs that are used to communicate with the physical devices. The piece of paper can be referred to or read over and over again, as can computer media.

It is easy to understand how one person communicates with another person as long as they both speak the same language, but it is difficult to understand how the software communicates with the hardware. Does the hardware actually interpret and understand instructions? The answer is that it does so electronically.

THE CENTRAL PROCESSING UNIT

The most important piece of hardware in any computer system is the central processing unit (CPU). This unit is composed of vastly sophisticated, high-speed circuits that are capable of transmitting electronic impulses at speeds measured in terms of nanoseconds (billionths of a second) and picoseconds (trillionths of a second). The exact nature of these circuits differs from one computer manufacturer to another, and one would need several courses in electrical engineering to comprehend the finer points of modern CPUs.

Central processing units generally consist of three basic subunits: a control unit (CU), an arithmetic-logic unit (ALU), and a primary storage unit (PSU) (see Figure A.4). Each of these subunits has a very specific function and purpose. The

FIGURE A.4   **Conceptual Design of a Central Processing Unit**

CU interprets instructions and directs the processing of the other physical devices. The ALU performs all arithmetic operations, including comparisons. The PSU stores instructions and data. Physically, these subunits can be either separate components or integrated. Many computers use an integrated circuit or microprocessor that combines the control unit and the arithmetic-logic unit on a common *chip,* which is a thin wafer of silicon or other type of semiconductor material. The primary storage units generally are separate components within the CPU that can be replaced and enhanced as needed.

The control unit is the most sophisticated component of the CPU. It is capable of interpreting instructions that have been converted into electronic impulses or codes and directing the physical operations of all of the other devices in the computer hardware system. The control unit alone determines the sequence of tasks performed by the physical equipment. Before assigning new tasks, it verifies that the preceding tasks have been satisfactorily completed.

The arithmetic-logic unit performs all arithmetic operations such as addition, subtraction, multiplication, and division. It can do this because all data are converted into numeric codes in the CPU before they are received by the ALU. Data used in computer systems consist of all the letters of the alphabet, the digits 0 through 9, and special characters such as commas, periods, exclamation marks, and so forth. Each of these has a unique numeric code that enables the arithmetic-logic unit to manipulate them as numbers. Because all characters are converted into numeric codes, operations that usually might not be considered as arithmetic, such as alphabetizing or sorting a list of names, becomes an arithmetic operation in a CPU. Alphabetizing or sorting actually becomes a series of "less than/greater than" or subtraction operations.

The primary storage unit stores instructions and data; thus, it is also referred to as the memory unit. There are generally two types of PSUs: random-access memory (RAM) and read-only memory (ROM). Random-access memory stores instructions and data temporarily as needed to perform a specific computer operation. It is used to store instructions (portions of computer programs) at the time they are to be processed by the control unit. It is never used to store instructions or data permanently. Read-only memory is used to permanently store a set of instructions that are to be used over and over again. Once a set of instructions has been stored on a ROM, it generally cannot be changed—hence the term "read only." Special versions of ROM do exist that can be changed but are not regularly used in computer systems. Programmable read-only memory (PROM) and erasable programmable read-only memory (EPROM) are examples. All CPUs must have RAM for the temporary storage of instructions and data. Those that have only RAM store instructions and data permanently on other non-CPU storage devices such as magnetic disks or tapes.

The primary storage or memory capacity of a CPU is measured in terms of characters, or bytes. A byte is the minimum amount of memory needed to store a character of information and is made up of binary digits, or bits. A bit is a single electronic circuit capable of being in either the "on" or "off" position, conceptually similar to an ordinary light switch. When it is on, the electrical current is flowing; when it is off, the electrical current is stopped. Eight of these bits comprise a single byte, or the amount of memory needed to store one character of data (i.e., one letter of the alphabet, one digit 0 through 9, or one special character).

An important characteristic of all CPUs is the memory capacity of the primary storage unit. The earliest computers in the 1950s had memory capacities measured in thousands of bytes. Modern computers are measured in millions of bytes. Most microcomputers purchased today will have a minimum of 128 million bytes of primary storage. Large-capacity mainframe computers may have many millions of bytes of primary storage.

The number of bytes of primary storage available in a CPU determines the size and the number of computer programs that can be resident (running) at any one time. Therefore, the larger the primary storage capacity, the more computer programs that can be running and hence the more computer processing that can be performed. Although not as critical on microcomputers, which usually run several programs (e.g., word processing, database management, e-mail, electronic spreadsheet) at a time, memory size is very critical on mainframe computers, which are designed to run hundreds of programs simultaneously.

A brief introduction to data representation may be helpful for visualizing how characters are actually stored in the primary storage unit of the CPU. The two basic coding schemes for storing characters are American Standard Code for Information Interchange, or ASCII (pronounced "as-key"), and Extended Binary Coded Decimal Interchange Code, or EBCDIC (pronounced "ebb-sih-dick"). Table A.1 provides the actual coding schemes used in primary storage units. Note that each individual character code is eight binary digits (bits) long or the length of a single byte. These bits represent individual circuits that can be turned "on" or "off." A bit turned on is represented by a 1, and a bit turned off is denoted by a 0. For example, the ASCII codes for the first three letters of the alphabet are as follows:

A = 0100 0001
B = 0100 0010
C = 0100 0011

The vast majority (99.9%) of people who use computers do not need to know these codes. However, knowing that they exist provides a broader understanding of how computers operate. A fundamental characteristic of all digital computer systems is that data must be converted into a series of bit patterns or codes to be processed. The frequently used term *digital* as applied to computer systems means the numerical representation of data in bit format.

The control unit interprets instructions that have been converted into electronic impulses or codes. As with data, the various instructions that a computer can execute, such as reading a file from an input device or displaying a data record on a video monitor, are coded as a series of bit patterns referred to as the instruction set. The instruction set for each manufacturer's computer is different, and there are no generally accepted standards. Like data, every single instruction has to be converted into an appropriate bit code before being interpreted by the control unit.

TABLE A.1   ASCII and EBCDIC Data Codes

Character	ASCII	EBCDIC
0	0011 0000	1111 0000
1	0011 0001	1111 0001
2	0011 0010	1111 0010
3	0011 0011	1111 0011
4	0011 0100	1111 0100
5	0011 0101	1111 0101
6	0011 0110	1111 0110
7	0011 0111	1111 0111
8	0011 1000	1111 1000
9	0011 1001	1111 1001
A	0100 0001	1100 0001
B	0100 0010	1100 0010
C	0100 0011	1100 0011
D	0100 0100	1100 0100
E	0100 0101	1100 0101
F	0100 0110	1100 0110
G	0100 0111	1100 0111
H	0100 1000	1100 1000
I	0100 1001	1100 1001
J	0100 1010	1101 0001
K	0100 1011	1101 0010
L	0100 1100	1101 0011
M	0100 1101	1101 0100
N	0100 1110	1101 0101
O	0100 1111	1101 0110
P	0101 0000	1101 0111
Q	0101 0001	1101 1000
R	0101 0010	1101 1001
S	0101 0011	1110 0010
T	0101 0100	1110 0011
U	0101 0101	1110 0100
V	0101 0110	1110 0101
W	0101 0111	1110 0110
X	0101 1000	1110 0111
Y	0101 1001	1110 1000
Z	0101 1010	1110 1001

MICROS, MINIS, AND MAINFRAMES

Classifying or categorizing computer systems is not, and never was, an easy task. In some ways it was like trying to hit a moving target, because as technology improved, the classification systems kept changing. The simplest classification system was originally based on the physical size of the equipment. Microcomputers were considered small systems because they took up a small amount of space on top of a desk; mainframe computers were large systems that took up as much as several thousand square feet of space; and minicomputers were something in between. However, with a technology demanding precision, these classifications were very inexact. At the beginning of the 21st century, microcomputers can be the size of a credit card, a small briefcase (as in laptops), or a standard typewriter. Some minicomputers are available that are larger than mainframe computers. Mainframes are available that are the same size as a microcomputer.

Another way of differentiating computers has been according to the speed of the central processing unit as measured by *megaflops,* or millions of mathematical calculations per second. For example, an Apple Macintosh IIfx microcomputer executed 0.23 megaflops; a DEC Vax 8800 minicomputer, 1.3 megaflops; and an IBM Risc System/6000 mainframe, 62 megaflops. Some supercomputers (very large mainframes) were measured in billions of mathematical calculations per second. Though impressive to computer engineers and scientists, these speeds do not hold much significance for everyday computer users, most of whom are satisfied if their computer systems provide an acceptable level of response time. Because computers are continually becoming faster, any classification system based on the speed of the CPU is subject to continual revision.

The storage capacity of the CPU as measured by millions of bytes (characters) has also been frequently used as a way of differentiating computer systems. However, as with speed, primary storage capacity regularly increases. For example, as in the middle 1970s, most large mainframe computers only had 1 or 2 million bytes of primary storage, and microcomputers only had 16,000 to 32,000 bytes. In the year 2000, mainframe computers were approaching a billion bytes of primary storage, whereas high-end microcomputers had in excess of 100 million bytes. In general, the primary storage capacities of computers are doubling every 1 or 2 years.

Possibly the best way of describing the differences among micros, minis, and mainframes is based on the number of physical devices (input, output, storage) that can be controlled by their CPUs. Microcomputers generally consist of one CPU or microprocessor that is capable of controlling several other devices, usually fewer than a dozen. The CPU on minicomputers generally contains multiple microprocessors that are capable of controlling dozens of other devices. In most such systems, each microprocessor has a control unit and an arithmetic-logic unit, with separate primary storage units being shared by all the microprocessors. Mainframe computers, including the largest supercomputers, have hundreds of microprocessors that are capable of controlling hundreds and, in some cases, thousands of other devices.

A practical way of differentiating computer systems is by their unit costs. Microcomputers generally cost from several hundred to several thousand dollars;

minicomputers from tens of thousands to hundreds of thousands of dollars; and large mainframes from hundreds of thousands to millions of dollars for advanced supercomputers. However, costs are also constantly changing as manufacturers attempt to remain competitive. The cost of computing decreases as demand and competition increase.

The final assessment of computer classification—specifically the micro, mini, and mainframe—is that maybe the concept itself has become obsolete. The technology has changed and will keep changing, so that any classification system will be subject to constant revision.

INPUT DEVICES

The central processing units of all computers receive instructions and data through input devices. The keyboard and the mouse are probably the most familiar. However, in the past 15 years, an assortment of other input devices (touch-sensitive screens, light pens, Koala pads, joysticks, etc.) have evolved that are appropriate for educational applications. They may be a bit more expensive now or require special software, but they will likely play a more significant role in the years to come.

The basic input device for computers is the *keyboard,* which has been the mainstay for all types of computer systems since the 1950s and continues to be so today. Whether used for developing software, maintaining records, or doing word processing, the keyboard is the essential input device for computer systems. The key arrangement is the same as a typewriter keyboard. When a key is depressed, an electronic signal is sent to the CPU with the code of the respective letter, number, or special character. In addition, keyboards have special function keys that can be programmed to perform certain tasks automatically, such as transferring the contents of a video screen to a printer or saving a file on a disk. Many keyboards will also have a number pad, which simulates a calculator and is an important time-saver for users such as accountants, bank tellers, and bookkeepers.

Standard on microcomputers, the *mouse* is a handheld input device electronically connected to a video screen. The mouse is used to position a pointer on the screen, then the user presses a button to select options depending on the software used. For example, Macintosh and Windows-based microcomputers allow users to choose basic computer operations, such as shutting the computer down, formatting a new disk, or discarding an old file, simply by pointing the mouse to the desired option and clicking. For young children, the mouse is an especially attractive input device and easier to use than a keyboard.

A *touch-sensitive screen* performs the same function as a mouse but allows users to point to one of the options provided on the video screen. Although similar to a mouse, a touch-sensitive screen provides a more natural connection between the person and the machine. However, the options provided must be displayed in areas large enough to be easily discriminated by the size of a person's finger. For this reason, the mouse may be more appropriate for certain applications because it allows for very small objects to be available for selection. A touch-sensitive screen is also more expensive than a mouse and requires a special monitor.

Light-sensitive pens likewise can be used to point to options provided on a video screen. They are versatile, allowing for a great deal of interaction between user and machine. Of all the various input devices, light-sensitive pens permit the greatest accuracy when pointing or selecting an option. They also may be used for painting or drawing on a screen and so have significant potential in educational applications. They require special software that may be expensive depending on the application.

Graphics tablets such as *Koala pads* are electronic surfaces connected to a CPU and include software that allows instant display of the surface on the video monitor. They come with a pen, stylus, or arm that is used to manipulate or alter the image on the tablet and simultaneously on the monitor. Depending on the accompanying software, they can also perform other functions. They are very popular for electronic drawing applications and are very easy to use. Graphics tablets are becoming common on handheld microcomputers and information appliances.

Joysticks, trackballs, and *game paddles* are commonly used input devices for computer and video games. They allow for faster manipulation of the pointer and other objects on the video screen. Trackballs, in particular, became popular in the 1990s and are being supplied as standard input devices on several popular laptop computers.

Voice recognition devices allow users to input data or instructions by speaking into microphones that convert human speech into electronic impulses. This technology has not achieved its original promise but continues to improve. Because speech is the most natural way for people to communicate, it is likely that voice recognition devices will eventually be the major way of communicating with computer systems. Various voice recognition devices are on the market and working well in limited applications. In education, these devices are being used more and more in special education classes whose students may have limited hand dexterity.

Optical scanning devices—which include optical mark recognition (OMR), optical character recognition (OCR), handheld wands, and digitizers—have been available as special-purpose input devices for many years. They are used for scoring tests, reading bar codes on labels, and converting paper images into digital form. A number of machines have come on the market in recent years, securing the future of optical scanners as important input devices because they can be significant time-savers in converting printed and graphic materials into digital form, which thereby obviates the need to manually key in extensive amounts of data.

OUTPUT DEVICES

The major purpose of most computer systems is to produce various types of output so that users can see or read the results of their input and computer applications. The two basic output devices are video displays and printers.

Cathode ray tubes (CRTs) are the most common type of video displays. They generally use an electron gun that generates a light beam that can be scanned across a video screen. These beams are displayed as a series of picture elements, also known as pixels, that appear as single dots of light in horizontal and vertical patterns. A pixel (derived from the words *picture* and *element*) is very small. For example, on a medium-resolution video monitor, 128 pixels are needed to display a single character of data. Generally, the quality of a picture on a video display is directly related to its *resolution,* which is the number of pixels that can be displayed on the screen. The resolution of video monitors ranges from tens of thousands to more than a million pixels per screen. In addition to the number of pixels, the number of colors that can be displayed is also a significant factor in terms of image quality. For example, an image displayed on a video monitor with 300,000 pixels and 16 colors will not necessarily look as sharp as the same image displayed on a monitor with 60,000 pixels and 256 colors. The reason for this is that the large array of available colors can refine the image quality and make up for less resolution or a smaller number of pixels.

The tendency in education is to acquire color monitors to take advantage of the vast array of graphics software that is available. In evaluating color monitors, the choices are extensive, and options include standard color, RGB (red, green, blue), CGA (color graphics adapter), EGA (extended graphics adapter), PGA (professional graphics adapter), and VGA (video graphics adapter). These options all refer to the resolution and number of colors available. For most student uses, a standard color monitor is sufficient. For classroom presentations, the higher quality color monitors should be considered. This is especially true if a CRT is to double as both video monitor for a computer and as a television receiver for viewing educational TV programs. Receiver/monitors are the most versatile video devices available and also the most expensive. Nevertheless, they are becoming widely used for classroom presentations. Software packages, particularly those that require a certain level of resolution or color, will indicate their requirements in their brochures.

In addition to CRT displays, there are *plasma display* and *liquid crystal display* (LCD) devices. Plasma displays use neon and argon gas to produce a very high-quality and bright image. Liquid crystal displays or flat-panel displays, which are used in watches and calculators, are also being used as monitors. Most portable and laptop computers have switched to LCD technology. A good deal of research and development has gone into improving the quality of the images produced on LCDs, and in years to come this technology will likely replace CRTs as the major video output devices for computer systems.

Computers' ability to generate paper has become legendary. Stories abound about reams of computer-generated reports "drowning" their users in paper. Despite the jokes, the popularity of printed material in computer technology and the importance of printer output devices cannot be denied. Many types of printers are available, differentiated by the technology used to generate characters and images on a page. For microcomputers, the basic types are ink-jet, laser, dot-matrix, and daisy-wheel printers. For large mainframe computers, the basic types are laser and line printers.

Dot-matrix printers are the least expensive, and are most commonly used with microcomputer systems. They generate a series of small dots to form images and characters. The quality of images produced on dot-matrix printers ranges from poor to near-letter quality.

Daisy-wheel printers use a wheel with all the characters appended to them. They get their name from the fact that the appendages look like daisy petals. The wheel spins at very high speeds, and the appropriate character appendages strike a ribbon similar to a typewriter. Daisy-wheel printers are considered letter quality, which means that the image is comparable to that produced by a standard typewriter.

Ink-jet printers use tiny droplets of ink sprayed from a nozzle to produce images. They are considered letter quality, are very quiet, and are capable of producing color. If an application requires good color output, ink-jet printers are probably the best solution.

Laser printers are letter-quality printers that use laser technology to produce whole images on a page similar to a photocopying machine. The fact that they are page printers is an important distinction from the other printers that produce one character at a time along a print line. An important feature of some laser printers is their ability to be programmed to produce different size and style images including print fonts. For this reason, they are extremely popular with desktop publishing applications. Because of their advanced technology, laser printers are also more expensive than other printers. However, as the technology improves and production becomes cheaper, they are becoming less expensive. Laser printers for microcomputers can range from several hundred to several thousand dollars, depending on their features and options. For large mainframe computers, they can easily cost tens of thousands of dollars.

Line printers are used on large mainframe computers. They are very high-speed devices, printing at speeds in excess of 3,000 lines per minute. They print a line at a time using little hammers to strike characters through a ribbon onto continuous sheets of paper.

Plotters are a special type of printer designed to draw graphic displays on paper. Plotters are available for all types of computers (micros, minis, and mainframes). They are extremely useful for applications in art and drafting for which high-quality and color images need to be produced.

Voice output or *audio-response units* use speech synthesis to replicate the human voice. Most examples of voice output are for special and limited-purpose applications such as toys, games, and telephone answering systems. Like voice recognition units, which are input devices, they represent the most natural way for humans to communicate. Because of this, their future as an important part of computer technology is assured. However, the technology still needs to improve to be used routinely and to become a standard component of most computer systems. In education, their application in special education classes, especially those for the visually impaired, shows great promise.

SECONDARY STORAGE DEVICES

Secondary storage devices are used to store data and instructions permanently or at least until the application no longer needs them. They are called secondary storage devices to distinguish them from the primary storage devices that are part of the central processing unit. They are also referred to as input/output (I/O) devices because they are capable of reading data and instructions (input) and writing them (output). The major types of secondary storage devices are magnetic disks, magnetic tape, and optical discs.*

Today, magnetic disks are the most basic type of secondary storage devices and include floppy disks, hard disks, and fixed-head disks. They all use a similar technology that stores characters of data or instructions electromagnetically on disks or platters. These disks can be hard or rigid (i.e., composed of a metallic material) or soft or "floppy" (i.e., composed of a plastic material).

The disk drives (see Figure A.5) on which the disks rotate are spindles similar to a phonograph player. They use microscopic read/write heads, rather than a stylus (phonograph needle), that are capable of electromagnetically decoding and encoding data in digital format (bit patterns) on the disk's surface. These read/write heads are mounted on an extension arm that can extend itself across the radius (from the center to the outer edge) of the rotating disk. Data and instructions are stored on the disk in a series of concentric circles called tracks. Through software instructions, the read/write heads can move across the rotating disks and directly access any information stored on the disk. For this reason, magnetic disks are also referred to as *direct access storage devices*, or DASD (pronounced "dazz-dee"). The fact that the read/write heads actually move or extend themselves has led to their being called *moving-head disks*.

Another type of magnetic disk has a series of stationary read/write heads, one for each of the tracks on a disk. Because the heads do not have to move to access any of the information stored on the disk, these disks are referred to as *fixed-head disks*. Their major advantage over moving-head disks is that they save time by not having to extend the read/write heads across the radius of a rotating disk. But because they

FIGURE A.5   **Magnetic Disk Drive Operation**

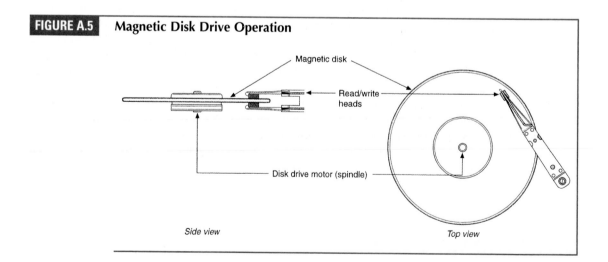

Side view   Top view

---

*According to the *Microsoft Press Computer Dictionary* (2002), "It is now standard practice to use the spelling *disc* for optical disc and the spelling *disk* in all other computer contexts (p. 1009). This approach is used throughout this book.

have a read/write head for each track (as many as 200), they are much more expensive than the single, moving-head disk drive. However, some extremely high-volume, high-speed applications require the additional speed, which makes these disks worth the additional cost.

An important characteristic of magnetic disks is their storage capacity. The smallest disks can store 1.5 million bytes of data. These are the familiar 3.5-inch floppy disks commonly available on microcomputer systems. Hard disks may be as large as 14 inches in diameter and can store from millions (megabytes) to billions of bytes (gigabytes) of data. Most mainframe computers use disk drives that can operate on a number or "pack" of disks stacked one on top of another. A stack of disks used for this purpose is referred to as a *disk pack.* On most microcomputers, there is a limit as to how many hard disk drives can be attached to a CPU. On large mainframe computers, many disk drives can be attached, which thereby increases a computer system's storage capacity to billions and trillions of bytes (terabytes).

Magnetic tape drives were the original secondary storage devices used on all computer systems. They operate similarly to a tape recorder; that is, a length of tape passes through an electromagnetic read/write (playback/record) head as it moves between two reels. Magnetic tapes were the major secondary storage devices used on large mainframe computers through the early 1970s. However, as magnetic disk technology developed with faster and greater direct access capability, magnetic tape (a device requiring the physical reading of all data records in sequence to reach the desired record) became too slow for many high-volume computer applications. As a result, the computer industry gradually moved to the use of disk equipment for most secondary storage needs. Magnetic tape is now used primarily to back up (make copies of) disk files and to transport large data files from one location to another.

The newest type of secondary storage is the *optical disc.* The term *optical* is used because the still-evolving technology depends on laser light for reading data from the disc surfaces. CD-ROM (compact disc read-only memory), WORM (write once, read many) discs, rewritable or erasable optical discs, DVD (digital versatile disc), and videodiscs are examples of the variety of devices available using laser technology for storing data. An important distinction among these different devices is the method of encoding data. They use either digital format—that is, bit patterns (on/off or 1 and 0) similar to all other digital computing equipment—or analog format similar to a series of video frames and sound tracks. Digital format can be directly accessed by CPUs and easily manipulated. Analog format cannot be directly accessed by CPUs and must pass through an analog to a digital converter or a video digitizer.

Optical discs that use digital format are already having a significant impact on secondary storage technology. Devices such as CD-ROMs are common on microcomputer systems. Although read-only, they are relatively inexpensive and capable of high storage capacities of 500 to 600 million bytes. They look like and are similar in size (4.75 inches) to CDs used for audio players. Compared with other secondary storage devices, they have high storage capacity for their size. For example, a CD-ROM can hold as much data as 400 of the original floppy disks (3.5-inch floppy disk with a storage capacity of 1.5 million bytes). Presently, a wide variety of computer applications are used with CD-ROM equipment—including reference works, software documentation, training manuals, and textbooks. WORM devices were the first attempt to develop a writing capability for optical discs. They are high-capacity (200 to 600 million bytes) and are similar in appearance to CD-ROMs. However, they provide the user with the ability to record or write data once on a disc surface. Data can then be accessed or read over and over again but can never be erased from the disc.

Erasable optical discs are also available. Their potential is significant—so much so that they may become the dominant secondary storage devices used on all computer systems, provided the technology for writing and erasing can be improved and the cost of manufacturing can be reduced.

IMAGE AND VIDEO TECHNOLOGY

Image and video technology, whether integrated with computer equipment or not, continues to play a significant role in education. Chapter 6 covers this topic in much greater depth, but a brief review of the major image and video media is appropriate here.

Image and Video Capturing

For individuals who use 35mm cameras and would like high-quality digital images, film developers such as Kodak will convert 35mm film into digital format for just a little more than the cost of normal film processing. To bypass the film-developing processing step, affordable digital cameras are available from major manufacturers such as Kodak, Canon, and Sony. They take the photographs, store them in digital format, and import them directly to a computer for subsequent processing. Once captured in digital format, photographs can be modified, edited, or enhanced through software.

For use in multimedia projects, the major video input media include camcorders, videotape, videodisc, CD-ROMs, and DVDs. Video boards are necessary computer components for using any type of video. Hardware and software are available that allow camcorders to connect directly to a computer's video board and subsequently convert the video into digital format. Most of this technology will accept camcorder input from the major manufacturers such as Canon, Sony, and Toshiba. Videocassette recorders and videodisc players can likewise be connected to a computer's video board for conversion to digital format.

Videocassette

Videocassette technology, which gained considerable popularity in the 1980s, remains an important technology for instruction. It is simple to use and graphically rich. Teachers and students alike have no problem dropping a videocassette into a VCR and hitting the Play button to provide video clips on subject matter. Teachers and students also increasingly have become familiar with using camcorders for creating videocassettes for classroom projects. A good deal of pedagogically valuable material is also available on videocassette from the Public Broadcasting Service (PBS), the Discovery

Channel, and other major educational software suppliers. The major limitation of videocassette technology is its noninteractive or passive nature. Viewing a videocassette in a class requires the teacher to stimulate discussions and activities. Videocassette is also a sequential medium with little or a generally clumsy Rewind/Playback facility for randomly selecting segments or clips from the larger videotape. As more advanced technologies (e.g., videodisc, CD-ROM, DVD) have evolved, the demise of the videocassette has been predicted many times. However, because of its simplicity, it remains an incredibly popular technology for instructional activities.

Analog Videodisc

Videodisc (or laserdisc) is an analog direct-access medium. Frames are stored on a series of concentric tracks on 12-inch or 8-inch metallic disks. Laser (light) technology is used to read the frames. Any individual frame or segment of frames can be accessed directly and played independently of any other frame. This technology has been popular for delivering instruction. Unlike digital video, videodisc may or may not be used with computer equipment, and because of its direct access capabilities, it is a much more advanced technology than videotape or other sequential media. Direct access also allows videodiscs to be integrated with computer technology to provide interactive video instruction as desired.

In the 1990s, a number of videodisc titles were produced specifically for education for the sciences, social studies, literature, art, and music. Optical Data Corporation, in particular, produced the highly acclaimed Windows on Science series. However, the future of videodisc technology is very much in doubt because most videodisc users are rapidly moving to new DVD formats.

Digital Versatile Disc Technology

Digital versatile (or video) disc (DVD) is a small plastic disc used for the storage of digital data and is the successor to the compact disc (CD). A DVD may have as much as 26 times the storage capacity of a CD; it also has better graphics and greater resolution. A DVD stores digital data as a series of microscopic pits on an otherwise polished surface. The disc is covered with a protective transparent coating so that it can be read by a laser beam. The playback or record heads never touch the encoded portion, and the DVD is not worn out by the playing process. Because DVD players are backward-compatible to existing optical technologies, they can play CD and CD-ROM discs; however, CD and CD-ROM players cannot play DVD discs.

At the time of this writing, a standard DVD format had not been established. DVDs can hold data in a number of evolving formats depending on the application. DVD formats include DVD-Video (often simply called DVD), DVD-ROM, and DVD-Audio. DVD-Video discs hold digitized movies or video programs and are played using a DVD player connected to a standard television monitor. DVD-ROM (read only memory) discs hold computer data and are read by a DVD-ROM drive hooked up to a computer. DVDs also include recordable variations. DVD-R (Recordable) discs can be written to sequentially but only once. DVD-RAM (random-access memory), DVD-RW, and DVD+RW (ReWritable) discs can be written to thousands of times.

The amount of content available in DVD format is growing significantly, especially for entertainment purposes. Educational content has begun to be developed and it is likely that this will grow significantly also. For example, Microsoft offers its Encarta Electronic Encyclopedia on one DVD—it used to require five CD-ROMs. Microcomputer manufacturers have begun to offer DVD drives instead of CD-ROM drives as standard equipment. Because of the backward compatibility mentioned earlier, most buyers are naturally opting for the newer DVD technology. All of this bodes well for the future of DVD.

DATA COMMUNICATIONS

Although the integration of computer technology and video technology is a relatively new development, computers have been routinely integrated with communications technology since the 1960s to provide an array of applications that transcend physical distance. The term *data communications* refers to the transfer of data between two or more digital devices over some physical distance. This distance may be several feet or thousands of miles.

The interconnection or "connectivity" of computer equipment transferring the data is called a *data communications network*. The most common interconnections use cable for short distances and telecommunications (i.e., telephone) for longer distances, although telephone systems can also be used for short-distance communications. Interconnecting computer equipment over some limited distance such as a room, building, or campus is commonly referred to as a *local area network* (LAN). Interconnecting equipment over longer distances such as throughout a large city, across a state, or spanning a nation or continent is called a *wide area network* (WAN). The 1990s saw the phenomenal growth of the Internet, which is the epitome of a wide area network.

Usually LANs use coaxial cable to connect various computer devices together, especially when confined to a single room, floor, or building. In addition to connecting the equipment physically, LANs also require specialized software to handle the transferring of data from one device to another. The sophistication of the software needed to control the network depends on how much interaction is required between the various devices.

Along with the number and type of devices, the amount of data to be transferred and the speed needed for transferring data are important factors in determining the software requirements. Central computer laboratories in many schools use a LAN to distribute instructional software. A typical network might consist of 20 or 30 microcomputers in a single room, with one microcomputer functioning as the central file server for the other microcomputers. The central file server usually has added hard disk storage so that it can contain a library of all the various software programs acquired by the school. Teachers or students using the other microcomputers access the central file server directly to select the individual program(s) needed. The central file server then downloads or sends a copy of the program over the network to the microcomputer that requested the program.

In the past few years, schools have begun to invest in *wireless local area networks* or WLANs. Conceptually, a WLAN is the same as a LAN without the connecting cables or wires, but instead uses high-frequency radio waves to send and receive data signals. While there are several variations, in a typical WLAN configuration a transceiver device, called an access point, connects to the school's wired network backbone from a fixed location using standard cabling. A backbone is a large data transmission line that carries data gathered from smaller lines that interconnect with it. Generally all LANs are connected to a network backbone in order to access the Internet and other wide area networks. The access point receives and transmits data between the WLAN and the wired network backbone. A single access point can support a number of users. Users access the wireless LAN through WLAN adapters, installed as PC cards in laptop, desktop, or portable (handheld) computers.

Although conceptually similar, WANs are more sophisticated networks than LANs because of the distances involved, the number of users, and the large amounts of data that can be transferred. However, the most important difference between WANs and LANs is that WANs require telecommunications or telephone facilities to connect the various devices on the network. In a LAN environment using coaxial cable, all the data transferred are in digital (bit pattern) format, and conversions are not required as the data pass from one device to another. In a WAN environment using telephone lines, this is not possible because telephone communications are not in digital but analog frequency format. This analog frequency format is a varying electric current that is generated from or converted into sound (i.e., human voice) by telephone transmitters or receivers, respectively. For computer equipment to use a telephone line, the computer's digital format must be converted into a frequency format and vice versa. To do this conversion, special equipment called *modulator-demodulators,* or *modems,* are needed. These are relatively inexpensive devices when used to connect a simple computing device such as a microcomputer, and most microcomputer manufacturers are now providing modems as standard devices. For larger computing systems, modems may be combined with other communications control equipment such as multiplexors and communications controllers, which in addition to modulating and demodulating signals are also able to perform complex message handling, protocol, and queuing operations.

The speed of modems as measured in bits per second (bps) varies significantly. Most microcomputers are being equipped with modems in the range of 56,000 bps. Modems for larger computer systems are usually measured in millions of bits per second. The growth of the Internet has generated a good deal of research and development in improving the speed of modems and other data communication devices. Broadband technology, for instance, which allows a single transmission circuit to carry millions of bits of data, is becoming more commonly available via cable modems, digital subscriber lines (DSL), and integrated services digital networks (ISDN). The costs for these broadband services have also been reduced dramatically so that many people can now afford them in their homes. Although WANs were originally designed and used by large corporations and public agencies for long-distance transaction processing such as making airline reservations and transferring funds, they are increasingly being used by everyone for a host of services. National networks such as America Online and AT&T provide electronic mail and shopping, reference, and financial services for modest fees to the general public. Many state education departments and large school districts have established WANs for record keeping and other administrative services such as reporting attendance, purchasing, and making library exchanges.

In view of the proliferation of the Internet, the telecommunications industry recognized the need for facilitating the integration with computing equipment and has moved rapidly to provide several high-speed digital data services, including wireless communication via satellite technology and fiber-optic cable-based services. The Internet established a standard protocol so that networks throughout the world could communicate with one another. The Internet promises to be the major source of all digital information in the years to come. Additional information on data communications technologies is available in Chapters 7 and 8.

COMPUTER SOFTWARE

Computer software is the instruction component of a computer system that directs the physical devices (hardware). Sets of instructions are called computer programs. These instructions may be communicated to the CPU through input devices such as a keyboard or a mouse, whereas instructions and programs that are executed over and over again are usually stored on storage devices such as magnetic disks.

There are two broad categories of software: system software and application software. *System software* directs, supervises, and supports the computer hardware system and all the tasks that are to be executed on it. *Application software* consists of all the computer programs "applied" to specific computer user activities such as word processing, record keeping, e-mail, computer-assisted instruction, and so forth.

The relationship of system software and application software is an important one for understanding how computers perform tasks. For clarification, compare two components of an automobile assembly-line plant. In the plant, the people who work directly on the assembly line are actually accomplishing the task of building cars. This is the application. However, for the assembly-line workers to complete their task, other workers must supervise and coordinate activities such as making sure that resources (e.g., raw materials) are available in sufficient quantities, that basic utilities (e.g., electricity) are functioning, and that certain tasks (e.g., quality control) are completed satisfactorily before commencing a new task. These activities are comparable to system software functions.

SYSTEM SOFTWARE

The most common example of system software is the *operating system,* which is a set of programs that all computer manufacturers provide for their computer systems. The operating system supervises and controls the activities of the physical devices and the application software. It is the master control program on which all computer processing depends. On larger mainframe computers, the operating systems are the most complex and sophisticated software programs being used, and the computer programmers who develop and maintain them are generally the most talented people on the technical staff.

Some computer manufacturers have actually named the operating systems used on their computers the *master control programs,* or MCPs. IBM has used names such as OS (operating system), DOS (disk operating system), and VS (virtual system). One of the most powerful, and one of the few machine-independent, operating systems is UNIX, developed by AT&T's Bell Laboratories in the 1970s. The UNIX operating system has proven to be especially effective in network environments and functioning as the server in client-server applications that are common on the Internet. A variation or hybrid of UNIX is an operating system named Linux, which was developed by Linus Torvalds in 1991. (Linux gets its name by combining *Linus* and *UNIX.*) Linux is open source software (OSS) that aims to be a viable alternative to proprietary operating systems.

On microcomputers, the operating systems are complex yet much easier to use and understand. Examples include Microsoft (MS)-DOS, Linux, OS/2, and Microsoft-Windows. Apple Computer popularized the concept of windows or a menu-driven operating system on its Macintosh computers. The menu can be displayed as small pictures or icons representing the available programs. Using a mouse, users click on the icon of the program or command they wish to execute.

Although operating systems differ from one manufacturer's computer system to another, almost all provide several fundamental programs or commands (see Table A.2). The three most important operating systems are supervisor programs, utility programs, and language translator programs.

Supervisor programs include job management, resource management, and data management programs. Job management programs allow users to execute their programs or tasks. They set job priorities and queues when there are multiple requests. Such ordering is critical, especially on mainframe computers capable of executing hundreds or thousands of programs simultaneously. Resource management programs allocate physical resources (devices) to programs and determine whether they are

TABLE A.2   **Basic Functions of Operating Systems**

Supervisor programs	Utility programs	Language processors
Job management	File copy	Assembler
Resource management	Disk copy	BASIC
Data management	Disk format	C
	Sort files	COBOL
	Merge files	FORTRAN
	Display files	PL/1
		Pascal

available. Computer systems with numerous physical devices require sophisticated resource management programs to control them. Data management programs allocate and retrieve data and programs on input/output devices such as magnetic disks. Because a major function of computer systems is to store data and programs, data management is critical on all computer systems. *Utility programs* that are used repeatedly are generally supplied in the operating system. Examples include programs for copying data files from one storage area to another, sorting data into alphabetical or numerical order, making backup copies of storage media such as magnetic disks, and preparing (formatting) new disks to store data.

Language translators, also referred to as *compilers* or *interpreters,* are programs that convert or translate commands into machine-readable or bit pattern instructions. Hundreds of programming languages are being used today. However, to use a particular language on a particular computer, a language translator program must be part of the operating system to convert instructions into a form that can be interpreted by the control unit of the CPU. Examples of language translator programs include the following:

> *BASIC (Beginner's All-Purpose Symbolic Instruction Code):* The most commonly used programming language available on microcomputers; developed by John Kemeny at Dartmouth University.
>
> *C:* A machine-independent language developed by Dennis Ritchie at Bell Laboratories in 1972. Because of its close association with the UNIX operating system, C has been especially popular in microcomputer-based networking environments. *C++* is an object-oriented version of C.
>
> *COBOL (Common Business-Oriented Language):* One of the first languages to use words (English) as the primary method of providing commands; the most commonly used language for business applications.
>
> *FORTRAN (Formula Translation):* One of the oldest programming languages, used mostly for scientific and mathematical applications; replaced by BASIC as the most commonly used programming language.
>
> *Logo:* A language designed for teaching young children how to program a computer; developed by Seymour Papert at MIT.
>
> *Pascal:* A highly structured language that is very popular for teaching proper programming style and techniques; developed by Niklaus Wirth in Zurich.
>
> *PL/1 (Programming Language 1):* A language originally designed to provide the best features of COBOL and FORTRAN.

Most of these languages use English-like words or commands such as *print, read, input,* and so forth, or arithmetic operators such as "+" (for addition) to provide instructions. These words, commands, or operators must be converted into a series of bit patterns (on/off codes) similar to the ASCII codes discussed earlier in order for them to be executed by the control unit. Simple programs may consist of several hundred instructions; more complex programs may consist of tens of thousands of instructions, all of which are translated before they are executed. The 1980s saw the introduction of object-oriented programming languages such as C++. These languages use a series of discrete objects that can be invoked to generate a series of commands or command structures. Object-oriented languages simplify programming by making commonly used tasks available at the click of a mouse. In all likelihood, the days of command-driven language translator programs may be numbered as object-oriented languages take their place.

DOS, MACINTOSH, AND WINDOWS

DOS is probably the most widely used operating system ever developed. Most users of microcomputers, especially those that have Microsoft Windows, would question this statement. However, Windows is basically a graphical interface for DOS on Intel-based microcomputers. So, every microcomputer that uses Windows also uses DOS. Developed for IBM machines by Microsoft, DOS originally was referred to as *PC-DOS* when used on IBM PC/PS microcomputers and as *MS-DOS* (the "MS" stands for Microsoft) when used on IBM-compatible computers. It was considered the standard operating system for all Intel-based microcomputers through the 1980s, and many other manufacturers besides IBM used it or something very similar on their own equipment.

DOS is a command-driven operating system, which means the user keys in a command on the keyboard to invoke a particular function. For example, the user would key in the command "Copy" to copy a disk file. Users are expected to commit these commands to memory or at least be able to look them up in a user's manual.

The Macintosh operating system, developed in the mid-1980s, is radically different from DOS and is patterned after operating system models developed in the 1970s at Xerox's Palo Alto Research Center (PARC). Though performing most of the same functions, the Macintosh is a menu-driven operating system that provides the user with a series of window selections from which a particular function can be invoked. Rather than key in a command on a keyboard, the user employs a mouse to select or click on a selection on a menu by pointing to it. The Macintosh operating system also introduced the extensive use of picture representations or icons to represent functions, files, and other system facilities rather than words or file names. The use of icons and menus that open as electronic windows is also referred to as a *graphical user interface,* or GUI (pronounced "gooey"). Other microcomputer operating systems have begun to move to the GUI style. As mentioned earlier, Microsoft's Windows operating system, for example, uses the GUI style as an interface for DOS. Because of this design, Windows has evolved to become probably the best-known operating system ever developed.

APPLICATION SOFTWARE

Application software includes the programs that actually perform the specific user tasks for which the computer system was acquired. In a bank, they would involve the financial record-keeping applications. In a hospital, medical record keeping and patient monitoring would be common applications. In a school, administrative and instructional applications are the two major categories; Chapters 4 through 7 are devoted entirely to the nature of these applications.

SUMMARY

This appendix introduces the basic concepts of computer systems. Covering the entire field of computer science is not possible here; only the major concepts and developments in hardware and software important to school administrators are included.

In terms of hardware, the computer system is made up of input, processing, output, and storage devices. The central processing unit (CPU)—which includes the control, arithmetic-logic, and primary storage units—is the fundamental hardware component of every computer system. Input devices such as keyboards provide data and instructions to the CPU. Output devices such as printers receive data and instructions from the CPU. Storage devices such as magnetic disk drives provide data and instructions and receive them from the CPU. All of these physical devices work together as a common hardware system to provide computer services to users. These are sometimes connected through data communications systems called wide area networks (WANs) and local area networks (LANs).

The physical devices or hardware can respond only to instructions that have been provided in the form of a computer program. Computer programs, developed by people, are communicated to the CPU by way of keyboards, magnetic disks, and other computer media. The two broad categories of computer software are system software and application software. System software is all the programs and instructions that control, supervise, and coordinate the physical devices and the application software programs. Application software is all the other programs that actually accomplish the specific tasks for which the computer is being used. In schools, the two major categories of application software are administrative applications and instructional applications.

KEY CONCEPTS AND QUESTIONS

1. A computer system is made up of interrelated hardware and software components. How do you distinguish hardware from software? What are some of the major hardware components? Are they essentially the same in all computer systems? Explain.

2. The central processing unit (CPU) conceptually is divided into three subunits: control, arithmetic-logic, and primary storage. How do these subunits differ? What is a microprocessor, and what is its relationship to the CPU? What is the difference between primary and secondary storage?

3. The terms *microcomputer, minicomputer,* and *large mainframe computer* are used to classify types of computer systems. How appropriate are these classifications? What are some of the characteristics on which these classifications are based?

4. Computer systems can include a variety of different input and output devices. Identify those devices that are appropriate only for specialized applications. Which are common to all applications?

5. Secondary storage devices have advanced significantly during the past 30 years. In particular, storage technology has favored direct access processing like that provided by magnetic disks. Why is direct access processing beneficial? What types of applications are dependent on it? What is sequential processing? What secondary storage device is most associated with it? What does the future hold for secondary storage technology?

6. Computer technology is gradually becoming integrated with other technologies such as video and communications. How has the integration of these technologies been progressing? What are the future implications?

7. Computer software is categorized as system software and application software. How do they differ? Is one dependent on the other? Explain. Are they different depending on the type of computer equipment being used? Explain.

SUGGESTED ACTIVITIES

To complete the Suggested Activities online, go to the Companion Website at **www.prenhall.com/picciano,** then to this chapter's *Suggested Activities module.*

REFERENCE

Microsoft Press Computer Dictionary. (2002). Redmond, WA: Microsoft Press.

For more information on competencies, go to the *Web Links module* for this chapter on the Companion Website at **www.prenhall. com/picciano**.

APPENDIX B

Educational Leader Competencies

This appendix attempts to identify some of the competencies required for educational administrators to be leaders in planning, developing, and implementing technology in their schools and districts. A more extensive set of competencies for administrators, teachers, and students has been developed by the International Society for Technology in Education (ISTE).

■ BASIC TECHNOLOGY

1. Educational leaders have an understanding of the principles of a digital computer system and other technologies used in schools and school districts.

2. Educational leaders have an understanding of the use of basic software applications (e.g., word processing, spreadsheet, office automation applications).

3. Educational leaders have had experience in making efficient use of complex electronic information resources (e.g., databases).

4. Educational leaders understand the power of data communications networks and are able to use these networks to facilitate communications and professional growth (e.g., e-mail, electronic bulletin boards, Internet and World Wide Web navigation).

5. Educational leaders understand the benefits of multimedia and presentation technologies for communication, teaching, and learning.

■ PLANNING, DEVELOPING, AND IMPLEMENTING TECHNOLOGY

1. Educational leaders model the effective use of technology in support of teaching, learning, and administrative functions in their professional activities.

2. Educational leaders are competent in leading and managing systemic change processes at the school building and/or district levels.

3. Educational leaders are able to initiate and support professional development processes and programs that respect the concerns of adult learners.

4. Educational leaders develop and maintain a knowledge of the current applications of technology related to administration, teaching, and learning.

5. Educational leaders are able to identify and maintain the financial resources needed to support technology applications at the school building and/or district levels.

6. Educational leaders are aware of the ethical, social, and equity issues related to technology (e.g., equitable access, fair use, copyright, free speech).

7. Educational leaders are aware of a variety of strategies and techniques for evaluating the outcomes of technology-related initiatives and projects.

8. Educational leaders understand the importance of integrating technology into an overall school building and/or district planning process.

GLOSSARY

access point A transceiver device that connects to the school's wired network backbone from a fixed location using standard cabling.

access time The time required to fetch data from a source once a request has been made. It is most commonly used to refer to accessing data from a primary or secondary storage device.

Advanced Research and Projects Administration Network (ARPANET) A worldwide data communications network established by the U.S. Department of Defense in the 1960s that evolved into the Internet.

ALN *See* asynchronous learning network.

ALU *See* arithmetic-logic unit.

analog A general term used to refer to a continuous physical property such as voltage, current, fluid pressure, rotation, and so on.

application software Programs that "apply" the computer to perform specific tasks or solve specific problems. Examples include word processing, electronic spreadsheets, and graphics programs.

arithmetic-logic unit (ALU) The part of the central processing unit that performs all arithmetic operations, including comparisons.

ARPANET *See* Advanced Research and Projects Administration Network.

ASCII An acronym for American Standard Code for Information Interchange, a coding scheme that represents letters of the alphabet, numerals, and special characters as a series of binary digits or numbers.

asynchronous Happening at different times. Asynchronous communication, for instance, is characterized by time-independence; that is, the sender and receiver do not communicate at the same time. An example is electronic mail.

asynchronous learning network (ALN) A form of distance learning that uses computer networking technology—especially the Internet—for instructional activities.

audio response unit Any device that produces a spoken word from a computer in response to a question or command.

authoring language A user-friendly programming language used to develop specific applications such as teaching presentations, computer-assisted instruction, and multimedia. Examples include HyperCard, HyperStudio, ToolBook, and PowerPoint.

authoring system *See* authoring language.

backbone A large data transmission line that carries data gathered from smaller lines that interconnect with it.

bandwidth In communications, the frequencies within which signals can be transmitted and received. Bandwidth directly relates to data transfer speed. The greater the bandwidth, the faster the data transmission speed.

BASIC An acronym for Beginners All-Purpose Symbolic Instruction Code, a high-level computer programming language developed by John Kemeny and Thomas Kurtz at Dartmouth University in the 1960s. Because of its general availability on most microcomputers, BASIC has become the most popular high-level language ever developed.

benchmark   A test used to measure the performance (i.e., speed or accuracy) of computer hardware or software.

binary digit   In the binary number system, either 0 or 1. *See also* bit.

bit   A binary digit. In the binary number system, the bit is either 0 or 1. In electronic storage, it represents the smallest unit of data and is characterized as being either "on" or "off." Groups of eight bits are combined to represent characters of data that are referred to as bytes.

broadband   A high-capacity communications circuit that is capable of transmitting data at high speed, up to millions of bits per second.

browser software (Web browser)   Software that provides facilities for accessing uniform resource locators (URLs) on the World Wide Web. Examples of Web browsers include Netscape and Internet Explorer.

bug   An error or problem in software or hardware.

byte   The minimum amount of primary storage or memory needed to store a character (letter, numeral, special character, etc.) of information. It is usually eight binary digits or bits.

C   A programming language developed at Bell Laboratories in 1972. Designed originally to work with the UNIX operating system, it has become widely popular on many micro-computers.

C++   An object-oriented version of the C programming language.

CAI   *See* computer-assisted instruction.

CAL   Acronym for computer-assisted learning or computer-augmented learning. *See* computer-assisted instruction.

cathode-ray tube (CRT)   The most common type of video display screen. It uses an electron gun to generate a light beam that is scanned across a screen.

CBE   *See* computer-based education.

CBT   *See* computer-based teaching.

CD-ROM   An acronym for compact disc read-only memory. It is a form of high-capacity optical storage that uses laser technology.

central file server   The central or host computer in a network that provides files and programs to other computers.

central processing unit (CPU)   The part of a computer hardware system that directs all pro-cessing activities. It consists of electronic circuitry and includes a control unit, an arithmetic-logic unit, and a primary storage or memory unit. On large computers, the term is used to refer to the entire main computer console. On some microcomputers, it refers only to the control unit and the arithmetic-logic unit.

character   A letter, numeral, or special character such as a comma or exclamation point that can be represented by one byte.

client server system   A distributed data communications system in which computers perform two important functions as either "clients" or "servers." The client function makes requests for data (i.e., files) from the server, which locates the data on the data communi-cations system and processes the request for the client.

clip media   Digital files or libraries containing images, video, sounds, and other media that can readily be incorporated into a multimedia program.

CMI   *See* computer-managed instruction.

CMS   *See* course management software.

COBOL   An acronym for Common Business-Oriented Language, a high-level programming language developed in 1959 that uses English-like commands. It became popular for business applications.

communications controller   A data communications device that is used to send and receive messages from multiple sources. A multiplexor is an example of a communications controller. In some networks, communications controlling is performed by computer programs that are also referred to as communications controllers.

communications control program   *See* communications controller.

computer   An electronic device that accepts input, processes it according to a set of instructions, and produces the results as output. Computers can be classified as supercomputers, mainframes, minicomputers, microcomputers, laptop computers, and so forth, depending on physical size, speed, and peripheral devices.

computer-assisted instruction (CAI)   The use of the computer to assist in the instructional process. One of the earliest used terms to generically refer to computer applications in education, it is used now to refer to tutor-type applications such as drill and practice and tutorials.

computer-assisted learning   *See* computer-assisted instruction.

computer-augmented learning   *See* computer-assisted instruction.

computer-based education (CBE)   A generic term used to refer to the broad array of instructional computer applications.

computer-based teaching (CBT)   A generic term used to refer to the use of a computer by teachers as part of an instructional presentation such as an interactive video.

computer chip   *See* integrated circuit.

computer hack   *See* hacker.

computer-managed instruction (CMI)   The use of the computer in an instructional process in which student progress is monitored and recorded for subsequent instructions and review. Most CMI applications are also able to adjust material to each individual student's level of understanding.

computer program   A set of instructions to direct physical devices to perform some task.

constructivism   Theory of learning that stresses the importance of experiences, experimentation, problem solving, and the construction of knowledge.

control unit (CU)   The part of the central processing unit that interprets instructions and directs the processing of the other physical devices.

course management software (CMS)   A set of computer software tools designed to enable users to create Web-based courses. Examples include CourseInfo, WEBCT, TopClass, and LearningSpace.

CPU   *See* central processing unit.

CU   *See* control unit.

cyberspace   Descriptive term for the Internet.

daisy-wheel printer   An impact printer that uses a daisy-wheel-type element to strike a character through an inked ribbon onto a sheet of paper.

DASD   *See* direct access storage device.

database   A collection of data files and records.

database management system (DBMS)   A package of computer programs that allow users to create, maintain, and access the data on a database.

data communications   The methods and media used to transfer data from one computer device to another. Common data communications media include coaxial cable, telephone, fiber optics, and satellite systems.

data disaggregation   The use of software tools to break down data files into various characteristics. An example might be using a software program to select student performance data on a standardized test by gender, by class, by ethnicity, or by other definable characteristics.

data-driven decision making   Using data analysis to inform when determining courses of action involving policy and procedures. An important aspect of this definition is that data analysis is used *to inform* and does not replace the experience, expertise, intuition, judgment, and acumen of competent educators.

data element   A grouping of characters (letters of the alphabet, numerals, special characters) to represent some specific data characteristic of a person, place, or thing. Examples include a person's name, street address, and gender. Also referred to as a data field or data item.

data element dictionary   A table used to identify the content and coding schemes used for all the data elements in a database. Can also refer to a document that identifies the content, definitions, and coding schemes used for all data elements in a database.

data field   *See* data element.

data file   A collection of related data records. Examples include a personnel file of all personnel records or a student file of all student records.

data item   *See* data element.

data mining   A frequently used term in research and statistics that refers to searching or "digging into" a data file for information to better understand a particular phenomenon.

data processing   A general term used for the systematic processing (storing, manipulating, sorting, etc.) of data on computer systems.

data record   A grouping of related data elements for a single entity such as a person, place, or thing. Examples include a personnel record, inventory record, and financial record.

data structure   The method by which data are organized in a database.

data warehousing   A computerized database information system that is capable of storing and maintaining data *longitudinally* over a period of time.

DBMS   *See* database management system.

desktop publishing   The use of computer equipment to develop text and graphics. It usually refers to software that provides enhanced facilities for displaying characters, pictures, and color.

digital   Related to digits. Computers are considered digital because all data and instructions are represented as binary digits.

digital versatile disc (DVD)   A small plastic disc used for high-capacity optical storage of digital data that uses laser technology. Same as digital video disc.

digital video disc   *See* digital versatile disc.

digitizer   Any device used to convert analog (continuous physical property such as voltage or current) signals into binary or digital format.

direct access storage device (DASD)   Any secondary storage device such as a magnetic disk or optical disc that allows users to access data in a direct or nonsequential manner.

directory   A grouping or catalog of filenames that reside on a secondary storage device such as a disk. On Macintosh microcomputers, a directory is referred to as a folder.

disk operating system   A generic term used to refer to any operating system that resides on a disk device and is loaded as needed into primary storage.

Disk Operating System   *See* DOS.

distance learning   A term for the physical separation of teachers and learners that has become popular in recent years, particularly in the United States. While used interchangeably with distance education, distance learning puts the emphasis on the "learner" and is especially appropriate when students take on greater responsibility for their learning, as is frequently the case when doing so from a distance.

distributed system   A form of computer processing that distributes and links hardware over some geographic area as in a network. It assumes that the local hardware can perform some tasks and expand its capabilities by connecting to other hardware.

DOS   An acronym for Disk Operating System, the most popular operating system for Intel-based (i.e., IBM PC and PC-compatible) microcomputers. It is also referred to as Microsoft or MS-DOS after the company that developed it.

dot-matrix printer   An impact printer that forms text and images as a pattern of dots.

downlink   The transmission of data from a communications satellite to an earth station.

download   In a computer network, the process of transferring a copy of a file from one computer, generally referred to as a central file server, to another, requesting computer.

drill and practice   A form of tutor software used to reinforce a lesson or material that has already been presented to a student. It is characterized by repetitive questioning or drills.

DVD   *See* digital versatile disc.

EBCDIC   An acronym for Extended Binary Coded Decimal Interchange Code, a coding scheme developed by IBM for use on mainframe and minicomputer systems that represents letters of the alphabet, numerals, and special characters as a series of binary digits or numbers.

electronic bulletin board   A group e-mail or mailing list that allows all participants to post and read messages.

electronic mail (e-mail)   The transmission of messages over a data communications network.

electronic spreadsheet   Application programming software that provides the user with an electronic grid of rows and columns similar to a ledger worksheet. It is used extensively for budgeting, forecasting, projections, and other number-based applications. Examples include Excel and Lotus 1-2-3.

e-mail   *See* electronic mail.

environmental scanning   A term used in planning that means engaging in activities to provide information outside of an organization or on the external environment.

EPROM   An acronym for erasable programmable read-only memory, which is a type of read-only memory that can be programmed or rewritten to.

E-Rate   A U.S. government-managed program that provides discounts on telecommunications technologies to schools. Discounts are based on the percentage of students in a school participating in the federal free lunch program.

ergonomics   The study and design of people in work environments. The objective is to develop comfortable and safe conditions so as to improve worker morale and efficiency.

Ergonomics is especially important in designing computer hardware such as keyboards and video display devices.

fiber optics　The method of transmitting and receiving light beams along an optical fiber that is usually made of a thin strand of glass. Fiber optics are destined to radically change the speed and nature of communications throughout the world.

file transfer protocol (FTP)　A popular protocol used for transferring data files on the World Wide Web.

floppy disk　*See* magnetic disk.

folder　A grouping or cataloging of filenames that reside on a secondary storage device such as a disk. The term is most commonly used on Macintosh microcomputers. It is similar to a directory on IBM PC and PC-compatible microcomputers.

FORTRAN　An acronym for Formula Translation, a high-level programming language developed in 1954. Although originally developed for scientific and engineering applications, it established several programming concepts such as variables, subroutines, input/output formats, and so forth, which continue to form the basis for many other programming languages.

frame rate　The number of frames or images per second displayed on a video device. Thirty frames per second is the full-motion video standard.

FTP　*See* file transfer protocol.

gigabyte　One billion bytes.

gopher　A database communications protocol used for locating data files on the World Wide Web.

graphical user interface (GUI)　The graphic display of software options in the form of icons and pictures that can be selected, usually by a pointing device such as a mouse. It is considered a feature of user-friendly software such as that provided with the Macintosh operating system, Microsoft Windows, and many application software packages.

graphics tablet　An electronic surface connected to a central processing unit. It comes with a pen, arm, or stylus to draw images that are automatically transferred to the CPU.

GUI　*See* graphical user interface.

hacker　Someone who seems overly involved with computer hardware and software. Also refers to people who gain unauthorized access to computer networks and databases.

handheld computer　A small portable computer capable of being used (held) in one hand.

hard disk　*See* magnetic disk.

hardware　The physical components of a computer system, such as the central processing unit, printer, keyboard, and so on.

high-level language　A programming language that uses common words and symbols that are translated into computer machine language instructions by way of a compiler or interpreter. Examples include FORTRAN, BASIC, COBOL, and Pascal.

HTML　*See* hypertext markup language.

http　*See* hypertext transfer protocol.

HyperCard　An authoring language designed for the Apple Macintosh microcomputer. It established several important new concepts—such as fields, buttons, and stacks—that have been copied by other authoring languages.

hypermedia　A computer-based information retrieval system for accessing sound, text, images, graphics, or video in a nonsequential or nonlinear format.

hypertext   A computer-based text and document retrieval system that can be accessed in a nonsequential or nonlinear format.

hypertext markup language (HTML)   Software language used to establish data files for access on the World Wide Web.

hypertext transfer protocol (http)   The most commonly used protocol on the World Wide Web. It runs in conjunction with TCP/IP.

ICAI   *See* intelligent computer-assisted instruction.

icon   A graphic image displayed on a video screen, representing an object—usually a file or command that can be referenced or executed by a user. Icons are common features of user-friendly software referred to as graphical user interfaces.

IIS   An acronym for integrated instructional system. *See* integrated learning system.

ILS   *See* integrated learning system.

information superhighway   Descriptive term for the Internet.

ink-jet printer   A nonimpact printer that uses droplets of ink sprayed from a tiny nozzle.

input device   Any device that is used to enter or bring data to a central processing unit.

input/output device (I/O device)   Any device that can be used to enter data to or receive data from a central processing unit.

instruction set   The set of machine instructions that the control unit of a central processor recognizes and can execute.

integrated circuit   Circuit that combines two or more electronic circuits (transistors, resistors, etc.) onto a thin wafer of silicon or other type of semiconductor material. A microprocessor is an integrated circuit that usually combines a control unit or circuit and an arithmetic-logic unit or circuit. Same as a computer chip.

integrated instructional system (IIS)   *See* integrated learning system.

integrated learning system (ILS)   A single computer package for delivering instruction that combines hardware, software, curriculum, and management components. It is usually supplied by a single vendor.

Integrated Services Digital Network (ISDN)   A high-speed (128 kilobits per second) data communications network evolving from existing telephone services.

integrated software package   A software package that integrates several programs into a single comprehensive program. An example is Microsoft Office, which combines word processing, spreadsheet, database, communications, and graphics.

intelligent computer-assisted instruction (ICAI)   Similar to CAI but also uses a substantial database of information for presenting material and selecting instructional paths.

interactive   Operating in a back-and-forth mode. It refers to user and machine dialogue or interaction in which both are active participants in a process.

interactive video   Combining computer and video technologies to provide an active video environment in which users can control and select options based on a given application. Interactive video is a major advancement over other video technologies such as film and television, which are considered "passive."

interface   The point at which two components meet. With computers, it is used for both hardware (when two physical devices connect to one another) and software (when two programs work with one another). It is also used to refer to points at which people connect to computer devices such as with graphical user interfaces.

Internet   The network of networks that provides the basic protocol standard for allowing data communications systems to link themselves together throughout the world.

Internet Relay Chat (IRC)   Computer software that allows multiple parties to participate in synchronous (same time) communications on the Internet.

intranet   In data communications, the adoption of the standard Internet protocol and software tools for a local network or establishing a mini-Internet within a local system.

ISDN   *See* Integrated Services Digital Network.

Java   An object-oriented programming language that attempts to operate across software platforms.

JavaScript   A programming language similar to Java that generally operates with World Wide Web browser software.

joystick   An input device popular with computer games and used to point to objects on a video screen.

kilobyte (KB)   One thousand bytes.

Koala pad   A form of graphics tablet or electronic surface connected to a central processing unit. It comes with a pen, arm, or stylus used to draw images on the tablet that are automatically transferred to the CPU.

LAN   *See* local area network.

laptop   A type of portable computer that can easily be used by resting it on one's lap.

laserdisc   An optical disc used to store video images and associated audio or sound information in analog format. Same as a videodisc.

laser printer   A nonimpact printer that uses laser technology to produce a high-quality image on a page.

light pen   An input device that allows the user to point to objects on a screen with a pen-shaped wand. It can also be used for drawing and designing shapes and figures.

line printer   An impact printer that prints one line at a time.

Linux   A variation of UNIX that is an open source operating system developed by Linus Torvalds in 1991.

liquid crystal display (LCD)   A flat-panel video display that uses electroluminescent (liquid crystal) material to produce a light image. Very popular in watches and portable and laptop computers.

LISP   An acronym for list processing. It is a high-level programming language developed in 1959 and used extensively in artificial intelligence applications.

local area network (LAN)   Connecting computer equipment using data communications over a limited geographic area such as a room, building, or campus.

Logo   A high-level programming language developed by Seymour Papert in 1968; a very popular programming language for teaching young children to use a computer.

machine cycle   The time required for a central processing unit to perform its fastest operation as determined by its internal clock.

machine language   Instructions that are represented in binary form (1s and 0s). All computer instructions must be converted or reduced to machine language instructions for the central processing unit to execute them.

magnetic disk   A form of secondary computer storage that uses electromagnetic technology to store data. A magnetic disk can be made of metallic (hard disk) or plastic (floppy disk) substances. Because the read/write head on a magnetic disk drive can move across the surface of a disk, this technology is used for direct or random processing. A magnetic disk is the actual platter on which data reside. The device that stores and retrieves data on magnetic disk is a disk drive.

magnetic disk drive   *See* magnetic disk.

magnetic tape   A form of secondary computer storage that uses Mylar tape to store data. Because the tape passes through a stationary read/write head, this technology is used strictly for sequential processing. Magnetic tape is the actual reel of tape on which data reside. The device that stores and retrieves data on magnetic tape is a tape drive.

magnetic tape drive   *See* magnetic tape.

mainframe   Large computer systems capable of processing extensive amounts of data and of controlling many peripheral devices. IBM and Hitachi are the major manufacturers of mainframe computer equipment.

media distribution system   A computer-based system that integrates several media sources (videotape, videodisc, computer, camera, etc.) and is able to distribute them to selected output devices.

megabyte (MB)   One million bytes.

megaflops (MFLOP)   One million arithmetic operations per second.

megahertz (MHz)   One million machine cycles per second.

memory   *See* primary storage unit.

menu   A presentation of options available that a user can select or request from a program. Menu-driven software anticipates user options and presents them in the form of lists or icons.

microcomputer   A small computer system that usually uses one central processing unit. Apple, COMPAQ, Dell, Gateway, IBM, and Sony are among the most popular manufacturers of microcomputers.

microprocessor   A central processing unit used for most microcomputer systems capable of being integrated on a single chip. *See* integrated circuit.

microsecond   One millionth of a second.

millisecond   One thousandth of a second.

minicomputer   A computer system, midrange between a large mainframe and microcomputer. Minicomputers are highly effective in network environments where they are used to control microcomputers and other minicomputers. Digital Equipment Corporation (now a part of COMPAQ) and Sun Microsystems are among the leading manufacturers of minicomputers.

MIP   An acronym for million instructions per second. Similar to megaflop.

modem   *See* modulator-demodulator.

modulator-demodulator (modem)   A data communications device used to convert computer digital signals into a telephone frequency or analog signal and vice versa.

monochrome   A video monitor that displays images in one color.

morphing   Relating to form or structure. Morphing software is designed to edit and manipulate graphics such as images and video.

mouse   A handheld input device that is electronically connected to a video screen and is used to position a pointer to make software selections by pressing a button.

multimedia   Combining sound, text, images, animation, and video. With computers, it refers to a variety of applications that utilize CD-ROM, videodisc, and audio equipment.

multiplexor   A data communications device used to control many messages by funneling them into a smaller number of communication lines or ports.

nanosecond   One billionth of a second.

narrowband   A low-capacity communications circuit that is capable of transmitting data at speeds of up to 56 thousand bits per second.

network   A group of computer devices connected by a data communications system. Two major types of networks are local area networks (LANs) and wide area networks (WANs).

notebook   A very lightweight portable computer, usually weighing less than 10 pounds, that can be easily carried under one's arm.

office automation   The use of computer and data communications equipment to perform office functions electronically rather than manually. Examples of office automation applications include word processing, electronic mail, and desktop publishing.

open system architecture   A term used to refer to any computer or hardware device that has published design specifications so that other (third party) manufacturers can develop compatible hardware components.

operating system   A type of system software that acts as a master control program and directs the processing of all physical devices and application programs. Examples of operating systems include DOS (Disk Operating System), Windows, and the Macintosh operating system.

optical character reader (OCR)   *See* optical scanning device.

optical disc   A secondary storage device that utilizes laser technology for storing data. CD-ROM is a form of optical disc.

optical mark reader (OMR)   *See* optical scanning device.

optical scanning device   An input device that uses light sensors to scan paper documents and convert images into digital format. Optical mark readers and optical character readers are types of optical scanning devices.

output device   Any device that receives data from a central processing unit.

Pascal   A highly structured, procedural programming language developed by Nicholas Wirth in 1967. It is very popular for teaching structured programming techniques to beginning programmers.

PC   An acronym for personal computer. *See* personal computer.

peripheral   Any hardware device—such as a printer, keyboard, magnetic disk, magnetic tape, and so on—that connects to a central processing unit.

personal computer   A generic term used for any microcomputer that is used by one person. It is also the model name (Personal Computer or PC) that IBM adopted for its microcomputers.

picosecond   One trillionth of a second.

pixel   Short for picture element. A point on a grid such as a video screen that represents a single dot of light. Text and images are developed by manipulating many pixels.

plasma display   A flat-panel video display that uses neon or argon gas to produce a light image. Also referred to as a gas-discharge display.

platform   The foundation hardware and operating system software technology of a computer system. Examples include Motorola/Macintosh and Intel/DOS/Windows platforms. The term *software platform* is also used to refer to only the basic operating system software.

PL/1   An acronym for Programming Language I. It is a high-level programming language developed in 1964, designed to combine the best features of FORTRAN and COBOL.

plotter   An output device used to draw charts, maps, diagrams, and other line-based graphics.

plug-in   A dynamic computer code module that performs a specific task, which generally is made available or functions with World Wide Web browser software.

portable computer   Any computer designed to be carried and moved about. Laptop, note-book, and handheld computers are examples of portable computers.

portal   A main point of entry to the Internet that provides a full range of Internet services such as e-mail, search engines, access to databases, and useful links to other Web sites.

primary storage unit (PSU)   The part of the central processing unit that stores instructions and data. Also referred to as memory.

probeware   Hardware and software used to conduct experiments of physical properties such as temperature, light, and humidity. Probeware is characterized by the use of probes to measure physical surroundings.

PROM   An acronym for programmable read-only memory, which is a type of read-only memory that can be programmed or written to once.

protocol   A general term for a set of rules, procedures, or standards used to exchange information in data communications. Examples include a code or signal indicating the beginning of a message, a code or signal indicating the end of a message, or a code or signal indicating that a device is busy with another task. Computer manufacturers have established various protocols for exchanging information on their equipment.

PSU   *See* primary storage unit.

query language   A user-friendly language that enables users to retrieve and display data from a database.

RAM   An acronym for random-access memory. A type of primary storage that can have data and instructions read from and written to it by a central processing unit. Also referred to as volatile memory because it can keep changing.

read/write head   The read and write or playback and record mechanism on secondary storage devices such as magnetic disk and tape drives.

relational database   A database structure that uses a table to relate or link one data element with another data element.

resolution   Clarity of detail available on a video monitor or printer.

response time   The time required for an operation to be performed once a request has been made. It generally refers to software but can also refer to hardware.

ROM   An acronym for read-only memory. A type of primary storage from which data and instructions can be read by a central processing unit. Because ROM is read-only, data and instructions on it can never be changed.

router   An intermediary device on a communications network that accepts and routes messages from one link (i.e., LAN) on the network to other links.

sampling rate   The rate, as measured in KiloHertz (KHz), at which sound can be recorded and played back.

search engine   Software that provides keyword and other search facilities for locating information on the World Wide Web. Examples include Yahoo!, Google, Lycos, and Alta Vista.

secondary storage   Input/output devices, other than the primary storage unit, that are used to store data and instructions. Common examples include magnetic disk, magnetic tape, and optical disc.

semiconductor   Any substance between a full conductor and a nonconductor of electricity. In computer electronics, silicon and germanium are the most common semiconductor materials used for manufacturing microprocessors.

simulation   A form of tutor software used to represent a real-life situation on a computer.

software   Computer programs and instructions that direct the physical components (hardware) of a computer system to perform tasks.

software platform   *See* platform.

sound board   A CPU component capable of generating and synthesizing sound.

sound capture   Term used for converting analog sound into a digital file.

speech synthesis   Producing spoken words from computer-generated or controlled equipment.

supercomputer   The largest, fastest, most expensive computers manufactured. They are used to process extensive amounts of data and to make very precise mathematical calculations. Cray XMP systems are examples of supercomputers.

synchronous   Happening at the same time. Synchronous communication, for instance, is characterized by time-dependence; that is, the sender and receiver communicate at the same time. An example is a telephone conversation.

system   A group of interrelated parts assembled to achieve some common goal or end. The three major components of most systems are input, process, and output. Examples of systems include computer systems, ecological systems, economic systems, political systems, and school systems.

system software   Programs that direct, supervise, and support the computer hardware system and all the tasks that are to be performed on it. An operating system is an example of system software.

TCO   *See* Total Cost of Ownership.

TCP/IP   *See* transmission control protocol/ Internet protocol.

terabtye   One trillion bytes.

T1   A dedicated digital circuit that uses broadband data communications to provide high-speed transmissions of data at the rate of up to 1.5 million bits per second.

tool software   One of the classifications of instructional software established by Robert Taylor. It assumes that the computer is used to assist in a learning activity. Examples include word processing, spreadsheet, database, and graphics software.

Total Cost of Ownership (TCO)   A yearly calculation used to represent the total cost of installing, operating, and maintaining hardware such as a computer workstation.

touch-sensitive screen   A video screen designed to recognize the location of touch on its surface. It allows users to use a finger to point to options provided on the screen by software. Also referred to as a touch screen.

trackball   An input device that functions very similarly to a mouse and is used for pointing to objects on a video screen.

train the trainer   An approach to staff development that relies on developing a cadre of well-trained individuals in an organization who train other staff.

transfer rate   The time it takes to transfer data from one location (device) to another. In computer hardware evaluation, transfer rate would be used to measure the performance of input and output devices.

transmission control protocol/Internet protocol (TCP/IP)   The standard protocol used on the Internet. Originally developed by the U.S. Department of Defense for ARPANET.

tutee software   One of the classifications of instructional software established by Robert Taylor. It assumes that the student possesses the necessary information and controls the learning environment. Examples include programming languages such as Logo, BASIC, and Pascal.

tutorial   A form of tutor software similar in style and appearance to drill-and-practice software. However, tutorials are designed to teach new material, whereas drill-and-practice programs are designed to reinforce material already learned.

tutor software   One of the classifications of instructional software established by Robert Taylor. It assumes that the computer possesses the necessary information and controls the learning environment. Examples include drill-and-practice programs, tutorials, simulations, and educational games.

uniform resource locator (URL)   An electronic address that identifies a unique location of a data file on the World Wide Web.

UNIX   A powerful multitasking operating system developed at Bell Laboratories in 1969 and written in the C programming language. Variations of UNIX enable it to run on IBM, Apple, and other manufacturers' computers. The UNIX operating system is especially popular for supporting the "server" function in client-server environments such as the Internet.

uplink   The transmission of data from an earth station to a communications satellite.

upload   In a computer network, the process of transmitting a copy of a file from a computer to a central file server.

URL   *See* uniform resource locator.

video board   A CPU component capable of accepting and generating video.

video capture   Term used for converting analog video into a digital video file.

videoconferencing   The use of analog or digital video technology to connect multiple parties simultaneously in a conference where participants can see and hear each other. Point-to-point video conferencing refers to a two-party conference. Multipoint video-conferencing refers to a multiple (more than two) party conference.

videodisc   An optical disc used to store video images and associated audio or sound information in analog format. Same as a laserdisc.

video display device   An output device capable of displaying text or images on a video screen.

virus   A computer program designed to reproduce (infect) as it is used in computer networks and copy programs. Some viruses are merely nuisances; others are designed to damage files or programs.

voice output unit   Any device that produces spoken words from a computer. *See* speech synthesis; audio response unit.

voice recognition device   Any device that can be used to recognize and record sounds. Frequently used with a digitizer to convert sounds into digital format.

WAN   *See* wide area network.

wave format   Digital file format used to store sounds as a pattern of oscillatory periodic electronic signals.

Web browser   *See* browser.

wide area network (WAN)   Connecting computer equipment using data communications over a widespread geographic area such as a town, city, or country.

Wi-Fi   A communications or signal standard for WLANs based on the Institute of Electrical and Electronics Engineers (IEEE) Wireless Standard 802.11b.

wireless local area network (WLAN)   A form of a local area network that uses high-frequency radio waves to send and receive data signals.

WLAN   *See* wireless local area network.

word processing   The use of computer equipment for entering and editing text. Popular word processing programs include WordPerfect, WordStar, and Microsoft Word.

World Wide Web   The protocol and file format software incorporating hypertext and multimedia capabilities for use on the Internet.

WORM   An acronym for write once, read many. It is a type of optical disc that allows the recording or writing of data once, which can then be accessed or read many times.

WWW   *See* World Wide Web.

INDEX